BELFAST

The publishers gratefully acknowledge
the generous financial assistance
of the Belfast City Council

BELFAST

An Illustrated History

by

JONATHAN BARDON

with picture research
by

HENRY V. BELL

THE
BLACKSTAFF
PRESS

For
my mother and father
and for
Carol, Jane and Daniel

British Library Cataloguing in Publication Data

Bardon, Jonathan
  Belfast
  1. Belfast (Northern Ireland) – History
  I. Title
  941.6'7   DA995.B5

ISBN 0–85640–272–9

© Jonathan Bardon 1982
Published by The Blackstaff Press Limited
3 Galway Park, Dundonald, BT16 0AN

Printed in Northern Ireland
by Nicholson & Bass Limited

Contents

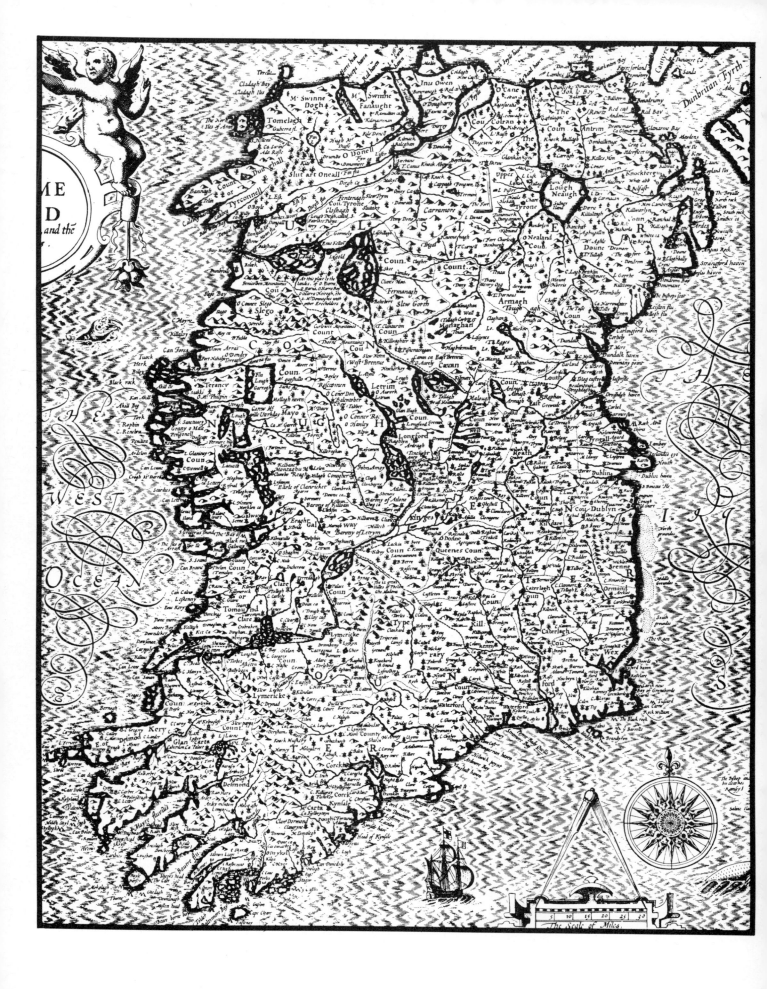

1
The Crossing Place
Earliest times to c.1603

Under Napoleon's Nose

Look up from the streets of the city,
Look high beyond tower and mast,
What hand of what Titan sculptor
Smote the crags on the mountain vast?
Made when the world was fashioned,
Meant with the world to last,
The glorious face of the sleeper
That slumbers above Belfast.
            'Mountain Shapes' by Alice Milligan

Few cities have such a magnificent setting as Belfast enjoys, as William McComb pointed out in his guide of 1861:

The situation of the town, at the debouchure of the river Lagan into Belfast Lough – a well sheltered, secure, and excellent harbour – on the confines of the two great counties of Antrim and Down. . . is peculiarly advantageous for the purposes of trade and commerce. . . The scenery in the neighbourhood of Belfast is agreeably picturesque. On the Western side, the fertile and populous plain of the Lagan, which it terminates to seaward, is skirted by a chain of mountains, bold in outline, and ranging from 900 to nearly 1,600 feet in height above sea level. One of these – the Black Mountain – seems to overhang the town, from the nearest suburb of which it is not more than a mile and a-half distant. The Cave Hill, the most northerly of the chain, presents a rugged front of beetling basalt cliffs, the 'sky line' of which as seen from the best point of view on a clear evening, soon after sunset, bears no remote resemblance to a Titanian profile of Napoleon the Great, fancy picturing the figure as in a prostrate or reclining position. From the declivity of any of the hills, but particularly from that of Collin, the prospect is very impressive. . .

M.J.B. Baddeley, in his *Thorough Guide* of 1902 advised that:

Every visitor should make this ascent for the sake of the fine panorama of Belfast, its lough and surrounding country. The hill has a bold escarpment, fronting east, and reminding the English tourist of Saddleback in Cumberland.

Up the railed path, 'bristling with trespass boards', the walker has to face a short stiff climb to the top – 'a bulwark of almost perpendicular basaltic rock, from which there is a fine bird's eye view of the country south and east. . .'

John Speede's map of Ireland 1610. Belfast, then only seven years old, was insignificant compared with neighbouring Carrickfergus (Knockfergus), the main stronghold of royal power in the north east.

1

The Cave Hill, visible from almost any point in Belfast. The fosse of an impressive promontory-fort, 'McArt's Fort', encircles the approach to the summit.
(Michael J. Collins)

Michael McLaverty sketches this panorama in *Call My Brother Back*:

At the top of the mountain they lay in the heather and gazed at Belfast spread out in the flat hollow below them, its lean mill chimneys stretched above the haze of smoke. Rows of red-bricked houses radiated on all sides and above them rose blocks of factories with many of their windows catching the sunlight. They saw their own street and could make out the splash of whitewash on the wall that Alec had daubed there as a mark for his pigeons; it was all very far away like a street scene through the wrong end of a telescope... Their eyes ranged over the whole city to the low ridge of the Castlereagh Hills, netted with lovely fields and skimming cloud-shadows, to the blue U-shaped lough covered with yachts as small as paper boats, and steamers moving up towards the docks where the gantries stood like poised aeroplanes.

But despite its fine setting, Belfast is not built on a perfect site. Much of the land is low-lying, prone to flooding, and composed of muddy sleech providing an uncertain base for buildings, as the leaning Albert Clock indicates; in dockland, after the Point Fields had been drained, wooden piles 30 to 40 feet long had to be driven through the blue clay to the bedrock underneath to take the weight of the larger buildings. The semi-circle of hills encouraged a pall of smoke to hang over the city – 425 tons of soot and tar per square mile were recorded as falling on the city centre in 1954. The choking atmosphere uniting with a penetrating dampness largely accounted for the alarmingly high rates of death from tuberculosis and bronchitis until very recent times. In the nineteenth century the outward and visible sign that a linen millowner had become prosperous was that he built a villa on the Malone Ridge or on the 50-foot contour line on the southern shore of Belfast Lough to be above the murk of the town. Good building stone is not readily available nearby: the villas and public buildings of nineteenth-century Belfast were generally built of Scottish sandstone; the City Hall is composed of Portland stone and Italian

The Giant's Ring: a megalithic tomb, surrounded by a massive earthen ring bank 600 ft in diameter, at Ballylesson, south Belfast. Only the tomb, fancifully described here as a 'druidical altar', is shown in this engraving from [G. Benn] *History of Belfast*, 1823.

marble; and though local clay made the bricks used to construct nearly all the city's dwellings, those bricks had to be fired with imported British coal. So uninviting, indeed, was the Lagan mouth that it was not until the seventeenth century that a town stood there at all.

The sandbank ford

Probably early Mesolithic Man prised out cockles and clams from the estuary mud but the low-lying country of the Lagan and its tributaries – where dense thickets of oak, willow and alder, entangled with thorns, formed the habitat of bears, wolves and wild boar – was then impenetrable and hostile to human beings. Higher ground was more easily cleared for grazing animals and it is here that traces of the first settlements have been found. Just beyond Shaw's Bridge to the south stands the Giant's Ring, one of the finest prehistoric monuments of the north; it may have been near this great amphitheatre that the Lagan was forded in ancient times. Later, perhaps following the rise of slob-land, the crossing was made where a small stream rising on Squire's Hill joined the Lagan. Here a sand-spit had formed which was to give Belfast its name.

It was the Celtic-speaking Irish or Erinn, who had mastered most of Ireland by the beginning of the Christian era, who called this crossing-place *Beal Feirsde*. The name literally means the mouth of, or approach to, the sandbank or crossing. The Farset stream, entering the Lagan almost at its mouth, takes its name from this sandbank crossing: *fertas* translated can mean a sandbank, a sandbar, a crossing-place or a ford. In the early Christian era this region was ruled by the Ulaid, a warrior caste of the Erinn, though it is likely that most of the inhabitants were the mysterious Cruithin, a people closely connected with the Picts of northern Britain. It was a battle between

3

KEY

■ above 400m
▨ above 300m
▨ above 200m
▨ above 150m
▨ mud or sand

ANTIQUITIES

🗿 cairn or dolmen
❚ standing stone
• earthworks rath or fort
■ motte
✛ site of church
⚎ site of castle

The site of Belfast before its foundation in 1603. Early inhabitants avoided the tidal muds on which much of the city now stands; the high ground later imposed severe limits on the direction of Belfast's outward growth.
(Henry V. Bell)

the Cruithin and Ulaid, recorded in the *Annals of Tighernach* as having been fought at the 'Fearsat' in 666 AD, that gave Belfast its first mention in history; later the *Annals of Ulster* explained: 'The Fearsat here alluded to was evidently at Belfast, on the river Lagan. . .'

Though the Erinn left their place-names and remains of their fortified farmsteads scattered about Belfast, they built no town here; indeed these Irish made no towns at all. At Drumbo a round tower still stands – now part of a Presbyterian Church – giving clear evidence that the Vikings nosed their shallow-draught longships up the Lagan, dragging their light craft overland at the rapids, to plunder the surrounding settlements. The Northmen erected stockades at Olderfleet and Strangford to protect their beached vessels but it was further down the east coast that they founded Ireland's first true towns. Belfast was still no more than a crossing-place when Anglo-Norman freebooters swept into Ulster towards the end of the twelfth century.

A Castle at Belfast

In 1177 John de Courcy, an Anglo-Norman knight adventurer intent on acquiring a fiefdom of his own and against the express orders of Henry II who feared the rising power of his vassals in Ireland, marched north from Dublin with 22 mailed horsemen and 300 footsoldiers. From then until Tudor times Antrim and Down became the setting of a many-sided conflict; native against Anglo-Norman, over-mighty Anglo-Norman vassal against kingsman, native

Elizabethan soldiery on the march: woodcut from *The Image of Ireland* by John Derricke, 1578. (Mansell collection)

against native, with Scottish marauders taking their chance against a shifting background of alliances and allegiance. It was sometime during the early Anglo-Norman occupation that a castle was built by the ford at Belfast. Much smaller than the great keeps of Carrickfergus and Dundrum, Belfast Castle must nevertheless have had a vital function in keeping watch over the principal passage from Down to Carrickfergus and the manors of the Route. We cannot be certain where it stood – it may have been by the ford at the bottom of what is now High Street, or perhaps further up the Farset stream at the present Castle Junction. Its strategic significance can be reckoned by the number of times it was taken, demolished and rebuilt – in 1476 the chief of the Tyrone O'Neills 'attacked the castle of Belfast which he took and demolished'; in 1489 Hugh Roe O'Donnell 'took and demolished the Castle of Belfast, and then returned safe to his house loaded with immense spoils'; in 1503 the King's deputy, Garret More Fitzgerald, sacked Belfast; in 1512 he did it again; and in 1523 his son, Garret Oge, wrote to Henry VIII:

I brake a castell of his, called Belfast, and burned 24 myle of his country.

The Tudor monarchs in their struggle for Ireland had three pre-occupations: Ireland should not become a base for foreign attack on England; it should not provide a base or breeding-ground for disaffected Englishmen; it should offer the wealth of its virgin forests and underdeveloped farmland to those English bold enough to seize them. Complete English conquest was seen as an urgent necessity by Queen Elizabeth: Western Christendom was rent by religious conflict, and Protestant England would at all costs have to prevent Catholic powers making alliance with the Irish – who, colonists and natives alike, had largely been untouched by the Reformation – to threaten the English crown from the west.

Ulster was the most Gaelic, the most impenetrable, and least known part of Ireland; the dense wolf-infested oak-woods, the myriad loughs and the bogs lying on ill-drained soil between the drumlins had long hampered invaders. The conquest of Ulster was to be the bloodiest and most costly venture of the Virgin Queen's reign, exceeding by far in expense the defeat of Spain. It was as a result of this war that the town of Belfast was built. Tragically the campaigns were fought at a time of intense religious animosity and they were to leave a legacy of sectarian bitterness which would endure and fester to

Carrickfergus circa 1540: dominated by its massive Anglo-Norman keep, the town was for many centuries the English government's principal foot-hold in Ulster. (British Museum)

blight the lives of the people of Belfast in later times.

Queen Elizabeth's first attempt on Ulster was a fiasco. In 1571 Sir Thomas Smith was given a pathetically small force of men and letters patent to possess Belfast, the Ards and other tracts of Clandeboye – in Irish, *Trian-Chongail*, a great semi-circle of land extending from the Upper Ards, curling round Belfast to Carrickfergus. The Clandeboye O'Neills not surprisingly rose in revolt.

'Belfaste is a place meet for a corporate town'

The Queen turned to Walter Devereux, Earl of Essex, who had already earned her gratitude by crushing Northumberland's rebellion and by foiling Mary Queen of Scots in her attempt to escape from Tutbury; surely he, one of the most powerful nobles in England, could succeed where Smith had failed? All previous grants were torn up and Essex was given Clandeboye, 'including the river of the Belfast', and much else besides. Setting out from Liverpool on 16 August 1573 with an impressive force, the Earl was soon safely arrived at Carrickfergus.

Sir Brian McPhelim O'Neill, chief of Clandeboye, at first was inclined to submit to Essex's authority, but when the Earl stole his cattle he called his warriors to arms. For a time the English 'were stayed at the ford of Belfast by the Rebels, who were gathered in great numbers upon the other side of the ford, to stop their passage'. The Earl routed Sir Brian's men at the ford 'and there encamped all night where we might hear their cries after their country

6

Carrickfergus Castle

fashion, for the loss of them that were dead'. From then on, to the end of his life, Essex set his heart on building a settlers' town here at Belfast. Carrickfergus he believed unsuitable 'both for lack of wood and convenient harbour for ships and for annoying of enemies which commonly keep themselves in the woods'. He continued:

therefore considering that near unto, Belfaste is a place meet for a corporate town, armed with all commodities, as a principal haven, wood and good ground, standing also upon a border, and a place of great importance for service, I think it convenient that a fortification be made there at the spring; the fortification for the circuit, and a storehouse for victuals to be at her Majesty's charges; all other buildings at mine, and such as shall inhabit it. . .

Essex did build a fort, possibly at Fortwilliam, but his fellow adventurers did not share his enthusiasm for a plantation of loyal subjects at Belfast. He complained to Queen Elizabeth that his captains 'not having forgotten the delicacies of England' had forsaken him 'feigning excuses to repair home' and 'the common hired soldiers, both horsemen and footmen, mislike of their pay. . .' The Earl did at least persuade Sir Brian to submit and, the *Annals of Ulster* record:

Peace, sociality, and friendship were established between Brian, the son of Felim Bacagh O'Neill, and the Earl of Essex and a feast was afterwards prepared by Brian, to which the Lord Justice and the chiefs of his people were invited, and they passed three nights and days pleasantly and cheerfully.

The Earl, however, could not forgive Sir Brian for shattering his dream of quick and easy success; while he was being so lavishly entertained in Belfast Castle, Essex prepared to have revenge on his host. The *Annals* tell us:

As they were agreeably drinking and making merry, Brian, his brother, and his wife, were seized upon by the Earl; and all his people unsparingly put to the sword, men, women, youths, and maidens, in Brian's own presence. Brian was afterwards sent to Dublin, together with his wife and brother, where they were cut in quarters.

Even the Queen's officials thought the treatment meted out to Sir Brian and his people was brutal and excessive. Essex claimed that 'this little execution hath broken the faction and makes them all afeard'; instead in a short time all Clandeboye was aflame and the Earl was forced to make an ignominious withdrawal. This failure notwithstanding, he did not abandon his dream as he informed the Queen:

I resolve not to build but at one place; namelie, at Belfast; and that of littel charge; a small towne there will keep the passage, relieve Knockfergus with wood, and horsemen being laid there shall command the plains of Clandeboye. . .

Elizabeth would not renew her support and Essex, and with him his hopes, died in 1576.

A small royal garrison remained at Belfast, however, and the Clandeboye O'Neills had won for themselves only a temporary respite.

Sir John Chichester at Belfast

Growing rivalry between England and Spain made the subjugation of Ireland a principal object of Queen Elizabeth's government – the Irish must not be allowed to ally with England's enemies. Munster was ruthlessly devastated and parcelled out; Armada crews cast up on the shores of Connacht were pitilessly put to the sword; and the writ of English law ran through three-quarters of Ireland. Then in 1595 Hugh O'Neill, Earl of Tyrone, banded most of the Gaelic chiefs of Ulster in a carefully prepared rebellion against the extension of English power to the northern province.

'What shall be done with the Castle of Bellfest,' the governor of Carrickfergus asked of the Lord Deputy, 'the which hath cost some money in fortefying and is made in reasonable good sort to be garded. . .' On 18 June 1597, when the officer in charge was drunk in Carrickfergus, Belfast Castle was taken by Shane McBrian O'Neill of Lower Clandeboye; '. . . all the English men in the ward were hanged', Anthony Dearinge reported, 'and their throats cut, and their bowells cutt oute of their bellyes by Shane McBrian'. Sir John Chichester was sent north to recover Belfast, which he achieved on 11 July, as he reported back, 'without anie loss to us, and put those wee found in yt to the sworde'. In a letter to Burghley, Chichester described Belfast as:

Being a place which standeth 8 miles from Kerogfergus, and on the river, wher the sea ebbes and flowes, so that botes may be landed within a butte shotte of the said Castell, for the recovery whereof I made choice that it should be one of my first workes.

Meanwhile the Earl of Tyrone was sweeping all before him and Chichester foolishly fell out with the neutral MacDonnells of the Glens. Four miles outside Carrickfergus Chichester and 180 of the English were killed. Then in 1598, Tyrone inflicted the most severe defeat ever suffered by English arms in Ireland – the 'Battle of the Yellow Ford', fought by the river Blackwater. For a time Elizabeth's position in Ireland was a desperate one; virtually all the Gaelic families and many of the 'Old English' joined the Ulster rebellion. Slowly, painfully, and at vast expense, royal troops recovered lost territory in Munster, Leinster and Connacht. Yet the Great O'Neill had the support of Spain and other Catholic powers, and again and again the English were thrown back in their attempts to penetrate Ulster.

Elizabethan conquest: Sir Arthur Chichester given Belfast

Ironically it was his alliance with the great European power of Spain which brought about Hugh O'Neill's downfall and with him fell the Clandeboye O'Neills. Where he had looked for aid, he found himself appealed to for rescue. The Spanish invading force under Don Juan del Águila which, landing in the south of Ireland, was supposed to trap the English between two fires, was itself soon trapped in the Co Cork port of Kinsale and appealed to Tyrone for aid.

The hard winter's march southwards exhausted the Ulstermen, and on Christmas Eve 1601 Mountjoy's cavalry shattered the disorganised Irish in the half-light of dawn. Kinsale marked the end of Gaelic Ulster. For two terrible years Tyrone fought a rear-guard action, but the English net around Ulster slowly drew tighter. Sir Henry Docwra, with over 3,000 men at Derry, advanced up the Foyle; Mountjoy with 3,000 men cautiously advanced from Dundalk; there was a small force at Lecale; and at Carrickfergus Sir Arthur

Hugh O'Neill, Earl of Tyrone: seventeenth-century copy of an Italian portrait. For almost nine years O'Neill led most of Gaelic Ulster in combined resistance to the extension of English royal power; his capitulation in 1603 led directly to the foundation of the town of Belfast. (PRONI)

Chichester with 1,000 men had high hopes of 'soon beheading that wood-kerne Tyrone'.

There were no spectacular battles in this closing stage of Elizabeth's last Irish war, but it was now that suffering was at its worst. Famine was the weapon Mountjoy used to crush the Great O'Neill. Relentlessly, as Tyrone's warriors were driven into the bogland and forests, the English rounded up the people's cattle, and the skies flamed with burning cornfields. Only rarely did either side take prisoners; any warrior captured, Docwra wrote, 'I caused the soldiers to hew in pieces with their swords'. In London, Cecil appealed to the Queen to let Tyrone submit 'for saving of Christian blood and of miseries of her natural people from hence hourly sent to the shambles'. But Mountjoy was anxious to destroy the harvest to deprive Tyrone of the means to continue his rebellion into the spring of 1603.

Clandeboye shared in this suffering, for the O'Neills of Clandeboye had briefly joined Tyrone at the height of his success. Fynes Moryson, secretary to Mountjoy, has left a grim description of the state of this part of Ulster:

Now because I have often made mention formerly of our destroying the rebels Corn, and using all means to famish them, let me by two or three examples show the miserable Estate to which the Rebels were thereby brought.

On their return from pursuing Brian McArt O'Neill, Sir Arthur Chichester, Sir Richard Moryson and their forces saw, on the Castlereagh hills,

. . . a most horrible Spectacle of three children (whereof the eldest was not above ten Years old) all eating and gnawing with their Teeth the Entrails of their dead Mother, upon whose Flesh they had fed 20 Days past, and having eaten all from the Feet

9

Sir Arthur Chichester, Lord Mountjoy's tireless lieutenant, who subdued Clandeboye and was granted the 'Castle of Bealfaste' in 1603. Appointed Lord Deputy in 1605, he masterminded James I's Plantation in Ulster. (PRONI)

upward to the bare Bones, roasting it continually by a slow Fire, were now coming to the eating of her said Entrails in like sort roasted, yet not divided from the Body, being as yet raw.

When, at the end of March 1603, Tyrone finally submitted at Mellifont, Captain Bodley saw warriors eating grass in Lecale and Moryson writes:

The Captain of Carrickfergus, and the adjacent Garrisons of the Northern Parts can witness, that upon the making of Peace, and receiving the Rebels to Mercy, it was a common Practice among the common Sort of them (I mean such as were not Sword-men,) to thrust long Needles into the Horses of our English Troops, and they dying thereupon, to be ready to tear out one another's Throat for a share of them. And no Spectacle was more frequent in the Ditches of Towns, and especially in wasted Countries, than to see Multitudes of these poor People dead with their Mouths all coloured green by eating Nettles, Docks, and all things they could rend up above Ground.

The very wolves were driven by starvation from the woods, and killed the enfeebled people.

Sir Arthur Chichester had come a long way since he had been forced to flee from England after robbing one of the Queen's tax-collectors. After being pardoned, he was captain of one of the Queen's ships on Drake's last voyage to the West Indies. He fought in Picardy, was knighted by Henry IV of France, and arrived in Ireland in 1599 when Essex appointed him Governor of Carrickfergus. He was one of the ablest and most ruthless of Mountjoy's lieutenants, and for his services to the crown he was given, in a patent dated 5 November 1603, 'The Castle of Bealfaste or Belfast, with the Appurtenants and Hereditaments, Spiritual and Temporal, situate in the Lower Clandeboye, late in the possession or custody of Sir Ralph Lane Knt., deceased'.

It was sweet revenge for the death of his brother; he was now possessor of the lands of those who had killed Sir John Chichester. Sir Arthur Chichester was to succeed where Essex had failed – he was the true founder of the town of Belfast.

10

2
Settlers' Town
c.1603–1750

'A place meet for a corporate town' is how Essex had seen Belfast, but it was not until the Gaelic lords of the north had been ruthlessly subdued that Chichester was able to realise that dream. Once James VI of Scotland became King James I of England, the union of crowns made it possible for English and Scots to work in harmony in colonising Ulster. In the continuing turbulence and bloodshed, Belfast was uniquely fortunate in escaping massacre and destruction; indeed the wars of the seventeenth century gave Belfast a special strategic importance, and occupying troops, in spending their pay, enhanced the wealth of the town's inhabitants. As a settlers' town, Belfast generally won government favour and escaped harsh reprisal and repression.

Belfast became a flourishing market town and a prospering port, but Thomas Phillips' claim in 1685 that it 'is now the third place of trade in this Kingdom' does not stand up to close examination. Belfast was merely the equal of Newry, Derry and Lisburn, and there were few signs as yet that it would be the nucleus of a great industrial city. Indeed, due to the indifference of the Chichester family and the development of the provisions export trade in the southern ports, Belfast's relative position slipped in the first half of the eighteenth century.

The Planting of Clandeboye

It was in Clandeboye, before the systematic confiscation of vast territories west of the Bann, that the Protestant colony in Ulster first put down deep roots. Sir Arthur Chichester dutifully set about rebuilding Belfast Castle, but he set a low value on his grant. 'When I have it att best perfection,' he wrote in complaint to London, 'I wyll gladly sell the whole landes for the wch others sell, five pounds in fee simple.' Soon afterwards he sublet the lands adjoining the Castle on generous terms to Sir Moses Hill. In any case, he had the government of all Ireland to concern him from February 1605, when he was appointed Lord Deputy. It was to be the success of the Scots in settling the rest of Clandeboye that eventually forced Chichester to give Belfast more of his attention.

Unwittingly Chichester gave the Scots their opportunity. In 'a grand debauch' at Castlereagh, Conn O'Neill, chief of Upper Clandeboye and the 'Great Ards', ran short of wine; obtaining fresh supplies in Belfast, O'Neill's men were attacked by English soldiers; deprived of their wine O'Neill's warriors counter-attacked and, as a result, Chichester had the chief thrown into Carrickfergus gaol. Hugh Montgomery, sixth laird of Braidstane, rescued the bewildered Conn and took him to Scotland where he promised to obtain a royal pardon for the chief in return for a share of his lands. Meanwhile another Scot, James Hamilton, appointed bursar of Trinity College Dublin on its foundation, had inherited from a London merchant the title to 'so much of the landes in the twoe Ardes, in the province of Ulster, as he or his nominee shall thinke fitt, to be parcel'. In April 1605 Hamilton, Montgomery and O'Neill divided Upper Clandeboye and the Ards between them. Chichester could not act against the king's favourites; James I approved the agreement, provided all three undertook 'to inhabit the said territory with English or Scotchmen'.

By November 1605 Conn O'Neill's estates had been surveyed, and early in the following year a stream of Scots settlers began to cross the North Channel. With over a million inhabitants, Scotland could spare these colonists, as Sir William Alexander wrote shortly afterwards: 'Scotland by reason of her populousnesse being constrained to disburden her selfe (like the painfull Bees) did every yeere send forth swarmes.' To Clandeboye came carpenters, masons, and smiths; farmers throwing off the oppression of the lairds and uncertain leases; fugitives from the king's harsh pacification of the Borders; and zealous Presbyterians chafing against the increased authority of Anglican bishops. As Protestant Lowland Scots, loyal to the crown, they could not but be welcomed by Chichester. Wood, running desperately short in Scotland, was cut at Slut Neal by the Lagan, floated down river to Belfast, and taken from there by sea to Bangor and Donaghadee. After only two years the colony was flourishing:

Now every body minded their trades, and the plough, and the spade, building, and setting fruit trees, etc., in orchards and gardens, and by ditching in their grounds. The old women spun, and the young girls plyed their nimble fingers at knitting – and every body was innocently busy. Now the Golden peacable age renewed, no strife, contention, querulous lawyers, or Scottish or Irish feuds, between clanns and families, and sirnames, disturbing the tranquillity of those times.

This is a highly romantic picture, but the success of the Scottish settlement in north Down could not be denied. The surnames of these Scots colonists were later to be found in abundance in Belfast.

'The towne of Bealfast is plotted out in a good forme'

In 1607 the principal Gaelic lords of Ulster, no longer able to bear the constraints of English rule, sailed out from Lough Swilly never to return. Until this 'Flight of the Earls' little more than church lands had been available for colonisation west of the Bann, and it was only after O'Dogherty of Inishowen had burned Derry and Strabane the following year that Chichester drafted an elaborate scheme of plantation. Here there was, Sir John Davies wrote enthusiastically, 'a greater extent of land than any prince of Europe has to dispose of'. It was the last major government-sponsored colonising scheme to enjoy success in western Europe and, in rural areas, the pattern of settlement can still be traced in detail by examining how Ulster people vote today. From this great hinterland industrial Belfast was to draw its inhabitants in the nineteenth century.

The Plantation in Ulster was to obsess Chichester to the end of his days. In 1610 he told King James that he 'would rather labour with his hands in the

Plantation of Ulster than dance or play in that of Virginia'. There was no need to include Antrim and Down in the scheme for in those counties, townships, bawns and stooks of corn were already providing evidence of successful colonisation. A little belatedly, Chichester now set out to make Belfast a model plantation town. In 1611 the Plantation Commissioners reported favourably on the progress made:

The towne of Bealfast is plotted out in a good forme, wherein are many famelyes of English, Scotch, and some Manksmen already inhabitinge, of which some are artificers who have buylte good tymber houses with chimneys after the fashion of the English palle, and one Inn with very good Lodginge which is a great comforte to the travellers in those partes.

The inn was probably 'Sir Moses' Cellars' which remained open until the early nineteenth century. The Commissioners found 'many masons, brick-layers, and other labourers aworke' building the new castle which they said was 'lyke to be finished by the mydle of next Somer'. Chichester 'hath ready made above twelve hundred of good Brickes, whereof after finishinge of the said Castle, house, and Bawne, there will be a good proportion left for the buyldinge of other tenements within the said Towne'. Sir Moses Hill had built a fort at Hillhall on the Plains of Malone and 'by the River of Lagan where the sea ebbes and flowes in a place called Strandmellis we found the said Moyses Hill in hand with buyldinge of a stronge house of stone 56 foot longe'. Belfast was not yet more significant than its near neighbours Bangor, Newtownards, Comber, and Donaghadee. Belfast Castle was smaller than Joymount, Chichester's great house near Carrickfergus, and Sir James Hamilton's house at Bangor. No town seems to have been built at Castlereagh; there the hapless Conn O'Neill watched Belfast rise up below him and piece by piece he sold off his share of Clandeboye to Montgomery and the rapacious Sir James Hamilton. Only a foetid stream in east Belfast, the Connswater, preserves his memory today.

The incorporation of Belfast

In 1613 Belfast was given a political importance which the town's small size did not yet warrant: it was granted a charter of incorporation. As Lord Deputy, Chichester attempted to enforce the king's policy that no toleration should be given to 'recusants' in Ireland. It proved impossible to persuade the Old English gentry in the south to abandon Catholicism, but Chichester did ensure that the Irish parliament of 1613 had a Protestant majority. Forty new boroughs were created and given the right to return two members each to parliament and to have limited local self government. Belfast was one of these, guaranteed to return Protestant members.

With minor alterations only, the charter of incorporation was to be in force for more than two hundred years. By placing the town's government firmly in the hands of the Chichester family, the charter at first gave Belfast the useful patronage of a great magnate. The 'Sovereign' and the twelve 'free burgesses' were named in the charter; they held their offices for life and vacancies were filled by the Sovereign and remaining burgesses. The Sovereign – an office equivalent to town mayor – was chosen by the burgesses from a short list of three drawn up by the head of the Chichester family, and the laws of the town

Corporation bye-law of 1638 prohibiting unauthorised malt kilns.

had to be drafted with the advice and consent of the lord of the Castle. There was provision for the creation of 'free commoners' who could be admitted on payment of a fee to the Sovereign. Apart from having some say in the assessment of rates, free commoners exercised no real political power. It was worth paying the fee, however; only freemen could be exempt from dues paid by outsiders selling goods in the Belfast market and only they could practise trades in the town. The two members of parliament were in effect Chichester's nominees.

In short, Sir Arthur Chichester, created Baron of Belfast in 1613, not only owned Belfast but also had complete control over its political life. Belfast was a 'close borough' governed by men controlled by the Chichester family; it was not long before the town's citizens were chafing against this self-perpetuating oligarchy. The future expansion of the town followed not as a result of, but in spite of the rule of the Corporation.

'A brave plantation'

Sir Arthur Chichester died in 1625 and was succeeded by his brother Edward, Viscount Chichester of Carrickfergus. In 1630, when Lord Edward married the Earl of Bristol's daughter, Belfast was valued at £400 a year; ten years later he found it worthwhile to pay £467.17s.6d. fine, or cash payment, to the crown to obtain final confirmation of his title to Belfast. The adjacent Chichester lands leased to the Hill family yielded £1,000 a year according to Brereton, who described them as 'a brave plantation'. 'Many Lancashire and Cheshire men are here planted;' he wrote, 'with some of them I conversed. They sit upon a rack rent, and pay 5s or 6s an acre for good ploughing land, which is now clothed with excellent corn.' Clearly there had been a dramatic rise in the value of the original grant which Sir Arthur had been prepared to sell even 'att best perfection' for £5.

Thomas Wentworth, Charles I's dynamic and ill-fated Lord Deputy, may have been, as he was to the Earl of Cork, 'a most cursed man to all Ireland', but Belfast had good reason to be grateful to him. Carrickfergus had long enjoyed the right to retain one third of the duties levied on imports and exports brought into and sent out of Belfast Lough. In 1637 Wentworth withdrew this privilege; Belfast could now trade on equal terms with its rival and Sir George Ratcliffe estimated that Carrickfergus lost £300 a year by this change.

Belfast was important enough to be chosen as the place where royal government attempted to bring Presbyterians to heel. Recalcitrant ministers were summoned for questioning to the Church of Belfast on 10 August 1636; Bishop Leslie of Down began with a text from Matthew: 'But if he neglect to hear the Church, let him be unto thee as an heathen man and a publican.' Next day Bishop Bramhall of Derry cut in on one minister's reply to say: 'It were more reason and more fit this fellow were whipped than reasoned with.' Five clergy were deposed for refusing to subscribe to Anglican doctrine and in September they set sail for America in a 150-ton vessel, the *Eagle's Wing*, built in Belfast. Storms forced the ministers to return, and they seem then to have been left unmolested. Belfast was already establishing its reputation for being a centre of religious controversy.

Presbyterians in the north were further alienated when Wentworth attempted to enforce loyalty by requiring all Scots in Ulster to take the 'Black

Corporate seal of Belfast, 1640.

Oath' of obedience to the king. Catholics had greater cause for resentment; the native Irish of Ulster, conquered and deprived of their most fertile lands, nursing their bitterness, eagerly awaited the opportunity for revenge.

1641: 'But for him we had Belfast'

On 24 October 1641 Lord Edward Chichester wrote in haste from Belfast a letter to King Charles: 'May it please your Majesty. I have had advertizement from some credible persons that certain Septe of the Irish of good quallities in the northern parts of your Majesty's Kingdom of Ireland two nights last past did rise with force, and have taken Charlemont, Dungannon, and Tanragee, and the Newry...' In a furious uprising the native Irish had thrown themselves on the British settlements, killing and maiming; in alliance with many of the Old English they threatened to uproot the plantation altogether. Certainly to Chichester the insurgents appeared to be closing in on Belfast: 'They are advancing near into these parts, and that this last night of all there hath been seen great fires so near as were discerned from this place.'

As exaggerated tales of wholesale slaughter flew about Belfast, Chichester and many other leading citizens made haste to flee from the town. Charles I, at war in Scotland and at loggerheads with his parliament, could send no aid. Captain Lawson, owner of the Belfast iron works at Old Forge, spurred the remaining townsmen to action:

I arose, calling two horsemen with me, and in the morning, being Monday, went down back again to Great Belfast, where I found most part of the inhabitants fled and flying, and carrying away their goods to Carrickfergus, and the old Lord Chichester, shipped aboard in a ship. So I went throughout the town, and blamed them for offering to leave the town, and intreated for some arms, either by buying or lending, but could not prevail. At last I found in Mister le Squire's house seven muskets, eight halberts, ready in the street to be shipped to Carrickfergus, which arms I took, and bought a drum, and beating the same through the town, raised about twenty men, who came with me again up to the Iron Works, having Mr Forbes, and some number with me, where I also gathered in all about 160 horse and foot.

That afternoon, Monday 25 October, Lawson marched to Lisburn where he arrived in time to find the Irish, led by Sir Conn Magennis, driving four hundred cattle at the gates in an attempt to breach them. Lawson held off the attackers long enough for reinforcements under Captain Chichester, Sir James Montgomery, Lord Hamilton and Arthur Hill to reach Lisburn to secure the town. 'But for him we had Belfast,' wrote one insurgent, Donal O'Kane, of Lawson: 'we did little dream any such action had been in him, if we had, we would have cut him short of his journey, but now no remedy.' When the Irish, led by Sir Phelim O'Neill, Sir Conn Magennis, and Major-General Plunkett, made a more impressive assault on Lisburn on 28 November, the colonists were strong enough to thrust them back. Belfast and Carrickfergus remained unscathed, vital bridgeheads for a relieving army from Britain.

Given a respite by the victories at Lisburn, the people of Belfast threw up a rampart to provide some kind of defence for what was an unwalled town. The rampart – known locally as the 'rampier' – appears to have run from the sea at the point where the present Corporation Street is met by Exchange Street; by Talbot Street west to North Street; south along the route of Queen Street until it reached out as far as College Square East, where it turned through the grounds of the City Hall to the water again at May Street. The rampart with its accompanying wet ditch was breached at two points: the North Gate, near where Royal Avenue cuts across North Street, and the Mill Gate, where Chapel Lane meets Castle Street.

The Scots army in Belfast

Over the next few years Belfast changed hands with bewildering frequency. In April 1642 General Robert Monro came to Belfast with a Scots army to assist the colonists. Colonel Chichester gave the reinforcements an enthusiastic welcome when they joined his men at Malone. As the Civil War broke in England, however, the Chichesters remained loyal to the crown and the Scots, augmented by more troops brought over by the Earl of Leven in September, for the moment supported Parliament. Fear of the Catholic Irish prevented open conflict – Monro billetted in Carrickfergus and Chichester held Belfast. When Chichester attempted to stop the Scots administering the Covenant to extirpate 'Popery, Prelacy, and Heresy', Monro took Belfast when it was momentarily unguarded, and ordered Colonel Chichester out of Belfast. In vain did Chichester appeal to Ormond, the King's viceroy in Dublin.

Ormond had arranged a 'cessation' of hostilities with the Irish insurgents. The Scots Covenanters in the north never accepted this truce and Monro marched into Tyrone only to be routed at Benburb on 5 June 1646. It was the most striking victory of the century for Irish arms; Monro lost all his guns and half his men. But the victor, Eoghen Roe O'Neill, could not follow up his success and Monro limped back to Belfast, which now gained a strategic importance second only to Dublin. With the triumph of Parliament in England, relations between the Presbyterian Scots and the Puritans deteriorated. When Parliamentary Commissioners sailed into Belfast Lough in November 1646 and requested that the Scots hand over Belfast to their forces, Monro politely but tenaciously refused. Further requests and a direct demand from Westminster were turned down in February 1647. Soon the Scots were at war with Parliament and it was Monro's nephew, Sir George Monro, who led them into England.

Colonel Monk, with a strong Parliamentarian force at Lisburn, received his orders at the end of August 1648: 'We have formerly written to you concerning Belfast which the Scots ought not to have had at all. . . And we again desire you to use all the means in your power to put the said town of Belfast in possession of the Parliament of England.' In October Monk complied, the gates of Carrickfergus were opened for him by the Captain of the Watch, Monro was made prisoner, and Belfast surrendered without a struggle. Shortly afterwards, when Monk returned to England, Belfast was reoccupied by Montgomery, Lord of the Ards, and Sir George Monro himself, for the crown.

'A barbarous nook'

The brief royalist reoccupation gave the Belfast Presbytery the opportunity to denounce the Sectaries in Parliament for opposing the Covenant. In their long declaration, dated 15 February 1649, the Belfast Scots denounced

Colonel Robert Venables takes Belfast in September 1649 – the town's first and last siege. A late-nineteenth-century impression by J. W. Carey. (Linen Hall Library)

Parliament's edict in favour of religious toleration. The Sectaries, they wrote, 'labour to establish by laws an universal toleration of all religions, which is an innovation overturning of unity in religion, and so directly repugnant to the word of God'.

This paper drew a furious and celebrated reply from John Milton in denunciation of the 'insolent and seditious representation from the Scotch Presbytery at Belfast in the North of Ireland'. He ridiculed them as 'Balaams', 'unhallowed priestings', and 'blockish presbyters of Clandeboye', and was at pains to point out the insignificance of Belfast which he described as 'a barbarous nook. . . Belfast, a place better known by the name of a late barony, than by the fame of these men's doctrine or ecclesiastical deeds, whose obscurity till now never came to our hearing'.

Belfast's only siege

In August 1649 Cromwell disembarked at Ringsend determined to halt the civil conflict which had torn Ireland for eight years. Having wreaked a terrible vengeance on the royalists in Drogheda, Cromwell turned south, leaving Colonel Robert Venables to subdue Ulster. Venables reached Lisburn on 27 September and from there he marched to Belfast to lay siege to the town for four days – the only siege in the history of Belfast. There was some sharp skirmishing at Buller's Fields outside the North Gate, but Belfast yielded without a serious struggle. The fifteen heavy guns and twelve barrels of gunpowder in the town now fell into the hands of the Commonwealth, which was to guide Ireland's destinies for the next ten years.

Cromwell's regime brought disaster for many of the Old English and Gaelic landowners as the most sweeping confiscations in the country's history were carried through. Belfast, in contrast, was relatively well treated. Its citizens were almost exclusively Protestant and they therefore escaped the harshest punishment. The Presbyterian Scots remained suspect as they had transferred their loyalties to the crown, but, valued as potential allies in the event of another Catholic rising, they were not unduly harried. Some defiant ministers were imprisoned in Belfast 'where none of the Lord's people durst come to visit them, nor hear them either preach, or join with them in prayer'. Presbyterian clergy who refused to recognise the Commonwealth's authority were summoned to Belfast in October 1652; even though they declared 'that they could not own the government as lawful, nor bind themselves by any oath or subscription to it', these ministers were allowed to return home if they undertook to 'make no insurrection in the country'.

Patrick Adair, Presbyterian minister of Belfast, was sent to Dublin to be questioned by General Fleetwood and the Council. During his defence, Allen, an Anabaptist member of the council, burst out: 'A Papist would and might say as much for himself.' Adair replied: 'Sir, under favour, it is a mistake to compare our consciences with Papists, for a Papist's conscience could digest the killing of Protestant kings, so would not ours, for our principles are contrary to it.' 'There being divers there who had a hand in the King's murder,' Kirkpatrick later remarked, 'all of them were struck with shame,' and Adair was hurriedly given an unconditional release.

The possession of Belfast had been of critical importance to all sides in the wars, yet the town had endured no protracted siege, no extensive plundering, and no massacre. The cost of billeting garrisons was more than balanced by the additional business brought by soldiers with money to spend. Cromwell's victories had been so crushing that peace, at least for a time, almost inevitably followed and trade began to recover. On the eve of the Restoration the seaborne trade of Belfast was more than six times that of Carrickfergus in value.

It was General Monk, who as a colonel had ousted the royalists from Belfast in 1648, who restored the monarchy in 1660. The citizens of Belfast, Scots and English alike, were royalist in sympathy; in gratitude they presented these verses to the General:

> Advance George Monck & Monck St George shall be
> Englands Restorer to Its Liberty
> Scotlands Protector Irelands President
> Reduceing all to a ffree Parliam^t
> And if thou dost intend the other thinge
> Goe on and all shall Crye God save y^e Kinge

From *The Town Book of the Corporation of Belfast 1613–1816.*

Venables returned to England to write *The Experienced Angler*, published with a preface by Izaak Walton in 1661. He certainly fished the Blackwater, the Main, and the Lower Bann; no doubt he had occasionally turned aside from his duties in Belfast for a throw or two on the Lagan, a river, Father McKenna observed in 1643, 'yielding a plentiful supply of salmon'.

'The third place of trade in this Kingdom'

During the reign of Charles II, Ireland's economy enjoyed the most striking advance of the century and Belfast, enhanced in importance and largely unscathed by the wars, grew rapidly. The plantation in the north, undisturbed by Cromwell, now yielded a significant surplus of agricultural produce and Belfast became the principal port of Ulster for sending this surplus abroad. 'The quantities of Butter and Beef which it sends into Foreign Parts are almost incredible;' Sacheverell observed, 'I have seen the Barrels pil'd up in the very Streets.' France took one third of the corn, half of the beef and beef products, and three quarters of the butter exported from Belfast.

The rapid recovery of the hinterland and growing importance of Belfast is reflected in a list of 1683 which shows that 4,610 barrels of beef, 33,880 cwts of butter, 12,445 hides, 3,769 cwts of tallow, and 7,067 barrels of corn were

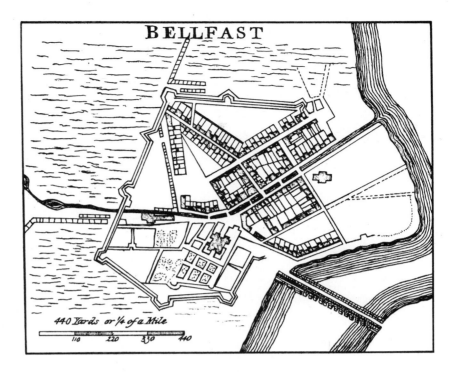

BELLFAST

440 Yards or ¼ of a Mile

110   220   330   440

A map of 1660 showing the rampart, and the Farset river flowing down the centre of High Street before entering the Lagan. Belfast Castle and its extensive grounds are shown just south of the Farset. (Linen Hall Library)

exported from the town. Linen was in its infancy; the list shows only 341 pieces exported. Despite trade restrictions, Belfast had a substantial trade with the American colonies and imported from there an impressive 382,640 lbs of tobacco. In return for butter, beef, corn, and – surprisingly – 162 cwt of bread, Spain sent to Belfast 108 butts of wine, anchovies, oranges and lemons, raisins, and other delicacies. France, however, was the most substantial partner in trade; in 1683 she sent 4,417 gallons of brandy and 213 tuns of wine. A century later, the ideas which travelled with these French cargoes were to have great consequence for Belfast.

No doubt Thomas Phillips exaggerated when he wrote in 1685 that Belfast 'is now the third place of trade in this Kingdom', but it had certainly become the most flourishing port in Ulster. 'It is one of the most considerable places in the Kingdom,' he added, 'having never less than 40 or 50 sail before it.' A shipping list of about 1663 names 29 Belfast-owned ships, 14 of them built in the port; another list of 1682 names 67 Belfast-owned ships. Yet Belfast was by modern standards still a small town. A map of 1660 indicates that the town covered no more than 86 acres, and a good part of this area was taken up by the extensive grounds surrounding the Castle.

The town's first street, High Street, followed the Farset from the Castle down to a dock where the stream joined the Lagan at the tide. The Farset ran down the centre of High Street, not to be covered in until the early nineteenth century; by Charles II's reign some of the wealthiest citizens had built several bridges across the stream with the permission of the Corporation. Upstream of the Castle the town's cornmill was powered by the Farset; the later Mill Street (now Divis Street) marked its site and Millfield was clearly the location of an adjacent field outside the rampart. By the Restoration there appear to have been five streets: High Street, Bridge Street, Waring Street, North Street, and Skipper Street. The rampart was still, therefore, an adequate boundary for the town.

Colonel Arthur Chichester, 1st Earl of Donegall: a Royalist commander who survived battles with the native Irish, disputes with the Scots, and Parliamentarian occupation to recover Belfast's fortunes after the Restoration.
(Linenhall Library)

The Chichester family continued to dominate Belfast. Lord Edward died in 1684 and was succeeded by his son, Colonel Arthur Chichester, 1st Earl of Donegall. After the Restoration Lord Donegall recovered full control over the Corporation, the town, and surrounding properties. The family seem to have lived as often now in Belfast as at Joymount, and impressive gardens were laid out around the Castle. Connected by cinder paths, there were plots for strawberries, gooseberries, and currants; a cherry garden and an apple orchard; a bowling green, an arbour, and private walks to the sea shore. The Chichesters had their land at Stranmillis and Woodburn under the plough, and cattle and sheep grazed on their fenced pastures at the Old Park and the New Park (Parkmount) and on the slopes of Squire's Hill and the Black Mountain. The leases to the Hill family were not renewed but Skegoniel, by the Milewater river, was rented out to Thomas Waring, the tanning merchant and shipper.

The Malone district is described by Dobbs in 1683:

From Lambegg the way leads direct to Belfast, which is all along for the most part furnished with houses, little orchards, and gardens; and on the right hand the Countess of Donegall hath a very fine Park well stored with Venison, and in it a Horse Course of Two miles, and may be called an English road.

The Donegall lands directly south of the town – the demesnes of Stranmillis, Cromac, and Friar's Bush – contained about 300 acres; the deer park mentioned by Dobbs was the 100-acre Stranmillis demesne. In short, the scene across from the Cave Hill and Black Mountain to the Castlereagh Hills was essentially a rural one. Belfast was by modern standards still a small provincial port with only two prominent buildings: Belfast Parish Church, which stood on the site of the present St George's Church at the bottom of High Street, and Belfast Castle, described by a visitor as 'the glory and beauty of that town'. The population of Belfast, about 1,000 in 1660, was still no more than 2,000 on the accession of James II.

An impoverished Corporation

As trade quickened during the reign of Charles II the power and confidence of the merchant families in Belfast began to grow. Thomas Waring had built Waringstown in Clanconnell and set up a tannery in Toome. His export business in hides was so important to Belfast that he was appointed Sovereign on several occasions, and in 1660 he moved his tannery to Belfast. He died in 1665, leaving a park beyond the North Gate to his wife Janet, £40 to the poor of Belfast, and another £20 for the poor, provided his ship, *Providence of Belfast,* returned in safety from San Sebastian. Waring was English, as were most of the prominent families in the early years, such as Vesey (the first Sovereign), le Squire (Chichester's agent), Leathes (shipowner), Theaker (lessee of lands at Cullingtree), and Martin (brewer).

It was probably during Monro's long occupation that the proportion of Scots in Belfast rose to around half of the population, and Scottish merchant families soon sprang into prominence. George Macartney, who came from Kircudbright in the 1640s, became the wealthiest man of business in Belfast in the seventeenth century. His ships sailed regularly to France, the Low Countries, and Spain. It may have been his dealings with Holland which encouraged him to set up the first sugar refinery in Belfast; sugar houses are recorded in the mid-eighteenth century as being in Sugar-house Entry (which ran between Waring Street and High Street, below Bridge Street) and in Rosemary Street; these were probably founded by Macartney. He built extensively in Belfast, leased lands from the Earl of Donegall, owned four water-powered corn mills, and set up a tuck mill for thickening and smoothing woollen cloth.

There was a flourishing iron industry for a time in and near Belfast; iron ore was imported from Cumberland and smelted by the Lagan at Old Forge and New Forge. Nearly 50 tons of iron were exported from Belfast in 1683, and the manufacturers, George Rawdon and Captain Lawson, had their own dock at Stranmillis. The industry was doomed, however; in less than a century the colonists of Ulster had felled the great woods of the province which had been the source of the charcoal for the forges.

The rising middle class clearly resented the indolence and exclusiveness of the Corporation, though the most successful merchants who were not Presbyterians, such as Macartney, were able to reach high office. The town records show that the Corporation could barely meet the expense of running the market out of customs dues and tolls levied on outsiders. A little extra money was raised from fines imposed by the Borough Court of Record and from fees for admission to freedom of the town. As the Corporation agreed on 25 June 1664,

there hath bean for a longe time past great want of a Court House or Towne Hall for this Corporacon whereby the decency Authority and well Governing of this Burrough hath received prejudice and determt. both in ye body Corporate and Politique (even to ye anihillating of that Antiquity Splendor and Majesty wherewith it has been adorned). . .

The Corporation was forced to rent a building for the purpose from the Sovereign, George Macartney; even then the annual rent of £5 (and £4 required for a new plush cushion for the town hall) had to be raised by a levy on the inhabitants.

Stone-carved shield ornamenting the keystone of the Long Bridge.

As 'ye River that runs through ye said Towne is very much defiled and greatly abused by all manner of sinks falling into ye said River and other nusances corrupting ye same', Macartney had to pipe pure water from his tuck dam to the town at his own expense; all the Corporation did to help him was to call for subscriptions to defray some of the £250 he had spent. The Long Bridge, begun in 1682 at the site of the old ford, was paid for by the counties of Antrim and Down. It was an impressive stone structure, 2,562 feet long with twenty-one arches. Weakened, it was said, by Schomberg's cannon, seven arches collapsed in 1692.

The government stubbornly refused to extend the powers of the Corporation and the Chichesters successfully deprived the freemen of what few rights they had in the original Charter. In vain did the Corporation propose to the Lord Lieutenant and Council in Dublin in 1671 that the Charter be altered to provide for a mayor, aldermen, a common council, and a grand jury, and that – to supply desperately needed income – 'all forran shipps and marchants not free in ye Corporacon pay wharfeage and Keage and Cranage...' The rejection of the petition meant that the Corporation continued to 'have neither lands Tenemts hereditamts Comons, Towne Stocke or pursse to pay or defrey any Publique Charge or Contingences of the Corporacon'.

The Jacobite occupation

On coming to the throne in 1685, James II received this effusive address: 'We, your Majesty's most humble and loyal subjects, the Sovereign, the Burgesses, Grand Jury, and Inhabitants of your Corporation of Belfast... prostrate ourselves at your Majesty's sacred feet as becomes your faithful and obedient subjects praying your gracious protection...' In a very short time these Protestant burghers were regretting their words as they watched the new favour granted to Catholics. The Corporation was not immediately punished for firmly refusing to provide a place of worship for Catholic soldiers in the town, but, in company with all other Irish corporations, Belfast was given a new charter in 1688. The number of free burgesses was increased to thirty-five and the monopoly of the Chichesters was broken. About half the burgesses were Catholic outsiders (as there were no propertied Catholics in the town) and the Sovereign (Thomas Pottinger the shipper) and remaining burgesses were Presbyterian.

On 4 November 1688, just three weeks after the new charter was applied, William of Orange landed in England. Early in the following year Captain Baldwin Leighton sailed from Belfast to take the inhabitants' pledge of allegiance to William who, in turn, reassured the citizens 'that we are resolved to employ the most speedy and effectual means in our power, for rescuing you from the oppression and terrors you lie under'. For the next two years Ireland became the cockpit of Europe, for the Jacobite-Williamite war was to decide not only the fate of Ireland but also the constitution of England and the balance of power in Europe.

On 12 March 1689 James II disembarked at Kinsale and two days later the Ulster Protestants were routed at the 'break of Dromore'. As a Belfast merchant, John Black, recalled later:

My father's family, by a night alarm at Belfast, left house and home furnished, on an express coming to town with a lamentable cry that after the break of Dromore the

22

Irish were coming down, sparing neither age nor sex, putting all to the sword without mercy; myself carried aboard my father's ship the 'John', which immediately set sail.

Protected only by a rampart, Belfast could not resist the Jacobite army. While Derry kept its gates resolutely closed, Pottinger opened those of Belfast and sought to prevent wholesale pillage. Leslie's account indicates that Pottinger was successful:

As the Irish forces marched over Belfast bridge, going to their quarters, their officers stopped them, and searched to see if any of them had taken any plunder in that expedition; and what they found, caused it to be delivered to Mr. Pottinger, then Sovereign of the town. . . Major Cologhan brake a soldier's head for taking a glass of ale at a door as he marched by.

Perhaps King James had been moved to restraint by the mass exodus from Belfast to Scotland; Black found the beaches of Stranraer thronged with fugitives, some sheltering from the rain under upturned boats. In an effort to attract back the refugees, James offered an amnesty in June but by this time Schomberg was preparing to bring a Williamite army to Ulster.

As the siege of Derry was being raised, a scout reported to Schomberg that Belfast Lough would be the most suitable place for bringing in his army:

It is a very bold and safe harbour; the biggest ships, if acquainted, may turn in with all winds and tides. Ships of 200 tons may go up the river within three miles of Belfast without being commanded by the Castle of Carrickfergus. Men-of-war may anchor and ride in the Lough out of command of the same fort or Castle, safe from all storms, winter and summer.

'God Bless our Protestant King, God Bless King William'

On 13 August 1689 Schomberg led his men ashore at Ballyholme Bay where 'the shore was all crowded with Protestants – men, women, and children – old and young falling on their knees with tears in their eyes thanking God and the English for their deliverance'. Carrickfergus surrendered and the Jacobite army left Belfast to retire rapidly southwards. After restoring the old Charter to Belfast, Schomberg marched to the Gap of Dundalk; there his army was so ravaged by disease that great numbers had to be shipped back to Belfast, as Story relates in his *Impartial History:*

Our ships came from Carlingford and Dundalk about the 13th of November to Belfast, and there were shipped at those two places, 1,960 men, and 1,100 of those came ashore but died at sea; nay, so great was the mortality that several ships had all the men in them dead, and nobody to look after them while they lay in the bay at Carrickfergus. As for the great hospital at Belfast, there were 3,762 that died in it from the 1st of November, to the 1st of May, as appears by the tallies given by the men that buried them. There were several that had their limbs so mortified in the camp, and afterwards that some had their toes, and some their whole feet that fell off as the surgeons were dressing them; so that upon the whole matter, we lost nigh one half of the men that we took over with us.

The epidemic spread to the rest of the town and Story found it impossible 'to come into any house but some were sick or dead, especially in Belfast where the hospital was. I have sometimes stood upon the street there, and

William of Orange: from letters patent of 1690. When he entered Belfast on 14 June 1690 'the streets were filled with bonfires and fireworks'. He is reputed to have rested at Orange Grove, now Cranmore, where the Royal Belfast Academical Institution has its playing fields. (PRONI)

seen ten or a dozen corpses of the townspeople go by in little more than half an hour'. For some of the survivors waiting for William's main army there was another hazard, as a letter from Belfast, dated 22 January 1690, indicates:

Several officers had occasioned their own deaths by drinking Irish Usquebaugh to excess, particularly Sir Edward Deering, Colonel Wharton, and Sir Thos. Gower. . . Colonel Herbert in his frenzy shot himself in the head with his pistol, and one Captain Garrot stabbed himself in the throat. A French officer in Lisburn threw himself out of a third story window. . .

At last, on 14 June 1690, William of Orange landed at Carrickfergus, met Schomberg at Whitehouse, and travelled in the Duke's coach along the sea-shore to Belfast, where

there were abundance to meet him at the North Gate, where he was received by the Sovereign and Burgesses in their formalities, a guard of Foot Guards, and a general continued shout from thence to the Castle of – God Bless our Protestant King, God Bless King William.

The citizens presented their deliverer with a verse address:

> Greatest of Kings, conquer what is your own,
> And add poor Ireland to sweet England's crown,
> Pull the stiff neck of every Papist down,
> Let captives free, who on the willow trees
> Hang useless harps that tuned such songs as these.

That night, writes Story,

the streets were filled with bonfires and fireworks, which were no sooner lighted than the alarm signal was given to the discharge of guns, so planted that from one place to another throughout the whole country all places had notice of the King's arrival, and in three hours made bonfires so thick that the whole country seemed in a flame.

Bonfires in the streets of Belfast would celebrate every year thereafter the Protestants' glorious deliverance.

After four days in Belfast, William marched south to victory at the Boyne. Though another year of hard campaigning followed, the war was over effectively for the town. The dogged rearguard action of the French and Irish Jacobites along the Shannon ended with the battle of Aughrim, fought on the 12 July 1691. The annual commemoration of these victories in Belfast would in later times be the occasion of tension and – at times – violence. The immediate significance of the battle of Aughrim was that it inaugurated the most peaceful century in Belfast's history.

The rise and fall of Presbyterian power

In the entrance of the Northern Ireland Public Record Office in Balmoral Avenue there hangs a painting of the Battle of the Boyne; in it Pope Innocent, peeping from the clouds and wearing his triple crown, gives his blessing to King William's army. The picture is a reminder that the Boyne, celebrated with Te Deums in Rome and Vienna, was a victory of a great European alliance which dealt a crushing blow to Louis XIV's schemes of domination. Yet James II's defeat also ended absolute monarchy in Britain: William's Dutch tolerance soon encountered stiff opposition from the men of property in the Westminster and Dublin parliaments. Ginkel's treaty with Sarsfield at Limerick, eventually signed by William and Mary, was overturned in favour of harsher terms: further extensive confiscations left all but 14% of the land of Ireland in Protestant hands. As a constitutional monarch, William had no choice but to sign laws voted by parliamentary majorities imposing severe restrictions on the rights of Catholics.

'We have not amongst us within the town above seven Papists,' wrote George Macartney, the Sovereign of Belfast, in 1708. As Protestants formed no more than a quarter of Ireland's population, the citizens of Belfast were privileged by comparison with the Catholic peasantry. Yet real power and wealth were monopolised by the Protestant Ascendancy, a narrow caste of great landlords and their relations. Ultimately the Ascendancy's exclusiveness would drive the Protestant middle class of Belfast into a potent alliance with Catholics in search of more basic rights.

King William could do little for the Catholics, but while he was still alive

An ACT for Baniſhing

all *Papiſts* exerciſing any Eccleſiaſtical Juriſdiction, and all Regulars of the *Popiſh Clergy* out of this Kingdom.

CHAP. XXVI

WHEREAS, it is notoriouſly known, That the late Rebellions in this Kingdom have been Contrived, Promoted and Carried on by Popiſh Arch-Biſhops, Biſhops, Jeſuits, and other Eccleſiaſtical Perſons of the Romiſh Clergy. And foraſmuch as the Peace and Publick Safety of this Kingdom is in Danger, by the great number of the ſaid Arch-Biſhops, Biſhops, Jeſuits, Friers, and other Regular Romiſh Clergy now reſiding here, and ſettling in Fraternities and Societies, contrary to Law, and to the great Impoveriſhing of many of His Majeſty's Subjects of this Kingdom, who are forced to maintain and ſupport them; which ſaid Romiſh Clergy do, not only rebearten to withdraw His Majeſty's Subjects from their Obedience, but do daily ſtir up, and move Sedition, and Rebellion, to the great hazard of the Ruine and Deſolation of this Kingdom. See

An early Penal Law.

Presbyterians in Ireland benefited from his protection. Grateful for Presbyterian loyalty, William, at 'our Court at Belfast, the 19th day of June 1690', had promised that all loyal subjects would 'enjoy their liberties and possessions under a just and equal government'. On his way to Hillsborough William sent an order to Christopher Carleton, collector of Belfast, for the payment of £1,200 a year to the Presbyterian ministers of Ulster, 'being assured of the peaceable and dutiful temper of our said subjects, and sensible of the losses they have sustained, and their constant labour to unite the hearts of others in zeal and loyalty towards us'. Schomberg may have restored the old Charter, but Presbyterians – by now the majority of the town's inhabitants – were appointed burgesses and appear to have been in control of the Corporation until shortly after William's death.

Lenient treatment of the Presbyterians came to an abrupt halt in 1704. The accession of Queen Anne brought the High Church Tories to power at Westminster and a new determination to extend the penal code against Catholics and incidentally against other non-Anglicans. The 1704 Act 'to prevent the further growth of Popery', the most vindictive and unenforceable of the Penal Laws, was accompanied by the Test and Corporation Act which required all office holders under the crown to take the sacrament in the Established Church. William Craford, one of Belfast's MPs and a Presbyterian, had to resign his seat, and on 29 July 1704 the Sovereign, David Burle, informed the burgesses: 'By a late Act of Parliament disabling disentors to serve in public office, I find it convenient for me to demitt the exercise of Sovereigne in yo[r] Corpora[n]. . .' George Macartney took Burle's place and, probably with some reluctance, removed eight other burgesses who refused to take the test. The chief impact, therefore, of the Penal Laws on Belfast was to deprive the Presbyterian majority of any say in the running of the town's affairs.

'Jet-black Prelatic Calumny'

Dr William Tisdall, Vicar of Belfast, was one of the most influential and intolerant of High Churchmen in Ireland. A close friend of Jonathan Swift, Tisdall shared Swift's view that Presbyterians were more to be feared than the Catholics themselves. Swift probably helped him to compose a pamphlet attacking the Presbyterians, ironically titled *A Sample of True-Blew Presbyterian Loyalty in all Changes and Turns of Government, taken chiefly out of their most authentic records*. Tisdall's greatest victory came when, in the last year of Queen Anne's reign, the 'regium donum' – the £1,200 granted annually to dissenting ministers – was withdrawn.

Tisdall did not have everything his own way, however. When he failed to collect 'house-money' in Belfast to improve the Vicar's income, he launched a suit against the Corporation. Citizens of all religious persuasions contributed to a fund to oppose him in court, and his suit failed. He also failed to oust his energetic opponent, John McBride, Presbyterian minister of Belfast. Tisdall accused McBride of being a Jacobite and the minister was forced to flee to Scotland in 1708; McBride returned soon after, however, to publish a popular denunciation of Tisdall, entitled *A Sample of Jet-black Prelatic Calumny*.

James Blow published and reprinted many of these pamphlets. Invited to come to Belfast by the Sovereign, Blow left Glasgow in 1696 to become the town's first printer; in partnership with his brother-in-law Patrick Neill he

26

printed the first bible in Ireland in 1704. Judging by his secret reprints, Blow seems to have scuppered Tisdall's attempts to impose censorship on the town. In vain did Tisdall obtain a warrant to seize copies of a scurrilous pamphlet. He wrote: 'I cannot positively assert that it was reprinted at Belfast though I am firmly of the opinion that it was published there with great caution and secrecy. . .' Other copies, not seized, continued to circulate freely.

It may have been Tisdall who persuaded Lady Donegall to complain to the Dublin government that Macartney, as Sovereign, had been evading the provisions of the Test and Corporation Act. Macartney faced more than eight hours of questioning by the Irish House of Commons in 1707, but he was acquitted on all charges. So strident was the High Church campaign against the Presbyterians that in 1713 eighty citizens of the Established Church in Belfast signed a declaration in favour of toleration of their Presbyterian neighbours when they were accused of unfair trading:

We do hereby certify that the Presbyterian inhabitants of Belfast deal and trade with us as freely and readily as they do with one another, though we are all of the Communion of the Established Church; that we have the greatest part of our trade from them, and that we do not perceive, know, nor believe that they use any unfair practices in confining trade amongst themselves. . .

Another declaration, signed by forty-one citizens, praising the Test Act for giving 'a seasonable check to the prevailing power of faction in our Corporations' never reached Queen Anne. She died, unmourned by the Presbyterians, and with the accession of George of Hanover in 1714 an era of greater toleration seemed certain.

A ground plan of Belfast in 1685. This attractive nineteenth-century copy is rendered somewhat confusing by South, contrary to all convention, being at the top of the plan. (Linen Hall Library)

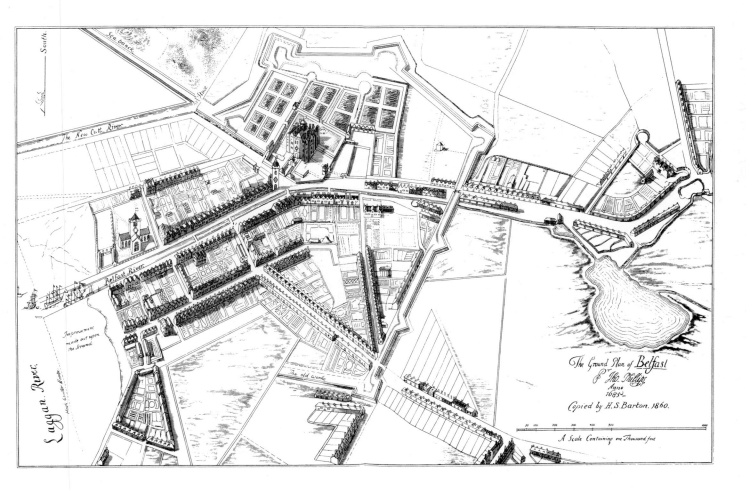

October.   FRANCIS JOY.   Numb. 113

The Belfast News-Letter,
And General Advertiser.

TUESDAY, October 3, 1738.

Founded by Francis Joy in 1737, the *Belfast News-Letter* is one of the oldest provincial papers in the world. It was printed at 'the Sign of the Peacock' in Joy's Entry, off High Street.

Catholics and Belfast

So comprehensive were the Penal Laws that George I's Lord Chancellor declared that 'the law does not suppose any such person to exist as an Irish Roman Catholic'. Yet the code, in, for example, depriving Catholics of the vote, parliamentary representation, the right to buy land, and entry into the higher professions, was directed principally against educated and propertied Catholics. The peasantry were only affected indirectly and laws restricting Catholic worship were fitfully applied. No serious attempt was made to convert Catholics to Protestantism – what use was privilege if shared by all? Catholics worshipping at Friar's Bush, where open-air Mass was celebrated on an oak table in a sand-pit, do not seem to have been disturbed. Shortly after the 1704 Popery Act, Father Brullaghan published in Belfast a detailed guide for pilgrims to Lough Derg, a pilgrimage which, although specifically forbidden in the Act, continued to flourish under the protection of the Protestant Leslie family.

Belfast was set in the most Protestant corner of Ireland; Macartney's report that there were only seven Catholics in the town also mentioned that 'by the return made by the High Constable there is not above 150 Papists in the whole Barony'. Perhaps it was because Catholics were in such a distinct minority that they appear to have enjoyed greater toleration in Belfast in the eighteenth century than in the rest of Ulster.

In 1708, during a Jacobite scare, Macartney attempted to protect the local parish priest, Father Phelomy O'Hamill, who had received orders from Primate Oliver Plunket in 1677, was parish priest for Belfast, Derriaghy, Drumbo, and Drumbeg; when the government ordered his arrest he willingly gave himself up to the Sovereign to be imprisoned. Macartney wrote to Dublin requesting permission to grant the priest bail: 'His behaviour has been such amongst us since, and was, upon the late Revolution so kind to the Protestants by saving several of their goods in those times, that I had offered me the best Bail the Protestants of this Country affords.' However, Macartney's letter was sent back from Dublin curtly endorsed: 'Let him Continue for the Present where he is.'

Even if Catholics did not live in the town, they did come in regularly to sell their produce; the Belfast market was regularly referred to as the 'margymore' (the great market), clear evidence that it was extensively used by native-speakers. The nearest Catholic churches to Belfast were Derriaghy and Hannahstown, though as the Catholic population in the town began to increase, Mass was said in a 'waste house' in Castle Street. Elderly people told the historian George Benn that they 'were obliged to take pieces of wood or bricks to kneel on, so mean and dirty was the place'. This description confirms the impression that there were no Catholics of great property and wealth living then in or around Belfast.

Friday, August 15, 1746.   F. JOY, and SONS.   NUMB.

THE Belfast News-Letter, AND General Advertiser.

With the freshest Advices Foreign & Domestick

'In a ruinous condition'

On 24 April 1708 Belfast Castle was gutted by fire; in the blaze three of the 4th Earl's sisters were burned to death. The tragedy was said to have been started by the carelessness of a servant who put on a large wood fire to air a room she had washed. An anonymous traveller wrote a few months later that the Castle stood 'separate from the rest of the houses, which, as it prevented the flames going further, so it cut off timely relief, in the midst of courts and gardens. . .' It was a disaster from which it could be said the Donegall family never fully recovered. Only two years before, the 3rd Earl had been killed at the siege of Monjuich, fighting in Spain with Marlborough's army. Now not only was the Donegall family headed by a weak-willed minor, Arthur Chichester, but it had also lost its principal home. Belfast lost its central focus and henceforth the Chichesters were absentee and negligent landlords.

'I live in the neighbourhood of Belfast and know it to be in a ruinous condition,' the 4th Earl's cousin, Lord Massareene, wrote in 1752. He believed the town would 'lose both its Trade and Inhabitants if it is not speedily supported by proper Tenures'. In 1754 an application to the Lord Chancellor for a Commission of Lunacy against the 4th Earl, made by Sir Roger Newdigate, uncle of the heir presumptive, failed by a narrow margin. The Law Lords admitted 'that his Lordship had not been much used to business or to care of his estates and concerns' and two relatives, Thomas Ludford and Richard Barry, were appointed trustees of the Donegall properties. The imbecility of the 4th Earl, legal wrangling, and the timidity of the trustees ensured that the Chichesters provided no initiative in improving Belfast.

Development of the town was stifled above all by short leases and tenancies which carried no obligation to carry out improvements. Merchants declared that unless they could obtain favourable leases 'they will immediately leave the Town and settle in Newry or Lisburn'. Opposed by Newdigate, a group of citizens sought an act of parliament to obtain long leases 'to promote or encourage the Rebuilding of the said Town'. The promoters stated:

The town of Belfast belongs to, and is the sole property of the Earl of Donegall, but as most of the Leases granted by the ancestors of the said Earl are now near expiring the Houses have been suffered to go out of repair, and so very old, ruinous, and unfit for habitation that is become necessary for the Preservation and Support of the Trade of the Town and for preventing the Inhabitants from quitting and deserting the same, that the said Houses should be rebuilt.

29

Belfast Castle destroyed by fire:
a late-nineteenth-century
impression by J. W. Carey.
(Linen Hall Library)

It was left to the 5th Earl, who succeeded his uncle in 1757, to grant the 99-year leases without which the rapid growth of Belfast in the late eighteenth century would not have been possible. Later the new leases were issued on such terms that they provoked resentment and violence. In the long term, however, those leases, together with the eventual disintegration of the Donegall family, were to clear the way for the mushroom growth of a mighty industrial city in the nineteenth century.

From the *Belfast News-Letter*,
15 August 1746.

3
Radical Town
c.1750–1801

In the first half of the eighteenth century the growth of Belfast had been almost imperceptible. Emigration to America drew away some of the most enterprising citizens and the town suffered from the neglect of the Donegall family. New leases issued by the 5th Earl were to be partly responsible for the 'Hearts of Steel' disturbances but they also ensured that Belfast had handsome buildings and well-laid-out streets by the end of the century. The town's population, which had been 8,500 in 1757, rose to 13,000 by 1782, and reached 20,000 by 1800. Expansion was due mainly to commercial growth but the cotton industry, too, helped to diversify the town's economy; it was in Belfast that the first industrial revolution had taken its deepest root in Ireland at the time of the Union.

In these years the town's Presbyterian middle class gave a lead in challenging the monopoly of the Ascendancy, giving Belfast a political importance out of all proportion to its size. For a time Belfast had the reputation of being the most radical and seditious centre in Ireland. Some Belfast democrats threw themselves into revolutionary conspiracy but the course of the 1798 rebellion was far removed from that which they had contemplated. Thereafter bourgeois idealism changed direction in the town and the enactment of the Union in 1801 was greeted there with comparative indifference.

Emigrants' port

'The humour of going to America still continues,' Dr Boulter wrote in 1729; 'and the scarcity of provisions certainly makes many quit us. There are now seven ships at Belfast that are carrying off about 1,000 passengers thither.' Throughout the seventeenth century Lowland Scots had poured into Ulster. In 1672 Petty estimated that there were 100,000 Scots in Ulster; another 50,000 came in during the fifteen years following the Battle of the Boyne; and by the close of Queen Anne's reign there were about 200,000 Presbyterians out of a total population of around 600,000 in the province. At this point immigration virtually ceased and for the next sixty years there was a spectacular out-pouring of 'Scotch-Irish' to America. By the middle of the eighteenth century it was reckoned that 12,000 were leaving Ulster every year.

Belfast was the most important port of departure, even though the most distressed areas were in the west of Ulster. Between 1750 and 1775 at least 143 emigrant vessels left Belfast for America, 65 of them with Philadelphia as their destination. For many, America was indeed, as one advertisement put it,

(a) Shipping advertisement,
Belfast News-Letter.

(b) Shipping advertisement,
Belfast News-Letter.

'the Land of Promise'; a notice in the *Belfast News-Letter* in 1766 informing the public that the *Falls* was shortly to sail from Belfast to Nova Scotia called on readers to embrace 'such a favourable opportunity by settling themselves to advantage by a removal to that country, a removal which cannot fail to give freedom, peace, and plenty to those who now wish to enjoy those blessings'. America was a land of limitless opportunity to Ulster Scots, where their skills in taming wild country would be highly valued, and where the Presbyterian work-ethic would receive its just reward, as de Crevecoeur wrote invitingly in 1782:

Welcome to my shores. . . bless the hour in which thou didst see my verdant fields, my navigable rivers, and my green mountains! – if thou wilt work, I have bread for thee; if thou wilt be honest, sober, and industrious, I have greater rewards to confer on thee – ease and independence. I will give thee fields and clothe thee; a comfortable fireside to sit by, and tell thy children by what means thou hast prospered. . .

'The humour has spread like a contagious distemper, and the people will hardly bear anybody that tries to cure them of their madness,' Boulter observed. He continued: 'The worst is, that it affects only Protestants and reigns chiefly in the north, which is the seat of our linen manufacture.' Catholics had neither the resources nor the inclination to go to colonies which were still overwhelmingly Protestant. The domestic linen industry, which had developed so rapidly in the eighteenth century, was export-based and therefore exceptionally sensitive to slumps and booms in international trade. A prolonged depression – as in the 1770s – could lead to a sudden increase in emigration. Ulster Protestants deeply resented the commercial restrictions designed to protect the mother country's interests when they had done so much to defeat the Irish Jacobites. Besides, earnings from linen were not enough to compensate for rent increases:

> For the rents are getting higher, and I can no longer stay,
> So fare well unto ye bonny, bonny Slieve Gallon Braes.

Rents quintupled in many areas between 1710 and 1770, and yet in the same period the average price of linen cloth rose only by 20%. As the population rose, and as land values increased with the return of settled conditions and the growth of linen production, landlords had no difficulty in obtaining high rents. For Protestant settlers in Ulster, the days of cheap land had gone:

> But these days are now all over, for I am far away,
> So fare well unto ye bonny, bonny, Slieve Gallon Braes.

The journey from Belfast across the Atlantic could be perilous, especially when fever broke out on board, or when ships were delayed by calms and contrary winds. In 1729, 175 people died on board two vessels from Belfast during the crossing. In 1741 the *Seaflower* sprang her mast en route from Belfast to Philadelphia; forty-six passengers died and six of their corpses were eaten in desperation by the survivors. A fortnight of storms drove the *Sally* off her course from Belfast to Philadelphia in 1762, and sixty-four passengers died. John Smilie survived this voyage and wrote an account of it for his father:

. . . Hunger and Thirst had now reduced our Crew to the last Extremity; nothing was now to be heard aboard our Ship but the Cries of distressed children, and of their distressed Mothers, unable to relieve them. Our Ship now was truly a real Spectacle of Horror! Never a Day passed without one of our Crew put over Board; many kill'd themselves by drinking Salt Water; and their own Urine was a common Drink; yet in the midst of all our Miseries, our Captain shewed not the least Remorse or pity. . .

Meanwhile the same hardship which sent some to hazard their lives crossing the Atlantic in search of prosperity, led on occasion to eruptions of disorder in Belfast.

'Provision for the begging poor': the Poor House

'All Order and Government here are now at an end,' George Macartney wrote from Belfast on 22 July 1756. Crowds of hungry people, unable to buy what little grain was for sale, were surging through the streets of the town, seizing sacks of meal and forcing shopkeepers to sell bread at below the market price. The rioting continued to the end of the month, as Macartney again reported:

The Town must in all probability be starved for none will bring in Meal either by Land or Sea till they can be secured of their Property which is impossible while the Mobb commands as is the present case, for no Justice dare Issue a Warrant against one of them.

Macartney's attempt to censor the town's only newspaper, the *Belfast News-Letter,* which had printed editorials sympathising with the hungry, had failed. Further disturbances followed in August; a grain store was looted and its owner, a woman, was dragged out forcibly, put on a cart, and taken to be ducked in the Mill Dam.

As the harvest was being garnered in, peace returned, but the unrest had shaken the men of property in Belfast and had given fresh urgency to the work of the Belfast Charitable Society. Founded in 1752, the Society set out to provide relief for the destitute and in particular to build a poorhouse 'for the vast numbers of real objects of charity in this parish, for the employment of idle beggars who crowd to it from all parts of the north, and for the reception of infirm and diseased poor'. Unlike England, Ireland had no Poor Law; the Donegall family shirked its responsibility and its creature, the Belfast Corporation, was even more out of touch with the needs of the town than before. The Society's target was £50,000, but lotteries brought in a profit of less than £2,000 in the first year.

The first response of the merchants to the 1756 riots was to form a posse in November to arrest the ring-leaders. In December, however, a scheme for the relief of the poor was adopted by 'a numerous meeting of the principal gentlemen of Belfast'. The town was divided into ten districts and twenty gentlemen were appointed to raise money every month to provide outdoor relief for the poor. This scheme was never sanctioned by law, but there is no evidence that resistance was made to the collection of this poor-rate.

The Charitable Society continued to run lotteries and by 1767 it had raised £7,592. The following July Lord Donegall granted to the Society an eight-acre plot of ground on the north side of what was then called Carrickfergus-Peter's

Hill. On 1 August 1771 the Sovereign, Stewart Banks, laid there the first stone of what is now called Clifton House. The great architect Thomas Cooley of Dublin was consulted, but the design adopted was an amateur plan drawn by Robert Joy. Busy though he was editing the *Belfast News-Letter* and building a great paper mill at Cromac, Joy found time to visit poorhouses in Liverpool, Birmingham, Manchester and Glasgow to seek guidance and inspiration for the Society. Unpretentious but imposing, the Poor House remains one of the finest buildings in Belfast today. It was opened in December 1774 and the following February this advertisement appeared in the *Belfast News-Letter:*

Provision being now made in this House for the greatest number of the Begging Poor, and new Badges provided for the Remainder with Licences to beg for a limited Time, until the House be fully fitted up for their Reception, it is expected that the Inhabitants will direct their attention to those and discourage all public Beggars, who, they may be assured, are not entitled to their Charity. And whoever shall apprehend and bring to the Poor House any such strolling Beggars will be paid 5s.5d. for each after next Saturday.

The money offered would, no doubt, have been better spent on outdoor relief. It would be too much to expect, however, that any other concept than that of there being deserving and undeserving poor would have been held by the Society at such an early date. It was in an effort to provide work for the inmates of the Poor House that Robert Joy was to bring the cotton industry to Belfast a few years later.

'The very marrow is screwed out of our bones': the 'Hearts of Steel'

On the morning of Sunday 23 December 1770 angry farmers gathered at Templepatrick Meeting House and, armed with firelocks, pistols and pitchforks, set out for Belfast. At the 'Stag's Head' on the Shore Road they stopped to collect reinforcements: as they approached Belfast they numbered 1,200 and were led by a man on horseback named Crawford, who carried crowbars wrapped in straw rope. Calling themselves 'The Hearts of Steel', they were intent on forcing the release of David Douglas, held on the charge of maiming cattle belonging to Thomas Greg, a Belfast merchant. Stewart Banks, the Sovereign, closed the North Gate and — with Douglas and twenty-five armed gentlemen — took refuge in the Barrack. The 'Hearts of Steel' surged round the Barrack and demanded the release of Douglas. A contemporary letter describes the sequel:

To this Mr Banks gave a direct refusal, on which they fired many shots at the gate and over the wall, but failing of the desired effect, a party proceeded to the House of Waddell Cunningham, broke it open, and were in the act of destroying the furniture when Dr Haliday, an eminent physician of Belfast, actuated by compassion, and dreading lest the town might be destroyed, mingled with the crowd assembled at Mr. Cunningham's house. After expostulating with them in vain he was taken prisoner by them and sworn, that he would immediately repair to the Barrack and procure the release of the prisoner. . . The Doctor had just reached the Barrack on this embassy, passing through an immense multitude consisting of the people from the country intermixed with those of the town, when the gate was thrown open by the military, who fired upon the assailants, killed five persons and wounded nine others. By the Doctor's humane interference farther firing was prevented. . .

'Hearts of Steel' attack on the Barrack, 23 December 1770: a late nineteenth-century impression by J. W. Carey. (Linen Hall Library)

In the meantime Cunningham's house at the bottom of Hercules Lane was burning fiercely, putting the whole town in danger. At one o'clock in the morning Banks saw no alternative but to give up the prisoner to prevent the destruction of Belfast.

The immediate cause of this assault was the eviction of tenants by the Upton family from their Templepatrick estate; poor tenants were ejected and replaced by solvent tenants including two Belfast speculators, Thomas Greg and Waddell Cunningham. The disturbances were widespread and coincided with the peak of Protestant emigration from the north. Their principal cause was a sharp increase in rents; on the Stewart lands in north Down, for example, the average rent per acre of newly leased land had risen from 4s.2d. in the 1740s to 12s.7d. in the 1760s. The great landowners – including Clotworthy Upton who relet 4,000 acres of land between Belfast and Antrim – preferred to let out their property for convenience to middlemen, described by Arthur Young as 'the most oppressive species of tyrant that ever lent assistance to the destruction of a nation'.

In the area around Belfast, however, the root cause of the unrest was the re-leasing of large parts of Lord Donegall's property from 1767 onwards. The extravagant 5th Earl was desperately short of money; to raise cash immediately, he relet farms at the old rents but at the same time he imposed heavy 'fines'. Many tenants could not pay these fines and were evicted, while others found that Belfast merchants had bid over their heads for leases of whole townlands. A lease was made, for example, to William Grey for the half-townland of Ballyclaverty in 1770, the rent being £57.10s.0d. but the fine being £400; Dr Haliday obtained a lease for Ballyduff at £120.10s.0d. rent and £500 fine; and Robert Wallace's lease for Ballymurphy specified a rent of £100.2s.0d. and a fine of £170.

'The first cause of those tumults sprung from my Lord Donegall's taking fines and granting long leases to several purchasers and putting the occupying tenants into their hands to covenant for their holdings as they could,' James Hamilton wrote in March 1772, and he continued: 'Many of them about Belfast gave up their lands and upon its being stocked, the cattle were maimed and houses burned.'

Throughout 1771 and 1772 the 'Hearts of Steel' continued what the local gentry described as 'a lawless, turbulent, and dangerous Spirit of Insurgency'. The Lord Lieutenant, Townshend, disapproved of the landlords' action, which would 'compel wretched tenants to go to America, or any other part of the world where they can receive that reward which is honestly due to their labour'. Nevertheless, Townshend sent troops northwards and some 'Steelboys' drowned attempting to escape from them across the Irish Sea in small boats. The plight of the tenants is stated poignantly in the Proclamation of the 'Hearts of Steel' in March 1772:

. . . betwixt landlord and rectors, the very marrow is screwed out of our bones, and our lives are even become so burdensome to us, by these uncharitable and unreasonable men, that we do not care whether we live or die; for they lay such burthen upon our shoulders that they cannot touch them with one of their fingers; they have reduced us to such a deplorable state by such grievous oppressions that the poor is turned black in the face, and the skin parched on their back.

John Wesley was in Belfast on 15 June 1773 when he recorded in his diary:

It is no wonder that, as their lives were now bitter to them, they should fly out as they did. It is rather a wonder that they did not go much farther. And if they had, who would have been most at fault? Those who were without home, without money, without food for themselves and families? or those who drove them to this extremity?

The rebuilding of Belfast

For the town of Belfast itself, the 5th Earl had other plans. Here, instead of imposing fines, he ordered a steep increase in rents. Prominent citizens had earlier promoted a Bill for longer leases and had obtained an Act of Parliament for this purpose in 1752. Leases tied to the duration of three named lives were issued, with higher rents and detailed clauses for improvement. The town was carefully surveyed and penalties were to be imposed if tenants – in the words of one lease – 'should lay or put upon any part of the Streets of the said town of Belfast, any Ashes, Dung, Filth, or Dirt whatsoever, and suffer the same to lie or continue there above the Space of twenty-four hours'.

New building standards were set. In Castle Place houses had to be 28 feet high; in High Street 25 feet; in Ann Street 18 feet; in Castle Lane 15 feet; and the cabins in Peter's Hill were to be 10 feet high. Important tenants had to undertake major projects: Thomas Greg, for example, had to build a mortared quay wall of 320 feet in length 'filled and paved to a depth of 35 feet' and to erect a 'draw-bridge across the east end of the dock of sufficient strength to carry loaded carts and carriages'.

A major rebuilding of Belfast was soon underway. Belfast has very little good local building stone, and Mourne granite was considered too gritty for general use. The result was that there was for a time an almost insatiable demand for brick. John Gordon, Donegall's agent, wrote in 1757: 'The Brick Grounds about the Town are most part run out, and Brick will be much wanted.' New brickworks were established in what is now Sandy Row. By 1783, when the town was 'deemed the third commercial town in the kingdom', the appearance of Belfast had been transformed.

In 1783 travellers from the south approached the town by the Malone Ridge – which marks the prehistoric shore-line of the Lagan and its estuary – passing Friar's Bush and the Plains before meeting the Turnpike Gate near the present Bradbury Place. The way leading into the town was through Sandy Row, an unprepossessing sight, according to one visitor in 1780:

. . . in my entrance into Belfast I was vastly surprized and hurt to see a long string of falling cabins and tattered houses, all tumbling down with a horrid aspect, and the seeming prelude to a pitiful village which was my idea of Belfast, untill I got pretty far into the town when I found my error, for indeed with some trifling improvements it might be made to vie with any town in Ireland save Dublin and Cork.

From Sandy Row to the Lagan ran the 'Pass Loning', now Donegall Pass, one of six paths through the extensive Cromac woods of oak and elm. The course of the Owenvarra, or Blackstaff, had been altered by a straight cut to the Lagan, and just above the cut the stream had been impounded to form the Mill Dam and Joy's Mill Dam supplying the paper mill. This cut had reclaimed land from the sea known as the Mall Fields and, further inland, as the Bog Meadows. The town proper could be reached by the Mall, which ran

View of Belfast from Lagan Village. The bottletower of the Ballymacarrett glassworks is clearly visible – an early indication that this area was later to become the industrial heartland of Belfast. (Morland, Ulster Museum)

View of the southern outskirts of the town from Joy's paper mill at Cromac. St. Anne's Church steeple is visible on the right. The warehouse and showrooms of the White Linen Hall (left centre) were used as a barracks in 1798: there were complaints in the *Belfast News-Letter* that ladies were shocked to see soldiers bathing in the mill-dam (foreground). (Ulster Museum)

from the paper mill to Castle Street, but the usual route was through Sandy Row, over the Saltwater Bridge (near the present Boyne Bridge), and right down Durham Street to Castle Street. Castle Street and High Street formed the town's main thoroughfare; here, though some thatched houses still remained, fine houses had been built for the gentry and merchants. This is how one traveller saw the town centre in 1772:

The houses are well built with brick and slated, with the streets pretty wide; the pavement is bad in some places, but not in general. Were conduits of water run through them, which I think might be effected at an easy expense, it would take off the dirt which unavoidably gathers, and this with shameful heaps in many streets, must be a very great nuisance to the inhabitants. . . A New Town Hall is now building; it is a gift of the Lord and on a handsome design, but scarcely long enough for its height. I hear the underpart is to serve for an Exchange, and the upper part for an Assembly Room. . .

The Exchange had been built in 1769 at the 'Four Corners' – the junction of Bridge Street, Waring Street, North Street and Rosemary Lane – with the Assembly Rooms completed in 1777. Sir Robert Taylor, Architect of the King's Works, designed the delicately ornate Rooms and an English craftsman, Samuel Kirke, was brought over to carry out the carving. As Kirke died of 'a Jaundice and Dropsy by Dram-Drinking', the work was completed by James Forbes, a local wood-carver, and was universally admired.

The Farset still flowed uncovered through High Street, where it was spanned by several bridges. 'As the river has been lately cleaned,' ran a notice in the *Belfast News-Letter* in 1761, 'it is requested that those who live opposite thereto, may as far as in their power prevent any thing from being thrown into it.' It was a vain appeal; three years later the Grand Jury declared: 'We present the several dunghills, rubbish, and filth lying or hereafter to be laid

High Street 1786: a late-
nineteenth-century copy of a
contemporary engraving. The
Donegall Arms (left
foreground) was the principal
hotel of the time. The dial-plate
of the Market House clock
(right foreground) fell and
severely injured a man earlier in
the century. (Ulster Museum)

down, in the streets of Belfast to be a public nuisance.' That there was no
improvement by 1780, is confirmed by a Scottish visitor:

It was about 10 o'clock on Sunday morning when I stopped at the Donegall Arms as I
meant going no farther that day. I strutted about the town; but Oh! Cleanliness,
Celestial Maid! What was my surprise at beholding piles of dunghills made up
through the middle of the whole town from one end to the other. . . I also observed
particularly in the main street, which is a very handsome one, that the pavements
before the doors were very indifferent, and not by any means calculated to throw off
the dirt having no descent from the houses to the channel. . .

High Street was flanked on either side by Ann Street and Waring Street,
which in turn were connected to each other by 'entries', the Cornmarket, and
Bridge Street. In September 1764, the *Belfast News-Letter* reported:

Six or seven new houses are now building, and will be finished this season on the
ground laid out for a New Street, and many others next spring. . . The New Street
will be very handsome – 600 yards, 60 feet wide, and the houses three stories high.
The Linen Hall ranging on one side of the street about the centre will add to its
beauty.

39

The Old Manse, Rosemary Street. Built for Rev Robert McBride of the 1st congregation about 1700: the birth-place of Dr William Drennan and Dr William Haliday.
(*Ulster Journal of Archaeology*)

New Street, later re-named Donegall Street, was planned and built by Roger Mulholland, an architect responsible for much of the rebuilding of the period. The new Brown Linen Hall did not stand for long as it was knocked down to make way for the new parish church of St Anne's, built entirely at Lord Donegall's expense in 1776; this elegant church was pulled down in 1900 to make way for St Anne's Cathedral. The church had serious design faults: the spire, for long a familiar landmark, was too fragile to hold the bell and the portico had to be rebuilt completely. Equally fine was the 1st Presbyterian Church in Rosemary Street, built by Mulholland in 1783. The Earl-Bishop of Derry, who subscribed 50 guineas towards its construction, declared that 'the beauty of the building does equal honour to the taste of the subscribers and the talent of the architect'. Wesley, who preached there six years later, recorded in his diary:

It is the completest place of worship I have ever seen. It is of an oval form; as I judge by my eye a hundred feet long, and seventy or eighty feet broad. It is very lofty, and has two rows of large windows, so that it is as high as our new chapel in London. And the rows of pillars, with every other part, are so finely proportioned, that it is beautiful in the highest degree.

In 1756 Robert Wilson and James Trail petitioned the Donegall trustees to obtain permission to widen the alley between Castle Street and Hercules Lane. The area remained run-down, however, and was filled with slaughter houses. As a correspondent of the *Belfast News-Letter* asked in 1785:

. . . is it not inconsistent in the inhabitants to be daily giving proof of taste and increasing opulence in opening new streets, in public erections, etc. when they never once turn their eyes to shambles that for nastiness have not their equal in the meanest village in Ireland – tho' they have been noticed by travellers and by some of them recorded to our discredit?

The Smithfield cattle market lay convenient to the butchers; this city centre site was then on the outskirts of the town where cattle grazed.

To the visitor the most prominent feature of Belfast was the seventeenth-century Long Bridge. Edward Willes described it in 1759:

The bridge over which we pass into the town is the longest in his Majesty's dominions. It is built over an arm of the sea and a lough, which is great part of it dry at low water; they say it is a mile long, but it is I really believe three quarters of an English mile. This bridge is the mall where all the company of Belfast take the air in a summer's evening.

The Stone Bridge was the business centre of Belfast, where ships discharged their cargoes at the quays and where financial deals were made at the Exchange close by. Here too was the post office and, in a narrow court off Joy's Entry, the offices where the *Belfast News-Letter* was published. It was adjacent to the bridge that, in 1769,

Mr Thomas Greg laid the corner foundation stone next the sea of the new Kay which he is building on the north side of the dock of Belfast. This Kay is 320 feet in length, and when finished will give room for the accommodation of a much greater number of ships and in deeper water than heretofore; and Mr Greg in commemoration of the birth of Lord Chichester hath called the said Kay Chichester Kay.

Shipping advertisement, *Belfast News-Letter*

THE DRAPER, Robert Moor Master, is now at the Key of Belfast, and ready to take in Goods and will sail for LIVERPOOL, on Thursday next, Wind and Weather permitting.

An Account of the ships which have sailed with Passengers to America from the Ports of Londonderry, Port Rush, Larne, Belfast & Newry from March 1771 to 25ᵗ March 1773 taken from the Advertisements in the Belfast News Letter.

From the Port of Belfast

	Ship	Master	Tons	Destination	Date		
1	Polly	Dd McCutcheon	200	Philadelphia	Mar. 71	80	80
2	Philadelphia	Jas Malcolm	250	Ditto	Apr. 71	256	300
3	Prince of Wales	C. McKenzie	250	New—	Apr. 71		60
4	Kitty & Peggy	D. Ferguson	300	Philadelphia	May 71	228	270
5	Polly	Dd McCutcheon	200	Ditto	Augt 71	130	150
6	Hopewell	J. Ash	250	Charlestown	Octr 71	220	260
7	Brittania	J. Clendenen	300	Savannah	Octr 71	300	350
8	Friendship	W. McCulloch	250	Philadelphia	Mar. 72	236	250
9	Prince of Wales	C. McKenzie	400	Ditto	Apr. 72	327	390
10	Philadelphia	Jas Malcolm	250	Ditto	May 72	242	287
11	Will & John	Jno Baker	150	St Johns Gulfs Lawren	May 72	106	106
12	Brittania	Jas Clendenen	300	Charlestown	Octr 72	84	105
13	Friendship	W. McCulloch	250	Philadelphia	Augt 72	69	76
14	Elizabeth	Dd Brown	250	Savannah	Octr 72	197	240
15	Hopewell	Tho: Ash	250	Charlestown	Sep 72	210	245
16	Pensilva Farmer	C. Robinson	350	Ditto	Octr 72	176	230
17	Friendship	W. McCulloch	250	Ditto	Mar. 73	248	280
			4450			3164	3679

From the Port of Newry

	Ship	Master	Tons	Destination	Date
1	Newry Packet	C. Robison	300	Philadelphia	apr. 71
2	Pensilva Farmer	A. Johnston	350	Ditto	Mar. 71
3	Betsy	Ger Brown	300	Baltre & Charlestown	Mar. 71
4	Dolphin	J. Finlay	300	Philadelphia	Mar. 71
5	Jenny & Polly	D. Lawrence	300	Baltimore	May 71
6	Venus	Jno Lloyd	250	Anapolis &c.	July 71
7	New York	Mos Rankin	400	New York	July 71
8	Robert	Mr Russell	300	Ditto	Sep. 71
9	Newry assist	Jas Chevers	300	Philadelphia	Sep. 71
10	Robert	M. Russell	300	New York	apr. 72
11	Pheby & Peggy	Dd McCulloch	350	Philadelphia	June 72

Shipping list 1771–3: the emigration of 'Scotch-Irish' to America was at its height at this time. (PRONI)

Ships still had to wait for high tide, nevertheless, three miles down the Lough at the Pool of Garmoyle, before they could tie up at Donegall Quay. Across the Long Bridge, Barry Yelverton, Lord Chief Baron, had bought Ballymacarrett from the Pottinger family. As the *Gentleman's Magazine* reported in December 1786, Yelverton,

seeing the advantage which must arise from building a town opposite to Belfast, formed an embankment of 300 yards in length, and marked out the places so inclosed into streets, which he let to tenants *in perpetuity*, in opposition to the custom of Lord Donegall, who set up his leases to sale, and let the premises to the highest bidder, without any regard to the interests of the old tenants.

This was too much for the Marquis of Donegall; in 1786 he bought out Yelverton and the way was prepared for Ballymacarrett to become the industrial heartland of nineteenth-century Belfast. In August of that year a glass-making factory, for making window glass and bottles, was put up at the Co Down end of the Long Bridge. The *Belfast News-Letter* reported: 'Its diameter in the clear is above 60 feet, and height about 120; being among the largest in Great Britain or Ireland.'

On the north side of the town, Peter's Hill, at one time noted for its racing and bull-baiting, was becoming a fashionable quarter. Nearby was one of the town's two theatres at Mill Gate; as the *Belfast News-Letter* recorded: 'On the 3rd of April 1770 Mr Ryder's New Theatre in Mill Gate opened with the Suspicious Husband and the Mock Doctor.' 'The Vaults', a playhouse in Ann Street, was of earlier origin; unfortunately, 'A new Ballad Farce never performed before in any place, called the Humours of Belfast', staged in 1776, has not survived.

On the south side, around and beyond the stump of Belfast Castle, lay the Castle gardens and meadows with its groves and walks. With the building of Donegall Place and the White Linen Hall this area was to become the hub of Belfast's social and commercial life.

The White Linen Hall

The White Linen Hall
(Benn, 1823)

Belfast did not play a leading part in the development of the linen industry which had become Ireland's second most valuable export – worth nearly £1½ million a year by the 1760s – just behind provisions. Belfast, however, was on the edge of the main area of production, one point of a triangle linking with Armagh and Dungannon, accounting for half the output of the province. Lurgan, Armagh and Lisburn were the principal markets, but Belfast was growing in importance not only as a port for export but also as a selling-place for linen. Early in the century most of Ulster's linen was sold in Dublin to be taken subsequently for sale in London, but as the century progressed an increasing proportion was sent out directly from Ulster and in particular from Newry, Londonderry and Belfast.

In 1782 there was a bitter dispute between the leading Ulster drapers and the Dublin merchants, when the merchants were accused of imposing unworkable regulations. As a result the northern drapers decided to by-pass Dublin and set up their own linen halls. Already Lord Donegall had built a Brown Linen Hall – for marketing brown or unbleached linen – in Donegall Street in the 1740s. Meanwhile, white or bleached linen was growing in importance, particularly when Westminster lifted the duty on white linen in 1779–80; as brown linen had been free of duty since 1696, Irish linen now had a privileged access to the British market. In 1783 Lord Donegall gave land for a white linen hall where the City Hall now stands: 'That parcel of meadow being part of the Castle Meadows situate on the south side of the Town and Castle of Belfast, in trust, to permit a Market House to be erected for the Sale of White linens to be managed by a Committee and for no other purpose whatever.'

In April 1783 the first stone was laid with great ceremony and, the *Belfast News-Letter* tells us,

there were deposited (besides the copper-plate inscription) a quantity of new shillings and halfpence, together with a large glass tube, hermetically sealed at both ends, so as not to admit the smallest particle of air. The procession was conducted by the Orange Lodge, so confessedly acknowledged the first in Europe, being composed of 150 gentlemen, among whom are noblemen and commoners of the very first distinction.

The 'Orange Lodge' was in fact a Masonic Lodge, No. 257, and was quite distinct from the lodges of the Orange Order founded in 1795. Though only partly built, the White Linen Hall was open for business in September 1784:

We can with truth inform the public that very large quantities of linens in boxes and packs are received in the Belfast White Hall from all the neighbouring counties. The quantity promises to be greater than the most sanguine friends of a northern hall can reasonably have expected. Some cloth was sold yesterday, and it is hoped the sales will at the close of the market secure the establishment of a hall in this place.

Most of the £17,550 guaranteed for the building was raised locally, including £100 from Roger Mulholland, who may have been the architect. It was a very functional two-storey structure put up to enclose a large quadrangle. In 1787 a meeting of subscribers was called to decide a plan for the central building. Well-proportioned with Venetian and round-headed windows, it was thought by some to be too plain and so in 1815 a handsome cupola was made. For many years much of the building, especially on the south side of the quadrangle, was left unfinished. Cavalry were quartered there in 1798 and during this occupation part of the building was accidently burned. As a market place for bleached linen the Hall was not a great success; drapers in and around Belfast had become prosperous enough to deal directly with the English market.

Donegall Street and the Brown Linen Hall. The original hall was knocked down to make way for St Anne's Parish Church.
(*Ulster Journal of Archaeology*)

Belfast was fast becoming a leading centre for bleaching linen, a process requiring a great deal of expertise and capital. Usually the cloth was laid out in fields to whiten in the sun and rain, and every draper had his secret ingredient. Arthur Young found urine and dung being used and in 1764 Dr James Ferguson of Belfast got a £300 Linen Board grant to develop a process using lime. Buttermilk and sour milk were used extensively; John Wolfenden of Dunmurry applied to Lord Donegall to rent land 'which he thinks would maintain 15 cows which would be a great help towards supplying him in sowr milk, absolutely requisite for whitening Linnen'. That barilla (the ash of burned seaweed) and potash were used for bleaching is clear from Wolfe Tone's account of his visit to William Sinclair's bleach works at Ligoniel, the largest in Belfast, in October 1791:

. . . a noble concern; extensive machinery. Sinclair's improvements laughed at by his neighbors, who said he was mad. The first man who introduced American potash; followed only by three or four, but creeping on. The rest use Barilla. Almost all work done by machinery; done thirty years ago by hand, and all improvement regularly resisted by the people. Mr. Sinclair, sen. often obliged to hire one, and sometimes two companies of the garrison, to execute what is now done by one mill. . .

Linen was of growing importance to Belfast but its domination of the town's commercial life was still far in the future. It was a more exotic textile, cotton, which was at the centre of Belfast's first major industrial development.

Belfast's first mills

Linen, cotton, and calico printing: Nicholas Grimshaw, from England, takes this method of acquainting the public that he has begun to carry on the printing business in all its various branches, from one colour to full chintz, at Greencastle within three miles of Belfast. . .

This *Belfast News-Letter* advertisement of July 1776 is the first indication of the arrival of the new techniques of mass production which were then revolutionising the economy of the north of England. Grimshaw, a Lancashire businessman, almost certainly brought with him knowledge of Arkwright's water-frame and carding-machine. Though Grimshaw, in partnership with Nathaniel Wilson, opened a water-powered cotton spinning mill at Whitehouse in 1784, the first mill in Belfast — and probably the first in Ireland — was set up by a local entrepreneur, Robert Joy.

Joy set out on a tour of parts of England and Scotland in 1777 to get ideas for finding employment for the inmates of the Poor House. There, as his son Henry tells us, he 'conceived the scheme of introducing into this then desponding Kingdom, the most intricate Branches of the Cotton Manufacture which had proved unfailing sources of Industry and Opulence to our sister country'. The linen trade had been brought to a low ebb by depression during the American War of Independence, and, as a result of this journey of industrial espionage, Joy was convinced that cotton would make a good alternative. As the minutes of the Charitable Society record:

In pursuit of this business of procuring various machinery for carding and spinning as weaving they cast their eyes on the children of the poorhouse as easiest to be instructed in the rudiments of a new manufacture, and they formed hopes that by their plan the business of the cotton loom might in due time be conveyed with correctness, along with the children into the town and neighbourhood of Belfast.

In 1777 Robert Joy formed a partnership with his brother Henry, the watchmaker Thomas McCabe, and John McCracken, a sea captain and owner of the first major rope-walk. While machines were operating experimentally in the Poor House, a mill was built in Francis Street, running between Smithfield and Millfield. It employed 90 workers — many of them children from the Poor House — and the machinery 'to spin twist by water, in the manner of Richard Arkwright' was driven by a 16-horse-power water wheel.

The partnership protested to the Irish Parliament because it had not been given any of the £5,000 grant made to promote the industry. Substantial government assistance was given soon after, commercial restrictions were eased in 1779, and a protective duty on cotton was enacted in 1794. The machinery was generally fitted into existing premises and it was not until later that tall purpose-built mills began to break the Belfast skyline. Other cotton mills soon sprang up in the town. The horizontal wheel in John Hazlett's factory in Waring Street, for turning carding machines and spinning jennies, was operated by a horse. Another mill in Millfield was advertised in 1796 as having a 32-foot-diameter wheel turned by one horse, providing power for six carding machines; James Wallace built the first steam-driven mill in Ireland at Lisburn in 1789; the first steam engine in Belfast was installed by Messrs Stevensons at Springfield where it was used to pump back to the top of the wheel the water of the stream that drove it.

The number of cotton spinning jennies in Belfast had leaped from 25 in 1782 to 229 in 1791. The machine-spun thread was sent to handloom weavers, working in their own homes but paid by the employers; by 1791 there were 522 looms weaving cotton in Belfast. Grimshaw, in giving evidence to the House of Commons in 1800, stated that, within a 10-mile radius of

David Manson, the progressive schoolmaster who emphasised the importance of play and enjoyment in education. The McCrackens and many other Belfast radicals attended his school in Donegall Street. (Ulster Museum)

Belfast, £192,000 was invested in the cotton industry, which provided work for 13,500 people.

The first industrial revolution had arrived in Ireland, and it was in Belfast that it took its firmest hold.

'The course of education an entertainment': 18th-century schools

Around 1666 the 1st Earl of Donegall had built a school at the Ann Street corner of Church Lane. By the middle of the eighteenth century it was known as the Latin School and the boys were taught by the curate of the Parish Church. Other schools were also set up and in 1754 Lord Donegall's agent, John Gordon, inserted the following advertisement:

The Earl and his Trustees have heard that some of the inhabitants do send their children to other schools. They have ordered me to acquaint the Inhabitants, as well as their other Tenants in the Neighbourhood, that they are not pleased with such treatment, and hope they will not be laid under the necessity of taking notice of any individual who shall continue to do so.

The Agent's warning went unheeded and the following year David Manson advertised an Evening School at his house in Clugston's Entry. Manson, who had come to Belfast from Cairncastle near Larne, was to become perhaps the most progressive educationalist Ireland produced in the eighteenth century. Having raised capital in a successful brewing business, he set up a school in High Street in 1760; he advertised that he would 'teach to spell, read, and understand the English Tongue without the Discipline of the Rod by intermixing pleasurable and healthful exercise with Instruction'. Eight years later he built a school in Donegall Street 'where there is a healthful air and delightful prospect of land and water'.

Manson was far ahead of his time in emphasising the value of enjoyment and play in education, in providing instruction on equal terms for boys and girls, and in denouncing corporal punishment. He encouraged achievement by reward – successful pupils became Lords and Ladies, Dukes and Duchesses, and (if they could memorise twenty-four lines) Kings and Queens. Finding that the children often carried playing cards, he made teaching cards for them, and these, together with his spelling books, grammar book and dictionary were widely circulated throughout Ireland. The school had its own bowling green and in bad weather the children played games in the Brown Linen Hall. He designed and built a velocipede for his pupils' enjoyment called the 'Flying Chariot'. As the *Belfast Magazine* observed:

Young ladies received the same extensive education as young gentlemen. He and the schoolmaster taught by him were the great cause of infusing into their delicate and tender minds the rudiments of the good sense and erudition for which our ladies during this age have been remarkable.

The most remarkable of such ladies was Mary Ann McCracken; it was significant that she, her brothers, and many other notable radicals attended Manson's school. Manson was made a freeman of Belfast in 1779 and was buried by torchlight in 1792. Few modern educationalists would quarrel with his advice:

Every tutor, should endeavour to gain the affection and confidence of the children under his care; and make them sensible of kindness and friendly concerns for their welfare; and when punishment becomes necessary, should guard against passion and convince them 'tis not their *persons* but their faults which he dislikes. . . These things are easily comprehended; but the great nicety lies in the execution: for *knowledge, diligence* and *sobriety* are not sufficient qualifications for this employment without patience, benevolence and a peculiar turn of mind, by which the Preceptor can make the course of education an entertainment to himself as well as to the children.

A woodcut by a Belfast craftsman: from *The Town Book of Belfast*.

The Presbyterians built the Belfast Academy in 1786 'in which the sons of gentlemen who could not conveniently send them to college, might receive a liberal education'. This indeed its most distinguished principal, Dr William Bruce, attempted to provide. Minister of the 1st Presbyterian Congregation in Rosemary Street, Bruce helped to lead the town's campaign for radical parliamentary reform; he was far from being, as Wolfe Tone asserted, 'an intolerant high priest'. Discipline, however, was more severe than it was in Manson's school and on 12 April 1792 eight boys declared war on the Principal and Patrons of the Academy until certain concessions had been made to them. Armed with five pistols, the boys seized loaves and beef from the kitchens, and shut themselves up in the mathematics room. The Sovereign, the Rev William Bristow, failed to induce the students to surrender; after the boys had fired several volleys, Academy Street was sealed off by a considerable force of armed men, smiths were brought in to break the locks, and slaters climbed the roof to pour water on a fire the defenders had started. Eventually, during the night, the boys capitulated. The school in the following century moved to the Cliftonville Road and continues to flourish as Belfast Royal Academy.

The Belfast Volunteers

On 13 April 1778 Paul Jones, the American privateer, sailed his ship *Ranger* into Belfast Lough and engaged HMS *Drake*. After an obstinate fight of forty-three minutes the British sloop struck its colours and was carried off by Jones. The American War of Independence was more than two years old and, just a few weeks earlier, France had joined the colonists' side. The people of Belfast were alarmed – had not Thurot captured Carrickfergus for the French eighteen years before? In response to a request for troops to defend the town, the Lord Lieutenant wrote from Dublin that he had only half a company of invalids and half a company of dismounted horse to send. If Belfast was to be defended it would have to be through the efforts of its own citizens.

The Protestants of Belfast had long experience of forming volunteer companies for the defence of the town. An independent company of Volunteers had been formed in 1715 during the Old Pretender's Scottish rising and in 1745, when Bonny Prince Charlie was on the march and when there were rumours of an assault on Ulster, two Volunteer companies were raised in Belfast in 'defence of ourselves, our *religion,* and *liberties,* against *Popery and arbitrary power*'.

When American colonists rose in rebellion against George III, the sympathy of the Protestants of Belfast was with them. As the Rev W.S. Dickson put it in a sermon made in Belfast: 'There is scarcely a Protestant family of the middle classes amongst us who does not reckon kindred with the inhabitants of that extensive continent.' Lord Newhaven told the Commons at Westminster that Washington was able to 'oppose our armies with our own Irish subjects, whom our own narrow policy had driven from their country'. Lord Harcourt reported to Dublin Castle that the Ulster Presbyterians were Americans 'in their hearts' and that they were 'talking in all companies in such a way that if they are not rebels, it is hard to find a name for them'. On 4 November 1775 a great meeting of 'the Merchants, Traders, and other principal Inhabitants of the Town of Belfast' agreed to send an address to George III, 'humbly and fervently imploring your Majesty to sheath in mercy the sword of civil war'.

The entry of France on the side of the colonists put the citizens of Belfast in a quandary: they sympathised with the Americans but the French were traditional enemies of Protestant liberties. Doubts were dispersed by Paul Jones; survivors of the Volunteers of 1745 met in the Donegall Arms on 16 April 1778 and gave 'their countenance and approbation to the spirit now springing up in the place for self-defence. . .' The 1st Belfast Volunteer Company had been formed on St Patrick's Day 1778, and now there were enough recruits to form a second company. Though Volunteers corps had been formed earlier in the year in Wexford and King's County, the Volunteers in Belfast were the first in Ireland to assume an organised military form, complete with uniforms of Irish manufacture, a full military band, and the Rev Bryson as Presbyterian chaplain. A remarkable phase in the history of Belfast was about to begin.

By the autumn of 1779 the position of the British government in Ireland was truly desperate – widespread distress followed the dislocation of trade by war; only an advance of £50,000 from the Bank of England saved the Irish Treasury from bankruptcy; Ireland had been stripped of troops to fight in America and no money could be found to finance the raising of a militia; and the Patriot opposition had at last won a majority in the Irish parliament. Now, at a time when Britain had been repeatedly defeated, when Spain had joined her enemies, and when she seemed to have not a friend in Europe, the defence of Ireland depended on some 45,000 Volunteers, entirely outside the government's control. The Volunteers seized the opportunity to wrest concessions from Britain which had been refused for decades.

Belfast was at the very centre of this movement, giving a radical lead to the rest of the country. Why? Over most of the island, Protestants were all too aware that they were a minority and a highly privileged minority at that. The rising Catholic middle class had not yet the confidence to seek their rights except in the most respectful terms, while the peasantry were too absorbed in the daily struggle for survival to take concerted political action. Over much of Ulster, Catholics and Protestants were roughly equal in number; as the population grew the competition for land intensified, keeping alive the hatreds of the seventeenth century. Belfast, in contrast, was in the most Protestant corner of Ireland, where Catholics were too poor and few in number to pose a threat. Commercial and industrial expansion created in the town a prosperous and confident middle class which deeply resented the exclusiveness of the Ascendancy.

Most of the citizens were Presbyterians, many of them following the tolerant 'New Light' or 'Arian' principles (that acceptance of doctrine was not essential, and that each should follow the dictates of conscience). The representative character of the Presbyterian Church contrasted sharply with the domination of the Chichester family, the supine Corporation, and the unrepresentative nomination of the two MPs for the borough. Strong trading connections with Scotland, France, and America helped to bring in radical ideas; the progressive *Belfast News-Letter* kept educated citizens informed and questioning; Manson's school and the Academy encouraged tolerance and new ideas; and Presbyterians, denied access to Trinity College Dublin by their non-conformity, travelled to take degrees at Edinburgh and Glasgow, at that time perhaps the most enlightened universities in Europe.

'Steady, Vigilant, and Prepared'

At the end of 1779 the government lifted many important commercial restrictions and on 6 March 1780 'this town was elegantly illuminated, and every other demonstration of satisfaction was testified on that agreeable occasion'. Almost immediately the Belfast Volunteers threw themselves into a campaign to win legislative independence for the Irish parliament – that is, to remove the 1720 Declaratory Act (by which Westminster could legislate for Ireland) and to modify the 1494 Poyning's Law (by which Bills from the Irish parliament could be altered or suppressed in London). On 23 March 1780 the Belfast Volunteers instructed the MPs for Belfast to work for 'the privilege of being bound only by laws enacted by the King and Parliament of Ireland'.

The campaign failed in the Irish parliament and so the Volunteers, notably in Belfast, flexed their muscles to bring pressure to bear on the government. Three days of manoeuvres and reviews were held in Belfast during July 1780. The Earl of Charlemont (commander of the Volunteers) and Henry Grattan (leader of the Patriot Party) were present at the review on 11 July: it began with a salute of seven guns which was answered by ships in the harbour. On 12 July a mock battle was fought, and the *Belfast News-Letter* observed:

It is difficult to say which called most for admiration, the spectacle, or the spectators? Three thousand men in arms, steady, uniform, obedient, *breathing the spirit of loyalty and liberty!* or thirty thousand spectators, building their hopes of peace and security on the skill and activity displayed by their neighbours, friends, and children, in the field. . .

Resolutions carried by the Belfast Volunteers were among the most fiery in the country. 'If the resolute defence of national rights and liberties be sedition,' the Belfast Battalion declared in August, 'we will not then scruple to denominate the Volunteers of Ireland traitors. . . we adjure our fellow Volunteers to continue, as we ourselves resolve to continue, *Steady, Vigilant, and Prepared.*' The manoeuvres of 20 July 1781 in Belfast were perhaps the most impressive ever carried out by the Volunteers in any part of Ireland. After reviews in the Poor House grounds, on the Falls Meadows, and on the Plains the previous day, a sham battle was fought along the Lough shores, eventually converging on Belfast. Operations began with an 'invasion' near Holywood and extended as far north as Fortwilliam, and ended with a 'victory' for defenders at the Poor House. One visitor, who arrived ten days early to be sure of finding accommodation, wrote:

The Review and the Sham Invasion took up three days; and the number reviewed was such that three thousand five hundred men were employed in the lines each day of the Review. The spectators during the first and second days were computed at 60,000 or 70,000, and on the third not less than 100,000. Every house, public and private, was full of guests; some merchants entertained a whole company with its officers. I never saw meat and drink in such profusion, yet during three days and four nights I did not hear of an individual being drunk or disorderly, except a Lord and two blackguard sailors.

The expected French invasion never came, but British arms met with humiliating defeat in America at Yorktown in October 1781. The Volunteers, especially in the north, demonstrated their impressive strength to press for their demands. Belfast was well represented at the Volunteer Convention at Dungannon in February 1782 when it was declared:

We know our duty to our Sovereign, and are loyal. We know our duty to ourselves, and are resolved to be free. We seek for our rights and no more than our rights; and in so just a pursuit, we should doubt the being of a Providence if we doubted of success.

The fall of the Tory government at Westminster a few weeks later prevented a dangerous clash between the Volunteers and Dublin Castle. The new Whig ministry granted all that was demanded even before it attempted to extricate Britain from the American War. For many in Belfast it was only the first victory in a long campaign.

St Mary's Chapel and the Volunteers

'Legislative independence' merely ensured that laws passed by the Irish parliament in Dublin's College Green would not be emasculated in London. The Irish government was still appointed by Westminster, and the Irish Commons remained utterly unrepresentative – Catholics could neither vote

Belfast Volunteer button, commemorating legislative independence in 1782. This one belonged to Henry Joy McCracken. (*Ulster Journal of Archaeology*)

Volunteer belt-plate. *(Ulster Journal of Archaeology)*

in elections nor sit in parliament, and most MPs were mere nominees of great landowners. In the words of a petition from Belfast citizens in 1784,

. . . although the borough of Belfast sends two Members to Parliament, yet those members are returned (under the immediate direction of a noble peer) by five or six Burgesses, in the appointment of whom your Petitioners have no share, and therefore the Members cannot in *any* sense, be deemed the Representatives of your Petitioners.

At Harristown in Kildare there was, one MP pointed out, 'not one house and but one tree inhabiting. . . Belfast is as much a rotten borough as Harristown; the number of inhabitants is nothing to the purpose, for those inhabitants could have no right to poll. . .' Little wonder, then, that delegates of thirty-nine corps, reviewed in Belfast in June 1783, resolved unanimously:

That at an aera so honourable to the spirit, wisdom, and loyalty of Ireland, A MORE EQUAL REPRESENTATION of the People in Parliament deserves the deliberate attention of every Irishman.

Perhaps no place in Ireland pressed the cause of parliamentary reform more strongly than Belfast. Waddell Cunningham, Henry Joy junior, Rev Kelburn, John Brown, and Robert Thompson represented Belfast at the great Volunteer Convention in Dublin in the winter of 1783–4. The campaign for reform failed; the Irish parliament refused to be intimidated, knowing well that the Volunteers were far too respectable to call the people to arms, and in any case the American War was over. When Henry Flood, the reformers' spokesman, presented the Volunteers' demands to the Commons in College Green, Barry Yelverton, Attorney General and owner of Bally-macarrett, protested: 'we sit not here to register the edicts of another assembly, or to receive propositions at the point of the bayonet'.

The Belfast delegates were bitterly disappointed not only because reform had been rejected but also because they had failed to convince the Volunteer Convention that Catholics should be given the vote. No Protestants in Ireland called more vociferously for Catholic emancipation than the Belfast Volunteers; undaunted by failure in Dublin, the Belfast 1st Volunteer Company resolved on 13 May 1784: 'That we invite to our ranks, persons of *every* religious persuasion' – the first Volunteers in Ireland formally to invite Catholics to enlist. The Belfast Volunteer Company, meeting at the Exchange, followed suit on 26 May. Four days later the Volunteers dramatically demonstrated their support for Catholic claims, as the *Belfast News-Letter* reported:

On Sunday last (May 30) the Belfast 1st Company, and Belfast Volunteer Company, paraded in full dress, and marched to MASS, where a sermon was preached by the Rev Mr O'Donnell and a handsome collection made to aid in defraying the expence of erecting the new Mass-house. – Great numbers of the other Protestant inhabitants also attended.

The modest chapel of St Mary's cost around £170 to build, but most of its parishioners were too poor to meet the cost; £84 was collected by the Protestants of Belfast and given to Father O'Donnell at the opening ceremony.

CASTLE STREET

Father O'Donnell published a letter of thanks from the Catholics of Belfast to the Volunteers 'for their generously enabling them to erect a handsome edifice for their celebration of divine worship. They know not in what adequate terms to express their feelings, excited by the attendance of so respectable a Protestant audience on Sunday last, at the opening of the House – the impression of which mark of regard is never to be effaced'.

In 1757 there were 556 Catholics listed as living in Belfast and by 1784 there were probably around 1,000. Catholics not only worshipped at Friar's Bush but also in the house of John Kennedy, cutler, in Castle Street almost opposite Fountain Street; more recently Mass had been said further along on the opposite side of Castle Street, facing on to Marquis Street. In 1782 Catholics obtained a 71-year lease on a house in Crooked Lane – now Chapel Lane – and here was built the first official Catholic place of worship in Belfast.

'Whilst such perfect concord distinguishes the Irish nation, what moderate demand founded in truth and right, can it ever make that can be long refused?' the *Belfast News-Letter* asked. But the campaign for parliamentary reform and Catholic emancipation failed. Belfast was considered too extreme; one MP described Belfast as a nest of traitors and rebels, and another described it as a town whom no king could govern nor no God could please. Lord Charlemont urged his Volunteers in Belfast 'to restrain *within the bounds of prudent moderation* that ardour, which. . . might plunge this country into the most serious calamities'. Dr William Drennan was disgusted at the collapse of the reform movement, and he wrote in March 1785: 'I was in Belfast lately for a day and among all the friends of Reform of all churches. Zeal is entirely sunk to the lower classes, and Reform is now but seldom the topic of conversation in any genteel society.' He was already sketching out for Dr Bruce a plan for a secret conspiracy. Events in France were to make it possible for him to realise his dream.

St. Mary's Chapel. (From [G. Benn] *The History of the Town of Belfast*, 1823)

'Friends and Brethren — Yes, generous Irishmen!': The Northern Whig Club

Issue by issue, week by week, readers of the *Belfast News-Letter* followed the detailed reports on the revolution in France in the summer of 1789. This, the first successful popular revolution in modern European history, had an electrifying effect on the business and professional classes of Belfast. 'Encouraged by the success of these glorious efforts of the French nation,' Henry Joy wrote, 'the friends of Liberty once more turned their undivided attention to the salutory measure of reform, and renewed those efforts from which they had been so ingloriously compelled to desist in the year 1785.'

In February 1790 Lord Charlemont encouraged his friend Dr Haliday in Belfast to set up a branch of the Irish Whig Club in the town. In Dublin the club was a moderate and respectable organisation, supported by the Patriots in the Irish Commons, which sought limited measures of reform. The Northern Whig Club, founded in Belfast on 16 March 1790, soon eclipsed in its support and fervour that of its parent in Dublin — a city ten times the size of Belfast. In June the Club did much to ensure the victory of radicals in the Co Antrim election. Belfast gave a magnificent reception to the new MPs, John O'Neill and Hercules Rowley, as the *Belfast News-Letter* reports:

A magnificent triumphal car having been prepared with much taste and expence in Belfast, the members were placed in it. . . In front of the two members a figure of HIBERNIA, holding in one hand a wreath, and in the other the *Cap of Liberty*, elevated on a pole, formed a prominent part of the embellishments. . . To gratify the anxiety of the people, the cavalcade, attended by a band of music, passed through every street of consequence. . . In the close of the evening the town was illuminated, a great bonfire was lighted in the market-place, the romantic summit of the Cave-Hill presented a similar ornament to the view of several adjoining counties. . .

Eight years later John O'Neill, by then Lord O'Neill, was to be slain in Antrim attempting to prevent a battle between the crown forces and some of those who now cheered him so rapturously. The Northern Whig Club reached the peak of its influence when it celebrated in Belfast on 14 July 1791 the second anniversary of the fall of the Bastille. The ecstatic report of the *Belfast News-Letter* tells us that 'together with such a multitude of our unarmed inhabitants as no former event ever was the means of assembling' the Belfast Volunteers marched from the Exchange down High Street, and behind them was carried:

THE GREAT STANDARD, elevated on a triumphal car, drawn by four horses, with two volunteers as supporters; containing, on one side of the canvass, eight feet and a half long by six in depth, a very animated representation of the "The Releasement of the Prisoners from the Bastile". . . The Northern Whig Club, and a body of Citizens, amounting to a very great number, formed in pairs, closed the procession. A green cockade, the national colour of Ireland, was worn by the whole body.

After three o'clock they moved forward in this order, passing through every street of any consequence in the town; and when arrived at the White Linen Hall, three *feu de joyes* were fired by the Battalion Companies, answered between each by seven guns from the Artillery. . .

There in the quadrangle of the White Linen Hall, the Volunteers solemnly agreed to send a 'Declaration of the Volunteers and Inhabitants at large of the

Town and Neighbourhood of Belfast' of appreciation to the people of France. The concluding paragraphs contained these words:

AS IRISHMEN, We too have a country, and we hold it very dear – so dear to us its *Interest*, that we wish *all Civil and Religious Intolerance* annihilated in this land. . .
   Go on then – Great and Gallant People! – to practise the sublime philosphy of your legislation. . . and not by conquest, but by the omnipotence of reason, to convert and liberate the World – a world whose eyes are fixed on you; whose heart is with you; who talks of you with all her tongues. . .

   In August addresses of thanks from Nantes and Bordeaux were printed in the *Courier de L'Europe*. That from 'The Friends of the Constitution at Bordeaux' included this fulsome tribute:

FRIENDS AND BRETHREN – Yes, generous Irishmen! receive this appellation which we have hitherto granted exclusively to Frenchmen, true friends of our Constitution. Receive it, notwithstanding the distance which separates us. . . your address, read the 12th of this month, at one of the public sittings of our society, and frequently interrupted by universal bursts of applause, has filled our souls with sentiments of delight. . . That day, friends and brethren, will arrive, when the different parts of the civilized world shall raise together their eloquent voice; which like that of Belfast, shall assert the rights of the People. . .

   The Protestant middle classes seemed almost unanimous in their support of the cause of reform. Yet there were already signs of the irrevocable split which would cause some to draw back and drive others to revolution.

Belfast radicals

A list of Belfast reformers and radicals would be, in effect, a roll-call of almost all the persons of property in the town. In this unique circle many were intimate friends and a considerable number were related to each other. All, without exception, were Protestants.
   The last journey of Francis Joy, founder of the *Belfast News-Letter,* had been made in 1790 to vote for the Co Antrim radicals; his sons Robert and Henry, joint editors of the family paper and owners of the Cromac paper mill, had been enthusiastic Volunteers; and Robert's son Henry Joy junior had represented Belfast at the 1783 Volunteer Convention. Robert Joy's house in High Street had been next to that of Captain John McCracken, owner of a sail-cloth firm and Belfast's first rope-walk; McCracken had married Francis Joy's daughter, Ann, and their sons, Francis, William, Henry Joy and John, were avid reformers (Henry Joy and William were to fight in 1798). Their daughters were all remarkable women – Rose Ann taught revolution to her husband Jim McGlathery, who led the men of Killead in 1798, and Margaret ran a muslin shop with Mary Ann, who as a revolutionary, a social reformer and an upholder of women's rights is perhaps the most famous woman the town produced.
   Captain McCracken and Robert Joy had formed a cotton business with a goldsmith in North Street, Thomas McCabe, who helped to found the United Irishmen; the McCrackens' minister, Rev Sinclaire Kelburn of the 3rd Presbyterian Congregation, was to be imprisoned for his revolutionary activities; a passion for traditional music brought the McCrackens, their

Joy's Paper Mill (*Ulster Journal of Archaeology*)

lodger Edward Bunting, and Henry Joy junior into close friendship with Dr McDonnell and Thomas Russell — McDonnell was not only an outspoken supporter of Catholic emancipation but also the founder of the Fever Hospital, the General Hospital, and the Dispensary; and Russell (better known in many a Belfast home as 'The Man From God Knows Where') became the first librarian of the Linen Hall Library before he died on the scaffold.

Henry Joy McCracken joined with fellow merchants to found the United Irishmen — Robert and William Simms, owners of the Ballyclare paper mill; Samuel Neilson, owner of the town's largest woollen drapery business at the Four Corners; Robert Getty, wine, timber and tea merchant; and Thomas Sinclair, founder member of the Northern Whig Club and owner of Belfast's largest bleach works. Many were present at Mrs McTier's 'coteries' and card evenings, where they met Thomas Greg and Waddell Cunningham — the latter survived the 'Steelboy' attack to become a Volunteer Commander. Mrs McTier's husband was an intimate friend of Dr Haliday, secretary of the Northern Whig Club, who had a professional link with Dr William Drennan. It was indeed, a letter sent to Sam McTier by Dr Drennan — who in turn was Mrs McTier's brother — which set Belfast on a course towards revolution.

The Society of United Irishmen of Belfast

How does your Whig Club? The one here literally does nothing more than eat and drink. They have no fellow-feeling with the people nor the people with them, and my own opinion is that every Volunteer should blush to quit his uniform and buy one for either Whig Club, northern or southern.

So wrote Dr Drennan from Dublin to his brother-in-law, Sam McTier, early in 1791. Son of the 'New Light' minister of the 1st Presbyterian Church in Rosemary Street, Dr Drennan had qualified as an obstetrician at Glasgow and Edinburgh universities. He believed that the reform movement was far too respectable and moderate. As early as 1784 he had sketched out for his boyhood friend, Dr Bruce, a plan for a society 'as secret as the Free-masons. . . to put into execution plans for the complete liberation of the country'. Even though he himself had once preached in his Volunteer uniform, holding his firelock in the pulpit, Dr Bruce was appalled.

McTier was more receptive in 1791 when Drennan drafted for him an elaborate proposal for 'a benevolent conspiracy — a plot for the people — no Whig Club — no party title — the Brotherhood its name — the Rights of Man and the Greatest Happiness of the Greatest Number its end — its general end Real Independence to Ireland, and Republicanism its particular purpose. . .' McTier put this scheme to his friends and on 1 April 1791 an organising committee met in Peggy Barclay's tavern in Crown Entry, off High Street. There they resolved 'to form ourselves into an association to unite all Irishmen to pledge themselves to our country, and by that cordial union maintain that balance of patriotism so essential for the restoration and preservation of our liberty, and the revival of our trade — Signed: Samuel Neilson, John Robb, Alexander Lowry, Thomas McCabe, and Henry Joy McCracken.'

Belfast reformers were greatly impressed by the Dublin Protestant, Wolfe Tone, author of *An Argument on Behalf of the Catholics of Ireland*; they

Henry Joy McCracken: in 1798 he led the United Irishmen at the Battle of Antrim and was subsequently hanged at Cornmarket. (Ulster Museum)

printed 10,000 copies of his pamphlet, made him an honorary member of the 1st Belfast Volunteers, and invited him to Belfast. Tone arrived in October 1791: 'Joy paid my fees to the Northern Whig Club, and signed the declaration. . . Dinner at McTier's; Waddell Cunningham, Holmes, Dr. Bruce, etc. . . A furious battle, which lasted two hours, on the Catholic question. . .' There he met the secret committee, helped to draft the declaration, and suggested a title for the organisation: 'The Society of United Irishmen'. Tone himself acknowledged that Drennan was the true founder. As Drennan's letter to McTier had been passed on to Dublin Castle, a conspiracy was out of the question, and so on 21 October 1791 the society was officially launched in public.

The Society of United Irishmen of Belfast was not yet revolutionary; it set out to achieve 'a cordial union among *all the people of Ireland'* and 'a complete and radical reform of the representation of the people in Ireland'. The members resolved that 'no reform is practicable, efficacious, or just, which shall not include *Irishmen* of every religious persuasion'. The power of public opinion, they believed, would achieve their ends. Nevertheless, many reformers in Belfast thought the programme too extreme.

55

The Belfast Harp Festival, 1792, in the Assembly Rooms: a twentieth-century impression by Frank McKelvey. (Ulster Museum)

'Strum and be hanged': The Belfast Harp Festival 1792

In December 1791 the following notice was issued in Belfast:

Some of the inhabitants of Belfast, feeling themselves interested in everything which relates to the honour, as well as to the prosperity of their country, propose to open a subscription which they intend to apply in attempting to revive and perpetuate the Ancient Music and Poetry of Ireland. . . In order to carry this project into execution, it must appear obvious to those acquainted with the situation of this country that it will be necessary to assemble the Harpers, those descendants of our Ancient Bards, who are at present most exclusively possessed of all that remains of the Music, Poetry and oral Traditions of Ireland. . .

Leading Protestant radicals of Belfast — moderates and democrats alike — were responsible for organising the first great revival of Irish traditional music. The four committee members — Henry Joy junior, Robert Bradshaw, Robert Simms, and Dr McDonnell — brought to Belfast ten harpers, including blind Arthur O'Neill, whose patron in Leitrim 'swore vehemently that if I did not go freely, he would tie me on a car, and have me conducted to assist in performing what was required. . .' The Belfast Harp Festival, arranged to coincide with the 1792 Bastille celebrations, entranced audiences of 'Ladies and Gentlemen of the first fashion in Belfast and its vicinity'. But Wolfe Tone, back in Belfast, was not impressed by the performances in the Assembly Rooms:

July 11th: All go to the Harpers at one; poor enough; ten performers; seven execrable, three good, one of them, Fanning, far the best. No new musical discovery; believe all the good Irish airs are already written. . . July 13th. . . The Harpers again. Strum. Strum and be hanged. . .

Edward Bunting, assistant organist of St. Anne's Parish Church. Inspired by the 1792 Belfast Harp Festival, he spent the rest of his life collecting traditional Irish music and songs. (Ulster Museum)

(From the *Ulster Journal of Archaeology*)

The McCrackens, however, were enthusiastic listeners, and they brought with them Edward Bunting, assistant organist of St Anne's Church, who had lived with them in Rosemary Street from the age of eleven. Bunting was immediately inspired and he spent the rest of his life touring the most remote corners of Ireland collecting airs and songs, many copies of which were put in the custody of Thomas Russell at the Belfast Library, now the Linen Hall Library. In 1797 Bunting published his first collection, which included 66 native airs never before printed. It was an incalculable service to Irish culture. The book caused a sensation; Mrs McTier wrote to her brother: '. . . to me they are sounds might make Pitt melt for the poor Irish'. In another letter, she asks Drennan: 'Have you got the Irish music – it is the rage here – it would be worth your while to try if you could hear him [Bunting] play his Irish music – sugar plumbs or sweetys is his greatest temptation, for he despises both money and praise. . .'

'Certain seditious and ill-affected persons'

In April 1792 revolutionary France declared war on her neighbours and in September the mob broke into the Paris prisons and ritually mutilated and massacred those held there. Mrs McTier wrote: 'I am turned, quite turned, against the French, & fear that it is all farther than ever from coming to good.' In January 1793 Louis XVI was executed and by February Britain was at war with France. In the view of the Westminster government and Dublin Castle the enthusiastic supporters of the French in Belfast were little better than traitors.

57

The Northern Star mast-head 1792: this was the newspaper of the United Irishmen. (PRONI)

Events abroad had not dampened the ardour of Belfast democrats. In January 1792 Samuel Neilson and the Simms brothers launched a United Irish paper, *The Northern Star*, which energetically promoted the radical cause. The badge of the United Irishmen of Belfast showed the harp without the crown with the motto: 'It is new strung and shall be heard.' In March 1793 the Secret Committee of the House of Lords reported:

An unusual ferment has for some months past disturbed several parts of the North, particularly the town of Belfast. . . The conduct of the French is shamefully extolled. . . At Belfast, bodies of men in arms are drilled and exercised for several hours almost every night, by candle-light; and attempts have been made to seduce the soldiery. . .

In the same month, as 'certain seditious and ill-affected persons in several parts of the north of this kingdom particularly in the Town of Belfast, have endeavoured to foment and encourage discontent', the Lord Lieutenant suppressed the Volunteers in Belfast, to the dismay of moderates and democrats alike. Soldiers ran amok in the town, wrecking taverns which displayed the portraits of Dumouriez, Mirabeau and Franklin. Sam McTier wrote that Colonel French 'swore by God if there was one Gun fired from any Window at any of his people he would immediately burn the Town. . .' The *Northern Star* was prosecuted in 1792, 1793, and 1794; the costs were so ruinous that Neilson was forced to mortgage his woollen warehouse facing the Exchange.

In an attempt to prevent Catholic men of property joining with Presbyterians, the Westminster government forced the Irish parliament to grant the vote to Catholics in 1793. However, instead of contenting the reformers, the government's action led them to believe that full Catholic emancipation was imminent. It was not. Lord Fitzwilliam was forced to resign as Lord Lieutenant in 1795 because he had openly supported a campaign to remove the last of the Penal Laws. On 4 March 1795 a town meeting of 'the inhabitants of Belfast' voted to send Fitzwilliam an address of support and to keep 28 March as a day of National Mourning. 'There was not a Shop or Counting-house open during the whole day,' the *Northern Star* reported, '— all was one scene of sullen indignation.'

With all hope of peaceful reform gone, the United Irishmen in Belfast began to prepare for revolution. In retrospect these Protestant bourgeois idealists of Belfast seem both naive and excessively optimistic, and perhaps they had much in common with the democrats of Bordeaux who had been so lavishly congratulated by them. The fire of their indignation against the Ascendancy had been blown white hot by the example of France. French victories, they believed, were triumphs for liberty and they were excited by French offers of assistance to all those seeking their freedom. They assumed the people would follow them and yet none, save Henry Joy McCracken, seem to have had members of the lower orders as close personal friends. Only

NUMBER 22—VOL. II.]   FROM WEDNESDAY MARCH 13, TO SATURDAY MARCH 16, 1793.   [PRICE TWO-PEN

The *Northern Star* mast-head 1793: note that the Crown has been removed, an early indication of the United Irishmen's drift towards revolutionary conspiracy. (PRONI)

one leader, Jemmy Hope, was a working man; apprenticed as a weaver, he had joined the Roughford corps of Volunteers and, in 1795, the Mallusk Society of United Irishmen. The Belfast United Irishmen were passionate supporters of Catholic emancipation and yet none appear to have had Belfast Catholics as companions and intimates. Only Jemmy Hope seems to have attempted to work out a plan for land reform, and few contemplated extensive social change. In 1792 the *Northern Star*, that champion of the rights of man, nevertheless printed this advertisement:

Caution: not to hire Jas. Smyth, without first inquiring his character from me, as he ran away from my service without the least provocation – Ballytweedy, May 4, 1792, Henry W. Shaw.

The Protestant middle class of Belfast were not united in their zeal for revolution, as has been asserted. Men such as Henry Joy junior, Dr Bruce, and Dr McDonnell, urged caution and loyalty to the crown; they shared the United Irish aims of parliamentary reform and Catholic emancipation but heartily disapproved of revolutionary action. Some, in the uniforms of the militia and yeomanry, would fight their former comrades in 1798. In brief, the politics of the town's population could be summarised as follows: the Episcopalians and a small group of Presbyterians were conservative supporters of the government; the overwhelming majority of Presbyterians had been liberals giving enthusiastic support to the Volunteers between 1778 and 1785; then in 1791 the liberals had split into two factions – the radicals for and the remainder against Catholic emancipation; the radicals themselves were divided from 1795 into those who were prepared to fight for their ideals and those who drew back from the brink of rebellion.

Meanwhile the Belfast revolutionaries confidently awaited the arrival of armed assistance from France.

'Two days that we passed on the Cave Hill'

Only family connections in high places prevented Wolfe Tone from being executed in 1795. Arrested for treasonable negotiations with a French spy, he was exiled and in May 1795 arrived in Belfast with his family to sail to America. He wrote in his diary:

Theobald Wolfe Tone. (National Museum of Ireland)

. . . parties and excursions were planned for our amusement; and certainly the whole of our deportment and reception at Belfast very little resembled those of a man who escaped with his life only by a miracle, and who was driven into exile to avoid a more disgraceful fate. I remember particularly two days that we passed on the Cave Hill. On the first Russell, Neilson, Simms, McCracken, and one or two more of us, on the summit of McArt's fort took a solemn obligation – which I think I may say I have on my part endeavoured to fulfil – never to desist in our efforts until we had subverted the authority of England over our country and asserted her independence. Another day we had the tent of the first regiment pitched in the Deer Park, and a company of thirty of us, including the family of the Simms, Neilsons, McCrackens, and my own, dined and spent the day together deliciously.

Meanwhile, Belfast democrats had sown a crop of United Irish societies in north Down and south and central Antrim; there, wrote Jemmy Hope, 'The republican spirit, inherent in the principles of the Presbyterian community, kept resistance to arbitrary power still alive.' In the autumn of 1795 these Protestant farmers and Belfast idealists gained unlikely allies. West of the river Bann the new ideas had made little progress; there – where Protestants and Catholics were roughly equal in numbers – seventeenth-century hatreds festered in the bitter rivalry to hold land close to the linen markets. Savage sectarian warfare reached a crescendo on 21 September 1795 when the Catholic Defenders were routed by the Protestant 'Peep-O-Day' Boys at the 'Battle of the Diamond' near Loughgall. The victorious 'Peep-O-Day' Boys founded the Orange Society, while the Defenders – first in mid-Ulster and later throughout Leinster – joined the United Irishmen en masse. As Ireland drifted towards civil war an extraordinary alliance was formed: the Presbyterian farmers of Antrim and Down, and the Protestant revolutionaries of Belfast joined the Catholic Defenders west and south of the Bann. The government, in turn, did not hesitate to enrol sectarian Protestants into the yeomanry, and ill-disciplined Catholic peasants into the militia.

'Every act of sedition originates in this town': Lake in Belfast

Belfast United Irishmen met regularly in Peggy Barclay's other tavern, in Sugar House Entry; this later became the 'Bambridge Bar', overlooked by the War Memorial Building destroyed in the 1941 Blitz. Their amateur preparations were soon exposed by spies and informers, notably John Hughes, who had a bookshop at 20 Bridge Street and Belle Martin, serving girl at the tavern. On 16 September 1796 Samuel Neilson, Thomas Russell, and Charles Teeling were arrested and the militia destroyed the presses of the *Northern Star* and threw the type out of the windows. Henry Joy McCracken was taken on 10 October and sent by coach to be held in Dublin's Newgate prison. In December 1796 a French fleet, with Tone on board as a French army officer, was in Bantry Bay. Though foul weather prevented a landing, Dublin Castle was well aware what 14,000 seasoned French troops could have achieved against poorly-trained militia men. The suppression of the revolutionary north could no longer be postponed.

'Belfast ought to be proclaimed and punished most severely, as it is plain every act of sedition originates in this town. . . Nothing but terror will keep them in order.' So wrote General Lake to Pelham in March 1797; appointed Commander of the Northern District, Lake imposed martial law in the north by issuing a proclamation in Belfast on 13 March 1797. All arms were to be handed in forthwith; Lake warned: 'I trust that an immediate compliance with this order may render any act of mine to enforce it unnecessary.' Almost immediately afterwards the General unleashed his troops on Belfast, for, as he wrote to Pelham, 'I much fear these villains will not give us an opportunity of treating them in the summary way we all wish. You may rest assured they will not have much mercy if we can once begin. . .'

The property of known democrats was destroyed, suspects were arrested and held without trial, men were flogged in the streets, and once again the

(From the *Belfast News-Letter*)

ANDERSON & GREERS,

PROPRIETORS of the Northern Mail Coaches, will ſtart the above Waggon from Dublin, on Saturday the 4th day of March next, and every ſecond Saturday after. All Goods will be received at the Waggon Stores, King's Inn ſtreet, adjoining Bolton-ſtreet, Dublin, where the Rates of Carriage and Regulations may be ſeen.— And a Waggon will alſo ſtart from Belfaſt, on Saturday the 11th of March next, and every ſecond Saturday after. The Proprietors at preſent engage to deliver Goods between Dublin and Belfaſt, on the fifth Day; and they ſhortly expect to be able to do it in much leſs time, and to run a Waggon each Way Weekly.

Newry, 20th Feb. 1797.

Belfast, March 13, 1797.

WHEREAS the daring and horrid outrages in many parts of this Province, evidently perpetrated with a view to supersede the Laws and the Administration of Justice, by an organized system of murder and robbery, have increased to such an alarming degree, as from their atrocity and extent to bid defiance to the Civil Power, and to endanger the lives and properties of his Majesty's faithful subjects. And whereas the better to effect their traiterous purposes, several persons who have been enrolled under the authority of his Majesty's Commissions, and others, have been forcibly and traiterously deprived of their arms; it is therefore become indispensibly necessary for the safety and protection of the well disposed, to interpose the King's troops under my command: And I do hereby give notice, that I have received authority and directions to act in such manner as the public safety may require.

I do therefore hereby enjoin and require all persons in this District (Peace-officers and those serving in a military capacity excepted) forthwith to bring in and surrender up all Arms and Ammunition which they may have in their possession, to the Officer commanding the King's troops in their neighbourhood.

I trust that an immediate compliance with this order may render any act of mine to enforce it unnecessary.

Let the People seriously reflect, before it is too late, on the ruin into which they are rushing; let them reflect upon their present prosperity, and the miseries in which they will inevitably be involved by persisting in acts of positive Rebellion; let them instantly, by surrendering up their Arms, and by restoring those traiterously taken from the King's forces rescue themselves from the severity of military authority. Let all the loyal and well-intentioned act together with energy and spirit, in enforcing subordination to the laws, and restoring tranquillity in their respective neighbourhoods, and they may be assured of protection and support from me.

And I do hereby invite all persons who are enabled to give information touching arms or ammunition which may be concealed, immediately to communicate the same to the several Officers commanding his Majesty's Forces in their respective Districts; and for their Encouragement and Reward, I do hereby promise and engage that strict and inviolate secrecy shall be observed, with respect to all persons who shall make such communication; and that every person who shall make it, shall receive as a Reward the full value of all such Arms and Ammunition as shall be seized in consequence thereof.

G. LAKE, Lieut. Gen.
Commanding the Northern District.

General Lake's proclamation imposing martial law: *Belfast News-Letter*, March 1797. A reign of terror followed immediately afterwards, highly effective in disrupting revolutionary plans in Belfast. (Linen Hall Library)

premises of the *Northern Star* were wrecked by the Monaghan Militia. It was a curious sectarian warfare: the largely Catholic militia acted for the crown in taking vengeance on the Protestant republicans of Belfast. 'The flame is smothered but not extinguished,' Lake reported, but Henry Grattan warned that 'the more you hang and the more you transport, the more you inflame, disturb and disaffect. . . The North complains that Belfast is persecuted and goaded to work her up and sting her to madness.' The French emigré De Latocnaye, in Belfast at that time, was nearer the truth when he observed: 'The people of this town, who were represented some time ago as about to rise, appear now in a sort of stupor hardly distinguishable from fear.' On 17 October the United Irishman, William Orr, was hanged at Carrickfergus; his last words were: 'Great Jehovah receive my soul. I die in the true faith of a Presbyterian.' In the Pool of Garmoyle below Belfast thirty-four leading suspects were held in the hulk *Postlethwaite*.

Lake believed that the people of Belfast were 'waiting with anxious expectation for the arrival of the French'. The French, however, were preparing to invade Egypt instead, and most Belfast republicans shrank back from revolution. Lake's ruthless repression may have provoked the great rebellion of 1798 in Leinster but terror was highly successful in Belfast. When

61

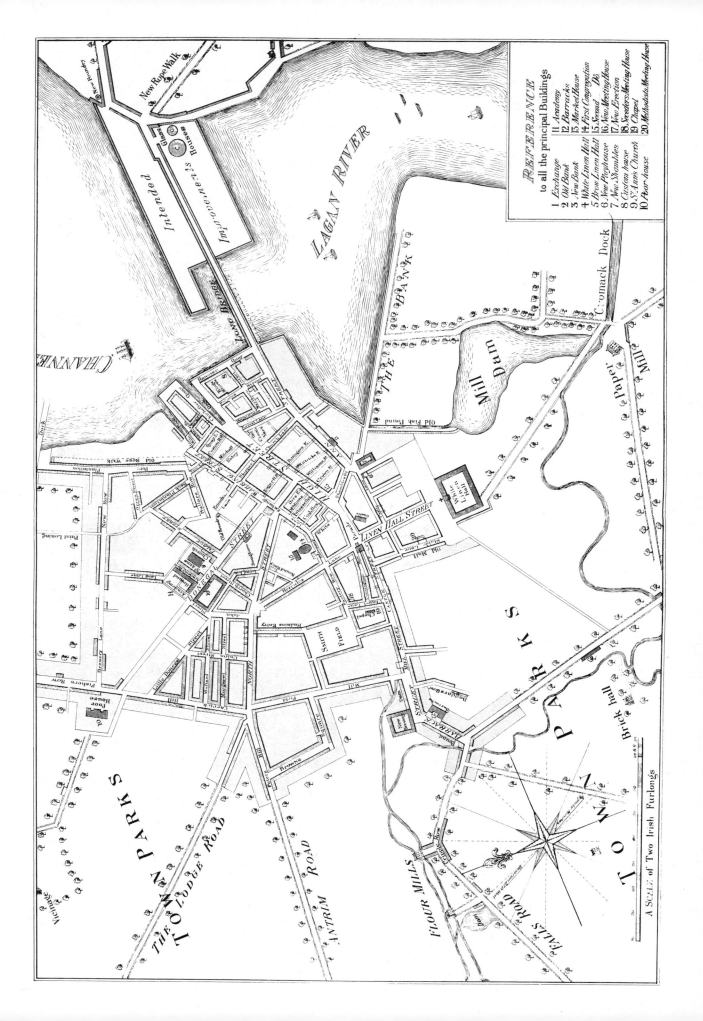

LAGAN RIVER

New Rope Walk

New Foundry

Intended Improvements Houses

Glass House

CHANNEL

THE BANK

Mill Dam

Cromack Dock

Old Fish Pound

Paper Mill

White L. Hall

LINEN HALL STREET

P A R K

New Row

Old Rope Walk

Plantation

Point Loining

Brewery Lane

Fletchers Row

the Poor House

Vicarage

T O W N   P A R K S

THE LODGE ROAD

ANTRIM ROAD

North Street

Brick hall

T O W N   P A R K

FLOUR MILLS

FALLS ROAD

A SCALE of Two Irish Furlongs

Mary Ann McCracken and her niece Maria. Maria was the illegitimate daughter of Henry Joy McCracken, and Mary Ann, with characteristic spirit, overcame family opposition and brought her up in the McCracken home in Rosemary Lane. (Miniature, owned by H. A. Aitchison, taken from *Mary Ann McCracken* by Mary McNeill [Alan Figgis, 1960])

the rising began in Carlow and Kildare in May 1798, there was no immediate response in the north.

The hanging of Henry Joy McCracken

Army of Ulster, tomorrow we march on Antrim; drive the garrison of Randalstown before you and haste to form a junction with your Commander-in-Chief. 1st year of liberty, 6th day of June 1798.

Released from prison for fear he would die of ill-health, Henry Joy McCracken was the only United Irish leader in Belfast prepared to fight. 'When all our leaders deserted us, Henry Joy McCracken stood alone faithful to the last. He led on the forlorn hope of the cause. . .', Jemmy Hope recalled. It was a forlorn hope: Belfast had the second largest garrison in Ireland. McCracken and Hope joined their men at Craigarogan rath near Roughfort, and set out towards Antrim through Templepatrick, Dunadry, and Muckamore. Their only gun was a brass six-pounder fixed on the wheels of an old chaise, hidden until then under the floor of the Templepatrick Presbyterian Meeting House. The very fact that they marched, wearing green sashes and singing the 'Marseillaise', on Antrim and not on Belfast was an indication that failure was certain. After being routed in a skirmish in Antrim town, McCracken evaded capture by taking refuge on Slemish and Divis mountain.

The rising in Down was more impressive, but once Major-General Nugent drew out his guns from Donegall Square, the Presbyterian farmers were doomed. McCracken heard the gunfire of the battle at Ballynahinch on 12–13 June; he himself was captured at Carrickfergus and brought to Belfast on 16 July where he was held in the Donegall Arms Hotel. Tried and convicted, McCracken was taken for execution to the Market House at the corner of Cornmarket and High Street, 'the ground of which,' his sister Mary Ann wrote, 'had been given to the town by his great-great-grandfather'. He asked for the Rev Sinclaire Kelburn to be brought to him, after which, Mary Ann recalled:

Map of Belfast 1791.
(Linen Hall Library)

63

South of the White Linen Hall (left centre) and Joy's mill-dam (right centre), Belfast was still essentially rural: 'Belfast', an engraving by John Nixon published in 1793. (Ulster Museum)

I took his arm, and we walked together to the place of execution. . . Harry begged I should go. Clasping my hands around him (I did not weep till then), I said I could bear any thing but leaving him. . . fearing any further refusal would disturb the last moments of my dearest brother, I suffered myself to be led away. . .

John Smith, then only a boy, remembered:

Hoarse orders were given by the officers, the troops moved about, the people murmured, a horrible confusion ensued, and in a minute or so the manly handsome figure on which the impression of nobility was stamped, was dangling at a rope's end. The body was soon cut down, and the only favour extended to it was freedom from mutilation.

The Union

The high ideals of the Belfast democrats — far from achieving 'a cordial union among all the people of Ireland' — had led on directly to ugly sectarian killing in the '98 rising in Leinster. As Lake smothered the embers of revolt in Wexford, and crown forces swept westwards to meet the French at Ballinamuck, Belfast was indeed in a 'stupor hardly distinguishable from fear'. Leading rebels, who refused to inform on their comrades, were hanged; they included Henry Munro of Lisburn and three Presbyterian ministers. 'Now boys, be merciful,' General Nugent had ordered as he achieved victory at Ballynahinch and by the standards of the time he restored peace in the north with considerable humanity. After imprisonment in Scotland Samuel

Neilson was able to emigrate to America and Robert Simms was allowed to return to Belfast, while William McCracken was freed on bail.

Partly as a result of the rising the extinction of the Irish parliament proposed by Pitt in 1799 provoked no great hostile response in Belfast. The 1st Marquis of Donegall opposed the Union, but he died in 1799; his son — mollified by being given command of a corps of yeomanry — threw his influence behind the measure. Manufacturers, led by Nicholas Grimshaw, made a successful plea for the retention of protective duties on cotton and were thus reconciled to the Union. When on 1 January 1801 the Union Flag was hoisted at the Market House, and a royal salute was fired by the royal artillery, there were no demonstrations of joy or rage in the streets of Belfast. Half a century later this indifference was transformed into passionate support for, and equally passionate opposition to, direct rule from Westminster.

Commercial Buildings at the corner of Waring Street and Bridge Street. Built in the early 1800s, the Buildings included a 'piazza' for the transaction of business, a news-room, an assembly room, and various shops and offices. (Benn, 1823)

4
Cotton Town
c.1801–1840

The Protestants of Belfast, the middle-class Presbyterians in particular, had little reason to regret the closing of the Irish parliament in 1801. Had not the Ascendancy repeatedly dashed the hopes of the people of Belfast who had done so much to win legislative independence in 1782? All efforts to obtain a greater representation of the people had been repulsed. Had it not been Westminster which had forced the College Green parliament to give Catholics the vote in 1793? Might not the people of Belfast get more justice in London than in Dublin?

Sectarian violence in Wexford in 1798 had dimmed the bright hope of a democratic republic. After the futile blood-letting at Antrim and Ballynahinch, only Russell and Hope believed that the struggle could continue. The country gentry and Orangemen blustered and threatened as the Irish parliament voted itself out of existence, but neither were strongly represented in Belfast. For the merchants, manufacturers and professional men of the town, the opening of the first graving dock and the improvement in local government brought about by the Belfast Police Act of 1800 were of greater immediate importance than the Union.

The liberal spirit of middle-class Protestants in Belfast did not die; bourgeois republicanism – which had little in common with the romantic nationalism of later times – was transformed into a liberal unionism which expressed itself in energetic attempts to improve the town. Unprecedented commercial and industrial growth, in spite of alarming fluctuations in trade, provided ample opportunities to the town's leading citizens to show their public spirit. The population of Belfast increased by almost 47% between 1801, when it was 19,000, and 1811, when it was 27,832. In 1821 the population was 37,277, rising to 53,287 in 1831 and 70,447 in 1841; as the town drew in more and more from the surrounding countryside the character of its inhabitants was profoundly altered. Forty years after the Union, Catholics formed nearly one third of the people of Belfast; in addition a high – but unmeasured – proportion of the town's Protestants had been born outside the town. The passions of the Ulster countryside were imported into Belfast with far-reaching consequences.

The Cotton Boom

'The distresses of the poor have for many months been very severe and still continue,' the *Belfast News-Letter* reported in July 1800; 'further aid must be had and that speedily, to alleviate the heavy calamity which still continues to press upon them.' Belfast was experiencing one of several severe jolts delivered to its economy by the long war with France. Yet Napoleon's attempts to prevent British and Irish exports from being sold on the continent of Europe helped to eliminate foreign competition in the British market and the conflict provided a vital stimulus to Belfast's industry.

British demand for food increased and corn and meat prices rose, bringing great prosperity to farmers, landlords and traders throughout Ireland, and it was in Ireland that most of Belfast's cotton was sold. As more and more solid-wheeled carts carrying cotton rattled through Sandy Row to markets far off in the south and west, the skyline of Belfast was increasingly broken by the tall brick chimneys of the mills. Growth had been slow since 1794, but there was a surge of new investment after 1800 and, in its issue of 16 December 1806, the *Belfast News-Letter* estimated that the cotton industry in the town was employing 2,108 persons. In 1811 the Rev J. Dubourdieu reckoned that the Belfast cotton mills contained 150,000 spindles and 15 steam engines and that 'besides these are six factories the machinery of which is wrought by horses or by hand, and twelve spinning mills driven by water'; his calculation that these mills employed 22,000, however, is now seen as a wild over-estimate.

John McCracken (brother of Henry Joy) had 200 workers in his mill close to Donegall Street (on the present site of the *Irish News* offices); his 6 h.p. Boulton & Watt engine burned 600 tons of coal a year. John Milford's mill in Winetavern Street was five storeys high and its 24 carding machines and 5,364 spindles were turned by a 10 h.p. steam engine. The Falls Cotton Mill had three factories; two were turned by water and the third – four storeys high – was driven by steam. McCrum, Leppers & Co, behind the Artillery Barracks, had a mill – 200 feet long and five storeys high – which was for a time the largest in Ireland; a great fire destroyed it in February 1813 but it was rebuilt in

Oldpark mill: in 1800 it was Lyons' linen bleach mill but became McPherson's cotton printworks in 1824. In the foreground are cottages built for employees, later known as Oldpark Terrace, and a flax beetling mill powered by water from the mill dam behind. A schoolhouse has been built to the left of the cottages. Lithograph, 'drawn from nature and on stone', published by Marcus Ward, c.1869. (Ulster Museum)

Mulholland's cotton mill, York Street: from *The Town Book of Belfast.*

the same year. Thomas Mulholland set up a spinning mill in Winetavern Street in 1816; when in 1822 he moved to the Point Fields his new mill exceeded McCrum's in capacity and became the largest in Ireland. In these years cotton was king in Belfast; it was estimated that between 1800 and 1812 £350,000 was invested in cotton machinery there.

Fortunes were made and lost with equal speed. Dramatic fluctuations in demand, and occasionally in supply, beset the new industry. Economic war between Britain and America in 1809 left the cotton trade in the town, according to the *Belfast Monthly Magazine,* 'in a state of the deepest depression'. In 1811, however, cotton wool worth £250,000 was brought into Belfast; when processed into cloth its value was estimated to be £1 million. Waterloo brought the war-time boom to an end; in 1816 prices fell between 30% and 40% and labour troubles were severe in 1817. After a short rally in 1818, depression returned in 1819. Even so, in 1819, there were 50 cotton manufacturers in Belfast and Ballymacarrett, and the town boasted four muslin warehouses, nine calico printers, and ten printed calico warehouses.

It is during these years that we get our first evidence – tantalisingly meagre though it is – about the living standards of ordinary people in Belfast. In the boom years factory cotton spinners were comparatively well paid; a spinner was reckoned to earn £2.7s.0d. a week in 1811. Weavers, by comparison, had very low earnings. There had been 129 linen looms in Belfast in 1791 but by 1806 there were only four remaining and 629 cotton looms. Jemmy Hope was employed as a hand-loom weaver by John McCracken for a time; in 1808 he wrote to Mary Ann McCracken that 'I was obliged to tell Mr John that I must Leave his Employment for want of wages, not being able Longer to support my family out of my small salary. . . Mr John, although he never Checked me much, he allwise treated me (when Ever I spoke to him about my own Situation) with a silence which in another I would have taken for Contempt. . .'

In 1811 weavers earned between 12 and 15 shillings a week, but out of that sum they had to pay for candles, assistance and – sometimes – the renting of a 'loom-stand'. Few cotton weavers worked for themselves; most were employed directly by manufacturers and paid 'prices' or piece-rates. Some hand-loom weavers worked in purpose-built factories like that containing 109 looms owned by James and Conway Grimshaw at the Francis Street corner of Smithfield. Others in the countryside could eke out their wages with produce from their farms, but most worked their looms in dank hovels in Smithfield, Brown Square, the Pound, Sandy Row, and Ballymacarrett.

Manufacturers unhesitatingly cut 'prices' in times of depression. 'Combinations', or trade unions, had been illegal in Ireland since 1780, but Belfast weavers periodically mobilised in attempts to prevent their employers reducing wages. In 1815 Francis Johnston, an employer living in Peter's Hill, was 'sworn out of trade' – that is, weavers took an oath not to work for him. On 15 August weavers set Johnston's house on fire and on 20 January 1816 another attack was made. As the iron bars on the windows were wrenched aside so that a home-made bomb could be thrown in, Johnston fired his blunderbuss at his assailants. While the weavers returned the fire, a servant pitched the bomb to the kitchen door where it exploded with tremendous force. Three weavers were arrested, tried, and finally hanged on gallows set up in Castle Street – the last public execution in Belfast. No one, however, was convicted when the weavers' spokesman, Gordon Maxwell, was mortally

Clifton House: built in 1774, it is still used largely for the purpose for which it was founded. From an engraving c.1815.
(Linen Hall Library)

wounded at Malone in March 1817. In the same year Johnston died of typhus, a fever which was said to have brought about the death of 7,000 Belfast weavers in three years. As in many English manufacturing towns, there was an impressive weavers' strike in June 1818 which forced employers to modify their wage reductions.

In November 1824, following the repeal of the Combination Laws, the weavers formed an association in the 'Weavers' Arms' in North Street; they declared that they were earning no more than seven or eight shillings a week. In 1825 around one third of the weavers in Belfast and its neighbourhood were unemployed, while the remainder endured a grim life in their cramped hovels by accepting below-subsistence wages. The weavers of Ballymacarrett lived in stifling two-storey houses; their families ate and slept upstairs and worked the looms on the wet earthen floors below. In years of depression the weavers worked from 4 a.m. to midnight seven days a week for a wage of 4s.6d. Wives served as unpaid winders, rent cost one shilling, and another shilling was needed for fuel and candles. The *Belfast News-Letter* reported in February 1830 that weavers in Ballymacarrett were forced to live on Indian meal unfit for cattle, and that they were reduced to skeletons from overwork and lack of sleep. A meeting of gentlemen at St Anne's Church on 17 February agreed to provide relief for the cotton weavers by selling them food at half-price and by finding them alternative work breaking stone.

The rapid growth of Ireland's population and the impoverishment of much of the countryside ultimately account for the weavers' distress. Poor labourers poured into Belfast faster than work could be created for them; Mulholland told Commissioners enquiring into the state of the poor in 1833 that 'persons will come 60 to 70 miles to be employed'. Wages could be kept at starvation level and therefore Belfast manufacturers had no incentive to set up power looms to cut labour costs. Soon Lancashire calico, muslin and cord – woven by steam and often finer than Belfast cotton – swept into Ireland, capturing the market. The end was in sight and in 1836 Parliamentary Commissioners declared that the Irish cotton industry was almost extinct. Belfast had been exposed to the cold blast of free trade; in vain did the mill owners there call for the retention of the Irish cotton tariff for in 1824 Westminster removed all duties on goods passing between Ireland and Britain.

It used to be assumed that the Belfast cotton industry expired because it was too inefficient to compete with British mills without the aid of protective duties. Recent research indicates otherwise. Belfast factories were not under-capitalised: in 1833 Leonard Horner showed that the average horse power of Belfast spinning mills was over 40 compared with an average of under 30 in England and Wales. Coal was dearer in Belfast than in Manchester but fuel accounted for around 2% only of production costs, while the level of wages – around 33% of production costs – was almost one third lower in Belfast than it was in Lancashire. Certainly Belfast was affected by unpredictable fluctuations in the cotton trade, but the slumps of 1817–19 and 1826–9 hit the industry all over the United Kingdom.

Cotton spinning in Belfast reached a peak in 1825 when 3,611 were employed in 21 mills in the town and its hinterland. If the industry was efficient why then were there only 15 mills by 1833 and a steady decline thereafter? The answer seems to be that the wet-spinning of flax, perfected in Leeds in 1825, offered Belfast manufacturers better opportunities for profit. There were only four cotton mills left in the town by 1850 but the decline in cotton was more than offset by the rapid growth in linen output. The valuable experience gained in making cotton was to be used to make Belfast the greatest centre for linen production in the world later in the century.

The Belfast Police Act

Throughout the eighteenth century the Corporation neither represented nor served the needs of the citizens of Belfast. The care of the poor had been left to the Charitable Society; the development of trade and the port had become the responsibility of individual merchants, the Chamber of Commerce and the Ballast Board; and even the supply of fresh water to the town was undertaken by seven 'Spring Water Commissioners' of the Charitable Society. The lack of local facilities was remarkable even by the standards of the time; to attempt to remedy this the Irish parliament in one of its last measures enacted the Belfast Police Act of 1800, or more exactly:

An Act for paving, cleansing, and lighting, and improving the several Streets, Squares, Lanes, and Passages, within the Town of Belfast, in the County of Antrim, and for removing and preventing all Encroachments, Obstructions, and Annoyances therein; and also for establishing and maintaining a Nightly Watch throughout the said Town and Precincts thereof, and for other purposes.

The Act was almost a declaration that the Corporation had failed to carry out its responsibilities. Two Police Boards were set up: the Committee of Police elected annually by ratepayers to act as a supervising executive, and the Commissioners of Police, a body of twenty-one men responsible for paving, lighting, and cleaning the town, for providing a fire service and a night watch, and for arresting suspects to be brought before a magistrate. The duties of the Commissioners were spelled out in detail in the Act and specific penalties were prescribed for fouling the streets and waterways. Fines of up to ten shillings could be imposed on anyone who

. . . shall throw, cast, lay, put or place. . . any ashes, dust, dirt, rubbish, dung, offals, or other noisome or offensive articles. . . in or upon any of the carriage or footways. . . or into any sewer, mill-race, or water-course, running through, along, or under any of the said Streets, Passages, Lanes, or other Places within the said Town of Belfast. . .

As 'the emptying of soil or filth from privies, necessaries, or bog houses, into or upon Streets, Lanes, or other Places in the said Town of Belfast, and the carrying of night soil through the same in the day time, are great and offensive nuisances', a twenty-shilling fine could be imposed on offenders and those who 'shall throw from any door or window into the same, any urine, ordure or filth'. Pigs could still be kept in the town, but any found wandering the streets could be seized, killed, and given to the Charitable Society 'for the use and benefit of the poor therein'. Bow windows and projecting shop signs were forbidden in the narrow streets, to ease the flow of traffic. A Night Watch began the regular policing of the town for the first time. The report for the night of 22 June 1812 includes:

Constables and guards went out at eleven o'clock. Second division returned at twelve o'clock: all quiet. . . Parties went out a second time a quarter before one o'clock; found a man perfectly intoxicated lying in the street near the Exchange; unable to tell his name, occupation or place of residence; brought into the guardroom and laid him down to sleep in such a manner as to prevent suffocation. . . Second division returned quarter before two o'clock; brought in a man called John King Macauley a dancing master intoxicated who was making a great noise in the street. . .

Though two months later, on 20 August, guards had to break up a vicious knife-fight between Portuguese sailors in Waring Street, and they reported, 'Whores very troublesome all night', Belfast clearly was not a town troubled as yet by organised crime and communal strife.

The bankrupt Marquis

The 5th Earl of Donegall, created 1st Marquis in 1791, died in 1799. His obituary noted that 'he laid out above £60,000 in the Lagan Navigation and the public buildings in this town, which were erected by his sole expense'. He was reputed to be the richest peer in Ireland, but he had lavished much of his income on art collections and on Fisherwick Park, the Chichester family's new home in Staffordshire. Towards the end of his life his financial troubles had been severe, and he had been forced to sell out most of his interests in the Lagan Navigation to Belfast merchants.

The 1st Marquis detested his eldest son, George Augustus, Lord Belfast, and with some reason. Within eighteen months of coming of age Lord Belfast had acquired debts of £30,000, languished in a debtor's prison for a time, and had secretly married the illegitimate daughter of Sir Edward May in 1795. A fresh batch of debts to gamblers and horse-dealers, amounting to £40,000, meant that the Chichester inheritance had to be resettled twice before the death of the 1st Marquis.

On succeeding, the 2nd Marquis was in a desperate position. Fisherwick Park passed on to his younger brother and – because of restrictions imposed by previous settlements – land could not easily be sold to eradicate debts which now reached at least £200,000. After agonising delays while the courts decided that the marriage of 1795 was legal, an elaborate new settlement of the Donegall estates was made in 1822. For most of the vast estates, leases were sold giving buyers a permanent right to lands and properties which they could now hold for ever at the old low rents. Altogether 1,520 leases were sold, 600 of them for properties in Belfast, its town parks, and the area immediately surrounding the town. Only landowners in acute difficulty sold leases 'in perpetuity' with rents which were fixed for all time. This the 2nd Marquis did for two thirds of his land – future income was sacrificed for immediate cash payments. Lawson Annesley, for example, paid the Marquis £150 for a lease of three plots in Church Lane, Castle Street and Earl Street; once the cash had been paid he was required only to pay an annual rent of £12.10s.0d. thereafter.

The businessmen, merchants, and manufacturers of Belfast had long been prising the Chichester family from its hold on the town. Many already enjoyed long leases at low rents but they seized the opportunity to buy perpetual leases as these documents not only gave them additional security for borrowing money but also conferred on them the prestige of being virtual owners of valuable property. No longer – as in 1767 – were strict rules made to regulate the height of houses; indeed, the buyers could do almost what they liked with their properties. The purchasers of land just beyond the town's limits got the best value of all for, as there were no restrictions, they could build or sublet to build and make enormous profits as the town grew. Indeed the 1822 settlement of the Donegall estates cleared the way for the spectacular expansion of Belfast in the nineteenth century. In 1812 Wakefield had remarked that every brick of Belfast was owned by Lord Donegall; by 1832 hardly a brick remained in his possession.

Martha McTier dined with Lord and Lady Donegall in 1803. 'The Marquis laughed like a Simon all the next evening I spent with him at Greg's;' she wrote, 'where She said they must retire to some country place, and eat boiled mutton and turnips.' The 2nd Marquis could not afford to be an absentee and was forced to live frugally in a modest house on the corner of Donegall Place (then Linen Hall Street) and Donegall Square North, where he could not even find the money to build a door frame.

In 1807 the Donegalls moved to Ormeau Cottage, a country house built in a farmhouse style in their townland of Ballynafeigh. Though Ormeau Bridge was built in 1815, the main entrance to Ormeau was from the Ravenhill Road, then the old road from Belfast to Newtownbreda. Once the 'fines', or cash payments, for the perpetually renewable leases began to come in from 1822 onwards, the Marquis was able to build the mock Tudor Ormeau House facing the Ravenhill Road, complete with a 'pheasantry' and 'race-course' nearby. Thomas Gaffikin remembered that 'a very extensive and expensive establishment was maintained there, which tended to make Belfast prosperous in trade'. He continued:

Game, such as hares and pheasants, frequented the plains from the preserves at Ormeau, and the gamekeepers – Adams and Sims – had to look sharply after them, it being so convenient to the town, hares being frequently taken near the Donegall Pass, and in the grounds now occupied by our Gas Works. . . The heron cranes were protected and encouraged to build their nests at Ormeau. The crane was conspicuous on the crest of the Donegal family, and the beautiful pillars which some will remember at the principal entrance, were topped with a gilt coronet and a crane about to swallow a struggling eel. A racing stud was kept at Ormeau, producing an occasional winner at the annual meeting on the Maze course.

PUBLISHED BY W. H. LIZARS, EDIN^R

Vignette showing St. Anne's Parish Church (left), the new Queen's Bridge (1843), and St. George's Church, High Street. (Linen Hall Library)

House at the corner of Chichester Street and Callender Street. (*Ulster Journal of Archaeology*)

'Belfast is really improving very fast'

'Belfast is really improving very fast, and though the landlord cannot do much for it at *his own* expense, yet want of money may operate to its advantage,' Mrs McTier wrote in November 1803. Even before the 1822 settlement Lord Donegall's difficulties ensured that few obstacles were put in the way of building expansion in the town. Though at times there were acute shortages of building materials, the prosperity of cotton manufacture and the rapid growth of trade during the Napoleonic Wars provided enough money for a continuous extension of the frontiers of Belfast.

The town's centre of gravity was shifting southwards to the White Linen Hall. Chichester Street and Wellington Place – then North and South Parade – had been started in the 1790s and most of the houses there were built in the first twenty years of the new century. Numbers 7 to 11 Chichester Street, for example, were put up in 1804; these were elegant tall brick houses in a Georgian style which remained popular in Belfast until the 1830s, long after it had gone out of fashion in Dublin. Adam McClean, an innkeeper's son who had made his fortune as a draper, had a fine row of houses built in Donegall Square South. On summer evenings the military band played for two hours in front of the White Linen Hall. Thomas Gaffikin remembered:

The main walk round the Hall was enclosed from this space by an iron railing on each side, with small gates for ingress and egress. The most respectable of the persons listening to the music were distributed on both sides, and it was the practice to turn and walk round between each piece, which rendered it necessary at times for the great crowds at the rear of the hall, to change sides in succession.

All the houses in Donegall Place – also known as the Flags – were private residences of merchants and the gentry. Sir Stephen May, Comptroller of

Customs, had his house where Anderson & McAuley's store now stands, and just opposite lived Thomas Stewart, Seneschal of the Castle. His garden wall, Gaffikin tells us, 'reached along Donegall Place from Castle Place and down Castle Lane, with large fruit trees hanging over the wall'. Lord Donegall's agent lived here with his hawks and falcons; when his hounds were taken out for exercise in the mornings their baying soon put to flight all other dogs in the streets. Nearby Arthur Street was second only to Donegall Place as a place for fashionable living. Here there were no shops as yet but the Belfast Theatre had opened there in 1793, superseding the theatre in Rosemary Street. Enjoying the patronage of the 2nd Marquis – who paid for a much admired drop scene of the Cave Hill – the managers Maywood and Talbot could afford to invite the leading stars of the time. The celebrated Mrs Siddons came three times to Belfast; after her performance of 1802 this letter appeared in the *Belfast News-Letter*:

Would you believe it Mr Editor? that as my youngest daughter was yesterday evening ironing some of her flounces, and as she fingered her white dimmity petticoat, I found her starting like an idiot and crying – Yet here's a spot! Out, out damn'd spot! then, darting her fiery eyes at me, she exclaimed 'No more o' that, my Lord! You mar all with this starting – To bed, to bed, to bed!' I started indeed, till I luckily recollected something of the sleeping scene in MacBeth. To bed too I went somewhat melancholy.

'Rusticus' Drumbo

High Street was still the main centre of business; its cleanliness had been improved by the Police Boards and the covering over of the Farset to make one broad thoroughfare. Designed by the Dublin architect, John Bowden, St George's Church was completed in 1816, its portico and facade being taken from Ballyscullion House, an unfinished palace intended for the Earl-Bishop of Derry. A low pole projecting from a barber's shop advertising 'Easy Shaving and Haircut, Threepence' was a constant danger to tall people opposite St George's. Here in High Street were the 'doctors' shops' (chemists) and at night bottles of coloured fluid glowed in their windows with the light of candles and oil lamps placed behind them. By day, in front of low-fronted shops with their tiny panes, tape-sellers cried, 'Broad, black or white, twilled or plain, penny tape, at a halfpenny a yard!'

Here stood McComb's bookshop. Tinware, cast-metal goods, and earthenware were laid out on the paths for sale, and Mrs McCallum sold tin whistles and marbles to children and tinder-boxes, turf, and potatoes to their elders. In the entries, sedan chairs were for hire. The old Market House in Cornmarket was pulled down in 1811, but here there were taverns such as 'The Mail Coach Passing Through Dromore Square' and the town's most fashionable hairdresser, Bourdet, whose father had been captured from Thurot's force at Carrickfergus in 1760.

At Fountain Street spring water from Monday's Well in Sandy Row was sold from barrels carried in by donkeys. Miss McElroy had her emporium of ladies' fashion in Castle Place, which also boasted the town's two leading hotels, Wilson's 'Donegall Arms' and Pat Lynn's 'White Cross'. Another hotel, together with a news-room and a piazza for merchants, was contained in the Commercial Buildings in Waring Street, a handsome granite building erected by John McCutcheon in 1822 and severely damaged during the 1941

High Street about 1830: view from the Town Dock, with Hanover Quay (left foreground) and (centre) the last bridge over the Farset, giving Bridge Street its name. (Ulster Museum)

Blitz. Miskelly's at the corner of Rosemary Street and North Street was not only a hotel but also a funeral parlour; each hearse was decorated with large black and white plumes, with a carved death's head, and crossbones on each side above the words TEMPUS FUGIT.

In 1829 the Belfast Savings Bank, with a large upstairs music room for the Belfast Anacreontic Society, was put up in King Street and in the same year May Street Presbyterian Church was built in classical style for the controversialist Dr Henry Cooke. Two years later the 3rd Presbyterian Church in Rosemary Street was completed, its four Doric columns cast in iron at Boyd's Belfast Foundry; the church was destroyed in the 1941 Blitz. Close by in Castle Lane, vegetables and fruit were sold at Tucker's or Weigh Bridge market. 'Ballinderry onions at a penny a pound!', 'Chelsea buns – all hot', and 'Hot mutton pies at a penny a piece – all hot', were cries Gaffikin remembered hearing there. Smithfield was a great open square with a large shed in the centre for the sale of hides and skins. Gaffikin described the scene:

Many people resorted to Smithfield on Friday evenings to witness the different spectacles and amusements provided by the grinning clowns at the show booths, and the recruiting parties playing the 'British Grenadiers' with fife and drum. On special days the entire military band escorted the party. The hum of voices, the bargaining for knacker's horses, the shouting of the cheap jacks and auctioneers, all combined to enliven the scene; whilst Jack Jeffers, the auctioneer, could have collected a crowd in a very few minutes by his sonorous bawling, even if it were only an old horse in dispute, or a seizure of household furniture in hand.

75

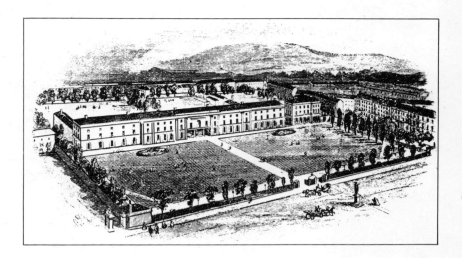

The Academical Institution, from a plate engraved about 1885: from *Royal Belfast Academical Institution: Centenary Volume 1810–1910.*

Unquestionably the finest public building of these years was the Academical Institution in College Square. At no charge Sir John Soane made 46 drawings but the completed structure had little of his recommended ornamentation; plain but elegant, this three-storeyed brick college was to be the centre of a furious controversy. In the 1820s and 1830s tall terraced houses were built around it for the well-to-do, stucco replacing brickwork in the later terraces. At the western end of College Square North, Christ Church opened in 1833; disfigured though it is by grime and wire, it still looks handsome today. Nearby, in Fisherwick Place, the town's prison or 'House of Correction' was built about 1817. Citizens passing its gateway could read the warning motto: 'Within Amend, Without Beware'.

The growing town

Donegall Square South still marked the southern limits of Belfast; beyond a small mill there with its belfry – used as a target by the constabulary during musket practice – lay green fields to Sandy Row. When this low-lying land was flooded in winter, the Mall Ditch was still the most convenient route by foot from the Academical Institution to the Saltwater Bridge. Joy's Paper Mill went out of production and its dam was drained ready for conversion into valuable building land, the heart of which was to be Joy Street. Bankmore House, now the site of Bankmore Street, was in the country, outside the borough boundary. Mount Charles and University Street were then but a market garden, and where the Botanic Gardens are today was McDowell's farm. The route to Dublin was still through Mill Street, Barrack Street, and Sandy Row. The Malone Road had been made to avoid the bad hills at Stranmillis. The toll-bar, where the Malone Road Methodist Church now stands, 'interrupted the progress of all vehicles except the Royal Mail Coach, which, with four fresh horses in front, and a couple of guards fully armed behind, took the hill at a canter'. Thomas Gaffikin continues:

It was a steeper hill than now. The farmers, coming out of town with heavy loads, often had to lighten their carts here. One side of the road was constantly studded with little heaps of manure left off, to be taken again at leisure.

The Lisburn Road was begun in 1817 and when it was completed in 1821 it became the most favoured way south; the toll-bar had then to be moved to where the Malone and Lisburn Roads meet. On the Malone ridge to the south stood a few gracious houses in an entirely rural setting. The finest of these was Cranmore at Orange Grove, owned by the Bridge Street merchant and noted botanist, John Templeton. Templeton interested William Thompson in the natural sciences and his son Robert became a world-famous naturalist. Mary Ann McCracken was a much loved and frequent visitor to Cranmore, which still stands in a ruinous condition in the Academical Institution's Malone playing fields.

On the north side of the town the chimneys of the cotton mills were competing for prominence with the spire of the Poor House. York Street began as an opening to the rear of John McCracken's mill in York Lane; between it and the river lay the Point Fields, often the scene of cock-fights, dog-fights, man-fights and bull baiting. At Lilliput, once owned by David Manson the educationalist, the road ran to Carrickfergus along the Lough shore without a house for three miles. At the Grove, the home of William Simms, Buttermilk Lane was the route through Skegoniel to Cave Hill, 'to which favourite hill', Thomas McTear recalled, 'it was the nearest road from the town and much more resorted to then than now, as it was quite open and free, and almost the only recreation ground of the people'.

North Queen Street – then New Barrack Street, named after the Artillery Barracks built in 1797 – was still the main route to Carrickfergus; substantial terraced houses were built here and in York Street in the 1830s. From about 1825 merchants' houses were put up in Great George's Street as were the more modest homes of sailors and cotton weavers in the network of side streets connecting with York Street and North Queen Street. Noisy horse fairs were held in York Street on 12 August and 12 November; 'All the juveniles prepared their whips for the fair,' Gaffikin remembered, 'and the contest was to see which could crack their whips the loudest.' The reputation of many a horse sold here would be made or broken at the July races at the Maze or the Ballyhackamore races on Christmas Day. At the head of Donegall Street, close to the Poor House, stood Greg and Boyd's Foundry and St Patrick's Catholic Church, consecrated in 1815. There was no road westwards except a crooked lane, now covered by Clifton Street and Duncairn Street. The Shankill Road was densely populated from North Street to Bower's Hill where Israel Milliken had his baths; a bath and a glass of punch could be had for two shillings. Close by, at Peter's Hill, was McNeice's Court for handball and 'racket playing'.

Across the Long Bridge, industrial Ballymacarrett was growing rapidly, soon to blend into and become part of Belfast. Here Robert Hyndman had his large bottle-house, and his works, making cut glass and watch glasses, extended to Short Strand. Further along at Lagan Village there was the foundry of Victor Coates, Son and Young, and adjoining this, Greg and Boyd's vitriol works. Ballymacarrett gave employment in weaving, lime-burning, salt-making and rope-making; it was also popular for its bathing by the Connswater in summer. From here to Holywood, Gaffikin tells us:

Wild fowl shooting in winter was another favourite recreation. Several parties had barrels sunk on the Holywood banks for the purpose. These barrels had to be bailed out between tides, as the birds sought after – such as widgeon, wild ducks and barnacle – avoided the shooting cots on clear nights.

It was where Belfast and Ballymacarrett were beginning to merge at the docks that momentous changes were about to take place.

Artillery Barracks (Benn, 1823)

Improvement of the port

The most serious threat to the future development of Belfast was the shallow depth of water from the docks to the Garmoyle Pool. At low water there were only between two and four-and-a-half feet of water at the quays; from there to the 'flats', two-and-a-half miles out to sea, was a narrow crooked channel which increased only to eight feet; from the flats to the Garmoyle Pool the channel did not exceed sixteen feet. Even at full spring tide, vessels with a draft of more than fourteen feet could not come nearer to the docks than the Garmoyle roadstead. Many vessels had to anchor three miles from the quays and have their cargoes and passengers taken in by light craft. The consequent delay, inconvenience and expense is illustrated by Gaffikin's account:

It was usually the fate of the *Old Eclipse*, the *Rob Roy*, the *Fingal*, or the *Chieftain* steamers to miss the tide, and stop between Whitehouse and Holywood. Then an open boat would come alongside, and any passenger anxious to get up to town had an offer of being rowed up 'in no time' for a shilling. After the wearying journey of twenty-two hours from Glasgow or Liverpool, many of the passengers were glad to leave the steamer on the terms; but after the shillings were collected the boatmen cried out, 'Can take a few more at sixpence'. When they had secured as many passengers as the boat could carry without a certainty of drowning them, they began their journey, the pleasures of which on a cold wintry morning were not much relished.

Attempts to improve the port in the eighteenth century had come to very little. The principal quays had been made by private initiative, notably Hanover Quay built between 1716 and 1720 by Isaac Macartney, and Chichester Quay begun in 1769. An Act of 1729 gave the Corporation power to supply ballast taken from the channel bed to outgoing ships but it was widely agreed to be an ineffective piece of legislation. Another Act in 1785 repealed that of 1729 and set up 'The Corporation for preserving and improving the Port and Harbour of Belfast'. Known to all in Belfast as the 'Ballast Board' this body worked strenuously to bring about improvement. The No. 1 Clarendon Graving Dock was begun on land prised at considerable expense from Lord Donegall and completed in 1800. A second graving dock (No. 2 Clarendon) was finished in 1826.

The Ballast Board knew that its main task must be to improve the approaches and though it insisted that ballast must be taken from the bed of the channel it realised that only a major project would solve the problem. The astonishing increase in Belfast's trade made improvement essential. Customs revenue had leaped from £101,876 (including excise) in 1784 to £393,512

Ritchie's Dock: painting by D. Stewart 1805. (Ulster Museum)

Ritchie's Dock (*Ulster Journal of Archaeology*)

(excluding excise) in 1813. In 1786, 772 vessels totalling 34,287 tons had entered Belfast Harbour; by 1820 the number had risen to 2,423 ships totalling 246,493 tons. William Ritchie wrote that when he first came from Scotland in 1791 Belfast owned only four sloops and four brigs; by 1811, he continued:

There are now in the London trade 10 brigs averaging 270 tons, and in the Liverpool trade 8 brigs of 160 tons each; there are also two brigs that trade to Bristol of 150 tons, one brig and two sloops in the Dublin trade averaging 90 tons. . . In addition to the above, there are 12 ships and brigs trading to the West Indies and other parts that will average 350 tons each, all armed and fitted out in the best manner; also a number of other vessels of various sizes that trade to different places. The greater part of the traders and West India vessels have been built in Belfast, several of them with Irish oak. . .

William Ritchie and his brother John had revived shipbuilding along the shore where Corporation Street now runs. On their arrival from Scotland they found only six jobbing ship-carpenters in Belfast; by 1811 they employed '44 journeymen carpenters; 55 apprentices; 7 pair of sawyers; 12 blacksmiths, and several joiners; the weekly wages about £120'.

For many years the Ballast Board attempted without success to win government aid for its schemes – that of John Rennie in 1821 to build a ship canal to Garmoyle would have cost £250,000. In 1824 the Board decided to rely on their own resources and paid for a detailed survey by Messrs Walker & Burgess. James Walker submitted plans in 1830 to make two cuts across the bends of the river to make one long straight channel to Garmoyle which would cost around £200,000. To carry out the works the necessary powers were sought by promoting a Bill at Westminster. When Lord Donegall opposed the Bill (probably to increase the money he would receive in compensation), the *Northern Whig* furiously condemned 'this most tyrannical and preposterous conduct of his lordship' and continued:

Reformers of Belfast, Lord Belfast has refused to present your Petition for reform; merchants and freeholders of Belfast, his papa has ordered him to oppose the very first Bill you apply for, to mend your quays and improve your harbour. However, the whole procedure admirably illustrates the base and villainous corruption on which our representative system is founded; and ought to urge us all the more strenuously to procure such a Reform as will extricate the people out of the hands of the Aristocracy.

It cannot have been easy to find parliamentary time for the Bill at a time

Belfast shipyard in 1812: painting by D. Stewart. Although shipbuilding began on the northern bank of the Lagan, it was to be on the south side that the most spectacular growth occurred later in the nineteenth century. (Ulster Museum)

when Reform seemed the only issue, but it got Royal Assent in 1831. A new Ballast Board was to be created; it took seven years to deal with objections but eventually the Board obtained the right to the bed of the Lagan from the Long Bridge to Garmoyle, an area of 885 acres. The Treasury would lend only £25,000 and although a loan of £60,000 was negotiated from the Board of Works, most of the money required had to be raised from the public by a bond issue. At last work began in April 1839 on the cut from Dunbar's Dock (at the northern end of Corporation Street) to the first bend in the river. Many other ports in Ireland and Britain had similar problems to those of Belfast, but few had men as tenacious as the members of the Ballast Board. Without their determination Belfast might not have become one of the greatest ports in western Europe and certainly the town would not have become the home for a time of the largest shipyard in the world.

In terms of value, Belfast's share of Ireland's exports had been one sixth in 1805. In 1835, even before work was begun on the first cut, Belfast's exports were worth £7,900,000 against Dublin's £6,900,000. Though second to Dublin in tonnage, Belfast had become the first port of Ireland in value of trade.

'Inst' and the Lancasterian Schools

'This town has for some years been in possession of an excellent plan of school education for which it is indebted to the Belfast Academy founded in 1786,' Dr Bruce wrote in 1806 in denunciation of 'visionary notions' to set up an Academical Institution. 'Though this project will in the end prove abortive,' Bruce continued, 'it may be persevered in so long as to dissipate a fund of money and public spirit. . . it should therefore be checked at its commencement. . .' The project was persevered in, however, and a town meeting in May 1806 approved of a plan to set up a college 'to facilitate and render less expensive the means of acquiring education; to give access to the walks of literature to the middle and lower classes of society; to make provision for the instruction of both sexes. . .' Lord Donegall made a site available, application was made to the government for a Charter of Incorporation, the foundation stone was laid in 1810, and on 1 February 1814 Dr William Drennan delivered an address at the opening ceremony.

Once established, the Academical Institution was sharply criticised by Dr Henry Cooke and other Presbyterian evangelicals for promoting 'New Light' or 'Arian' views. In 1825 Cooke published a 10,000-word letter to refute a declaration by the Professors that they did not teach Arian doctrines. In 1829 the Commissioners of Irish Education after a detailed investigation disagreed with Cooke and the Institution continued to flourish and win academic acclaim.

Meanwhile others had been turning their attention to the education of the poor. Henry Joy McCracken had gathered poor children into the Market House and given them free tuition. About 1803 the 'Belfast Weekly or Sunday School' was launched

. . . to afford the means of mental improvement to the children of the lower classes by communicating to them useful instruction and teaching them habits of good order and regularity of conduct, in the hope of guarding them from the vices attendant on ignorance and an early course of idleness. . .

80

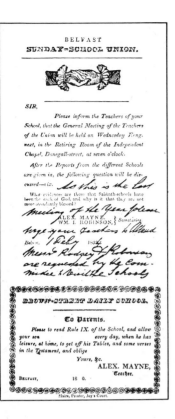

Idleness was unlikely to be a vice for children used to working six days a week from an early age. Instructed 'to come to school with their hair combed, hands and face washed and their apparel as clean as circumstances will admit', 149 children 'of all religious persuasions' were being taught by May 1806. The fifteen teachers gave their services free and the pupils made their first letters in sand, later graduating to slates and paper.

Not satisfied with a school for Sundays only, the committee planned a daily school, and building began on a site in Frederick Street, off York Street, in 1810. The school – which was eventually pulled down in 1963 – was known as the 'Lancasterian School' because it followed the scheme invented by Joseph Lancaster of London. Lancaster, who visited Belfast to give the committee his advice, claimed that by his 'mechanical System of Education. . .paradoxical as it may appear, above One Thousand Children may be taught and governed by one Master only, at an expense now reduced to Five Shillings per annum. . .' By his method the teacher taught the eldest children; they in turn passed on what they had learned to the next eldest; and so on downwards to the beginners. This rote-learning must have been soulless and often useless, but Lancaster was regarded as a progressive. He insisted that pupils should never be asked whether they belonged to 'Church, Meeting or Chapel' and, in a lecture given in the Belfast Theatre in 1811, he denounced all attempts to impose religious doctrine on children.

Another Lancasterian school was later built at Brown's Square. Numerous other private schools catered for the well-to-do at the time, including Shaw's next to the Donegall Arms, Bullick's at 82 High Street, Telfair's in Ann Street, David's in Castle Street, and Rev Dr Drummond's at 'Mount Collyer'.

'Resembling the clear effulgence of a cloudless atmosphere illumined by the moon': gas lighting

On 21 December 1821 two London engineers, John and George Barlow, signed a contract with the Commissioners and Committee of Police to supply Belfast with gas light for £800 a year for the first seven years, 'the said gaslight to be equal to that supplied to the public lamps in London and to be three times greater in brightness than the oil light now existing in said town of Belfast'. A rival scheme to produce gas from the oil of Irish basking sharks had been rejected. The contractors agreed not only to put up cast-iron lamp posts in all the main streets but also to 'erect a column twenty feet high at the head of the dock terminating High Street bearing an extra large light in the form of a dolphin's head, and three stars on the Long Bridge, one star at the White Linen Hall, a few ornamental lights at the Commercial Buildings. . .'

On the evening of 30 August 1823 the correspondent of the *Belfast News-Letter* was in the streets to see 'immense multitudes of people assembled to witness the lighting of our streets with gas' and he remarked that they 'were highly gratified with the mild radiance flowing from the lamps, particularly when contrasted, by memory, with the gloomy twilight or rather darkness visible, which formerly issued from our dull and sombrous globes'. The light at the end of High Street powered by twelve bat-wing burners was so bright 'that a letter was read by it near the quay, 60 yards distant from the pillar'. He continued:

The light now used is of the purest kind, shedding on the streets a brilliant lustre –

pleasing but not dazzling – and more resembling the clear effulgence of a cloudless atmosphere illumined by the moon, than any artificial beams heretofore produced by the imitative power of man.

Living objects in our streets thus illuminated were distinctly seen, even at remote distances – and did not as formerly resemble shapeless masses, now moving in obscurity, and now tinged, in part, with a doubtful gleam of light twinkling upon them from dull or expiring lamps. . .

The light, the reporter asserted, was 'superior in quality to any we have seen either in this kingdom or in Great Britain' and American experts visiting the town 'gave their decided opinion, that those of Belfast were the best constructed and most complete which they had ever beheld'.

The gasworks themselves were built on the Ormeau Road and the Retort House there was 100 feet long and 36 feet high, with a brick chimney 97 feet high. Fourteen miles of pipes had already been laid, issuing from 45 retorts heated by four coke ovens. Altogether the whole enterprise cost around £40,000; it demonstrated a civic zeal and a readiness to adapt to modern industrial technology which the rulers of Belfast retained to the end of the century. The *Belfast News-Letter* rapturously concluded:

Thirty years ago if any man had predicted that such works would be completed on the Ormeau Road, and that shops and streets in remote parts of Belfast would be illuminated by means of coals burned near the Cromac highway, on the banks of the river Lagan, he would have been laughed at, as a dreamer of dreams and seer of visions.

'Raw, uneducated Catholic labourers from the South and West'

One day in October 1810 Father Hugh O'Donnell and Hugh Magill called at the 'Donegall Arms' hotel in a vain attempt to obtain an interview with Lord Castlereagh. Undaunted, the aged parish priest of St Mary's and his companion went to the Long Bridge and stood there in a niche until the great statesman should pass by en route for Mount Stewart. The carriage drew up and the two men explained that they were seeking subscriptions for a new Catholic church in Belfast; Castlereagh handed them 100 guineas. The incident not only is an illustration of the complexity of Castlereagh's character but also demonstrates the continued friendliness of educated Protestants towards Belfast Catholics.

The Catholics of Belfast were in need both of a new parish church and of Protestant contributions. In 1784 there had been only 1,092 Catholics, forming 8% of the town's population; by 1811 Gamille was observing: 'The population in a random way may be estimated at thirty thousand of which four thousand are Catholics. These are almost entirely working people. A few years ago there was scarcely a Catholic in the place.' In 1812 when Father O'Donnell retired, Bishop McMullan appointed the Rev William Crolly in his place and made Derriaghy a separate parish. On Friday 3 March 1815 the new Catholic chapel in Donegall Street, St Patrick's, was consecrated and a week later the Catholics of Belfast published a vote of thanks:

Resolved – That we felt it a duty which we owe to our much esteemed Protestant and Dissenting Brethren of Belfast, and its vicinity, to express publicly our grateful acknowledgments for the disinterested generosity which they manifested. . .

82

Protestants — including the Marquis of Donegall, Thomas Verner the Sovereign, and High Sheriff James Farrel — had contributed £530.16s.7d. A school-house attached to the chapel was opened in 1828, and became Donegall Street National School, receiving state support, in 1833. In 1831 a temporary chapel, the future St Matthew's, was opened in Ballymacarrett and two years later St Malachy's diocesan seminary was founded.

As the rising prosperity of Belfast drew in more and more people of both religions from the countryside, the increase in the numbers of Catholics markedly affected the religious balance in the town. In 1834 there were 19,712 Catholics in Belfast, forming 32% of the town's population. The following year the Commissioners on Public Instruction calculated that there were 25,939 Presbyterians, 22,078 Catholics, and 17,942 members of the Church of Ireland in Belfast; Barrow observed: 'Within a few years some four or five thousand raw, uneducated Catholic labourers from the South and West had poured into the city.' No longer did the Catholics of Belfast form a tiny unobtrusive minority and the hitherto harmonious relations between Protestants and Catholics in the town began to disintegrate.

It was not until towards the end of this period that there were frequent reports of sectarian incidents in the town. During the first quarter-century after the Union the middle-class Protestants of Belfast, disillusioned and shaken by the events of 1798, tended to avoid contentious politics; instead they re-directed their public spirit towards improving the intellectual, cultural, and social life of the town.

'The Northern Athens'

On Tuesday 5 June 1821 eight scholars from the Academical Institution met in the home of Dr James Drummond, Professor of Anatomy, to form the 'Belfast Natural History Society'. In a short time members accumulated impressive collections of antiquities and botanical, zoological, and mineral specimens; the Society outgrew the accommodation provided at first in the Institution and later in the Commercial Buildings. On 4 May 1830 the Marquis of Donegall laid the foundation stone of the Belfast Museum of Natural History in College Square North, and eighteen months later the building was completed — the first museum in Ireland to be established by public subscription.

The Museum gave a new impetus to scientific inquiry in the town. John Templeton developed a passionate interest in botany in the beautiful seclusion of his Cranmore estate; his *Catalogue of Native Plants* and unfinished 'Flora Hibernica' made the museum a treasure store for scholars long after his death in 1825. Robert Templeton, his son, won renown as a zoologist, and during his travels to Latin America, Mauritius and Ceylon painted delicate water-colours of insects and invertebrates, many of them new to science. William Thompson succeeded Dr Drummond as President of the Natural History Society and became the acknowledged expert on Irish invertebrate fauna; he died in 1852 while organising the British Association's first meeting in Belfast. Members of the Society were also responsible for founding the Botanic Garden in 1827; its first site was a small piece of ground adjacent to the Malone turnpike; later, 14 acres were obtained from Lord Donegall as the nucleus of the present gardens; and the handsome palm-house — now faithfully restored — was put up in the 1850s, possibly to a design by the local architect, Thomas Turner.

The Industrial School (1801); the Belfast Literary Society (1801); the House

Mary Ann McCracken (1770–1866) in later life. She abandoned radical politics to become for many years the indefatigable secretary of the Ladies' Committee at Clifton Street Poor House.
(Ulster Museum)

of Industry (1809); the Cosmographical Society (1811); the Anacreontic Society (1814); the General Hospital (1817); the Female Society for the Clothing of the Poor (1820); the Belfast Medical Society (1822); the Mechanics Institute (1825); the Society for the Relief of the Destitute Sick (1826); and the Belfast Lunatic Asylum (1827) – this is but an incomplete list demonstrating the energy of a growing bourgeoisie with confidence in the future of their town. Dr James McDonnell initiated most of the medical charities of the day and was active in literary circles.

Mary Ann McCracken worked tirelessly to improve the condition of her poorer fellow-citizens. She withdrew from radical politics after the execution of her friend Thomas Russell in 1803, and, with her sister Margaret, ran a muslin business at 37 Waring Street until its failure in 1815. Her campaign for the humane treatment of children in factories cannot have pleased her brother John; a letter she wrote in the *Belfast News-Letter* of 17 May 1803 concludes:

In short the proprietor of a Factory is in duty bound to consider himself as the parent of a numerous family, and to do all those things which a sensible and virtuous parent would do; for it is obvious that nothing short of such conduct will prevent *emaciation*, *ignorance*, and *vice*, or e'er long the following exclamation – *Live Morality! – Perish Factories!*

She threw herself into the work of the Poor House; her compassion is revealed in the minutes she wrote for the Ladies Committee and in her scorching letters to the 'Gentlemen' of the Poor House when they called for frugality and inflexible discipline. Other women of her time may have shared her humane and radical convictions but none in Belfast was as indefatigable as Mary Ann McCracken in putting them into action.

It was probably John Lawless, the ebullient editor of the *Irishman*, who first described Belfast as 'the Northern Athens'. This pretentious title was justifiably ridiculed in 1826 by the anonymous author of 'Northern Athens, or Life in the Emerald Isle, a serio-comico-ludicro-satirical poem' – Belfast was not especially notable as a haven of culture in the nineteenth century.

The versatile Dr William Drennan wrote verse (a collection, *Fugitive Pieces*, was published in 1815) and it was he who first named Ireland 'the Emerald Isle' in his poem 'Erin':

> Arm of Erin prove strong, but be gentle as brave,
> And, uplifted to strike, be ready to save;
> Not one feeling of vengeance presume to defile
> The cause of the men of the Emerald Isle.

Robert Anderson, a pattern-drawer in the Mossley cotton works, had numerous poems published in the local press; he was born in Carlisle and, indeed, many nineteenth-century writers in Belfast were not native to the town. Sent up from Dublin in 1853 to be surveyor of the post in the northern counties, Anthony Trollope took lodgings for a time in the Lisburn Road; Belfast can hardly take credit, however, for *The Warden*, the first Barsetshire novel, completed when he moved to Whiteabbey. Though he lived most of his life in Donegal, William Allingham was educated at the Academical Institution and worked for some years in the Belfast Custom House. Allingham's poetry was immensely popular in Victorian Britain and his first collection, published in 1850, was praised by Tennyson for its interpretation of nature. His

Book-plate of the Linen Hall Library. United Irishman Thomas Russell, hanged at Downpatrick in 1803, was the first librarian of the 'Belfast Society for Promoting Knowledge'.
(Linen Hall Library)

influence on the early poetry of W.B. Yeats is striking, and most Irish people over the age of forty are familiar with his poem, 'The Fairies' (1849):

> Up the airy mountain,
> Down the rushy glen,
> We daren't go a-hunting
> For fear of little men.

Samuel Ferguson, born at 23 High Street in 1810, was the most original writer Belfast produced in the nineteenth century. Taught Irish by Patrick Lynch, together with other Protestants of the town, he turned for inspiration to the largely forgotten epics of ancient Ireland. His best-known works – 'The Tain-Quest', 'The Burial of Cormac', 'The Naming of Cuchullin', and 'Deirdre' – stimulated intense interest in the cultural heritage of his country's distant past. Appointed Deputy Keeper of the Records of Ireland in 1869, he earned such distinction as an archivist and archaeologist that he was knighted ten years later.

The Belfast Society for Promoting Knowledge, founded in 1792, carefully collected books in Irish for their library which opened in the White Linen Hall in 1802. Edward Bunting, whose first book was financed by the Society, lived on to complete his greatest collection of Irish music in 1840. Indeed, it could be said that Belfast Protestants had done most to found the nineteenth-century Gaelic Revival which caused so much revulsion to their descendants.

The Catholic Association, Brunswick Clubs, and the Reform Society

Liberal Protestants continued to campaign for the right of Catholics to sit in parliament; in 1818, for example, a town meeting in the Brown Linen Hall called for 'an immediate and total repeal of that part of the penal code which still remains on the statute book against our Catholic fellow-subjects'. John Lawless, who founded the *Irishman* in Belfast in 1800, was more aggressive in his approach; he caused a furore at a dinner given for Lord Donegall in 1822 by putting a foot on the table and attempting to make a speech amid cries of 'Down! Down! – Out! Out! – Hear him, hear him – Put him out!'

When Daniel O'Connell and the Catholic clergy, no longer content to let Protestants lead the campaign, launched a highly-disciplined mass movement for emancipation, some in Belfast were alarmed. A branch of the Catholic Association was set up in Lennon's tavern, Cromac Street, in 1824, and Dr Henry Cooke testified to a parliamentary inquiry that there was a growing feeling amongst Protestants of the north against emancipation. Moderator of the Presbyterian Synod, and afterwards minister of May Street Presbyterian Church, Cooke feared for the Protestant Church; 'with us whenever we hear of the destruction of the Protestant Church,' he said, 'the common people think of the year 1641.' Dr Henry Montgomery, of the Academical Institution, represented the views of the liberal Protestants who incidentally entertained Dr Crolly when he was made the Catholic Bishop of Down and Connor in 1825.

The alarmed government suppressed the Catholic Association and to avoid a similar fate the Orange Order reconstituted itself as the 'Brunswick Clubs'. The Belfast Brunswick Club, established in September 1828, petitioned parliament to maintain 'the Constitution in its Protestant essentiality'. This

was in vain, for the following year Westminster voted to allow Catholics to sit in parliament. The magistrates of Belfast, fearing trouble, issued an appeal to prevent the victory being celebrated: 'As Magistrates we are determined to prevent it as far as lies in our power, under the impression that such a step may lead to disorder and breaches of the peace.'

Cooke may have failed to stop emancipation but at the Synod of 1827 he had driven out Montgomery and the more radical Presbyterians; they, who could not subscribe to any man-made profession of faith, formed what is now the Non-Subscribing Presbyterian Church. Cooke drew the Presbyterian majority into closer alliance with the Established Church; at a meeting in Hillsborough he proclaimed: 'Between the divided churches I publish the banns of a sacred marriage.' The *Northern Whig*, founded in 1825 by F.D. Finlay, denounced Cooke in the following words:

He is the most implacable of enemies, and the most vulgar, too. He had the impudence to speak of the Belfast merchants as a set of grocers and hucksters. Why, the low-bred fellow, if he had not an ingrained and grovelling vulgarity of nature, he would have shrunk from the use of language which would put a chimney-sweep to shame.

It was the *Northern Whig* which played a leading part in launching the 'Reform Society of Belfast' in November 1830 to support the Whigs who had just come to power at Westminster. These 'wealthy and influential inhabitants' expectantly awaited the reform of parliament, and when in October 1831 the Lords rejected the Reform Bill passed by a large majority in the Commons, the issue of the *Northern Whig* announcing the news appeared in mourning with black borders on all its pages. The Reform Society meanwhile denounced the misrepresentation of Belfast:

What has our member, Sir Arthur Chichester, ever done for this town? He represents only twelve burgesses. Where have we any record of his talents or his public exertions? No such record exists. He has done nothing for Belfast.

In June 1832 the Great Reform Bill became law and Belfast's representation at Westminster was increased from one to two members, and, for the first time, all owners or tenants of property worth £10 or more a year could vote. An election was fixed for December 1832. 'And now, Electors of Belfast! the issue is in your own hands,' said Dr Robert J. Tennent in his electoral address as a Whig candidate; 'For more than fifty years yourselves and your ancestors have been struggling for the privileges which you at present possess.' The other Whig candidate, William Sharman Crawford of Crawfordsburn, later a noted champion of tenant right, promised: 'I shall not solicit any Landlord for the votes of his Tenants.' The Tory candidates were Lord Arthur Chichester and James Emerson Tennent (connected by marriage with his Whig opponent): they condemned the Whigs as *ungrateful manufacturers* [who] not content with turning their own backs on the best of men, and kindest of Landlords, the Marquis of Donegall, endeavour to induce his tenants to follow their pernicious example, and thus endeavour to break a sacred tie. . .'

The 1832 election – like almost all subsequent elections in Belfast – was a bitter and acrimonious one.

The Hercules Street riots: December 1832

When the results of the election were announced at the Court House in Howard Street on Saturday 22 December, the Reformers were aghast. They who had championed free elections for so many years had been roundly defeated. Lord Arthur Chichester headed the poll with 848 votes; J.E. Tennent got 737 votes; while Dr R.J. Tennent and Sharman Crawford were beaten into third and fourth place with 613 and 597 votes respectively. The *Belfast News-Letter* and the *Northern Whig* both agreed that only 200 Protestants had voted for the Whig candidates and that the rest of their support had come from Catholics.

Around noon a mob of Tory supporters attacked the mainly Catholic Hercules Street; after two hours of fierce fighting, the *Northern Whig* reported, 'The assailants, however, were completely driven back, by the butchers' boys of Hercules-street, although repeated and furious attacks were made against them, by a ferocious mob, armed with bludgeons.' Meanwhile, in front of the Tory committee rooms, bands played party tunes including 'The Protestant Boys' and 'The Boyne Water'. Then, the *Northern Whig* continued,

Mr Boyce, a noted Orangeman, harangued the mob, from Mr Emerson's Committee-room window. He flourished a staff exultingly, and told them, that the Protestants had gained this victory, and that they would continue to maintain their ascendancy: they had trodden down their enemies, and they would keep them down. . .

The Tories decided to chair their newly elected members in triumph through the streets:

The procession then got into motion, Lord Arthur taking the lead. The respective Committees walked in order, bearing wands, with ribands; and a crowd (not very large) of mean-looking individuals, surrounded the whole. The chairs were then dragged round the Linen-Hall, down High-street, up Donegall-street, and through Church-street. Throughout this line of march, the shops and windows were shut, owing to a well-grounded fear of outrage from such an assemblage.

The procession turned into Hercules Street – now Royal Avenue – and as the town police arrived there were shouts from the Tory mob of 'Here is the Protestant Police; come on, now, and wreck Tennent's house!' The Catholics, armed with knives, once again drove back the Protestants; Chichester was rescued by the police while James Emerson Tennent made a difficult escape through the Post Office, over walls, through backyards, and into Donegall Street. The police loaded their guns, advanced half-way down Hercules Street and opened fire into Torrens Place and down Hercules Street towards the Bank Buildings. Four were killed – two elderly men and two boys aged between twelve and fifteen. Evidence given at the inquest, which filled several columns of the *Belfast News-Letter*, seemed to indicate that the Catholics had fired first with blunderbusses, but no firm conclusions were arrived at.

For the next half century Belfast was to be convulsed periodically by sectarian violence. Even the peace of Christmas Day was shattered by 'a very serious affray' in 1833, not previously mentioned by historians. It began at the Point Fields where many had gathered to shoot wildfowl, 'and something about "orange and green" having disturbed the equanimity of those present a riot was commenced,' the *Northern Whig* reported. It continued:

Four or five Catholics were chased into York-street, by a very considerable body of vagabonds, who shouted 'To Hell with the Pope', 'Five Pounds for the face of a Papist', etc; suiting their actions so well to their words, as to inflict very severe wounds on the heads, faces, and bodies of those whom they hunted through York-street into town. . .

Later that afternoon there was severe rioting around Millfield and Peter's Hill and that night a young man was killed 'by the blow of a bludgeon' in a lane off Waring Street. In the 1835 election James Emerson Tennent was re-elected but a Whig linen merchant, John McCance, beat Lord Arthur Chichester into third place. The angry Tory mob attempted to wreck McCance's tally rooms, and as the *Belfast News-Letter* reported on 20 January 1835:

A crowd assembled daily opposite Emerson's committee rooms and on their way home smashed the windows of almost every Roman Catholic, whose house they passed, and the windows of not a few Protestants whose political sentiments were supposed to differ from theirs, while another mob attacked the houses of some Orangemen.

Order was restored only by a cavalry charge. Almost every year there was violence during the Twelfth of July celebrations. These early riots were on a small scale, however, compared with those of the next few decades when Belfast grew to be a great industrial city.

Early steamship: from *The Town Book of Belfast.*

5
Linen Town
c.1840–1870

Belfast was in festive mood on 12 August 1839 as thousands gathered in Great Victoria Street to watch the opening of the Ulster Railway. The engine raised its steam by coke instead of coal that day to avoid causing discomfort to passengers in the open carriages and, cheered by people standing in the railway ditches all the way to Lisburn, the train completed the journey in twenty minutes. The directors of the company ignored the warning given by the Presbytery of Belfast that wickedness and vice would result if passengers were carried on Sundays; one minister declared that the railway was sending souls to the Devil at the rate of 6d a head: 'Every sound of the railway whistle is answered by a shout in hell,' he said.

The opening of Ulster's first railway seemed to give a new impulse to the growth of Belfast. As tentacles of track were pushed out from the town, so the Harbour authorities built new docks and completed the cut to Garmoyle to cope with the doubling of sea traffic in these years. The new town council, elected in 1842, embarked on an ambitious programme of building and improvements. Little stood in the way, then, of the most spectacular development of the period, the concentration of the Irish linen industry in the steam-powered mills of Belfast.

The official status of Belfast remained that of a town; the Rev W.H. O'Hanlon described it in 1853 as a 'monster town' and by 1870 it was in reality a city. Captain Gilbert, in his report of 1852–3 which recommended the increase in the borough area from 1½ to 10 square miles, pointed out that Belfast had become the first port in Ireland, not only in value, but also in tonnage. The population of the town more than doubled: in 1841 it was 70,447; in 1851, 87,062; in 1861, 121,602; and in 1871, 174,412. Leitch Ritchie wrote in 1838: 'Dublin and Cork are great cities, but they are strictly Irish cities, while Belfast, if transported with its population to England, could be a credit to the country.' Many visitors observed that the town was not typical of Ireland: 'The cleanly and bustling appearance of Belfast is decidedly un-national. That it is in Ireland but not of it is a remark ever on the lips of visitors from south or west,' Mr and Mrs S.C. Hall wrote in 1843, and H.D. Inglis concluded that 'the town and its neighbouring districts have nothing in common with the rest of Ireland'.

Speaking in the New Music Hall in May Street, the Young Irelander Thomas Francis Meagher said: 'Your fate has been as singular as that of Robinson Crusoe and your ingenuity in making the most of a desert island has been no less remarkable.' The great increase in Belfast's prosperity coincided with the near-collapse of Ireland's rural economy. The thousands who migrated from the countryside of Ulster and beyond to Belfast were not only drawn in by

Doffers in the spinning room of Chartres' Falls Mills. Doffers – women who replaced the bobbins – were constantly drenched by spray thrown off by the machines and, as a result, were afflicted by phthisis (a lung disease), 'papular' and 'pastular' eruptions, and onychia (a painful affliction of the toe). (From Hall's *Ireland*, Vol 3)

employment opportunities but also pushed by famine and destitution. The town benefited from their cheap labour but their poverty created new problems. The new immigrants – Protestants and Catholics alike – brought with them their folk-memories, and the quarrels of the countryside were to be fought again with a new ferocity in the streets of Belfast. In this important respect, Belfast was essentially an Irish town.

'The new El Dorado in York Street': the first linen mills

On Sunday 10 June 1828 the sexton's wife hurried up the aisle of St Anne's Church during morning service to call out the military officers from their pews: Mulholland's York Street cotton mill was on fire. The officers' help was of no avail; the raw cotton burned so fiercely that for many hours the flames could be seen from several miles away. Undaunted by this disaster, the Mulhollands rebuilt the mill in Henry Street, just off York Street, not, however, for cotton spinning but for the power spinning of flax. It was a decision of vital importance in the history of Belfast's industrial development.

Until then flax had proved impossible to spin by power machinery. Flax fibres are bound together by a gummy substance which makes the strands to be spun slightly greasy. The hand-spinner could coax the strands into yarn with her fingers, but the strands either stuck together or snapped altogether in power-driven roving machinery. In 1825 James Kay of Preston discovered that a six-hour soaking in cold water made the flax slippery enough to be drawn by power-spinning machines into fine yarn without dissolving out the gum. Thomas Mulholland had acquired a Manchester expert, John Hinds, as his manager and together they experimented with flax spinning in premises in Francis Street. When the cotton mill in York Street burned down 'it was decided,' John Hinds' son wrote later, 'that as English and Scottish competition in the cotton-spinning business was so great, and as the linen trade was the natural business of Ireland, it would be advisable in rebuilding the mill to adapt it for the spinning of flax by machinery, which was accordingly done.'

Mulholland's linen mill, York Street. (Ulster Museum)

Thomas Mulholland and John Hinds travelled to England to make some discreet investigations. Fortunately for Belfast, Kay failed in his attempt to patent his discovery, and so the Mulhollands were able immediately to apply the results of their industrial espionage. Wet-spinning machinery was ordered from MacAdam's Soho Foundry in Townsend Street and in the spring of 1830 the first linen yarn was spun in the new mill. As a fellow manufacturer, Hugh McCall, wrote later, 'not only did flax-spinning by mechanical power succeed beyond the most sanguine expectations of the firm, but the yarn produced was so much cheaper and so superior to the finger spun article that it gave quite a new impulse to the manufacture of linen'. The York Street mill began with 8,000 spindles; by 1846 there were 17,000 spindles and 1,000 employees turning 800 tons of raw flax into yarn; and by 1856 the mill was probably the biggest of its kind in the world, housing as it did 25,000 spindles. As McCall wrote:

. . . the profits of the York Street concern exceeded the dreamiest imaginings of the proprietors; but like wise men, they had the good sense to preserve perfect silence on a subject which few can resist the temptation to talk about. Wealth, however, like its opposite, can hardly follow any one's exertions without some evidence of its track. Several of the far-seeing merchants of the Northern Athens began to surmise the truth respecting the new El Dorado that had been discovered in York Street, and no long time elapsed until other tall chimneys began to rise in different parts of the town.

Only two mills spun flax by power in Belfast in 1830 but by 1846 there were 24 mills. Before 1830 all of Ireland exported not more than 4½ million pounds of yarn in a year; from Belfast alone 9 million pounds were exported in 1857 and 28 million pounds in the boom year of 1865. The brief boom in cotton had created capital, promoted expertise, and brought in thousands from the countryside to work in Belfast. In 1824 the monopoly of the Bank of Ireland was restricted to a radius of 50 miles round Dublin, and Belfast was then free to form joint-stock companies. The Northern Bank was reconstituted on a joint-stock basis in 1824 and the following year the Ulster Bank and the Belfast Bank were set up as joint-stock concerns. All three banks had their head-offices in Belfast and the linen business there had at its disposal the credit needed for rapid expansion.

Cotton had concentrated in Belfast because it was there that the raw cotton was brought in. An important reason why linen concentrated in Belfast was that the coal for raising steam in the mills could be shipped there cheaply from English and Scottish coalfields without any further overland transport charge. The hand-loom weavers followed the tens of thousands of spinners who flocked to the town from rural areas to join those already there who had acquired their skills manufacturing cotton. The linen boom therefore not only brought unprecedented prosperity but also created acute problems – some similar to those experienced by the growing industrial centres of Britain but others uniquely and unhappily Irish.

'The corporation. . . confers on the inhabitants no benefit': Municipal Reform

In 1833 the government ordered an inquiry into the municipal corporations of Ireland and after two years of detailed investigations the thirteen commissioners picked out Belfast Corporation as one of the worst in the country: the burgesses had excluded the freemen from any role in decision-making, the constitution had long operated 'virtually to vest the whole of the corporate powers in the lord of the castle of Belfast,' and, they reported, 'No Roman Catholics have been admitted since the relaxation, in the year 1793, of the penal laws previously affecting them.' In short, the commissioners bluntly concluded, 'The corporation, as now conducted, embraces no principle of representation, and confers on the inhabitants no benefit.'

The list of criticisms covered many pages: the Corporation conducted its affairs in secrecy, justice was not administered impartially, tolls were imposed illegally, and, the commissioners believed, the 'abuses which may result from the existence of a public body so constructed, are clearly exemplified in the dissipation of the charitable funds intrusted to the management and distribution of the corporation of this borough'. The commissioners felt it their duty to refer to:

. . . the melancholy particulars of the 'Sandy-row riots', arising out of the unchristian practice of hooting at, insulting, and attacking persons attending the funerals of deceased Roman Catholics; of the 'Brown-street riots', which grew out of a custom of annually erecting an 'Orange arch' across a public street on the 12th of July, by the Orange party; and of the 'Hercules-street riots', which took place upon the collision of the exasperated parties on the occasion of the chairing of the Members for the borough after the general election in December 1832.

Lord Melbourne's Whig government at Westminster introduced the Irish Municipal Corporations Bill but, opposed by the Tories – including the Belfast MPs Tennent and Dunbar – and delayed by the Lords, it did not become law until 1840. Ballymacarrett was combined with Belfast for the first time and the whole municipal area was divided into five wards – Dock, St Anne's, Smithfield, St George's and Cromac. Each ward was to elect two aldermen and six councillors; one third of the councillors every year and half the aldermen every third year had to stand for re-election. The Town Clerk was to be responsible for drawing up the electoral register; those who were rated as £10 householders and who had paid their rates before 31 August were eligible for registration as voters. Belfast at last possessed a representative system of town government. Unhappily, much-needed municipal reform coincided with a heightening of political and sectarian tension which came close to breaking strain during Daniel O'Connell's visit to Belfast in 1841.

'To Hell with the Big Beggarman!': O'Connell in Belfast 1841

'My friend Bully Cooke, the cock of the North,' Daniel O'Connell told the people of Dublin, 'has written the most insulting letter he could pen.' O'Connell had announced his intention of visiting Belfast and Dr Henry Cooke had challenged him to a public debate. 'I believe you are a great bad man engaged in a great bad cause,' Cooke had written but the 'Liberator' was not discouraged; he had won emancipation for the Catholics and valuable reforms for Ireland and now he would settle for nothing else but repeal of the Act of Union.

Troops and police lined the streets when O'Connell's carriage drew into

Belfast on the evening of Saturday 16 January 1841. 'The news of his arrival spread like wildfire,' reported the *Vindicator,* O'Connell's Belfast newspaper, and next day 'not the slightest disposition to break the peace or disturb the general tranquillity was evinced, although the streets were at times densely thronged. . . we do think that the beating up the streets and squares with bodies of armed dragoons was a proceeding, that was, at that period, wholly uncalled for. . .

The following Tuesday, however, O'Connell's stentorian voice was drowned by hooting and groaning when he attempted to address a meeting in Donegall Square. That evening, while he was attending a 'soirée' for St Patrick's Orphan Society in Upper Arthur Street, mobs surged through the streets breaking windows, attacking the Royal Hotel and St Patrick's chapel, stoning the homes of known repealers, and besieging the *Vindicator* office. 'While we write,' the *Vindicator* reported, 'they are after being repulsed by the police, in the fifth attempt to break open the door; and there is scarcely a whole pane in the front of the office. . .' A great crowd roared 'To Hell with the Pope!', 'To Hell with the Big Beggarman and his tail!' and 'Down with rebellious Repeal!' outside the New Music Hall where O'Connell was attending the soirée. The *Belfast News-Letter* believed that had the authorities not been fully prepared Belfast would 'have presented to the view of a spectator, only a heap of ruins'.

As O'Connell left Belfast, escorted by four cars full of police and a body of police cavalry, Dr Cooke addressed a massive open-air demonstration against Repeal:

I would show Mr O'Connell what he did not yet see – that is, the wonders of Belfast. It is true, that within only a comparatively recent period, our town was merely a village. But what a glorious sight does it now present! Turn in what direction we will, our eyes meet new streets and public buildings – numbers of new manufactories rise up on every side – and look where we may, we see signs of increasing prosperity. . . And to what cause is all this prosperity owing? Is it not to the free intercourse which the Union enables us to enjoy with England and Scotland – to that extension of our general

'Who cares about the bloody blackguards of Sandy Row!' a Repealer cries, but Daniel O'Connell and his 'Tail' needed police protection from the 'bludgeon-men' as they left Donegall Square to catch the mail packet from Donaghadee. (Ulster Museum)

commerce which we derive through that channel? I can fancy I see the genius of industry seated upon the hills which look down upon our lovely town. . . while, accompanied by the genius of Protestantism, her influence is shed, from that point, over the length and breadth of Ulster (Hear, hear and loud cheers). . . Can there be any religious liberty, I would ask him, in a community. . . where freedom of conscience is unknown?

Fear of religious persecution, and Belfast's dependence on free trade within the British Empire – these were the two main arguments Cooke put against the restoration of the Dublin parliament. These arguments were to be advanced repeatedly in the years to come. Belfast had become and was to remain the principal bulwark of the Union.

The rule of John Bates: 'unscrupulous in action – prompt, energetic and determined'

O'Connell's visit to Belfast probably increased Protestants' anxiety about what would happen to them if a Catholic-dominated parliament were set up in Dublin. The national question certainly had an important bearing on the first elections for the new Town Council which were not held until the autumn of 1842. It seemed likely that all Catholic electors would support the Liberals (formerly the Whigs) and that almost all Church of Ireland electors would cast their votes for the Conservatives (formerly the Tories). How would the Presbyterians vote?

All forty seats in the Council were won by the Conservatives. Even the outgoing Sovereign, Thomas Verner, failed to win a seat and Lord Donegall, who had campaigned vigorously on his behalf, burst into tears when he learned of 'this most dishonourable transaction'. Clearly the great majority of Presbyterians had abandoned the political radicalism of their fathers. Most Catholics were too poor to qualify as electors in any case and the Protestant Liberal merchants and mill-owners seem to have been remarkably inept at organising support. This, however, was not the complete explanation of the Conservative triumph.

The lack of secret voting and the complicated system for the registration of electors created many opportunities for corrupt electoral practice. John Bates, a solicitor who was the Conservatives' agent from the parliamentary election of 1832 onwards, had mastered the technicalties of registration. He made sure that known Conservatives were put on the list of electors and he used all his legal skill to disqualify Liberals; in 1835, for example, he had 80 Liberals disenfranchised because they had described their premises as 'house and shop' instead of 'house, shop'. Almost all of those in charge of registration and polling seem to have been Conservatives. Bates set up Conservative registration committees in every ward and he was probably responsible for the unexplained closing of the tax offices throughout August 1842 – those who had not paid their rates before then were automatically disqualified. At the first meeting of the Council on 4 November 1842 – the anniversary of the landing of William of Orange – George Dunbar, formerly Conservative MP for Belfast, was chosen as Mayor. John Bates was elected Town Clerk, a position which gave him official control over registration; in effect, he was absolute ruler of Belfast until his death in 1855. A critic, Durham Dunlop, described Bates as:

Ready in conception, unscrupulous in action – prompt, energetic and determined – capable of sustaining great bodily and mental fatigue, with a mind fitted to embrace all the ramifications of the machinery with which he had to work.

Even without any of Bates' sharp practices, it is likely that the Council would have been dominated by the Conservatives. As it was, the Council was completely united by party and religion, and energetically it set about governing the town. Vigorous action was needed: the town's population had increased by 32.2% between 1831 and 1841, and was to rise by another 23.6% in the next decade. The Donegall family had long before lost its power to control building and development. Indeed, the 2nd Marquis had signally failed to pay his debts and when he died in 1844 his son, George Hamilton Chichester, was forced to raise £100,000 immediately from the remaining estates. Acts of Parliament in 1845 and 1846, and the Encumbered Estates Court in the 1850s, led to the outright sale of most of the Donegall properties. As most of the purchasers already held leases in perpetuity, the change was largely symbolic — the commercial and industrial barons now had full title to property they had been controlling for decades. In the eighteenth century the Chichesters had regulated building and now in the mid-nineteenth century the Town Council confidently resumed the task.

The Belfast councillors were perhaps the most uncharacteristic Conservatives in Ireland, and, perhaps, in the United Kingdom. Their zeal for improvement was matched only by the most progressive Liberals in England — perhaps in this respect Protestant radicalism remained alive amongst Belfast Conservatives. By 1848 only 29 out of 178 municipal corporations in England and Wales had applied for optional powers to pave streets and carry out other improvements; in Manchester even the radicals opposed the compulsory purchase of houses for street widening and objected to the cost of 'cursed improvements'. In contrast, the Belfast Town Council immediately set about applying for additional powers. Despite protests and an appeal to the Queen's Bench Division, the powers of the Police Committee and Police Commissioners were taken over in 1844. In 1845 the Corporation applied for and obtained an Act of Parliament giving the Council powers to borrow up to £150,000, mainly for widening old streets; building new streets; paving, cleaning and lighting parts of the town; laying sewers; buying land for markets; and providing fire engines.

Next year the Corporation obtained 'An Act for the better Lighting and Improving the Borough of Belfast' which gave the Council the right to set up a gasworks and to borrow another £50,000. 'An Act for the further Improvement of the Borough of Belfast' in 1847, and another Act in 1850, authorised further borrowing mainly for 'the abatement of the Blackstaff nuisance' between Bradbury Place and the White Linen Hall, and laid down that all new buildings had to comply with certain minimum standards — all new houses had to have a small yard with a lavatory and ash-pit. The Council gave enthusiastic support to the 1847 Factory Act, which limited hours of work for women and children in textile factories to ten hours a day, and to the 1850 Act which extended the ten-hour day to male textile workers.

The most immediate results of this legislation were the establishment of much-needed markets, particularly at May's Fields, and the building of Corporation and Victoria Streets on the site of decaying and evil-smelling docks. The Liberals, meanwhile, failed to win a single Council seat until 1855; deeply resenting the high-handed rule of John Bates and the blatant corruption of his political machine they awaited their opportunity for revenge.

Clifton Street Poor House: from Benn (1823).

The Union Workhouse

In 1836 a government inquiry painted a grim picture of poverty in Ireland:

We cannot estimate the number of persons in Ireland out of work and in distress during thirty weeks of the year at less than 585,000, nor the number of persons dependent upon them at less than 1,800,000, making in the whole 2,385,000.

Ireland had no official system of poor relief whatever; any relief available was given by private charity. The inquiry commented favourably on Belfast: the Clifton Street Poor House in November 1833 was providing accommodation for 233 old people and 195 children, and the House of Industry was giving bread to an average of 116 people a day, supplying 794 women with spinning wheels and flax in a year, and giving out rations regularly to 626 families in distress. In 1838 the government – despite well-founded arguments that the English system was inappropriate for Ireland – set up Poor Law 'unions' throughout the island; the resident Poor Law Commissioner, George Nicholls, united the parishes of the country into 130 unions, each to be governed by a Board of Guardians, elected by the ratepayers.

The Belfast Union covered not only the town itself but also the districts of Ballymacarrett, Ballygomartin, Ballyhackamore, Ballymurphy, Ballysillan, Carnmoney, Castlereagh, Dundonald, Greencastle, Holywood and Whitehouse. Seven Justices of the Peace held ex-officio positions on the Board; the other twenty-two Guardians elected were for the most part substantial owners of property. The Guardians bought a site on the Lisburn Road for £2,130 and on it Messrs Williams built a workhouse at a cost of £10,122. Opened on 11 May 1841, where the City Hospital now stands, the Belfast Union Workhouse was designed to accommodate 1,000 inmates and was one of the largest and best-equipped in Ireland. The Workhouse had, however, to comply with the rigid standards laid down by the Irish Poor Law Commissioners in 1839:

The style of building is intended to be of the cheapest description compatible with durability; and the effect is arrived at by harmony of proportion and simplicity of arrangement, all mere decoration being studiously avoided.

All inmates had to work and 'for the able-bodied it should be of such a nature as to be irksome and to awaken or increase a dislike to remain in the workhouse'; women did the chores of the house and the men broke stone or picked oakum (unravelled old ropes). The workhouse food 'must on no account be superior or even equal to the ordinary mode of subsistence of the labouring classes of the neighbourhood'. In Belfast able-bodied adults got 10 ounces of oatmeal, 3 pounds of potatoes and 2 pints of buttermilk per day, with some soup two days a week. Uniforms had to be worn; in 1842:

The clothing of the adult males consists of a coat and trowzers of barragon, cap, shirt, shoes and stockings. The female adults are supplied with a striped jerkin, a petticoat of linsey-wolsey, and another of Stout cotton, a cap, shift, shoes, and stockings. . .

Discipline was deliberately severe; smoking, playing cards and drinking alcohol were forbidden and adults could be locked away and boys flogged if they were 'refractory'. The harshest rule of all was that families were broken up; husbands and wives, brothers and sisters, and parents and children were separated. Much depended on the Master and the Matron. The first pair at the Belfast Workhouse, Mr and Mrs Arthur Conor, were forced to resign because they both assaulted the schoolmistress of the Workhouse, Catherine Evans. The police had to compel them to allow witnesses to appear and, after fining them ten shillings each, the magistrate felt it necessary to say:

If I find that the slightest violence or ill-treatment is shewn to any witness, in consequence of this trial, I shall certainly feel it my duty to send the offending party for trial to the Assizes.

The Commissioners in Dublin were perpetually afraid that the poor would treat the Workhouse as a kind of hotel and for a time the severity of the Workhouse regime kept inmates to manageable numbers. The annual report for 1844 showed that in the first three months of that year the Belfast Workhouse admitted 802 adults – 214 of these were widows and 51 were women deserted by their husbands – and 666 children, of whom 196 were either orphans or had been deserted by both parents. Had the Irish economy been as sound as that of Belfast, the workhouse system could have coped with poverty by the standards set by the Poor Law Commissioners. In 1845, however, the Irish economy was on the brink of disaster.

'Misery met the eye at every step in every street': the Famine

In 1845 blight struck the potato crop over most of the south of Ireland; the last great famine in western Europe had begun. Not touched by the disease and at the heart of the most prosperous corner of the country, Belfast that year was largely unaffected. In 1846 the potato crop was a complete failure throughout Ireland and in the winter of 1846–7 – the most severe in living memory – millions faced total destitution. At Christmas in 1846 the *Belfast News-Letter* reported that 'starving wretches hourly swarm into the streets from the country', and a government official in the town wrote that 'in many of our back lanes and courts there are families in the veriest wretchedness, with scarcely enough rags to cover their shivering emaciated bodies'; he found the destitute huddled around dying embers, one pathetic group attempting to fan into flame a small heap of damp sawdust.

Its very prosperity made the town a magnet for those who had nothing. Many came from thickly populated areas west and south of the Bann – Armagh, for example, was the most densely inhabited rural area in the United Kingdom. Over the previous decade spinners and handloom weavers there had been ruined by competition from the linen mills and, now that their basic food had been reduced to a blackened, rotting mass by blight, thousands streamed along the roads to Belfast. Dr Andrew Malcolm, who worked tirelessly to treat the sick and the dying at this time, observed:

We well remember the aspect of the hordes of poor who thronged into the town, from all parts. Famine was depicted in the look, in the hue, in the voice, and the gait. The food of a nation had been cut off; the physical strength of a whole people was reduced; and this condition, highly favourable to the impression of the plague-breath, resulted in the most terrible epidemic that this Island ever experienced.

Indeed, the deadly companion of hunger was fever. A deputation from the Belfast fever hospital informed the Board of Guardians 'that from the great

'The Emigrant Ship' by John Glen Wilson; this ship is putting out from Clarendon Dock. A similar vessel, the *Swatara*, brought a typhus epidemic to Belfast in 1847.(Ulster Museum)

increase in fever and sickness generally the hospital was so overcrowded that many cases requiring medical and surgical treatment were refused admission. . .'; as a result the Board, in its minutes of 20 October 1846, observed that 'the alarming increase of typhus fever renders it imperative on this board to prepare without delay for the approaching epidemic'. Of the several fevers which raged in the town, typhus was the deadliest; carried by body lice, typhus caused vomiting, delirium, gangrene, massive swelling and blackened features before death gave its victims rest. A loathsome stench accompanied the disease and one doctor wrote that he was 'always seized with the most violent retching' when treating patients.

It was a vessel carrying Irish emigrants from Liverpool, *The Swatara*, which was blamed at the time for bringing the typhus epidemic to Belfast. Delayed by contrary winds, this ship was forced twice to put into Belfast in March 1847; in the cramped conditions on board fever spread rapidly and, once in port, throughout the town. There followed a typhus plague, in Dr Malcolm's words, 'in comparison with which all previous epidemics were trivial and insignificant'.

Leading citizens set up a Board of Health in May 1847 to attempt to provide accommodation for fever victims. Sheds were put up in the grounds of the Frederick Street Hospital, the Workhouse infirmary was hastily enlarged, a hospital was organised at the Academical Institution and buildings used during the 1832 cholera epidemic were re-opened. Still there were not enough beds as fever claimed victims at the rate of 50 a day. The epidemic reached its height in July; weekly hospital admissions reached 660 and to provide for them tents were erected in the Workhouse grounds. The recorded fever admissions for 1847 in Belfast were 13,678. 'It may be safely affirmed,' Dr Malcolm wrote, 'that one out of every five persons in Belfast was attacked during this year.' The *Belfast News-Letter* reported on 20 July:

The hospitals are crowded, and every new building erected for patients is filled to overflowing as soon as completed. Yet hundreds – for whom there remains no provision – are daily exposed in the delirium of this frightful malady, on the streets, or left to die in their filthy and ill-ventilated hovels. . . It is now a thing of daily occurrence to see haggard, sallow and emaciated beings, stricken down by fever or debility from actual want, stretched prostrate upon the footways of our streets and bridges, unable to proceed further than the spot where they had fallen down. . . Misery met the eye at every step in every street.

The total number of those who died in Belfast from famine and fever cannot be estimated with any accuracy. Certainly the cemeteries were full; the Rt Rev Dr Denvir and the Rev Bruce urged the Guardians to make more ground available: 'The only grounds available for this purpose will speedily cease to be so. The ground which the Charitable Society have granted for the purpose cannot admit of any fresh burials after 1st July if the present rate of mortality continues. The Shankill burying ground is full; a month more will completely fill that of Friar's Bush. . .' An additional burden for the Guardians was that British Poor Law Unions tended to repatriate Irish immigrants to Belfast as the most convenient port and, as John Holden told the Board in January 1848, those sent from Glasgow 'are unfurnished with food or money, and several apparently just discharged from Hospital. . .'

The government allowed the Union to provide some 'outdoor relief' to the poor in the form of soup, but Lord John Russell, the Prime Minister, declared: 'It must be thoroughly understood that we cannot feed the people.' Private charity attempted to meet the needs of the famished. A fund was opened from 15 January 1847 in Belfast; Andrew Mulholland & Son and Richardson Bros headed the list with £200 each and eventually £7,000 was raised which was used to provide relief not only in Belfast but thoughout the country. Charities in Belfast provided soup for as many as 15,000 a day, mainly from kitchens in York Street and Howard Street. Dr Malcolm observed:

This great movement well became the capital of the North. It was the crowning act in her History, and made her, for a time, an example for the world. Well may she boast of her prosperity, when she can point to such noble deeds, to show, that in the midst of her increasing wealth, she has preserved intact the purity of the Christian virtues.

And yet the suffering and the dying continued.

'God save your Majesty and the whole of yez!' Victoria in Belfast 1849

On the morning of Friday 11 August 1849 the Royal Squadron entered Belfast Lough and, as the band of the Young Men's Total Abstinence Society on board the SS *Ranger* played appropriate airs in welcome, huge crowds gathered from the quays to the Lisburn Road. Though the Town Council had been given very short notice of the royal visit, the *Belfast News-Letter* reported:

Many hundreds of handsome banners and flags almost over-arched the leading

Ships richly dressed to welcome Queen Victoria to Belfast on 11 August 1849. A specially-erected pavilion, flying the Royal Standard, can be seen (left) standing on the filled-in old Town Dock, later the unstable foundation of the Albert Clock. (*Illustrated London News*)

thorough fares. Whole plantations of laurel and other evergreens were transferred to the fronts of the houses. Expensive draperies, of every hue, festooned the balconies. . . the coup d'oeil was sparkling and animated beyond anything of the kind ever witnessed before in Belfast. . .

At two o'clock the booming of artillery signalled that the royal party had transferred to the SS *Fairy* to take them from the Garmoyle roads to the pavilion erected at the quays. After receiving loyal deputations, the Queen, Prince Albert, and the Prince of Wales in sailor trim, were drawn in Lord Londonderry's carriage towards High Street, under a 32-foot-high Triumphal Arch with the words 'Caed Mille Failthe' magnificently mis-spelt in dahlias.

For the length of several hundred yards in front of the Royal arch, an unbroken line of galleries on each side, effectually concealing the blanks caused by the recent opening of Victoria-street, gave the scene the appearance of a vast theatre; the graduated tiers of the benches were filled with thousands of gaily-dressed and animated spectators, whose acclamations, as the cortege passed by, rose like the roar of the wind in the forest. . .

Expensive oil paintings of the Queen and Prince Albert were displayed on the balcony of McGee's the tailors; 'Welcome' was inscribed in immense gold letters over the Northern Bank; and in front of one house was written:

Up goes my caubeen
For Erin's own Queen!

In Donegall Place the National Anthem was played and at 2.55 p.m. the royal family entered the White Linen Hall (passing under an arch composed of two orange trees laden with fruit from Robert Langtry's Fortwilliam conservatory) to visit an exhibition of the linen industry 'from flax in the growth to the splendid damask'. Thereafter the royal party drove through Wellington Place, up Great Victoria Street, past the Malone turnpike, to the Lisburn Road where the Workhouse children gave three shrill cheers. The Botanic Gardens and the new Queen's College (now Queen's University) were visited; a poor woman ran beside the carriage crying:

Och, the Lord love her purty face, for goodness is in her. Look at the way she bows and smiles to everybody – God save your Majesty and the whole of yez – hurra!

After driving down Howard Street, past the Clifton Street Poorhouse, and

Queen Victoria stops in Donegall Street to see an exhibition of the linen industry 'from flax in the growth to the splendid damask' in the White Linen Hall. The Royal Standard is flying over the Library wing. *(Illustrated London News)*

down Henry Street to view 'the magnificent factory of the Messrs Mulholland, where a large platform, crowded to excess, and decorated with flags, was erected', the Queen re-embarked. That night the Mayor gave a sumptuous banquet at the Donegall Arms:

The dinner was of the most *recherche* kind, and comprised all the delicacies of the season, served in the most excellent style. The wines were of the choicest vintage; and the dessert profusely supplied with the rarest fruits, etc.

Behind these opulent scenes the greatest distress prevailed in the densely inhabited warrens of the poor. The government had declared the famine to be at an end, but the depredations of the blight and the consequent starvation continued. To add to the prevailing misery, cholera swept through Belfast in 1849, reaching peaks in March and July. The authorities were well prepared, for this Asiatic disease had moved across Europe like a dark cloud as the last embers of the 1848 revolutions were being ruthlessly extinguished. The Belfast Sanitary Committee had been formed as early as March 1848; in the summer it issued notices on the importance of cleanliness and ventilation, and in October Health Visitors were sent out to advise the poor on how best to avoid the disease. Even so, at the dispensary station alone, 2,282 cases of cholera were recorded in 1849; 997 of these cases died, indicating a far higher death-rate than in the 1831–2 epidemic – 33% as compared with 16%. Above all, the Sanitary Committee concluded, the disease was largely confined to the poor whose living conditions appeared to have worsened over the previous decade.

Walks among the poor of Belfast

The Sanitary Committee produced a damning report in 1849 on the condition of working-class districts. It found Little Ship Street and much of the Dock area in a 'filthy, flooded, and neglected state'; Sandy Row and the Pound were full of open drains; off the New Lodge Road there were 'several open drains of semi-liquid filth'; in Cromac there were 'large cesspools and open drains'; and the courts around Smithfield were 'especially victimised by sanitary neglect'. 'A more neglected portion of the town cannot be well conceived,' the Committee observed of Ballymacarrett; here it found:

An almost complete want of drainage, extensive accumulations of liquid manure here and there immediately in the rere of dwelling houses, and a general absence of house accommodations, are its chief characteristics.

The driving force behind the Committee almost certainly was Dr Malcolm of the General Hospital. In a detailed report on the sanitary state of Belfast, published in 1852, Dr Malcolm showed that many of the problems arose out of bad drainage:

At high tide, the sea-water passes up into the main sewers of all the level districts of the town – as those of Victoria Street, High Street, North Street and Great George's Street – to a very considerable distance. . . Thus, for several hours before full tide, a large portion of the solid refuse, which would have been under other circumstances carried out in suspension, has time to deposit in all the main lines of conduits.

He estimated that only 3,000 out of 10,000 houses in the town had piped water, and even in many of these there were no cisterns; 180 thoroughfares were unpaved; 3,000 houses were without yards of any description; and there was 'a lamentable deficiency' of street cleaning in poorer areas leading to an 'accumulation of offensive remains'. He praised the opening up of new thoroughfares:

. . . where nought but vice, death, and poverty, held their fearful orgies, has risen, as if by enchantment, a splendid array of marts and emporia of trade and commerce. . . Our main streets, for width and regularity of outline, are proverbially a model; but we cannot say so for the myriad approaches to the poorer residences. Upwards of 1,800 houses, in courts, etc., are accessible only by a covered archway. . . of a total of 579 streets, lanes, and courts, 331 of the residence-ways of the poorer classes are under twenty feet in breadth!

Dr Malcolm's statistics were given added force by the Rev W.M. O'Hanlon's *Walks Among the Poor of Belfast,* letters to the *Northern Whig* published as a book in 1853. O'Hanlon had come from Lancashire to be minister of the Congregationalist Church in Upper Donegall Street between 1849 and 1854; the Irish Evangelical Society withdrew their grant to him, possibly because he concentrated his energies on writing vivid descriptions of poverty in the town. His first letter is an account of the Dock area where he found entries and courts 'mostly crowded with human beings in the lowest stage of social degradation'. The sight of seven people living in one room in Brady's Row, off Grattan Street, he found 'revolting, disgusting, and heart-rending. . . It haunts one like a loathsome and odious spectacle, from which the eye and the thoughts cannot escape'. Nearby, there were five brothels in one short street '. . . a very sink of iniquity, a gate to perdition, both a fountain and a focus of the crime and brutality of the whole neighbourhood'. In his next letter, O'Hanlon began:

Let me first direct your eye to some of the purlieus of North Queen-street. . . plunging

102

into the alleys and entries of this neighbourhood, what indescribable scenes of poverty, filth, and wretchedness everywhere meet the eye! Barrack-lane was surely built when it was imagined the world would soon prove too strait for the number of its inhabitants. . . no pure breath of heaven ever enters here; it is tainted and loaded by the most noisome, reeking feculence, as it struggles to reach these loathsome hovels. These are, in general, tenanted by two families in each, and truly it is a marvel and a mystery how human beings can, in such a position, escape disease in its most aggravated and pestilential forms.

Dr Malcolm produced much evidence to support this view: in the whole of the United Kingdom the mortality rate was 1 in 50 per year whereas in Belfast it was 1 in 35. In the 1847 epidemic 70% of houses 'deficient in sewerage' had fever but only 19% of houses in the better drained districts suffered. He listed the origins of 1,141 cases of fever recorded at the dispensary in 1848: 'In first class streets, none; in second class ditto, 22; in third class ditto, 81; and in lanes, courts, entries, alleys, rows &c., 156 — making a total of 259 localities.' O'Hanlon noted that in Dawson's Court, off Durham Street, the landlord insisted on complete cleanliness and, as a result, there was not a single case of cholera there in 1849: 'The pestilence was rebuked at the threshold; it looked down, but, finding no encouragement to enter there, it turned aside to scenes where it could riot at its pleasure.' He observed that, as he crossed the Blackstaff, 'I felt as though actually pursued by grim Pestilence and Death.' On the outskirts of the town, however, the poor were better favoured:

. . . let us enter Sandy-row. This locality is not unknown to fame. . . I had heard of its bludgeon-men, and, even though on a peaceful mission, I thought it just possible we might fare ill among men of blood. But our fears were groundless. . . Its suburban situation is greatly in its favour. . . The mountain breezes play upon their dwellings, and they have only to look around to catch some glimpses of the country, not yet quite eaten up by the insatiable appetite of our monster town.

The Rev A. McIntyre blamed low wages for much of the wretchedness he found. In his diary for 8 December 1853, he records a visit to a family living at 12 Little Donegall Street; there a widow and her daughter embroidered cloth as piece-work and her little boy cut stone. Margaret Lyons, the widow, he described as

. . . an old skeleton, having the appearance of one lately risen from the grave, seated on a stone and surrounded by slates, pieces of old mortar, the floor flooded with water and no fire that I could see before her. The entire top of the house had fallen in. There was not one particle of it remaining. She complained that she had got her death from the rain and frost that came down upon her in bed. I asked her why she did not go to the Workhouse. She said she did not like to be separated from her children.

Though he found women in entries off Little Patrick Street veining muslin for as little as 7d a week, O'Hanlon believed that strong drink was the principal scourge of the poor. He saw twenty spirit stores in Smithfield as 'exhibiting unmistakeable marks of a brisk and lucrative trade'; the proprietor of a store in Little Patrick Street told him that he had sold 9,380 gallons of whiskey alone in 1852; in a tavern-brothel off North Queen Street 'all herd together in this place as in a common hell, and sounds of blasphemy, shouts of mad debauch, and cries of quarrel and blood, are frequently heard here through the livelong night'; and in Pepper-hill-court near Carrick Hill 'whiskey-drinking and lewd singing relieve the monotony of the scene, and the lazy and laden atmosphere is duly stirred at times by the frantic shouts of low bacchanalian orgies'.

In a recent study Peter Froggatt has shown that Belfast had much in common with British industrial city-ports such as Bristol, Liverpool, Edinburgh and Glasgow which had emerged for much the same reasons and at much the same rate. These ports had similar laws and bye-laws; their age structures were similar; they shared in the cholera epidemics of 1831–2 and 1848–9; they all practised vaccination and had much the same range of medical and Poor Law services; and their philanthropic effort had much in common. Belfast did not have the grim cellar dwellings of many English cities but wages in the cotton and linen mills were lower in Belfast than in either England or Scotland. Though it is difficult to compare British and Irish statistics, it appears that mortality rates for those aged between 6 and 45 years were higher in Belfast than in comparable British cities. While Belfast had much in common with other British industrial city-ports, it was – as the only major industrial area – quite unique in Ireland. Dr Froggatt, looking at the 1841 census, concludes:

In every age group except one (46-55 years) the Belfast mortality rates exceed those of other civic districts which in turn everywhere exceed the rural district rates. In younger groups in fact the Belfast mortality is over twice that for the country as a whole. . . the results can be interpreted as showing significantly higher mortality in Belfast than elsewhere in Ireland: since it is most marked in the pre-16-year-old age groups it is likely to be due to living in, rather than working in, Belfast *per se*.*

* P. Froggatt, 'Industrialisation and Health in Belfast in the Early Nineteen Century', in Harkness and O'Dowd, *The Town in Ireland* (see bibliog), p. 173.

In short, though the statistics are unreliable, Belfast had the worst death rate in Ireland. It may even have had the worst death rate in the United Kingdom. In 1981 the life expectancy for women was 76 years, and 70 years for men. In 1852 Dr Malcolm calculated that, due to the 'absolutely excessive' infant mortality, the average life expectancy in Belfast was *nine years*.

The fall of John Bates and the borough boundary extension

Perhaps the greatest failure of the Town Council in these years was that it had done little more for the sanitation of Belfast than provide public wash-houses for the poor. But for its vigorous programme of street improvement, however, conditions might have been worse still, and there is little evidence that the Liberals would have been as energetic as the Conservatives. In 1850 James Simms, editor of the *Northern Whig*, Robert Grimshaw, William Dunville, Thomas Verner and other Liberals organised a protest meeting against the Bill seeking permission to drain that hazard to health, the Blackstaff; even after the Bill became law Liberal mill-owners were largely responsible for frustrating the scheme. When the Council applied for an extension of the municipal boundary, the Liberals refused to give evidence to Captain Gilbert, sent by the Lord Lieutenant to investigate Belfast's claim. Gilbert found that in 1852 the population had increased by 10,000; that the rapid growth of the town 'is concurrent with, and chiefly consequent upon, the thriving state of the linen manufactures in the town and neighbourhood, and the favourable position of Belfast as a seaport, and an outlet for the trade and produce of the province of Ulster'; and that the additional powers granted to the Council from 1845 to 1850 'appear to have been judiciously exercised for the improvement of the borough'.

Gilbert's recommendation that the boundary be extended to increase the area of Belfast from 1½ square miles to 10 square miles was accepted. The boundary extension of 1852 was of the greatest benefit to Belfast as the Council could now draw rates from and regulate the suburbs; the Poor Law valuation was raised from £156,645 to £250,000. In contrast, Dublin failed to extend its city frontier and suffered from severe inner-city decay because it was not able to impose rates on the prosperous middle classes living beyond the urban boundary.

The Liberals were hopelessly divided: Catholics wanted urban improvement while Protestant employers resented the rate increase brought about by the boundary extension. They were united, nevertheless, in resenting the arrogant domination of John Bates and the Conservatives. In 1853 John Rea, a solicitor who had fought in the Young Ireland rebellion of 1848, filed a suit in the Court of Chancery in Dublin against the Belfast Town Council. The Corporation, and Bates in particular, were accused of borrowing more than had been permitted by the Acts between 1845 and 1850; of buying the May's Fields instead of the gasworks; and of fraudulently borrowing £84,000. Bates himself was charged with tampering with the accounts books and with exacting £32,000 exorbitantly for his services as Town Solicitor.

This was the opportunity the Liberals had been waiting for, and when in June 1855 the Lord Chancellor found all the allegations proved, Rea was received rapturously by his supporters in Belfast with bonfires and a torchlight procession. John Bates resigned both as Town Clerk and Town Solicitor and died three months after the judgement. In the 1855 Council elections six Liberals were returned including the first Catholic to hold office in Belfast, Bernard Hughes. The Conservatives were in disarray, particularly as the special respondents in the case were held personally responsible for £273,000 which had been raised illegally or misapplied. When the Conservatives attempted to put forward a private indemnity Bill to clear the special respondents, Liberal opposition was so vociferous that they made no progress in parliament.

The government appointed a Royal Commission to inquire into the Belfast borough. When it reported in 1859 the Commission absolved the Corporation from many of the charges upheld in 1855; it found 'no specific instances of waste or misapplication of moneys'; 'that an extension of market accommodation was required'; that it had not been necessary to buy the gasworks, 'while at the same time they were enabled to apply to the other purposes contemplated by the Improvements Acts, the moneys authorized to be borrowed thereunder'; and that street-improvement 'was necessary to keep pace with the increasing population, commerce, and manufacture of the town'. The Commissioners, however, were strongly critical of the failure to drain the Blackstaff, and recommended that its filthy tributary, the Pound Burn, be diverted into the sewers.

The report was a blow to the Liberals, especially as the question of the £273,000 was to be referred to arbitration. For a time the Conservatives were contrite; they made room for seventeen Liberals on the Council in 1859 and in 1861 not only did the Liberals get half the seats but Sir Edward Coey was also elected as the first and last Liberal Mayor of Belfast. Thereafter, the Conservatives reasserted themselves – attending with care to the register – and by 1864 there were only five Liberals left on the Council. Wealthy Protestant Liberals were not prepared to undertake the menial task of supervising the

Engraved by J Thomson Belfast

The Long Bridge c.1823,
replaced 20 years later by the
Queen's Bridge. (Benn, 1823)

register, and preferred more and more to be members of the Harbour Board
and the Chamber of Commerce.

Lanyon's Belfast

> Spanning the Lagan, now we have in view,
> The Great Long Bridge, with arches twenty two

To which Percy – who must rank with McGonagall as one of the worst poets in
the English language – added this note: 'It has only 21, but as a poetical licence,
and for the sake of rhyme, I had to add another arch.' Those arches were
crumbling by 1841 when the grand juries of Antrim and Down agreed to pull
down the Long Bridge and replace it with another, the Queen's Bridge.
Completed in 1843, the bridge was the first commission Charles Lanyon
obtained in Belfast. Born in Sussex and trained as an engineer in Dublin,
Lanyon has been described by the architectural historian, Charles Brett, as
'certainly the greatest single name in the development of Belfast'.

The list of major buildings designed by Lanyon is formidable: the Deaf and
Dumb Institution (1845); the old Exchange refurbished for the Ulster Bank
(1845); Crumlin Road Gaol (1846); the Queen's College (1849); the County
Courthouse (1850); the Northern Bank Head Office in Queen's Square
(1852); the Assembly's College (1853); the Custom House (1857); and the
Ulster Club in Castle Place (1862). In addition, he is said to have designed
fourteen churches in the diocese between 1838 and 1844. Contemptuously
setting aside Belfast's long-standing admiration for chaste Georgian lines,
Lanyon used a kaleidoscope of styles with imagination and flamboyance.

106

None of his buildings is truly great, and too often his employers insisted on the use of cheap materials, but Lanyon's work reflected most magnificently the rising importance of Belfast. He became an enthusiastic and not too scrupulous Conservative politician; he was elected as Mayor in 1862, sat as an MP for Belfast between 1866 and 1868, and was knighted in 1868.

W.J. Barre, from Newry, was Lanyon's bitterest rival; an exuberant exponent of the Gothic revival, he too made his mark on Belfast. Barre's first commission was for the Unitarian Church in York Street in 1855 and in 1860 he won the competition, against forty-one other entries, to build the Ulster Hall. His love of ostentatious ornamentation was given full scope in the Provincial Bank of Ireland in Castle Place begun in 1867; in that year he built the Albert Memorial (known to all in Belfast as the Albert Clock), began work on Belfast Castle, and died at the age of thirty-seven. Barre was responsible for many sumptuous mansions ordered by the linen lords, including the Moat, Strandtown, and Danesfort on the Malone Road. The middle classes were moving from Donegall Place and adjacent streets to airy suburbs, especially on the Malone Ridge. William McComb in his *Guide to Belfast,* published in 1861, mentions that

. . . during the last few years groups of continuous, semi-detached, or single villas, in highly-tasteful styles of architecture, have sprung-up, and been designated by the fashionable names of Windsor, Balmoral, Kensington, Sydenham, Brandon Towers, Richmond, Wellington Park, Cliftonville, &c.

By 1861 Belfast had 55 churches – 20 Presbyterian, 20 other nonconformist, 10 Church of Ireland, and 5 Catholic. Most were undistinguished; the three finest were St Malachy's in Alfred Street by Thomas Jackson, John Carey's Elmwood Presbyterian Church, and St Peter's Pro-Cathedral in Derby Street designed by Father Jeremiah McAuley.

The working classes remained packed into the warrens of Ballymacarrett, the Docks, North Queen Street and Frederick Street, Millfield, Smithfield, the lower Shankill, the Pound, and Sandy Row. Most were comparatively recent immigrants and they had chosen where they had settled with care. Belfast has been described as a collection of villages; certainly, almost self-contained communities clustered round the mills but the invisible dividing lines running through these districts were primarily a reflection of sectarianism imported from the Ulster countryside. Here, where the low-paid majority eked out a wretched existence, religious hatreds had ample opportunity to fester in brutalising conditions. Sectarian clashes were frequent and in 1857 they reached a new peak of intensity.

'Guns levelled, firing without intermission': the 1857 riots

Of old times lords of high degree, with their own hands, strained on the rack the limbs of the delicate Protestant women, prelates dabbled in the gore of their helpless victims. The cells of the Pope's prisons were paved with the calcined bones of men and cemented with human gore and human hair. . . The Word of God makes all plain; puts to eternal shame the practices of persecutors, and stigmatises with enduring reprobation the arrogant pretences of Popes and the outrageous dogmata of their blood-stained religion. . .

With these words the Rev Dr Drew addressed members of the Orange Order from the pulpit of Christ Church on Sunday 12 July 1857. Born in Limerick and educated in Dublin, Drew had attracted attention since his arrival in Belfast in 1833 by his concern for the poor, his fervent evangelical views, and his Orange songs and pamphlets. Christ Church stood on the frontier between the Pound and Sandy Row, and the force of Town Police outside the railings soon attracted a hostile Catholic crowd. Fierce fighting ensued and only after Sub-Inspector Bindon brought in armed 'peelers' of the Irish Constabulary was order temporarily restored. That night, however, shots were exchanged between Sandy Row and the Pound.

This incident set off ten days of continuous rioting in Belfast. On Monday night, while mobs hurled stones and insults at each other across the wasteland alongside Albert Street, Catholics at Millfield wrecked a spirit-grocer's store and beat two Methodist ministers with sticks. On Tuesday night Protestants from Sandy Row made a determined attack on Quadrant Street in the Pound, smashing windows with long poles and setting houses on fire, and, while Catholics wrecked a Methodist church on the Falls Road, the police, constabulary, and Hussars arrived. The *Belfast News-Letter* reported:

The police then got the order to fix bayonets and 'charge' the mob, which they accordingly did. . . the police were again attacked by a perfect shower of stones. 'Charge' was given once more. . . This crowd then dispersed; but it would appear that they re-assembled in Cullingtree Road, where they began to attack some of the houses with large stones, or 'pavers', as they were called. . .

Sub-Inspector Bindon on one occasion 'rushed forward with naked sword and routed the mass single-handed'. Next day in the Belfast Police Court a policeman admitted having said: 'I don't want to make a prisoner, but I want to break his skull.' William Tracy RM, who had accompanied the Hussars, described the scene that Tuesday night:

We would liken it to nothing but a rabbit warren, for the moment we appeared, they ran into holes and entries, and the moment we were gone round they came out and pelted us. They were too cowardly to do so before us, but they pelted us behind our backs and over the houses.

The riots slowly built up to a climax on 18 July, a Saturday, when the mills stopped work at two o'clock. Paving stones had been prised from the streets, and walls running behind houses had been demolished to provide ammunition which was heaped in piles along the roads. The police were swept aside as the mobs clashed in ferocious combat on the waste ground in front of the Pound. For hours the fighting and destruction continued until the constabulary advanced in order with loaded carbines. The crackle of gunfire continued through the night and resumed on Sunday afternoon. Head-Constable Henderson from Quadrant Street saw a ditch on the edge of the wasteland 'closely lined with men, having guns levelled, firing without intermission'.

On 1 August a Catholic mill-girl was shot dead by a bullet from Sandy Row and on 6 August Catholics formed a gun-club at a meeting in Smithfield. An uneasy truce followed, but on 23 August Catholics attacked a street-preacher at the Customs House steps. Here, Frankfort Moore remembers, 'as a medium for replying to such points in the preacher's discourse as were not altogether acceptable to their ears, these cobble pavements could scarcely be surpassed'.

After this 'warm interchange of opinion on a basis of basalt', the Belfast Parochial Mission cancelled the remainder of its programme of open-air sermons; the Rev Hugh Hanna, minister of Berry Street Presbyterian Church, declared that he would preach 'despite the Romish mobs or the magistrates'. On Sunday 6 September at four o'clock Hanna began to address Protestants waiting to hear him in front of the Duncrue Salt Works. Catholics, expecting him at the Custom House, the *Belfast News-Letter* indignantly reported, 'came rushing along Donegall Quay, yelling at the top of their voices, and, when they reached Corporation Square, they commenced firing vollies of stones at the peaceable and orderly congregation which surrounded the minister. . .' A Town policeman ordered Frankfort Moore's nurse:

Take them childer out o' this or I'll not be tellin' ye. Don't ye see he's read the Riot Act. Heth! you're a gierl bringin' them wee'uns intill a crowd like thon!

It took several charges by the Hussars to clear the squares and streets and the Lord Lieutenant ordered an inquiry which reported on 20 November. The report of the commissioners was inconclusive though it criticised Orange festivals 'leading as they do to violence, outrage, religious animosities, hatred between classes, and, too often, bloodshed and loss of life'.

Harbour development and the making of Queen's Island

'I believe your trade will prosper to a degree that will astonish yourselves,' remarked J.B. Farrell, the Admiralty surveying officer, to members of the Ballast Board at the close of his investigations. The Board had applied to parliament for powers to borrow money to carry out further improvements to the docks and port of Belfast.

Farrell had clearly been impressed by the energy and efficiency of the Board which had carried out its functions without any of the corruption, wrangling and sectarianism which had been surrounding the activities of the Town Council. The first cut from Dunbar's dock had been completed in 1841 and in 1845 the Donegall, Cunningham's, Hanover, Chichester and Merchants' Quays had been bought up, together with other properties, from their private owners. Now, in 1847, on Farrell's recommendation the Belfast Harbour Bill became law: the Ballast Board was replaced by 'The Belfast Harbour Commissioners' composed of the Lord of the Castle, the Mayor, and 15 elected members.

Within six months of the passing of the Act the Harbour Commissioners signed a contract with William Dargan, Ireland's most successful railway engineer, to make another cut to give easy access to the docks from the Garmoyle Pool. On 10 July 1849 the cut was opened by senior Harbour Commissioner, William Pirrie, and named the Victoria Channel. The *Northern Whig* described the scene:

. . . a gentle breeze, just sufficient to keep unfurled the thousands of flags of every variety and colour, size and shape, with which the shipping in the river were made gay, blew from the northward. . . all Belfast was making holiday, so thronged were both banks of the river, the decks of the various steamers preparing for the excursion, and all the shoal of small craft flitting to and fro upon the tide.

At the same time Donegall Quay was extended into the channel, the old

'Clarendon Dock and the Harbour Office' by A. C. Stannus, 1859. Clarendon Dock was later filled in to become the Liverpool cross-channel terminus in 1966. The Harbour Office was designed by George Smith in 1854, with additions by W. H. Lynn in 1895. (Belfast Harbour Commissioners)

Limekiln, Town and Ritchie's docks were filled in, and the Clarendon graving docks were extended. Even so, the Commissioners reported in 1851 that '. . . in consequence of the rapid increase of trade which proceeds year after year at an accelerated rate, the quay and dock accommodation provided within the last ten years is likely to become inadequate to the wants of the Port'. This proved to be correct: the tonnage cleared from the port had risen from 288,143 (2,724 vessels) in 1837 to 538,525 (4,213 vessels) in 1847 and would reach 1,372,326 (7,817 vessels) by 1867. In 1852 Captain Gilbert included in his report the following:

In the Report of the Boundary Commissioners in 1836, Belfast was ranked as the third port in point of commercial importance in Ireland. It is now the first, the number of vessels and tonnage being greater than at any other port in Ireland. . . In the year 1836 the value of the exports and imports amounted to £5,700,000; the same for 1852 amounted to £12,600,000, exclusive of an immense coasting trade. This increase, in sixteen years, is fully 120 per cent., goods increasing in a greater ratio than tonnage.

In 1854 the Commissioners had applied for and got passed an Act to allow them to buy and reclaim land on the Co Down side; 50 acres of this land were made into Victoria Park and given to the Corporation. Contracts were made with local and English firms to construct a floating dock, the Abercorn basin, on the Co Antrim side, and a graving dock, the Hamilton dock, on the Co

Down side of the harbour; both were opened formally by the Marquis of Abercorn, then Lord Lieutenant, on 2 October 1867.

Meanwhile the mud excavated when making the first cut had been heaped on the eastern side as a training bank to modify the direction of the river. First known as Dargan's Island and later as Queen's Island, there was little indication as yet that this reclaimed land would become the engineering heartland of Belfast. As the Botanic Gardens were normally closed to the public, Queen's Island became the main pleasure park of the town. After the Queen's visit an Amusement Committee was formed to hold an annual fete there. Entertainments arranged for the 1851 fete included dancing on platforms to military and quadrille bands, a Punch and Judy show, Scotch dancing, tub races, tilting at the ring, and, the Committee's minutes record:

Dr Murney suggested to have a 'Monte' table at the bazaar. . . That Mr Carrothers be requested to make arrangements for having sub-marine explosions. . . That Messrs Usher and George Murney be requested to call upon the Rt Rev Dr Denvir to know if he would consent to exhibit an electric light. . .

A Crystal Palace was built on the island which Rev McIntyre took his Sunday school children to visit on Monday 4 July 1856, as he records in his diary:

They were admitted free through the kindness of Mr Hanlon, to the Island and to inspect the interior of the Crystal Palace. With the latter they were greatly delighted, very many of them not having been on the Island before. They were regaled with cakes and fruit on the grounds and the weather being very fine and the band playing some of its favourite airs the children and young people enjoyed a perfect treat and returned late in the evening without any accident occurring. There were about 150 in all.

However, the great development of the port brought unforeseen problems. In Frankfort Moore's opinion, the riots of 1864 'were due to the importation the previous year of some hundreds – perhaps thousands – of navvies to dig a new dock, and it was found out that a large proportion of these men were Roman Catholics. The balance of the fighting power among the belligerent classes was thereby disturbed. . .'

'At children in Brown's Square school stones we did throw': the 1864 riots

On Monday 8 August 1864, Catholics, who had attended a great ceremony to lay the foundation stone for a monument to Daniel O'Connell in Dublin, returned by rail to Belfast. Protestants from Sandy Row resented this massive display of nationalist strength at a time when Orange processions were illegal under the Party Processions Act of 1832. As the Dublin train steamed into the Great Victoria Street station around 9 p.m., a huge crowd advanced to the Boyne Bridge – built across the railway above the Saltwater Bridge – and set alight a huge effigy of O'Connell:

> And what do you think they do in Belfast
> Just as, in the Sandy Row we came past?
> They burned Dan O'Connell, I saw him aglow
> But 'twas only his effigy, Kitty, you know!

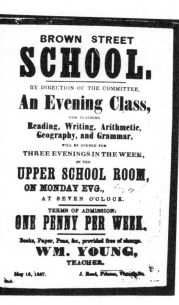

The following evening, after an attempt to bury the ashes of the effigy at Friar's Bush was foiled, a mock funeral ended when a coffin was thrown into the Blackstaff. From then until the end of August there was continuous warfare between the Pound and Sandy Row, so severe that many mills and factories closed. On Friday 12 August, while Protestants stoned Bishop Dorrian's house in Howard Street and Bankmore House convent, Catholics broke the windows of Dr Cooke's Church and looted shops in Arthur Square. The *Belfast News-Letter* observed next morning:

Women, in several cases, fought with a courage that would have done honour to their sires. . . The whole thing seemed like a burlesque on an invasion by a Gothic horde on a Roman province.

Monday 15 August was a Holy Day of Obligation for Catholics. About 400 Catholic navvies gathered round St Malachy's Church, and finding that no Orange attack was imminent, they marched into the town centre. An indignant citizen described the scene: 'About twelve o'clock noon an immense mob came into High Street from Bridge Street. They at once proceeded to the shops of Mr Currie, ironmonger, and Mr Neill gunsmith, and seized on all the firearms and every other weapon they could lay hands on.' Another eye-witness, L.D. Millar, wrote: 'At last they reached the shop of Mr Gibson, and here on feasts of jewellery they seemed to glut their desires, and with all the audacity of a hungry bear to seize and carry off their valued prey.' After being enthusiastically received in Hercules Street, they marched up North Street to Peter's Hill and the Shankill Road; here they turned left and made for Brown's Square National School. The *Northern Whig* described what followed:

The Brown Street School, which at the time contained about 1,200 children, was assailed with stones, bricks, and even shots were fired through the windows. The teachers and children were in a state of absolute frenzy; the poor little children were hidden under the forms; and the teachers did all they could to preserve their lives from the fury of the savages by concealing them in the yard of the school and other places. Several of the children are very badly injured; and one fine child has had its eye gouged out by a blow from a large stone. . .

Protestant workers from the neighbouring Soho Foundry surged out to repel the invaders, as a verse from a satirical Orange ballad recalled:

> We marched in procession, and windows we broke;
> And those fine policemen a word never spoke:
> At children in Brown's Square school stones we did throw
> But Och! We were chased by the boys of Soho.

When the navvies returned to the Pound, fighting was resumed at Albert Crescent, and a contingent from Sandy Row gathered at the Ulster Hall around 4 p.m. to make an assault on St Malachy's Church and on Bankmore House. Though the Protestants succeeded in setting fire to the convent hay-stacks, they were driven back by deadly gunfire from the church windows. The mobs were dispersed eventually by cavalry charges made down Ormeau Avenue. Thomas Gaffiken ordered a cab for a man he found still living though he had three bullets in his head. That night the government sent from Dublin a train of 27 wagons carrying two field guns and reinforcements, raising the

Rioting in Sandy Row: sketch of uncertain date by an unknown artist. The Boyne Bridge formed the frontier with the Pound. (Ulster Museum)

total engaged in restoring order in Belfast to 1,300 soldiers and 1,000 armed constabulary. Still the internecine warfare continued.

'But woe to you, ye navvies!': the 1864 riots

'The prosperity of our town, which is the envy of the rest of Ireland,' the *Northern Whig* observed on Tuesday 16 August, 'brought to it for the formation of our new docks this horde of assassins; and the greatest punishment that could be inflicted upon them would be, not to send them to jail, but to dismiss them, and send them starving from our town, as starving they came to it.' As an Orange ballad of the time recalls, the shipwrights of the Shankill were preparing a more summary retribution:

> But woe to you, ye navvies! for before another sun
> You will sup a heap of sorrow for the ruin you have done;
> We'll come upon you like a storm, or like a sudden flood,
> And we'll send you helter-skelter, writhing, wriggling through the mud.

That Tuesday morning while the shipwrights gathered their forces, people from Sandy Row attacked the Dublin train in the belief that it was conveying carters and dockers to assist the navvies. Sub-Inspector John Caulfield, sword in hand, led the constabulary into Durham Street where he was greeted by volleys of bullets and paving stones; one Town policeman was seen urging on the mob and another was arrested for throwing stones at the constabulary. Caulfield drew up his men on the Boyne Bridge and ordered them to fire: John McConnell of Sandy Row fell dead and others were seriously injured.

113

18 August 1864: John McConnell's funeral. The hearse, attended by armed Protestants, passes the Bank Buildings before turning down High Street. In the background, armed Catholics throng Castle Street and Hercules Street (later widened to become Royal Avenue). (Ulster Museum)

Meanwhile the shipwrights marched into the town centre, plundered gun shops and hardware stores in High Street, and returned to attack St Peter's Pro-Cathedral in the Falls. At Millfield, however, they met their match in the 84th Regiment. Lieutenant Clayton, in command of the detachment, reported:

A party of about seventy men and women advanced down Wilson Street, keeping up all the time an intermittent fire. . . I advanced my sub-division to the corner of Wilson Street, wheeled to the right and fired a volley at the mob. . . No one was killed on the spot, but it had the effect of entirely quieting and dispersing the mob.

In retaliation for the previous day's attack on Brown's Square School, Protestants destroyed Malvern Street National School. 'It was all done calmly and deliberately,' the principal said later. 'The mob worked intently, like furniture removers. And the inhabitants of Malvern Street stood at their doorways watching all.'

It was while they were at work that the Catholic navvies were most vulnerable. Next day, Wednesday 17 August, while most of the police and soldiers were searching Sandy Row and the Pound for arms, the shipwrights made a concerted attack on the navvies at work close to Garmoyle Street leaving them no line of retreat but the mud and the water. Neal Fagan was mortally wounded by the blow of a ship-adze; others fled before sustained gunfire as far as the Garmoyle Pool. Military officers were later to express amazement at the failure of local magistrates to take immediate action. As darkness fell Frankfort Moore recalled: 'that night when going to bed I stood for some time at an open window and heard the report of shot after shot coming from the north of the town'.

The following day, Thursday, a huge procession of Protestants openly carrying arms followed the coffin of John McConnell through Wellington Place, Donegall Place and High Street to the cemetery at Knock. Even though there were now in Belfast six troops of the 4th Hussars, half a battery of artillery, the 89th Regiment of infantry, 1,000 Irish Constabulary, 150 Town Police, and 300 special constables, the fighting continued. The Union Hospital and the General Hospital were filled to capacity with the wounded, and Clifton Street Poorhouse was asked to make its private ward available. Surgeon David Moore of the General Hospital wrote on 20 August:

I beg to report that during the past week there were admitted to the hospital 75 patients. . . Upwards of 50 of these were the result of the present riots in the town, 30 of them being gunshot wounds, and the remainder contusions, lacerations, fractures, and other injuries of a serious character.

He treated another 60 as outdoor patients who refused to remain in hospital 'in consequence possibly of a fear of detection by the authorities'. By 18 August, 11 had been killed, Dr Murney estimated, and next day another man was shot dead in Brown's Square. It is likely that others were buried without the knowledge of the authorities.

'Shortly afterwards,' Frankfort Moore wrote, 'the usual autumn monsoon set in: . . . while rioters do not mind the hottest fire, they object strongly to a cold shower of rain. There was no show after the first deluge.'

'Belfast is liable to periodic disturbances'

The causes of the 1864 riots were investigated more thoroughly than those of 1857. The commissioners of inquiry put much of the blame on the partiality of the Town Police:

As a matter of fact, it certainly is somewhat remarkable that in this body of 160 men, only five Roman Catholics are to be found; the proportion of Roman Catholics (of all sects) in Belfast being a third, and in the class of life whence the police is recruited, considerably higher. . . It must then be regarded as strange that in these circumstances Roman Catholics are to be found in the Belfast Police force in the proportion of only one to thirty one, compared with Protestants. . .

The recommendation that the force be disbanded was accepted by the government and from the end of June 1865 the policing of Belfast was left entirely to the Irish Constabulary. The 1864 report concluded:

Belfast is liable to periodic disturbances on occasions well known as the Orange anniversaries. . . if the celebration of these anniversaries be attended with such risk we might well ask why any party should obstinately adhere to it. In other countries good feeling and good sense have buried in generous oblivion the memory of civil strife such as they commemorate. Why is it otherwise in Ireland?

That question was not answered in 1864, nor is it likely that completely satisfactory answers can be given today.

Belfast was not unique in Ulster in the nineteenth century in being periodically convulsed by sectarian rioting; the riots were on a large scale simply because of the town's great size. Belfast had been unique in the eighteenth century in being free of sectarian strife but at that time Catholics formed only a tiny proportion of the town's population. For that period, only the views of the educated propertied elite have been recorded and there is a lurking suspicion that enthusiasm for the French Revolution arose partly out of admiration for the revolutionaries' anti-clericalism. The reforming zeal of educated Protestants did not evaporate after the Union; some threw themselves into projects to alleviate the sufferings of the poor and sick while others either joined the Liberals or avoided municipal politics altogether by working through the Chamber of Commerce and the Harbour Board to develop the town.

For much of the nineteenth century the majority of the inhabitants of Belfast were comparatively recent immigrants. Unfortunately the enumerators made no distinction between those born in Belfast and those who had come into the town from Antrim and Down; the proportion of inhabitants from the rest of Ulster was 10.5% in 1841, 15.8% in 1861, and 13.8% in 1881. Only a negligible proportion came from Leinster, Munster and Connacht: 2.1% in 1841, 3.3% in 1861, and 3.05% in 1881 – these figures do not support the popular belief that a large number of Catholics had come from the south. Indeed, a greater percentage of immigrants came to Belfast from Britain: 2.36% in 1841, 5.14% in 1861, and 5.17% in 1881. The overwhelming proportion of immigrants, Protestants and Catholics alike, came in from the Ulster countryside.

One of the consequences of immigration was that Catholics formed a significant minority; in these years the proportion of Catholics in Belfast hovered around one third – 32% in 1834, 33.9% in 1861, and 31.9% in 1871. Faced with this Catholic presence, educated propertied Protestants re-assessed the liberal views of their parents and grandparents; many were repelled by the uncouth ways of so many impoverished refugees from rural destitution and alarmed by Catholic opposition to the Union which so many Protestants regarded as the source of Belfast's prosperity. Some leading Conservative politicians, such as John Bates, exploited Protestant fears. What is certain is that employers and politicians did not create sectarian feeling. That feeling may always have been there but it was certainly increased by the immigration of so many, bringing with them memories of ancient hatreds. The eighteenth-century warfare west of the Bann between the Peep-O-Day Boys and the Defenders was transferred by industrial concentration to battles between Orange and Green in the narrow streets of Belfast.

Commissions of inquiry blamed provocative Protestant celebrations for fomenting strife, and several modern writers see the Orange Order as the main cause of sectarianism. The Order, which had been poorly represented in Belfast at the beginning of the century, had 35 lodges in Belfast in 1851 with a membership of 1,335; by 1858 Belfast had the greatest number of lodges in Co Antrim and became a County Grand Lodge in 1864. The Orange Order was frankly sectarian and undoubtedly helped to trigger off religious rioting. Street preaching and the great Protestant revival of 1859 – when 35,000 attended a monster meeting in the Botanic Gardens – also helped to emphasise religious divisions in the town. Catholics joined Ribbon societies and Fenian circles which were usually more sectarian in character than their parent bodies in the south; little is known about these as secret oath-bound organisations were unreservedly condemned by the Catholic Church.

Some historians have been a little too ready to blame the symptoms rather than search for the underlying causes of this sectarianism, which had its roots deep in Irish history. Unemployment was not at that time the cause of conflict; the depression of 1857 came only after the riots of that year, and the riots of 1864 came when Belfast was in the middle of the great linen boom of 1862–7.

116

The Great Linen Boom

In 1864 the columns of the Belfast newspapers were filled not only by detailed accounts of the local riots and the Prussian invasion of Denmark, but also of fighting in the United States. The American Civil War – perhaps the bloodiest conflict of the nineteenth century – had a very direct impact on the development of Belfast. The cotton-growing states were devastated and, starved of their raw material, the Lancashire cotton mills almost ceased production. Linen was the closest available substitute for cotton and thus from the start of the war in the spring of 1862 Belfast enjoyed a spectacular boom.

Belfast was ready to take advantage of the 'cotton famine' only just in time. Ulster had been slow to develop the weaving of linen cloth by power machinery for, as William Charley wrote in 1862, 'So long as a man's labour could be had at the handloom in Ireland for a shilling a day, it was felt no power loom could work much, if at all cheaper.' Between 1828 and 1852 piece wages for cambric weaving fell by 69% for fine cloth and by about 40% for coarser webs. It was only after the great exodus to America during and after the Famine had reduced the surplus of labour and raised wages above starvation levels that, Charley observed, 'it was admitted that the power loom was at length required'. In 1850 Britain had 3,660 power looms for linen while all Ireland could muster only 58, though most of these machines were for weaving coarser grades. 'It is true there are power-looms at work, here and elsewhere, capable of weaving certain kinds of linen,' a member of the Royal Flax Society wrote in 1852, 'but what is required is a power-loom that will weave ordinary quantities of linen yarn into ordinary descriptions of linen cloth.'

When the technical difficulties of weaving fine linen by power were overcome, progress was not sudden as the machines produced only four times as much cloth as a handloom weaver. Power looms increased in number from 218 in 1853 to 4,900 in 1861 and more rapid weaving called for greater supplies of linen yarn; the number of spindles rose from 326,000 to 593,000 in the same period. As the American Civil War began, Belfast linen firms had caught up with and by-passed their British competitors and were thus equipped to take full advantage of the opportunities presented. The price of cotton rose from around 9d per ounce in 1861 to £1.4s.0½d. an ounce in 1863, and the boom in linen continued without interruption even after the war came to an end in 1865. The linen industry's capacity had risen to over 12,000 power looms and 900,000 spindles by the end of the boom in 1867. In that year there was 'a cataclysmic reversal of fortune', the *Linen Trade Circular* reported:

. . . in the mercantile history of the nineteenth century the year 1867 will occupy a place painfully prominent by the disastrous events which its records will of necessity enfold. After a period of great prosperity, the sinews of industry had become paralysed, as the partially silent spindle and noiseless loom only too clearly testify.

The following year 60,000 spindles and 4,000 looms were idle. Expecting the boom to continue, the industry had borrowed heavily and over-extended its capacity. The supply of cotton wool returned to normal in 1867 and the depression in linen continued until 1869. Belfast, however, had become the greatest centre of linen production in the world and its domination continued when demand recovered in 1870.

The linen mills: 'Five o'clock the horn does blow'

On Saturday a woman named Sarah Jane Quinn, a worker in the mill of Messrs. Rowan of York Street sustained a very severe accident. . . She was engaged at the carding part of the machinery and her head by some means got entangled in the machinery in which the greater part of the scalp was removed from the head and the skull was severely injured. She was conveyed to hospital but little hope was entertained of her recovery.

Belfast News-Letter, 1 May 1854

The danger of being maimed or killed by exposed machinery in the linen mills was very great. The large cylinder of the carding machine, for example, was studded with iron pins which turned very rapidly, and it was easy to lose a hand or an arm in the hackling machine. In 1854 a thirteen-year-old boy was injured when a belt on a revolving drum broke and, because the belt was makeshift, his employer, George Herdman, was fined £10. When, on appeal, the conviction was quashed this observation was published in the *Belfast News-Letter* on 27 October:

It is but a false, mawkish and mongrel humanity which cares not though trade should go to the dogs lest an impudent little larking scamp. . . should fail to get his cut fingers salved with a ten pound note. . .

Proposals to enforce the fencing-off of dangerous machines provoked passionate opposition from the millowners. In March 1855 Belfast linen manufacturers joined the 'National Association of Factory Occupiers' (Charles Dickens called it the 'Association for the Mangling of Operatives') to oppose legislation. An Act in 1856 to make owners place guards on their machinery was largely evaded and a further Act was required in 1876; even so, at the end of the century inspectors complained that it was difficult to obtain convictions for breaches of the regulations.

Perhaps the main cause of accidents was exhaustion from long hours of work in the mill:

> Five o'clock the horn does blow,
> Half past five we all must go.
> If you be a minute late,
> Oul' Jack Horn will shut the gate
> So early in the morning.

Before 1874 the usual working day began at 5 a.m. and ended at 7 or 8 p.m. with only two half-hour breaks. Employers had circumvented the 1847 Act, limiting hours of work for women and children to ten a day, by introducing a relay system and it was not until 1874 that hours were cut down to ten every weekday and six on Saturdays. Even then employers introduced an extra duty of cleaning machines after hours to compensate for the effect of the 1874 Act. Until the beginning of the twentieth century the working weekday began at 6.30 a.m. and finished at 6 p.m., with three-quarters of an hour for breakfast and three-quarters of an hour for lunch. The minimum age for starting at the mill was ten years in 1874, eleven years in 1891 and twelve years in 1901; these juveniles or 'half-timers' attended school either in the mornings or afternoons, or on alternate days; then a year or two later they shared the long hours with their elders. These young people were the principal victims of the health hazards of dust, heat and vapour.

The linen mills: hazards to health

While employers were urging the need to keep costs down, some others were drawing a grim picture of the effect of mill work on the operatives' health. After being taken from the retting dams and dried, the flax was taken to the mills for 'hackling'. The first part of this process was 'roughing', described by Dr John Moore in 1867:

The process consists in drawing the fibres of the flax across a coarse iron comb. The atmosphere in which they work is certainly not one of the purest, the dust and fine particles of the flax load the air, and consequently a good deal of bronchial irritation results.

From the roughers the flax was sent to the machine boys to be combed to separate the 'tow' – or short fibre – from the 'line' – the best long fibre. Dr C.D. Purdon, certifying surgeon of the Belfast factory district, wrote detailed reports in 1877 of the effect of flax dust, or 'pouce', on the lungs of machine boys:

The first symptom is a sensation of dryness in the throat. . . Thence into the lungs, soon bringing on the attacks of cough and dysnoea, which seize them, especially in the morning and at night. In severe and well marked attacks, the paroxysm of cough and dysnoea lasts for a considerable time, and does not pass off until the contents of the stomach are ejected, and often blood is spat up. During this period the worker seizes any article that may be near, in order to enable him to get over the attack more easily. In the case of a machine boy suffering from a severe paroxysm whilst at work, the table at which he is engaged is caught with both hands, and when thus observed by his companions, he is said to be poucey.

Dr Purdon noted that army surgeons had forbidden recruiting sergeants to enlist any men from the hackling departments, and he observed: 'When about thirty years of age their appearance begins to alter, the face gets an anxious look, shoulders begin to get rounded – in fact, they become prematurely aged, and the greatest number die before 45 years.' Next, the 'sorters' arranged the different qualities of flax given to them; one told Dr Purdon that when he became 'real poucey' he felt as if his neck was 'a drawing down into the chest, and his limbs beginning to get weak, the hands and forearms often beginning to get stiff'; attacks ended 'in vomiting or in expectorating a glairy mucus'.

The next process was 'preparing' and 'carding' which Dr Moore looked on as 'the dustiest, most disagreeable, as well as the most unwholesome and most dangerous of all the departments connected with the spinning of flax'. Here women and girls did most of the work. 'These suffer in the same manner as the males, but in a far more aggravated degree,' Dr Purdon wrote, and he gave an example of the attacks suffered by one woman:

Now when they come on, she has to lie across one of the 'cans' in order to get relief, and the paroxysm does not cease till she throws off the contents of her stomach, and sometimes blood. Has to get up at five o'clock in the morning in order to be dressed in time for the mill at six, as she is often obliged to stop on account of the paroxysm coming on.

The most dangerous work of all was the spreading of the 'long line' in the 'preparing room', as the dust was so fine; one manager said of this work: 'It is sure death.'

After preparing, the flax passed through a frame in the 'roving room' where it was twisted onto bobbins and removed from the machines by the 'rovers':

Do you want to breed a fight? We are the rovers!
For it's if you want to breed a fight, Oh, we are the jolly fine rovers!
Ha! Ha! You had to go, you had to go, you had to go,
Ha! Ha! You had to go, riding on a donkey.

The rovings were taken to the 'spinning room' which was hot and steamy, as the cold wet-spinning had been replaced by the faster hot wet-spinning. Here, again, Dr Purdon found lung disease prevalent: 'Phthisis is always acute among those that are employed in the spinning room.' The girls who replaced the bobbins here – often 'half-timers' – were known as 'doffers':

You would easy know a doffer when she comes into town
With her long yellow hair and her ringlets hanging down
With her rubber tied before her and her pickers in her hand
You would easy know a doffer for she'll always get a man.

The 'pickers' lifted the bobbins and the 'rubbers' or aprons did not prevent the girls being drenched by spray thrown off by the machines. Doffers suffered from chest complaints, 'mill fever', swollen legs and ankles, 'papular' and 'pastular' eruptions, and – when older – from varicose veins. Dr Moore observed that long standing caused the crushing and flattening of the arch of the foot and described 'onychia', a most painful affliction of the toe:

It is a most inveterate disease, and requires for its remedy a most painful operation, either the dissecting out or wrenching out the entire roots of the great toe-nail. It results, I believe, from the custom which is universal here with that class of going barefooted while at work; the water which has filtered through becoming more or less impregnated with the brass and other metal of the machinery.

Belfast in 1860: steel-engraving by Marcus Ward & Co. The Queen's Bridge, in the foreground, replaced the Long Bridge in 1843. The Lagan has been widened and deepened to make the Victoria Channel (1849), enabling the ships seen here to come up to the quays. On the right, the Belfast & County Down railway terminus and, on the left, Lanyon's Custom House (1857). (Ulster Museum)

The spun yarn was prepared for the weavers by the 'reelers' and 'winders'. The winders' reply to the rovers' song goes:

Raddy daddy and we're not beat yet.
Raddy daddy and we're hardly!
Raddy daddy and we're not beat yet.
A button for your marley.

The reeling room was well ventilated and free of dust, and for that reason women no longer fit for the other departments were sent to work there. Before being woven the yarn had to be dressed with a mixture of carrageen moss, flour and tallow. As the heat in the 'dressing room' was kept between 95°F and 125°F to dry the yarn, only men over 18 years free of chest infections were employed; Dr Purdon remarked that 'as it is considered that their lives were shortened by several years they are paid very high wages'. The atmosphere in the 'weaving sheds' was hot and damp, encouraging chest infections, but generally – with better pay and working conditions – the weavers were envied by the doffers:

You would easy know a weaver when she comes into town
With her oul' snuffy nose and her snatters hanging down
With a shawl around her shoulders and a shuttle in her hand
You would easy know a weaver for she'll never get a man.

Messrs Hinds piped steam into their hackling, preparing and carding departments and reported in 1877 that 'all our workers find a great benefit from this arrangement, as it lays the dust, and makes a dusty room more comfortable than without steam'. The real answer was the powered fan, not made compulsory until 1906. Professor Hodges invented an alternative preparation for dressing yarn which did not require a high temperature; there is no record of its general adoption.

The linen mills chiefly employed women at very low rates of pay, and by themselves they could not have given Belfast the prosperity it enjoyed in the late nineteenth century. Fortunately, works manufacturing textile machinery were springing up to provide better pay for the men, and on Queen's Island Harland & Wolff were about to make Belfast a shipbuilding and engineering giant.

6
Shipbuilding and Engineering City
c.1870–1900

On 1 September 1870 the first *Belfast Evening Telegraph* was issued from the offices of William and George Baird in Arthur Street. The *Belfast Morning News,* established in 1855 and to become the *Irish News* in 1891, had been Ireland's first penny newspaper, compelling the *Belfast News-Letter* and the *Northern Whig* to reduce their price also to a penny shortly afterwards. The *Belfast Evening Telegraph* was Ireland's first half-penny newspaper; that it flourished to such an extent that it could move to impressive new premises in the recently completed Royal Avenue was an indication not only of good management but also that Belfast was the only part of Ireland where there were enough skilled artisans sufficiently prosperous to buy a daily newspaper. Lord O'Hagan, born in Belfast and in 1868 the first Catholic to be Lord Chancellor of Ireland asked this question:

Is it a vain boast to say that Belfast has outrun in the race of progress many of the proudest cities of the Empire, and exhibited to the world the spectacle of an Irish community, aided by no physical advantages, trusting to no adventitious support, fostered by no patronage of Cabinets or Parliaments, pampered by no doles from the treasury of the State, by its own inherent energy and determined purpose, exalting itself to industrial eminence and social importance with a speed almost unparalleled and a success beyond expectation or belief?

No answer seemed necessary even though Lord O'Hagan died in 1885, before the most spectacular growth of the period had begun. The official recognition in 1888 that Belfast was a city seemed somewhat overdue; the population had risen from 174,412 in 1871 to 349,180 in 1901, the increase for the years 1891 to 1901 alone being over 36%. No city of comparable size in Britain could show such a rate of growth in this period. In part the expansion was brought about by developers who built good houses cheaply and ahead of demand. Linen continued to play a vital role in the city's economy. Above all, it was the emergence of a great shipbuilding and engineering industry which made Belfast the biggest city in Ireland and the third most important port in the UK. By 1900 the Belfast yards had launched *Oceanic II,* the biggest ship afloat, and had the greatest shipbuilding output in the world.

Yet the existence of four daily newspapers – three unionist and one nationalist – emphasised the sectarian divisions in the city. Any comfort Protestants might have got from the diminishing proportion of Catholics in Belfast – from 31.9% to 24.3% between 1871 and 1901 – was more than offset by the nationalisation of Irish politics. Belfast's prosperity contrasted more sharply than ever with the continued poverty and famine in the west. The widening of the franchise gave nationalists an effective voice at Westminster,

Belfast from the Cave Hill about 1883. In the foreground can be seen the Mineral Tramway connecting the Cave Hill limestone quarries and Belfast harbour. (Ulster Museum)

raising Catholic hopes of a Dublin parliament and generating alarm amongst Protestants. Sectarian rioting reached its bloodiest level of the century in 1886 and in the years that followed Liberals and Conservatives sank their differences to make Belfast the centre of resistance to Home Rule.

Linen still the biggest employer

'Our country is not in a position to bear this legislation. It will ruin our trade, and perhaps, leave Belfast a forest of smokeless chimneys': this was the *Belfast News-Letter*'s indignant comment on the 1874 Factory Act which limited the hours of labour in textile mills to 56 a week. Yet the following year the number of spindles in the linen industry was 925,000 – the highest recorded in the nineteenth century. In 1878 factory legislation was extended to the linen workshops, prompting the linen merchant Robert Lloyd-Patterson to say in a speech to the Belfast Chamber of Commerce on 15 February 1879:

I think we have had too much restrictive factory legislation of late years. Last summer, in the course of a journey on the continent, I visited some manufacturers and found the general weekly hours of labour were seventy-two, and sometimes more. . . Much more of this paternal legislation will have the tendency to legislate the trade out of the country.

The spectacular growth of shipbuilding notwithstanding, linen continued to give more employment in Belfast than any other industry. The numbers employed in the Irish linen industry were 55,000 in 1871, 56,000 in 1875, 62,000 in 1885, and 69,000 in 1896; as Belfast had over 80% of the spindles and 70% of the power looms in the country in 1870, only a small proportion of millworkers were outside the city. Employers, however, did have cause for concern. Factories in Belgium, Russia, Austria-Hungary and France became more efficient and could obtain home-grown flax and – in some places – labour more cheaply than in Belfast.

The spinning capacity of Belfast mills fell slowly to 828,000 spindles in 1900; by that year the UK was importing 25 million pounds of linen yarn from abroad. If the number of power looms did not fall this was mainly due to the steady decline of the hand-loom. While Britain continued her free trade policy other countries – the United States in particular – raised high tariffs against foreign cloth and thus prevented any further expansion of the Belfast linen industry. Cotton was cheaper than linen and could be finished in a greater variety of ways – it was this fact above all which kept the price of linen declining steadily in the last quarter of the nineteenth century. A linen mill required up to four times as many operatives as a cotton mill with the same number of spindles. It was therefore the united opinion of Belfast linen mill-owners that wages must be kept down.

A detailed American investigation of the textile industry in the UK in 1913 concluded that wages in the linen mills were lower than in any other, the jute mills not excepted, and this seems to have been the case throughout the latter half of the nineteenth century. Lacking the protection of trade unions, mill hands were unable to prevent a cut of 10% in their wages between 1874 and 1884. Wages rose by 20% between 1886 and 1906; 'Nevertheless,' concludes D.L. Armstrong, the chief authority on the industry for this period, 'the standard of living of the great majority of the linen workers was still terribly low at the end of the century, even by contemporary standards.' The average wage in the industry was 11s.0d. in 1875, 10s.6d. in 1884, 11s.0d. in 1886, and 12s.0d. in 1906. Men engaged in skilled and heavy work were relatively well paid; in 1886 roughers earned 18s.6d. and sorters £1.3s.6d. a week. However, men formed only a small part of the mill workforce: in 1886, 68% of linen workers were female and 26% were juveniles under the age of 18. In that year, despite a recent wage rise, spinners earned 8s.5d., weavers 11s.6d., reelers 8s.11d. and preparers 6s.10d. a week. These did not include deductions for lateness and poor work:

> Oh what is Mary weeping for?
> Oh weeping for, Oh weeping for?
> Oh what is Mary weeping for?
> On a cold and frosty morning?
> . . . perhaps it was her wages!

'Not fit to afford shelter to domesticated animals': mill housing

Linen manufacturers were the most important developers of working-class housing in Belfast at the beginning of this period; they needed a constant supply of inexpensive labour, and local contractors could not put up houses on the scale millowners required. Very early starting times, long working hours and low wages forced mill hands to live as close as possible to their work in dwellings which cost no more than three shillings a week in rent. Ewarts laid out nine streets, including Hooker, Kerrera, Butler, Chatham, Elmfield and Herbert Streets, beside their Crumlin Road mills in 1869 and in 1875 submitted a single plan to build 111 houses in these streets. Adjacent to its weaving sheds in Agnes Street, the Brookfield Spinning Company put up 36 houses in Arkwright and Glentilt Streets. Other linen families which built cheap dwellings beside their mills included the Charters of the Falls Mills, the Mulhollands of York Street Mill, the Malcolmsons of the Blackstaff Works, Murphy & Stephenson of the Ulster Works in Sandy Row, and the Rosses of Clonard.

As a result of this building there were dense clusters of 'kitchen houses' scattered across Belfast. In the 1860s, when houses near the town centre (at Millfield and Brown's Square for example) were already decaying into slums, Belfast's built-up area was pushed westwards by the erection of mill dwellings in the lower Falls and the Shankill. In the 1870s, working-class housing pressed out from a line running from Agnes Street, Northumberland Street and Albert Street. Kitchen houses were built at Bridge End and Connswater until the two areas merged; around Lagan Village; and in the vicinity of the brickfields at Ormeau.

These tiny houses were cramped and often insanitary; some were so poorly built that later, in 1885, housing commissioners condemned them as 'barely capable of keeping the draught away from their inmates'. On 18 January 1873 the medical officer at Ligoniel, Dr Robert Newett, wrote to the Belfast Board of Guardians:

Gentlemen, I am desirous of bringing before your notice the condition of some recently-erected houses, which in my opinion, are not fit to afford shelter to domesticated animals, much less to our fellow-creatures... The privy accommodation is public, and so small and abominable that I do not consider it decent. These houses are one storey high. The construction of them is flimsy, the walls being, as I am informed, four inches back and front. They have flat roofs, made of wood, covered with tar and felt... I was in some of the houses – it had rained for some hours. In one of them I saw the rain drop on a bed; a bed for children was placed on the floor, and some heavy rain-drops were falling so fast as to necessitate a vessel being placed along the side of the bed to catch the water. The floor was so wet that ashes had been sprinkled on it to sop up some of the wet. The floor of the back room was quite saturated with sewage matter from a privy outside, which easily soaked in through the flimsy four-inch wall. In the time of frost I picked pellicles of ice off ceilings and walls.

In fairness, most mill houses were more durable than this. The real problem was that linen workers earned barely enough to keep their families at subsistence level and, to keep down costs, crowded densely together. Dr Strahan, medical officer of the York Street area in the 1870s, found that houses inhabited by factory hands '... are almost invariably sub-let. Sometimes a whole family inhabit a room, but there seems to be a good many females who are not living with their parents, and are unmarried and board together, two or sometimes more, and hire a room. I frequently meet cases where the original tenant is a married man, who, with his family, occupies the ground floor, all the other parts being sub-let.' The house accommodation, he observed, 'is generally bad, sometimes wretched'.

Dr Spedding, in the Shankill area, reported: 'Millworkers' houses are generally overcrowded, and badly ventilated; the chimney is usually stuffed with straw. Very many families in this district sleep three or four in a bed in a small close apartment.' Dr Clements, in the area from Smithfield to the docks, observed: 'The small two storey houses are in many, or most cases, occupied by two families (6 to 8 or more in each). In many of the streets, as Marine

Street, New Andrew Street, New Dock Street, Trafalgar Street, the ground floor – the sole residence of a family – is subject to periodic flooding from high tides.'

The living conditions of the unskilled workers were blighted not only by overcrowding, poor drainage and low wages, but also by inadequate diet. Dr Strahan believed that too often 'the diet of Factory hands consists of tea and white bread three times daily, sometimes I see butter used sometimes not – potatoes or meat rarely'. Dr Spedding argued that tea boiled and re-boiled 'confines the bowels very much'. Again and again medical officers deplored the return of mothers to work only a few days after giving birth; such women suffered 'prolapse of the womb, uterine displacements, chronic leucorrhoea, and ulceration'. Babies and small children were 'minded' by old women or older children. Dr Purdon found workers 'leaving the care of their offspring to the "Baby Farmer", who feeds them on improper diet – tea and whiskey – and in order to keep them quiet, different preparations of opium'. The sale of laudanum and opium, more cheaply bought than whiskey, he discovered was 'enormous and increasing'. 30.1% of the factory class died under the age of two-and-a-half years:

> Oh Kathleen, Oh Kathleen, your true love is dead,
> But we've sent you a letter to turn back your head.

Vigorous action by the Corporation helped to bring about a marked improvement in the quality of housing in the final decades of the nineteenth century. A local Act of 1864 made all landlords of houses below £8 Poor Law Valuation responsible for rates and repairs; in 1865 bye-laws laid down that all streets should be properly paved and sewered; in 1878 it was enacted that each house should have a back access of nine feet, that the height of buildings should not exceed the width of the street, and that all streets should have kerbed pavements; and in 1889 damp courses were to be installed in all new dwellings. Above all, the rapid growth of well-paid employment in engineering and shipbuilding ensured that a greater proportion of workers could afford to rent better accommodation.

Iron shipbuilding

Yesterday, shortly before twelve o'clock, the splendid iron sailing ship Alexandra, for the East India trade, was launched from the ship-building yard of Messrs. Harland & Wolff, Queens Island. There was a large concourse of people at the quays, a great many of whom had come in from country districts to spend their Easter holidays. When the blocks which kept the vessel steady in her cradle were cleared away, she was projected with great rapidity into the river, and then brought up at the Northern part of Queen's Quay. The arrangements were admirably carried out, under the superintendence of Mr Harland. The Alexandra is 230 feet long, the breadth of the beam is 36½ feet; her registered tonnage is 1,500 tons. . .

The prominence given by the *Belfast News-Letter* to this launch in its issue of 8 April 1863 indicated that Belfast now had a shipbuilding industry of some importance. Sixteen years before, the *Belfast People's Magazine* had seemed unduly optimistic when it predicted that iron shipbuilding would become 'a permanent and profitable channel of industrial enterprise in Belfast, employing a large number of workmen'. Cork had been the shipbuilding centre of

Bird's Eye view of Belfast 1889.
(Ulster Museum)

Ireland in the first half of the nineteenth century and the three Belfast firms building wooden vessels – Ritchie & MacLaine, Charles Connell & Sons, and Thompson & Kirwan – had launched only 50 ships, most of them small, between 1820 and 1850.

Belfast, not being close to sources of iron and coal, appeared to have few of the assets needed to become a great shipbuilding centre. It is to the Harbour Commissioners that credit must first be given for making the most of what advantages Belfast did have. Only after the excavation of the Victoria Channel and the creation of ample space at Queen's Island could shipbuilders make use of the shelter and depth of water available in the Lough. The Commissioners concentrated the trading docks on the Co Antrim side of the Lagan, leaving the Co Down side free for shipbuilding and laying out small yards on Queen's Island between 1849 and 1851 in anticipation. In 1851 Thompson & Kirwan moved across the river to the Island and in 1853 the Commissioners built another yard there for Robert Hickson. Soon after, the Commissioners were able to report:

. . . that the business has been commenced in a spirit that augurs well for its future success and importance, the vessels contracted for being of a very large tonnage and the proprietor already finding it necessary to ask for additional space. It is also proper to observe that the other yards for timber-built ships are extending their business and laying down vessels of a much larger burthen than formerly.

Hickson was an ironmaster who had set up in Eliza Street in 1851; by turning to shipbuilding two years later he hoped to find an outlet for his iron plates which he found difficult to sell in the teeth of English and Scottish

127

competition. He needed an expert to manage his new enterprise, the craft of which he knew little, and found one in Edward Harland, a twenty-three-year-old Yorkshireman. Son of a physician who had invented a steam carriage and been three times Mayor of Scarborough, Harland learned his trade with George Stephenson on the Tyne and a firm of marine engineers on the Clyde. The new manager at once showed the ruthless determination he was to display all his life; he reduced the shipwrights' wages and, when they went on strike, dismissed them and replaced them with men from the Tyne and the Clyde.

The yard flourished and over the next four years two iron steamships, four iron sailing ships and a paddle tug were launched. Harland then attempted to set up on his own at Birkenhead; the history of Belfast would surely have been very different had not the City Council of Liverpool refused to make land available. Hickson sold out to Harland in 1858; the £5,000 needed was largely provided by G.C. Schwabe of Liverpool whose nephew, Gustav Wolff, had just joined the business as a personal assistant. The talents of all three men – Harland, Schwabe and Wolff – were needed to bring the glittering success of the years to come. Harland provided the managerial skill and, above all, the imaginative and innovative engineering expertise.

Towards the end of his life Wolff replied to a toast in these words:

Mr Chairman: Sir Edward Harland builds the ships for our firm; Mr Pirrie makes the speeches, and as for me I smoke the cigars for the firm.

Wolff did much more than this: he brought with him the financial prowess he had acquired in Hamburg and Liverpool, and a unique talent for supplying the Belfast yard with orders. G.C. Schwabe, a partner in the Bibby Line of Liverpool, was able in turn to obtain ships from his nephew's firm which exactly met his specifications. The first order was for three barque-rigged steamers, the *Venetian* and *Sicilian* completed in 1859, and the *Syrian* in 1860. Eighteen of the first twenty-five ocean-going ships built by Harland & Wolff were for the Bibby Line. The *Istrian, Iberian,* and *Illyrian* launched in 1867 created a sensation in the shipping world; disparagingly called 'Bibby Coffins' by rivals, their special feature was their great length and narrowness of beam. That the rivals were proved wrong was due to Harland's design, which maintained strength by the fitting of iron decks, while the square bilges and flat 'Belfast bottom' ensured stability. Seeing their greater speed and increased capacity, admirers described the new ships as 'ocean greyhounds'.

It was the signing of a contract in 1870 with the Oceanic Steam Navigation Company of Liverpool, better known as the White Star Line, which set Harland & Wolff on course for becoming the greatest shipbuilding yard in the world. The growth of American economic power after the Civil War and the continuing high level of emigration from Europe led to a huge increase in transatlantic traffic. Only those lines which ensured speed, safety, low fares for the emigrants, and luxury for the rich could survive. In 1850 only 5% of the total tonnage of the UK was steam-powered, but between 1863 and 1872 fuel consumption fell by 50% as low-pressure engines and paddle wheels were supplanted by more efficient compound engines and screw propulsion.

Harland & Wolff was in the van of this revolution and its first White Star ship, *Oceanic,* can be regarded as the first modern liner. For the first time, accommodation was extended to the full width of the ship and first-class passengers were placed amidships away from the vibration and roll

Oceanic I (1871) the pioneer steam ship of the White Star line which set new standards of first-class passenger luxury, described as being 'as comfortable as a Swiss hotel'. (Harland & Wolff)

experienced aft. The design and record-breaking speeds made all other North Atlantic liners obsolete. The *Oceanic* was launched on 27 April 1870 and had three sisters – *Atlantic, Baltic,* and *Republic* – all in service by 1872. The slightly larger *Adriatic* left the slips in 1872; 3,888 tons gross, she measured 437½ feet by 41 feet, was the first ship to be lit by gas generated on board, and like the *Oceanic* she remained in service until 1896.

The established lines soon replied to the White Star challenge and this in turn led the White Star to order two larger ships from Harland & Wolff, the *Britannic* and *Germanic,* launched in 1874. Four-masted barques with two funnels, they were 'flyers' which cut the Atlantic crossing by a day; the *Germanic* won back the Blue Riband from the Inman Line by reaching America in 7½ days at between 15 and 16 knots. Later sold to Turkey, torpedoed by a British submarine in the Great War, and subsequently salvaged, the *Germanic* was not broken up until 1951. The White Star Line won renown for Harland & Wolff but, equally, it was Harland & Wolff which made the White Star Line. In the forefront of shipbuilding design and construction, Belfast was poised to meet the challenge of the next revolution in ocean transport in the late 1880s.

Steel shipbuilding

Edward Harland believed that other Irish ports could be as successful in building ships as Belfast provided there were first generated the spirits of enterprise, industry and honest hard work in 'an environment of true patriotism'. The celebrated author of *Self-Help,* Dr Samuel Smiles, held up Harland as an example to the world of what riches could be won by

129

determination and application. The Harland & Wolff workforce had risen from 500 in 1861 to 2,400 in 1870, and by 1900 it would be 9,000.

In 1880 the firm acquired more land from the Harbour Commissioners, increasing the extent of its yard to 40 acres, and by then it had 10 building slips. In the same year Harland & Wolff built its own engine works on the Island and from now on the yard was virtually self-sufficient, from the laying of the keel by the shipwrights to the completion of intricately-carved oak panelling in the first-class cabins by the carpenters.

The control of Harland & Wolff was passing slowly to others. Harland was chairman of the Harbour Commissioners between 1875 and 1887 and sat as an alderman for St Anne's Ward between 1883 and 1887. He revelled in public life; he was Mayor of Belfast in 1885 and 1886; he accepted a baronetcy in 1886; and between 1887 and his death on Christmas Eve 1895 he was the unopposed Conservative MP for North Belfast. Gustav Wolff, too, withdrew from the business and sat as Conservative MP for East Belfast from 1892 to 1910. 'I had no idea when I came to Belfast in 1858 I would be a permanent citizen. I have no regrets I stayed,' he said on being made an honorary burgess in 1911, and recited a verse he had composed:

> You may talk of your Edinburgh and the beauties of Perth,
> And all the large cities famed on the earth,
> But give me my house, though it be in a garret,
> In the pleasant surroundings of Ballymacarrett.

It was William Pirrie, a native of Belfast, who presided over Harland & Wolff during its greatest years. His grandfather, Captain William Pirrie, had been a distinguished member of the Ballast Board and the Harbour Commissioners, and had been given the honour of opening the Victoria Channel in July 1849. Joining the firm in 1862, William Pirrie was successively a draughtsman, Works Manager, and – in 1874 – a partner at the age of 27; 'Pirrie won his place in the firm by dint of merit alone, by character, perseverance and ability,' Harland said later. Virtually in full control, Pirrie depended heavily on Walter Wilson who had been taken on by Hickson as the 'first gentleman apprentice' in 1857; many of the firm's innovations had been Wilson's, including the single-plate rudder, lapped tied butts for joining ships' plates together, and the use of electric current to reduce corrosion.

The shipyards faced difficult times during the 1881–5 trade depression. In January 1884 riveters and platers were laid off until they accepted a cut in wages; in March boilermakers struck unsuccessfully in protest against a 10% wage reduction; and in the summer Harland & Wolff locked out 900 riveters and helpers for a month. Another 10% reduction was reluctantly accepted by all trades in the yards in 1885, and by the middle of 1886 the work force of Harland & Wolff had been reduced from 5,000 to 3,500. There was no sign that the Belfast yards were on the brink of the most hectic expansion in their history.

In 1882, for the first time in the UK, the tonnage of new steamships equalled the tonnage of new sailing ships and steady development thereafter put steam further and further ahead of sail. Steel replaced iron, making hulls lighter and stronger, and more efficient engines increased ship space for passengers and crew by reducing the hold space required for coal. Shipping lines had to re-equip or go out of business, and having more than established its reputation in the 1870s, Belfast received an unprecedented flood of new orders for vessels.

The creators of the White Star –
Harland & Wolff partnership.
Left to right: G. W. Wolff, J. H.
Ismay, W. J. Pirrie and E. J.
Harland. (Harland & Wolff)

With the launching of the *Teutonic* and the *Majestic* in 1889, Harland & Wolff ushered in the new era; Harland, always the master of innovation, had submitted the designs for these twin-screw ships to the White Star Line as early as 1880 and despite the delay the two vessels were acclaimed immediately as the most advanced on the Atlantic run.

The *Majestic* was just under 10,000 gross tons; 565.8 feet long and 57.8 feet wide, she could accommodate 300 first-class, 175 second-class and 850 steerage passengers – the funnels were widely spaced so that all first-class passengers could be seated together in one great dining room. Sophisticated triple-expansion engines – outdating the four-cylinder compound engines then current – gave great power and efficiency. The *Teutonic* achieved the record maiden Atlantic passage time of 6 days, 17 hours and 25 minutes, and attended the 1889 Spithead Review, for she and her sister were the first merchant ships built for conversion – if necessary – into auxiliary cruisers.

The boom in shipbuilding continued through the 1890s; output at Harland & Wolff rose from just over 1,000 tons a year in 1880 to an average of 100,000 tons a year in the 1890s; by the end of the century the workforce was 9,000. Harland & Wolff's success tended to mask the growth of other shipbuilding firms. McIlwaine & Coll moved from their 'Ulster Iron Works' at the Abercorn Basin to Queen's Island and began building ships the following year; between 1885 and 1893 the firm built 58 vessels up to 5,000 tons, fitting its own triple-expansion engines. McIlwaine & Coll was taken over by Workman Clark & Company, who set up their 'Belfast Shipyard' on the Antrim bank of the Lagan in 1880; their first vessel, the steam coaster *Ethel*, had her compound engine made by J. Rowan & Sons, Belfast, but from 1891 the 'wee yard' made its own engines.

131

The Harbour Commissioners again were quick to respond to the growth of trade and shipbuilding. In 1885 the Prince of Wales re-opened Donegall Quay when its reconstruction was finished, while the Princess turned the first sod of the Alexandra graving dock, formally opened by Prince Albert Victor in 1889. The Duke of York opened a branch dock formed out of the Spencer basin – the York dock – in 1897, and in July 1898 an Act of Parliament gave permission for a deepening and widening of the channel and other extensive improvements.

Engineering

The growing needs of the linen and shipbuilding firms helped the emergence of a successful engineering industry in Belfast. It was in iron founding that engineering began. Stewart Hadski set up a foundry in Hill Street in 1760 and until about 1798 he made pots and pans, and boilers for linen bleaching; between 1786 and 1816 Benjamin Edwards had a foundry attached to the glassworks in Ballymacarrett making bottle moulds, grinding machinery and boilers; at the Short Strand the 'Lagan Foundry' began production in 1799 and passed into the ownership of Victor Coates 1802; in 1811 Boyd built his 'Belfast Foundry' in Donegall Street; and in 1846 John Rowan & Sons moved their concern to Belfast. By 1870 there were 20 foundries in Belfast, though Dublin remained more important as an ironfounding centre.

With easy access to cheap fuel, British foundries could under-sell Irish producers in their own market – most traditional three-legged pots were imported from Scotland. Even Harland & Wolff and Workman Clark found it more economic to have foundries on the Clyde. Belfast foundries, therefore, could only remain in business by making machinery and by 1910 only two out of eighteen firms in the city were not in engineering. After 1825 Belfast became the main centre in Ireland for manufacturing steam engines: Coates made water turbines and just before the firm closed in 1905 it made a 3,000 h.p. triple expansion engine to generate electricity for the Newcastle-on-Tyne tramways; McAdam Brothers built steam pumps at their Soho Foundry for irrigating the Nile; Rowan's invented piston rings still in use; in 1883 J.H. Greenhill began making electric dynamos; and Combe Barbour built quadruple-expansion engines for cotton mills in India.

Belfast could not compete with Manchester and Leeds in the making of cotton machinery and linen looms. Hackling, beetling and spinning machinery for flax had no counterparts in the cotton industry, however, and Belfast was to become the world's most important centre for the production of linen machinery. From 1853 James Combe was making hackling engines at his Falls Foundry; George Horner from Leeds set up the Clonard Foundry in 1859 and his 'Duplex' machine which hackled both ends of the flax sold world-wide; Stephen Cotton's Brookfield Foundry, established in 1865, became famous for its spinning and drawing frames. Two brothers, James and Peter Reynolds, began business in McClenaghan's Court off Mill Street and then fell out with each other: James built the Linfield Foundry and Peter the Northern Foundry, both in Grosvenor Street. James Scrimgeour began making textile machinery in Albert Street; when the business went into liquidation it was taken over by its manager James Mackie, also a Scot, who had first come to Ireland to install steam engines at a flax-spinning mill in Drogheda. Mackie made spindles, fluting rollers, flax cutters, bundling presses and twisting frames, and by 1892 was producing 100 wet-spinning frames a year.

By the end of the century, Mackies and the rival Combe Barbour – which became Fairburn Lawson Combe Barbour Ltd in 1900 – were the two largest engineering firms outside the shipyards. Between them the two businesses made the whole range of flax machinery; engineering firms, an 1874 guide to Belfast observed, were 'surrounded by spinning mills and were visited almost daily by the spinners, who thus were able to see the progress being made in the execution of their orders, and to point out their exact requirements and the defects of previous machines' which led to improvements which 'placed the Irish spinners and makers of flax machinery in a deservedly high position in the commercial world'.

During the Crimean War in the 1850s the supply of hemp from Russia had been cut off, putting the dozen small 'rope-walks' in Belfast in jeopardy. Harland needed a large and reliable source of ropes for his ships and helped to set up the Belfast Ropework Company in 1873; Gustav Wolff was chairman but the director with most talent was W.H. Smiles, son of Dr Samuel Smiles, author of *Self-Help*. The company imported Manila hemp from the Philippines which, when bathed in oil, produced the finest rope for shipping; it also made binder twine for the new reaping machines, window-blind cord, trawl nets and fishing lines. By the end of the century the Belfast Ropeworks were the biggest in the world.

Other firms which became leaders in their fields were Musgraves, Davidsons, and Gallahers. From the 1850s Musgrave Brothers won an international reputation for their patent stable and house fittings; by the end of the century they had cornered the luxury end of the international market and supplied such people of title and wealth as Krupps of Essen, the Prince of Wales, M Eiffel and the Khedive of Egypt. Samuel Davidson went out from Belfast to the Assam tea plantations in 1864, returned in 1870 to take out patents for tea-drying machinery, and set up his own works in Belfast in 1881; by the end of the century the 'Sirocco' works had become the world leader in ventilation and fan manufacture. In 1863 Thomas Gallaher transferred his tobacco firm from Derry to Belfast and by 1891 he had 45 tobacco spinning machines at work in York Street; it was not until 1902 that he began making cigarettes. Murray Sons & Company also won an international market for their tobacco processed at their factory beside the Boyne Bridge.

Modern methods of mass production were also applied to the whiskey distilling industry. William Dunville and his partner James Craig built a very large and modern plant on the Grosvenor Road in 1870, the Royal Irish Distilleries, with grain lofts which could store 6,000 tons of grain, fermenting vessels which could hold up to 35,000 gallons each, and which produced 2½ million gallons of proof spirit in 1890. The Irish Distillery at Connswater could produce 2 million gallons annually by the end of the century and the Avoniel Distillery had an annual output of around 850,000 gallons. By 1900 Belfast was sending out 60% of Ireland's whiskey exports.

Belfast was important for its manufacture of agricultural implements. At the Queen's Bridge the Union Foundry of William Gregg, Sons, and Phenix made 20,000 steel spades and shovels annually for sale in Ireland and all over the Empire; the firm, founded in 1873, produced 2,000 tons of nails every year using the latest American self-feeding machines. Joseph Braddell & Son, established in 1811 in Castle Place, specialised in making shot-guns and 'Ulster Bulldog' revolvers, and could claim in 1893 to be the largest gun manufacturer in Ireland.

Wm Gregg, Sons & Phenix, Union Foundry, Belfast, 1882

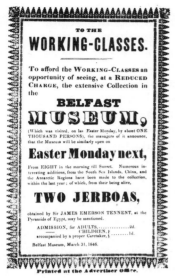

Artists, scientists and inventors

The backward state of the Arts in Ireland, and more particularly in the North, compared with other parts of the Empire, has been remarked with regret, by those who take comprehensive views of their capabilities. . .

It is not easy to deny the truth of this observation made in the catalogue for an exhibition of paintings in Belfast on 5 September 1836. Nevertheless, 217 works of art were shown in the Museum's great hall that day; while most of the paintings are of interest now only because they illustrate the growth of the town, the work of some local artists did rise above the level of mediocrity. The most striking pictures hung were those by Andrew Nicholl; born in Church Lane, Nicholl learned his craft in F.D. Finlay's printing shop, and later enjoyed the patronage of Sir James Emerson Tennent. Nicholl's landscapes are arresting and dramatic, typically showing towering cliffs, raging seas and mysterious ruins; of the many paintings of the Cave Hill his is by far the best. Shortly after he died in 1886 at the age of eighty-two, nearly 300 of his paintings were displayed at 55 Donegall Place. James Howard Burgess was a more technically accomplished but a less original painter of the developing town. Dr James Moore, consultant surgeon to the General Hospital, was a skilful and sensitive water-colourist, and the few surviving paintings by John Glen Wilson – in particular 'The Harbour Steps' (1851) – tantalisingly reveal talent of a high order.

In the late nineteenth century many Belfast artists were trained by the firm of Marcus Ward: the business began in Cornmarket in 1843; thirty years later it owned the Royal Ulster printing works in Ormeau Avenue, had an office in London, and listed 150 books in its catalogue; it printed Vere Foster's writing copy-books; and the Ramblers' Sketching Club was formed entirely from its employees. Hugh Thomson left Marcus Ward to become a witty and accomplished book illustrator for London publishers, while J.W. Carey stayed to depict, in a prolific output of delicate water-colours and sketches, his native city at the height of its economic power. Not until the twentieth century, however, did Belfast produce any artist of international standing.

In 1870 the Government School of Art opened in a wing of the Academical Institution. T.M. Lindsay, the headmaster, said that the school's aim was to 'impart instruction of practical value to the operative no matter by which craft he earns his daily bread'; the teaching there was directed towards perfecting technical skill rather than cultivating the creative imagination. Indeed, it was in the sciences rather than in the fine arts that Belfast excelled in the nineteenth century. The Academical Institution and the Queen's College were nurseries of some of the most distinguished medical researchers of the period; Sir Almoth Wright, in particular, became an internationally-renowned pathologist and bacteriologist. William Thomson, created Lord Kelvin in 1892, was born in Belfast in 1824 though it must be admitted that he left his native town for Scotland at the age of eight; he described his absolute temperature scale (now given in degrees Kelvin) in 1848, made mathematical analyses of magnetism and electricity, and earned a fortune from his submarine cable patents. Kelvin did more than anyone else in Britain to lay the foundations of modern physics, and, together with his older brother James, and Sir Joseph Larmor (also educated in Belfast), prepared the way for Einstein's theory of relativity.

Belfast was particularly proud of those citizens who made inventions of

134

immediate practical application. The cup anemometer, still widely used for measuring wind speed, was invented by Thomas Romney Robinson, who first attracted attention by precociously publishing a book of verse at the age of thirteen. John Boyd Dunlop came from Ayrshire to practise as a veterinary surgeon in Belfast in 1867 and made the first working pneumatic tyre for his son's tricycle in 1887. He set up a company to make tyres in Belfast in 1890 – the nucleus of the multinational firm which today still bears his name. Though devised as an improvement for the bicycle, Dunlop's invention was made just in time to ensure the success of the motor car; the era of the internal combustion engine had not yet arrived, however, and transport in Belfast was still dependent on the steam locomotive and the horse tram.

'Do ye mind the old horse trams a long time ago?'

In 1868 the Corporation published bye-laws for regulating transport in the town; vehicles mentioned included 'Carriages, Chariots, Landaus, Sociables, Jaunting-cars, Gigs and Cabs Plying for Hire'. Passengers could not be charged fares of more than 6d a mile.

Most people in Belfast could not afford to spend money on transport at that time; nevertheless, several horse-omnibus services were operating for the fortunate minority who could pay. In 1849, when the Great Victoria Street railway terminus opened, the Railway Omnibus Company ran a service from Malone to the town centre and by the following year five services – all run by hotel proprietors – took passengers to and from the railway. From 1860 the General Omnibus Company operated between Lower Donegall Street and the Co Down railway terminus at Bridge End; as the first omnibus did not leave daily until 8.30 a.m. and as the fares ranged from 2d to 4d, there could be no hope of attracting working-class passengers. In 1870 Lyons & Company had omnibuses pulled at regular intervals as far as Sydenham, Fortwilliam and Windsor.

Metal tracks, by reducing friction, made it possible to pull heavier loads with fewer horses, but the capital needed to lay tramlines was very great. It was not until 1872 that a group of British businessmen sought and obtained parliamentary approval to set up the Belfast Street Tramways Company. The first line ran from Castle Place to Botanic Gardens, with passing loops at intermediate points; at night the single-decked trams were parked at Wellington Place and the horses taken to stables in Wellington Street. Double-deckers pulled by two horses each had been introduced by 1878 when the lines extended as far as Dunmore Park in the north and Ormeau Bridge in the south. Poor management ensured that the omnibuses could comfortably hold their own with the trams until, in 1881, the London directors of the Belfast Street Tramways Company sent over Andrew Nance as general manager.

Nance controlled the destiny of most of Belfast's public transport until 1917. Immediately on his appointment he took action which ensured the ultimate ruin of the omnibuses; fares were reduced to 2d for any journey, cars ran at five minute intervals on the main routes and, when Royal Avenue was completed in 1884, the terminus was moved to Castle Place – it was Nance who renamed it Castle Junction. To take advantage of great numbers visiting graves on Sundays, tramlines were taken to the principal cemeteries. Parliamentary approval for track extension was given in 1884, and the lines pushed out to Newtownbreda in 1885, Malone Park in 1888, Sydenham and

Palm House, Botanic Gardens. (From *The Industries of Ireland*)

Tennent Street in 1889, and Ligoniel in 1892. The circle of hills around the city made it necessary to post 'trace boys' with fresh horses to help the trams up the steep gradient:

> Do ye mind the old horse trams a long time ago
> As they passed through the city at jog, trot or slow?
> On the level they cantered, but the pace it did kill
> When they got to the bottom of Ligoniel Hill.
>
> But the trace boys were those with a heart and a hand,
> They let down the traces and buckled each band.
> The passengers sat on, contented and still,
> When they saw the bold trace-boys of Ligoniel Hill.

By 1893, when the Belfast Street Tramways Company lease was due for renewal, Nance had a fleet of 94 double-decker tramcars and a stable of 800 horses. The year before, the last omnibus service had expired, after the 1d stage tramfare had been introduced; tramlines had been laid along Bedford Street and the Dublin Road to Shaftesbury Square, and from Corporation Street to Fortwilliam Park, and the whole system had been linked up to the lines of the Cavehill & Whitewell Tramway Company, set up in 1882 – Kitson steam engines pulled large double-bogied double-decker trailers or open toast-rack trailers from Chichester Park to Glengormley. Nance offered his whole operation to the Corporation for £63,000 and the short-sighted refusal of the offer resulted in Belfast being one of the last major cities in the British Isles to transfer to electric traction. The Corporation did pay for eight miles of line extension to Knock, Strandtown, Balmoral, Ravenhill, Stranmillis and Cliftonville.

A powerful railway lobby thwarted Nance's plans to push his tramways beyond the suburbs. A network of railways centred on Belfast had developed independently of Dublin; the Ulster Railway had reached Portadown and Armagh, for example, before the link was made with Dublin in 1853. By the 1880s there were three companies operating services from Belfast: the Great Northern Railway with its terminus at Great Victoria Street and suburban stations at Windsor, Adelaide and Balmoral; the Belfast and County Down Railway with its terminus at Bridge End and halts at Sydenham, Victoria Park, Ballymacarrett and Kinnegar; and the Belfast and Northern Counties Railway with its terminus at York Street and only one suburban station at Greencastle. The Ulster Railway had become part of the Great Northern Railway in 1876.

A consortium of London businessmen, believing that existing railways were not tapping potential commuter traffic, formed the Belfast Central Railway in 1864 to connect the three termini. The company survived only with the help of the Board of Works in 1872, partly because the GNR and BCDR were reluctant to have their termini superseded by the BCR's Oxford Street station. It was not until 1878 that passengers could cross the city by rail, with halts at 'Ormeau', 'Windsor', and 'Ulster Junction' (on the Blackstaff Loney, later the Donegall Road). On the cramped site at Oxford Street, shunting was awkward and time-consuming, and the journeys were too slow to attract enough passengers; the company was bankrupt by 1885 when it sold out to the GNR for £127,500 on condition that the BCR debt of £100,000 was also paid.

The building boom

The White Linen Hall with its massive quadrangle of warehouses photographed by R. J. Welch about 1888. The château roof of Richardson Sons & Owden's warehouse (later the Water Office) was destroyed in the 1941 Blitz. (Ulster Museum)

The development of a cheap, regular and sophisticated transport system did much to encourage the steady migration of Belfast's propertied classes out from the town centre. In 1843, 47% of the 'nobility, gentry and clergy' had lived in the fine Georgian houses around the White Linen Hall and College Square and in the tongue of stucco houses projecting southwards by Great Victoria Street and the Dublin Road to the raised beach beyond Shaftesbury Square. The Turnpike Abolition Act of 1857 abolished the payment of tolls at the borough boundaries and therefore removed an obstacle to middle-class movement to the suburbs. Luxurious terraces for those who could afford private carriages were built in the 1850s and 1860s on the framework of turnpike roads radiating out from the town, particularly on the Lisburn, Antrim, Ormeau and Crumlin Roads. Spacious houses were also put up on the interconnecting roads, particularly at Windsor (on the old Malone turnpike), Richmond (on the new Antrim turnpike) and Sydenham (near the Holywood turnpike). These fashionable villas were to be the forerunners of the greatest building boom in the history of Belfast.

Belfast is pre-eminently a late Victorian city though it is rapidly becoming less so as bull-dozers and JCBs demolish and clear row after row of decayed inner-city housing. Between 1870 and 1900 Belfast's housing stock quadrupled. The boom began in the 1860s, gathered strength in the 1870s, faltered during the recession of the early 1880s, and reached its height in the prosperous 1890s; almost 56% of all houses built in Belfast between 1861 and 1917 were put up in the 1880s and 1890s. In the 1890s the city's population increased by more than a third, 60% of the increase being accounted for by immigration. Had linen remained the only great employer of labour this hectic expansion would not have taken place – wages in the mills were too low and

137

the hours worked too long to make it possible for flax workers to move out of their cramped warrens adjacent to the factories.

It was above all the growth of shipbuilding and engineering which led to the spectacular development of housing in the late nineteenth century. Men working in the new heavy industries earned around three times the average wage paid to mill workers, male and female; for example, men employed in the foundries and engineering works of west Belfast earned average weekly wages of over £1.10s.0d. In Britain it has been calculated that the 'aristocracy of labour' – the skilled and well-paid – formed between 10% and 15% of the population in 1900; in Belfast more than a quarter of male workers were skilled artisans. Such workers could not afford to buy houses, but they could pay higher rents for newly-erected kitchen and parlour houses which were more comfortable than the mill houses they had often left behind.

In the 1880s the clusters of working-class housing expanded around the mills, foundries and engineering works, and the built-up edge of the city moved outwards, particularly in the west and the north. In the 1890s the gaps between these clusters were filled in. On the Co Antrim side of the Lagan river the kitchen housing beside the Gasworks and around mills at Jennymount, York Street, the Crumlin Road and the Falls Road merged into one great belt of working-class homes. On the Co Down side the pockets of dwellings at Bridge End, Lagan Village and along the Connswater were identifiable no more; the gaps between them disappeared as developers created a solid mass of kitchen houses with limbs thrusting out along the Woodstock, the Ravenhill and the Beersbridge Roads. In his impressive study of transport and housing in Belfast in these years, P.G. Cleary observes:

> . . . the continuously built-up area of low-rental housing stretched from the Bog Meadows at Donegall Road in the west to the Woodstock and Beersbridge Road area in the east, and from the Skegoniel district on York Road in the north to the Essex Street area off the Ormeau Road in the south.*

* P. G. Cleary, 'Spatial Expansion and Urban Ecological Change in Belfast 1861–1917' (see bibliog), p. 400.

On the fringes of this vast area of working-class housing, parlour houses – distinguished from kitchen houses by having tiny front gardens, decorative tiles and an additional room – were built between the Ballygomartin and Woodvale Roads, on Manor Street and Cliftonpark Avenue, and along parts of Duncairn Gardens in the north; around Alexandra Park Avenue and Gainsborough Drive in the north-west; in the area bounded by the Ravenhill Road, Ravenhill Avenue and Cregagh Road in the east; and in the vicinity of Stranmillis Road in the south.

The expansion of suburbs for the middle classes was equally impressive in these years. In their steady exodus from the town centre, business and professional classes were confronted by a solid ring of working-class dwellings except in the south and even there the route to the Lisburn and Malone Roads was hemmed in by Sandy Row to the west and low-lying marshland around the Blackstaff to the east. The Encumbered Estates legislation removed the last restrictions on building in south Belfast, which was firmly established as the leading fashionable suburb by the building there of Queen's College (1849), the Presbyterian Assembly's College (1853) and Methodist College (1868). Here along the Malone Ridge, on land which was comparatively well drained and free of smoke, large estates were broken up for the erection of small villas and terraces along avenues connecting the Lisburn and Malone roads.

Continuous outward migration from the York Street/Donegall Street area was blocked by the congested working-class housing at Carrick Hill and North Queen Street; a new residential area for the better-off had begun at Carlisle Circus in the 1850s and 1860s and by 1900 middle-class housing had extended along the Antrim Road as far as Belfast Castle. In east Belfast the phalanx of working-class dwellings was by-passed as developers built comfortable suburbs on the 'Henryville' and 'Shamrock' estates in Mountpottinger; at Ormeau and Ballynafeigh; and from the mid-1880s McConnells developed a 17-acre estate at Rosetta to build sumptuous residences for the well-to-do.

The departure of the middle classes to suburbs extending as far as the tramlines helped to ease overcrowding for the working classes. Congestion had been at its worst in 1851 when there were 6.72 persons per inhabited dwelling; by 1901 there were only 5.20 per dwelling. Most of the inner-city residences became business premises and the people of Belfast did not suffer the fate of the Dublin poor who thronged into the draughty and decaying tenements abandoned by the gentry.

'The unending procession of carts of bricks': developers and builders

A striking feature of the building boom in Belfast was that dwellings of all kinds were built ahead of demand – indeed, many newly-built houses remained unsold for several years. The developers, speculators and builders therefore played an important role in promoting the growth of the city. The good quality and comparatively low rents of houses were often given by immigrants from Glasgow as reasons for coming to work in Belfast. If more houses were needed for the poor it was due to inability to pay the rents and not to a shortage of houses.

The Donegall family – its fortunes improved when Harriet, daughter of the 3rd Marquis, married the 8th Earl of Shaftesbury – took no part in this development of housing in the city. Some other landowners and leaseholders were responsible for minor developments: Baron Templemore promoted building in Castlereagh Street; the Marquis of Downshire opened up an estate at Cregagh; the Houston family prepared building lots on a 52-acre property fronting the Crumlin Road; and the Ashmores laid out Wilton, Conway and Ashmore Streets on a 58-acre property. Others were opportunists: they included Cliftonville Football Club which laid out eleven houses on spare land on Cliftonville Street in 1894; a Methodist minister who developed Buller and Baden-Powell Streets with twenty-two houses, a school and a bakery on vacant land beside the Oldpark Methodist Church; the McCrorys – a family of solicitors – who laid out a 34-acre estate between the New Lodge and the Limestone Road; and E. Walkington – a wholesale chemist – who prepared his 'Snugville' estate beside the Shankill for low-rental housing. Most of the developers, however, were full-time professionals.

As soon as the Corporation laid down stringent building standards and made landlords responsible for repairs, the linen lords ceased to build for their workers. Harland & Wolff built no houses, not even in streets with such names as White Star, Harland, and Teutonic. The massive increase in dwellings in the last quarter of the nineteenth century was achieved principally by the building societies, estate agents, builders, and land and investment companies. Helped by capital and services provided by building societies and estate agents, the

land and investment companies carried out the real work of development; in the early stages of the boom the four most important companies were the 'Royal', the 'Bloomfield', the 'Ulster', and the 'Belfast Provincial'. The 'Bloomfield', for example, opened up Cyprus Avenue and built semi-detached three-bedroomed cottages on the Beersbridge Road in the 1880s, and built extensively in east Belfast in the 1890s on such streets as Sintonville and Martinez Avenues. Towards the end of the century the greatest developer of all, and probably the largest firm of its kind in Ireland, was R.J. McConnell & Company. With its head office in Royal Avenue and branch offices in Mountpottinger, Cliftonville and the Shankill, McConnells built all over the city and for every class; in the 1880s the company had divided Harrybrook, Upper Snugville, Queensland and Tasmania Streets into building lots, and, at the same time as it was selling villas in Rosetta Park for £700 each, it was selling kitchen houses in the Shankill in lots of five for £345.

No less than 174 builders were listed in the 1898 Belfast Directory. Among them was Hugh Scott who put up 304 houses between the Central Railway and the newly built Donegall Road, particularly on Colchester, Dorchester, Barrington and Abingdon Streets – probably the biggest single house-building project in Belfast until after the Second World War. John McCurdy began in a humble way in Sandy Row; in the 1890s he was the main builder of houses on the eastern side of the Ormeau Road; and in 1897 he was at work on sites at Stranmillis, Donegall Road, Woodstock Road, Oldpark Road and on newly-drained land bought for £10 an acre in the Bog Meadows which became Tavanagh Street. By far the biggest builders, contractors and brick makers in Belfast, and almost certainly in Ireland, were H. & J. Martin; from their 'Ulster' building yard on the Ormeau Road they controlled 300 acres of building land and brickfields dotted all over the city. They built extensively at

140

Malone, Ormeau, Ravenhill, Rosetta, Donegall Road, Cregagh and the Shankill. McLaughlin & Harvey, founded in 1853, depended largely on Corporation contracts and orders for major buildings but they too were responsible for building dwellings at this time, including kitchen houses put up in James Street off the Shankill in the 1880s and expensive villas in Osborne Park in the 1890s.

The cost of building was probably lower in Belfast than anywhere else in Ireland. Steady immigration from the impoverished west of the province kept down the cost of labour which was, in the words of the 1885 Housing Commissioners, 'lower than in other centres of industrial production in the sister islands'; the highest paid bricklayers earned 7½d per hour and worked a 56½ hour week. Labour was cheaper still in other parts of Ireland and it was the low price of raw materials, above all, which kept costs down. Builders had easy access to the docks and imported supplies of Baltic timber and Welsh slate, and, when the Penthyn quarries were closed by a bitter industrial dispute in the 1890s, Belfast bought £125,000 worth of American slate – 54% of all that was imported into Ireland. The marls and tills on which much of Belfast is built provided ample supplies of clay for the 33 brickworks in the Belfast area. At their 'Laganvale' brickworks on the Ormeau Road, McLaughlin & Harvey not only mass-produced ordinary building bricks but also specialised in making the terra-cotta ornaments and panels which largely replaced stucco in the 1890s. H. & J. Martin's 'Haypark' and 'Prospect' brickworks, also on the Ormeau Road, were the largest in Ireland; in 1888 their output achieved a record 60,000 bricks a day and at £1.1s.0d. per 1,000 in 1885 they were half the price of bricks sold in Dublin. The landscape artist, Paul Henry, who was brought up in Ulsterville Avenue in the 1880s, remembered the rapid building of the time:

From the Botanic Gardens and up the Malone Road, the roads were kept clean by clumsy contrivances known as scrapers: the mud which had been allowed to accumulate was put into carts and taken off to any depression in the fields and there dumped to form the groundwork and foundations for new houses which were springing up everywhere. For Belfast was growing up... There were very large deposits of the red loam from which bricks are made in the neighbourhood of Belfast, and there were limestone quarries of considerable extent on the Cave Hill. In my childhood there was no more familiar sight than the unending procession of carts of bricks with which Belfast was feverishly built...

Belfast becomes a city: 1888

The completion of Robinson & Cleaver's magnificent store on the corner of Donegall Place and Donegall Square in 1888 was another sign that improved transport was drawing the propertied classes to the suburbs, leaving the centre of the town to trade and commerce. The pamphlet celebrating its opening noted that:

The materials used in construction include 400,000 bricks, 30,000 cubic feet of sandstone, 29,000 cubic feet of timber (including the massive staircase of Australian jarrah-wood), 360 tons of iron, 4,300 square feet of polished Aberdeen granite, 11,500 square feet of polished plate glass, 25½ miles of electric wire, 30,000 square feet of polished teak and mahogany, and about 3,000 square feet of mirrors, mostly with bevelled edges...

Each front was enriched by

finely modelled heroic-sized busts illustrating some of the most distinguished of
Messrs Robinson and Cleaver's customers: the Queen, the late Prince Consort, the
Emperor and Empress of Germany, the Maharajah of Cooch Behar, Lady Dufferin. . .

1888 was also the year when Belfast obtained from Queen Victoria a charter
which converted the town into a city and recognised that not only was Belfast
the largest town in Ireland and first in manufacturing and commerce but also
the third port in the UK, its customs revenue being exceeded only by London
and Liverpool. Another charter in 1892 raised the Mayor to the rank of Lord
Mayor. The Corporation, chastened perhaps by the earlier and humiliating
judgements of the Court of Chancery, displayed a more conscientious desire to
cope with the problems of the growing city. The Gasworks were taken over by
the borough in 1874; the butchers' shops of Hercules Street were swept away
in 1880 to make way for Royal Avenue; Ormeau Avenue was opened in 1884;
Queen's Bridge was widened and the Albert Bridge – which collapsed
dramatically in 1886 – was rebuilt; Ormeau, bought by the Corporation in

142

1869, was made into a public park and by the end of the century the Falls, Dunville, Victoria, Woodvale and Alexandra Parks had been opened to the public; in 1894 Purdysburn estate was bought as a site for an asylum; and a free public library was built on a grand scale in Royal Avenue.

The Corporation health department built an abattoir to replace the insanitary slaughterhouses of Hercules Street and recommended a modern system of sewage. The Blackstaff was culverted in the 1880s but it took from 1887 to 1894 to lay sewers to serve the whole city. Even so, public health was still a cause for concern; 27,000 people caught typhoid in 1897 through direct infection, the consumption of shellfish collected from polluted water, and the drinking of tainted water. It was not until 1893 that the Belfast Water Commissioners began their great project to pipe water from the Mourne Mountains to the city.

Though the Nationalist councillors could never hope to rule Belfast, through the powerful influence of Irish Party MPs at Westminster they had considerable control over the Corporation. For example, in 1887, when the Corporation was promoting its private Main Drainage Bill, Thomas Sexton, MP for West Belfast, carried an amendment introducing household suffrage — that is, a vote in Corporation elections for every male householder — 12 years before it was granted to other Irish boroughs. Again, when application was made for an extension of the city boundary in 1895, Irish Party MPs insisted on having a say in drawing up the boundaries of the new wards; it was agreed that two wards — Smithfield and Falls — should be created to ensure permanent Catholic majorities. It was the opinion of Joseph Devlin, then 25 years old, that the 1896 boundary extension would perpetuate sectarian divisions which showed no sign of diminishing in these years.

'What if the serfs should get the upper hand over their masters?': William Johnston of Ballykilbeg

We will have an Orange Party, please God, after a while in the House of Commons. . . for all the good some of the Ulster members do the Orange cause they might as well have been selected from the Deaf and Dumb Institute. . .

With these words William Johnston of Ballykilbeg proclaimed himself, in a Twelfth of July speech in 1868, to be the true spokesman of the Protestant workers of Belfast. A small landowner from Co Down, Johnston had already proved himself indomitable in the defence of popular Orangeism by defying the 1832 Act forbidding party processions; he led a massive demonstration to Bangor in 1867 and earned himself a month in prison. Given a magnificent reception in the Ulster Hall after his release, Johnston was nominated as parliamentary candidate for Belfast by the United Protestant Working Men's Association of Ulster. The Conservatives refused to endorse his nomination and instead put up the architect, Sir John Lanyon, and John Mulholland, the owner of the York Street Spinning Mill who had won distinction in negotiating the Cobden-Chevalier commercial treaty with France in 1862.

The Conservatives paid the price for failing to realise the implications of the 1867 Reform Act which had given the vote to skilled artisans. 'What if the serfs should get the upper hand over their masters?' the *Northern Whig* had asked. A highly unorthodox alliance of Liberals and Orange workers led to the election of Johnston and the Liberal, Thomas McClure, a tobacco manufacturer who, in Frankfort Moore's opinion, could not 'make a speech that did not violate every rule of grammar and pronunciation'. The election was an impressive demonstration of the growing power of the skilled Protestant workers of Belfast. For a time Johnston proved to be a sturdy opponent of the men of property: he supported the 1874 Factory Act, opposed though it was by the Conservatives and mill owners; unlike the Conservative shipowner, J.P. Corry, he voted for the enforcement of the Plimsoll Line to prevent the overloading of vessels; and in 1870 – to the joy of his supporters – he secured the repeal of the Party Processions Act. The skilled trades of Belfast were almost completely dominated by Protestants and the new awareness of the strength of the working classes was not matched by a decline in sectarian rivalry. Indeed, in the view of Frankfort Moore, the legalisation of political demonstrations began a new round of sectarian rioting:

Between the years 1870 and 1886 there were several outbreaks in the seismic area of the city – that part in which the streaks of disagreement lie in parallel lines running northward. . . Now, anyone passing through these localities will perceive, on being made aware of the respective creeds of the inhabitants and of the spirit of animosity which is inhaled by all from their earliest years, how easy it is for a riot to be started.

'The appearance of a place that had been sacked by an infuriated army': the 1872 riots

Perhaps because there had been unremitting rainfall which had caused severe flooding in Sandy Row, the Twelfth of July parades of 1872 had passed off without serious incident. On Thursday 15 August Catholics gathered in great numbers in the Pound, the Falls and in Hercules Street to take part in Belfast's first Nationalist parade. Eight years before to the day Catholic navvies had made their notorious assault on Brown's Square School and now the Rev Hugh Hanna declared that the Nationalists intended to destroy St Enoch's, his recently erected Presbyterian Church at Carlisle Circus.

The parade was led by Joseph Gilles Biggar, member of the Town Council, Chairman of the Board of Water Commissioners, President of the Belfast Home Rule Association and later famous at Westminster for his interminable obstructive speeches. Biggar agreed to a police request not to go through Carlisle Circus; nevertheless the re-routed parade was attacked by Protestants using clubs, bricks, bottles and guns at brickfields at the top of Divis Street. When the procession reached Hannahstown, 30,000 Nationalists cheered when Biggar called for the release of Fenian prisoners: 'I have no doubt they will be released,' he said, 'and I have no doubt Ireland will get the kind of government she is entitled to – a government of her own.'

Meanwhile 500 shipyard men had stopped work early and, marching in a body towards Carlisle Circus, fought a running battle with the police. Head-Constable Robert Irwin was severely injured when struck on the head with a cudgel. Captain J.C. O'Donel RM declared: 'These men were an illegal body in their formation, illegal in their march through town and in their conduct. Every step was illegal. They came into town in a tumultuous manner, in a manner highly calculated to inspire peaceable citizens with terror.' That night while Hanna was being carried shoulder-high through the Shankill, Protestants – after setting fire to tar barrels on the Boyne Bridge – emerged from Sandy Row to clash with Catholics from the Pound near Great Victoria Street railway terminus, and by midnight the casualty wards of the General Hospital

J.G. Biggar boring the House of Commons. (National Library of Ireland)

in Frederick Street were full.

Friday 10 August began with the shooting of several people on their way to work; at midday Catholics were driven out of their homes in Malvern Street; at six o'clock sectarian mobs, totalling about 3,000, fought each other with stones; and later in the evening Catholics wrecked St Stephen's Church in Millfield. When Trinity Church in Stanhope Street was threatened, the sexton tolled the bell, bringing thousands of Protestants to rally to its defence; only after at least two men had been killed during repeated charges of mounted police was order temporarily restored. Next morning the Mayor, Sir John Savage, issued a proclamation warning that 'in case it becomes necessary to read the Riot Act previous to the use of force for the dispersion of any mob, the military and police will forthwith act as directed by the officers in command. Dated this the 17th August 1872.'

That Saturday the rioting reached its highest pitch. Another man was found shot dead on the Falls Road in the morning as Protestants looted Catholic-owned public houses in the Shankill. The constabulary had fired two volleys directly at the looters when General Warre arrived and drove off the rioters with a sabre charge. About three o'clock that afternoon, Protestant gunmen were seen advancing from the Shankill to the brickfields adjacent to the Pound and for an hour a deadly sectarian battle was fought there before the military arrived. It took the troops – the 78th Highlanders forcing back Catholics with fixed bayonets, and the 4th Dragoon Guards galloping into the Protestants – three hours to separate the combatants. The 'Battle of the Brickfields' was celebrated in verse by the *Northern Whig*:

> With guns and pistols, and blades like crystals,
> And stick and bludgeon, and stone and sling,
> And the police eyein' the brickbats flyin'
> And the kilties dancin' the Highland Fling.
>
> But for powder scanty, Och! not one in twenty
> Would have survived, as each party owns,
> And we were all stranded till the women banded
> And politely handed round the paving stones.

This battle was only one of many fought that Saturday, and the rioting continued with great ferocity until Wednesday 21 August. The correspondent of the *Daily Telegraph* wrote that Belfast 'presented the appearance of a place that had been sacked by an infuriated army', and continued:

There are entire streets wherein a whole pane of glass is not to be found, the very casements being shattered to pieces, while the feathers from a hundred mattresses strew the roadway, and piles of embers here and there show the spots in which the furniture of the victims of one side or the other has been reduced to ashes. In the middle of these ruins and between the half-quieted savages of Sandy Row and the Pound is encamped a force nearly four thousand strong.

One of the worst features of the riots was the large-scale eviction of Catholics living in Protestant areas and Protestants living in Catholic areas. The religious dividing lines running through Belfast became more abrupt and, as the *Belfast News-Letter* reported on 21 August, the evictions caused much suffering:

Several very harrowing scenes have occurred in connection with these compulsory flittings. Here, for example, is a picture of what was seen in Donegall Street yesterday evening about 7 o'clock, and we can assure our readers it is no isolated instance but one typical of a vast number of cases of expulsion from houses. A poor man, very indifferently clad, but apparently very decent for his rank in life, was going along with a handcart laden with some miserable furniture, a bed-tick, a table, one or two chairs and a bag of coals. A friend trudged behind, carrying a clock in one hand and a pendulum in the other, while his wife, a poor frightened and dejected-looking woman, went wearily along with a child in one arm and a looking-glass in the other.

'Is them'uns bate?': the First Home Rule Bill 1886

The Third Reform Act of 1884 trebled the Irish electorate and the Redistribution of Seats Act of 1885 increased Belfast's representation at Westminster to four seats. The election that followed in 1885 proved to be perhaps the most significant of the nineteenth century in Ireland. In South Belfast Johnston won with ease; in East Belfast the Orange candidate E.S. de Cobain defeated the Conservative Sir James Corry; in North Belfast the Conservative Sir William Ewart easily defeated the Liberal secretary of the Belfast Trades Council, Alexander Bowman; and in West Belfast – the only marginal seat for unionists – the Conservative J.H. Haslett in a poll of 7,500 defeated the Nationalist Thomas Sexton by a perilous 37 votes. In 1868 there were 40 Conservatives and 65 Liberals representing Ireland at Westminster; now, secret voting and an extension of the franchise reduced the Conservatives to 18 and not a single Liberal was returned.

The 85 Nationalist MPs – members of the Irish Parliamentary Party – now held the balance of power between the Liberals and Conservatives at Westminster. 'No man has the right to set a boundary to the onward march of a nation,' Charles Stewart Parnell, the Protestant landlord who had welded the Nationalists into a disciplined party, had said in January 1885. On 27 January 1885 the Irish Party put Salisbury's Conservative government out of office, and the new Liberal Prime Minister, W.E. Gladstone, announced that he would introduce a Bill to give Ireland Home Rule, that is, a parliament of her own in Dublin. The Nationalists of Belfast were overjoyed, as Frankfort Moore recalled:

'Our turn is coming now,' cried one of them to me, 'and, by God, we'll learn you what we can do!'

On 22 February 1886 the prominent Conservative, Lord Randolph Churchill, landed at Larne and, after travelling by rail to Belfast, spoke that evening at a monster demonstration of Unionists in the Ulster Hall. 'The hall was crowded to excess,' the *Belfast News-Letter* reported. 'Two excellent bands – the Ballymacarrett Brass Band and the Britannic Flute Band – were placed in the balcony, and before the commencement of the formal proceedings played a number of loyal airs. . . the great ovation was, of course, reserved for Lord Randolph Churchill. He entered, accompanied by Lord Arthur Hill, Rev. Dr Kane, Mr James Henderson, and others, and was cheered to the echo.' For one-and-a-half hours Churchill held the rapt attention of his audience. He said:

I am sure you appreciate the extremely grave nature of the crisis which is impending over you, and the vital necessity of rallying all you can to your standard and your ranks. . . On you it primarily rests whether Ireland shall remain an integral portion of this great empire sharing in its glory, partaking of all its strength, benefiting by all its wealth, and helping to maintain its burdens, or whether, on the other hand, Ireland shall become the focus and the centre of foreign intrigue and deadly conspiracy directed against the efficiency of a dominion with which I believe is indissolubly connected the happiness not only of the Eastern but of the Western world.

Churchill concluded:

> The combat deepens, on ye brave
> Who rush to glory or the grave;
> Wave Ulster, all thy banners wave,
> And charge with all thy chivalry.

Churchill had urged loyalists to organise and prepare so that Home Rule might not come upon them 'as a thief in the night', and in an open letter, published shortly afterwards, he proclaimed: 'Ulster will fight and Ulster will be right.' Some Ulster loyalists took Churchill at his word and began to purchase arms. Most Ulster Liberals deserted Gladstone and when William Pirrie was asked whether or not he would transfer Harland & Wolff to the Clyde if Ireland got Home Rule he replied: 'Most certainly this would be done.' Very early in the morning on 8 June 1886 the vote was taken at Westminster; 93 Liberal MPs voted against the Bill, which was defeated by a margin of 30 votes. Frankfort Moore got the news in Belfast by electric telegraph:

I remember that as I made my way homeward on the lovely June morning when the Bill was thrown out, although it was only four o'clock, I was met by groups of working men who had risen two or three hours before their usual time and came forth from their homes to learn the result of the division in the House of Commons; and when I told them that the Bill had been defeated, the cheers that filled the air at the news surprised the policemen at the corners. . . I met scores of the same class of the population who had left their homes in the side streets, and especially in the ultra-Protestant Sandy Row, the scene of many a fierce encounter between two religious factions, to put to me in their own idiom and staccato pronunciation the burning question:
'Is them 'uns bate?'
And when I assured them that the unspeakable Nationalists had been beaten by a good majority, once more cheers were raised. I was slapped familiarly on the back by half-dressed 'Islandmen' (the shipwrights) with shouts of 'Bully wee fella!' as though the defeat of the measure was due to my personal exertions.

Already, however, the most serious riots Belfast experienced in the nineteenth century had begun.

'Seven martyrs to loyalty have fallen': June–July 1886

On 4 June 1886, at noon, shipwrights marched out of Queen's Island to Alexandra dock; they were seeking revenge for the expulsion by Catholics the day before of a Protestant navvy who had been told by them that once Home Rule became law 'none of the Orange sort would get leave to work or earn a loaf of bread in Belfast'. The yard men attacked with such ferocity that ten Catholic navvies had to be taken to hospital and another, 18-year-old James

Curran, drowned in full view of the combatants.

During Curran's funeral on Sunday 6 June mounted police skilfully kept Protestant and Catholic mobs apart; nevertheless, the following day the Mayor, Sir Edward Harland, telegraphed Dublin Castle to request additional police and soldiers. On Tuesday, when the Home Rule Bill was defeated, Catholics generally followed their priests' advice to remain indoors. People in the Falls did set their chimneys on fire, however, to lament the Bill's failure; this smoke, mingling with the fumes of burning tar barrels and bonfires lit by the Protestants in celebration, created a pall 'as thick as London fog'. That evening 400 police reinforcements pulled into Great Victoria Street railway station only to be led into action almost immediately against Protestants looting a public house beside the brickfields; assailed by stones and window glass, the constabulary were reduced to firing buckshot at the rioters. The pattern for these protracted riots was now set: clashes between Protestant and Catholic mobs were not nearly as frequent or as serious as battles between the police and the Protestants. The Irish Constabulary – renamed the Royal Irish Constabulary after their success in putting down the Fenian Rising in 1867 – were loathed by Belfast loyalists as southern Catholics, though nearly all the officers were Protestant. Their most vocal critic was the Rev Hugh Hanna who called for their expulsion and the reinstatement of the Town Police.

It was on Wednesday 9 June that some of the bloodiest fighting took place. While most of the police were attempting to restore order in Donegall Street, constables – mostly strangers to Belfast – were fighting a losing battle around the Bower's Hill barracks on the Shankill. Trouble began when police tried to prevent the looting of a liquor store; then the police infuriated the Protestants by fiercely batoning men returning from work from the Falls Foundry; finally, after they had been driven by a mob of 2,000 to take refuge in the barracks, the constabulary fired repeatedly at their attackers. The salvoes of paving stones were so heavy that the telegraph apparatus was destroyed. As the *Belfast News-Letter* reported, the paving stones had been

strewn over the road by a number of vicious young women who carried them in their aprons, dropping them at convenient intervals. A terrible scene ensued. Hundreds of people stoned the police in a desperate manner. The police charged them with batons, but without avail. . . and when the stone-throwing waned for a moment girls and women came to the front and uttered the most desperate threats to the men who desisted. It was evident the police would soon be overwhelmed. It must be remembered there was no opposing mob.

The police firing was indiscriminate: of the seven killed only two were rioting. The dead included Mary O'Reilly, a serving girl watching from an upstairs window; James McCormack, killed as he drank inside a public house; 13-year-old Hugh Henderson; Minnie McAllister, a clothing worker; and James Kyle, killed as he ran to her assistance. When troops finally cleared the area around 10 p.m. several children were found unconscious due to the effects of drinking looted alcohol.

The police fired on looters again on Thursday but a temporary peace returned over the weekend. On Sunday 13 June, Hanna declared from his pulpit in St Enoch's:

We must see to it that the terrible massacre on Wednesday last shall, if possible, be brought home to the perpetrators. At the door of the Government lies the guilt of bloodshed on that occasion, the guilt of seven innocent lives sacrificed to avenge the resistance of a loyal people to a prefidious and traitorous policy. . . Seven martyrs to loyalty have fallen. Their names we shall devoutly cherish. To their memory we shall raise a monument.

Violence resumed on the night of 13/14 July when mobs from the Falls and the Shankill fought anew over the brickfields battlefield. The police killed two rioters with buckshot; a soldier of the West Surrey Regiment was shot dead on the Shankill; and looters mortally wounded Head-Constable Gardiner. And the worst of the bloodshed was still to come.

The 1886 riots: July-September

Protestants in conflict with the Royal Irish Constabulary. (Mansell Collection)

Sunday school excursions had been postponed by the rioting and when, on Saturday 31 July, the St Enoch's outing returned to the Co Down railway terminus, Orange bands insisted on accompanying the children in procession through the town back to Carlisle Circus. Before High Street was reached the constables were grappling with drunks accompanying the procession; in Donegall Street Catholics threw stones over the heads of the police at the bands; and the evening ended with police firing volley after volley at looters in North Boundary Street. Though a formidable force of troops and police was on duty, Protestants attacked Catholic children of St Joseph's parish when they returned from an excursion on Sunday; Catholic dockers counter-attacked; and the police fired volleys of buckshot. Frankfort Moore was there; he had seen riots in Cape Town, Trafalgar Square and rural Ireland but, he believed,

None of the principals in these actions knew anything of strategy, compared with those who engineered the sacking of York Street upon that dark night in August, 1886. . . scarcely a light was to be seen; still I had no difficulty in making out the movements of the dense crowds surging in every direction, and shot after shot I heard above the shouts that suggested something very like Pandemonium. Once or twice I was carried along in the rush of people before a police charge. . . I felt that I had learned something of the impotence of every arm except artillery in the case of street fighting.

Thirteen died violently that weekend. The following Saturday almost all Catholics were driven from the shipyards and the police, trapped in Dover Street, killed three people as they shot their way to safety. Fighting was at its worst in the Springfield area on Sunday. Another twelve were either killed or mortally wounded that weekend. Fighting the constabulary became a kind of sport as this story indicates:

> 'Who have you there, Bill?'
> 'A policeman.'
> 'Hold on, and let me have a thump at him.'
> 'Git along out of this, and find a policeman for yourself.'

The riots continued into mid-September when torrents of rain began to fall. 'That rain lasted, as a shower does in Ulster, for three days,' Frankfort Moore observed, 'and, as a dreadful rascal who had taken part in the campaign told me a long time afterwards, that rain "took the heart out of the fighting".'

About 50 people had been killed, 371 police had been injured, 190

Catholics had been expelled from the shipyards, 31 public houses had been looted, and the damage to property had been very great. The report of the government inquiry exceeded 600 pages and put much of the blame on the fighting talk of politicians earlier in the year. As the Liberal shipyard owner, John Workman, put it in the evidence he submitted:

I may say that I am strongly Unionist in my views, but at the same time I think that putting forward the idea of appealing to force was exceedingly unwise on the part of respectable people. It was unwise to use such words, as they were likely to cause the poorer classes to carry out what they only talked about and threatened. . .

The 1886 rioting in Belfast was probably the worst episode of violence in Ireland in the nineteenth century. Certainly the riots caused more blood to be spilled than in the 1803 Emmet rebellion or the 1848 Young Ireland rising, or the 1867 Fenian rebellion, or the Land War of the 1870s and 1880s.

'We will not have Home Rule!': the Ulster Unionist Convention 1892

Though Home Rule had been defeated, the loyalist cause in Britain had been discredited by the Belfast riots of 1886. In 1892 Home Rule once again seemed imminent when Salisbury's Conservative government resigned and a general election was called. Once again Gladstone promised that, if elected, he would introduce a Bill to give Ireland a parliament of her own; once again the pivot of resistance for all those opposed to Home Rule was Belfast. Careful preparations were made to ensure that this resistance would be peaceful, responsible and united. In the common cause Conservatives and Liberals in Ulster sank their differences, and to show their unity and determination a great demonstration was held in the Botanic Gardens on 17 June 1892 – the Ulster Unionist Convention.

12,000 delegates from unionist organisations all over Ulster gathered with their supporters in Belfast that morning. The GNR ran fifteen special trains into the city, with the general and assistant managers both in Belfast to direct the traffic arrangements; and the Northern Counties Company brought in over 20,000 people. The *Northern Whig* reported:

In the forenoon all the termini were thronged in a style the 'Twelfth' has never witnessed, and the thoroughfares on both sides of the river were in a similar condition. Festoons of bunting imparted a festive aspect. Ordinary business, save on the tramlines, was practically suspended before noon. The islandmen and most of the factory operatives knocked off work at eleven o'clock.

The *Freeman's Journal* found it 'an agreeable feature that there were no bands, and we were therefore spared the ear-splitting sounds which are so inseparably associated with Orange and other demonstrations in Ulster'. All journalists were impressed by the orderliness of the proceedings; an English visitor, in a letter to *The Times,* wrote: 'The streets were thronged with a vast multitude, all orderly, all moving, scant of speech but with an air of quiet resolution, in one direction – to the hall.'

A special hall had been built for the Convention on the Plains at Stranmillis; put up in less than three weeks, it covered an acre of the ground – the glass in the roof being one third of an acre in extent – and was the largest structure ever used for political purposes in the United Kingdom. Immediately above the entrance were the arms of Ulster, and above this was a shield eight feet square, on which were quartered the arms of England, Ireland, and Scotland, surmounted by a trophy of Union Jacks; across the panel were the words 'Ulster Unionist Convention 1892' and 'God Save the Queen'. 'As far as sight could reach, sat row upon row of sturdy men packed closely together,' the English visitor wrote: 'There was no singing of patriotic songs; these hard-featured Ulstermen were come together for business, not for noise.' The *Northern Whig* declared:

There were the rugged strength and energy of the North. There sat men of opposed political creeds: still Liberal, still Conservative, on this occasion and in this cause they know but one name – that of Unionist.

The proceedings began with a prayer from the Church of Ireland Primate who asked God: 'Shed abroad upon us Thy Holy Spirit to guide our deliberations for the advancement of Thy Glory, the safety of the Throne, and the integrity of the Empire.' After the Presbyterian ex-Moderator had read verses from the 48th Psalm, the entire convention sang the hymn 'God is our refuge and our strength'. The Duke of Abercorn made a faltering start but concluded with energy:

Great danger is hanging over our heads. This plot of Home Rule is being hatched in darkness. It will not bear the light. . . You are fighting for home, for liberty, for everything that makes life dear to you. . . Men of the North – I say – We will not have Home Rule!

'At these words,' the *Northern Whig* reported, 'the house rose en masse, cheers rent the air, hats and handkerchiefs were freely waved, as every delegate forcibly endorsed the Duke's determination.' It was Thomas Sinclair, the Liberal Unionist, who nevertheless made the most effective speech. 'We will have nothing to do with a Dublin parliament,' he said. 'If it be ever set up we shall simply ignore its existence. Its acts will be but as waste paper; the police will find their barracks preoccupied with our own constabulary; its judges will sit in empty court-houses. . .'

The speeches carefully avoided hostile references to Catholics, and the highly organised respectability of the Convention was clearly designed to impress public opinion in Britain. When the meeting broke up at 2.45 p.m. the Botanic Gardens – not normally open to the general public until 1892 – filled with great crowds, estimated by the *Derry Standard* to total 300,000: 'The whole Gardens presented a moving mass of humanity, interlined with sunlight, shrubbery, white tents, and gloriously foliaged trees.' Speakers addressed audiences from three platforms, one on the principal lawn, the second on the rosary slope, and the third in the oak lawn. The *Northern Whig* regretted that no 'blandishments of Flora had the slightest effect' upon the crowds who 'recked little that this meant death to a poor floral victim. . . We fear Mr McKimm's excellent herbacious department, which he recently rearranged with much care for botanical purposes, must have suffered badly. . .'

This disciplined demonstration of unionist solidarity did not prevent Gladstone returning to office. The Second Home Rule Bill passed through the Commons on 21 April 1893 and the following night nationalists lit fires in celebration on Carrick Hill; the Bill's defeat, however, was assured in the

Waiting for the Islandmen. A brief moment of respite for the R.I.C. as they patrol the predominantly Catholic Carrick Hill, a flash-point during the intense rioting of 1886. (Ulster Museum)

Lords. The political leaders, the Belfast Orange Grand Master, and the employers worked hard to ensure that there was no repetition of the ugly violence of 1886, and W.J. Pirrie – unlike Harland in 1886 – made it clear that he would not permit the expulsion of Catholic workers from his shipyard. In 1895 the Conservatives returned to power at Westminster and for the next ten years Belfast loyalists had nothing to fear. The building boom was well under way, business was prospering as never before, and Harland & Wolff prepared to launch the world's biggest ship.

'She stirs! she starts – she moves': *Oceanic II*, 1899

At the close of the century Harland & Wolff was indisputably the greatest shipbuilding firm in the world. Leaving the ways on 12 October 1897, the *Cymric,* with a displacement of 23,000 tons and 6,800 horse power provided by quadruple-expansion engines, was the largest and most powerful cargo ship in the world, and was the thirty-sixth White Star vessel to be built at the yard. White Star now faced a formidable challenge, however: in 1897 North German Lloyd put the 14,300 ton *Kaiser Wilhelm der Grosse* into service and

Hydraulic rivetting: yardmen at work on the keel of *Britannic II*. (R. J. Welch: Harland & Wolff)

the new Cunard liners were nearly as large. As a result White Star made sure that 1899 was a busy year in Belfast; three sister ships – *Afric, Medic,* and *Persic,* each just under 12,000 tons – were built for a new Australian service, but the proudest moment was the launching of *Oceanic II.* 17,274 tons gross, 685.7 feet in length, with a 68.3 foot beam and two screws powered by four-cylinder triple-expansion engines putting out 28,000 horse power, the 1899 *Oceanic* was not only the largest ship afloat but the first to exceed Brunel's ill-starred *Great Eastern* in length. Probably the most elegant vessel ever launched by Harland & Wolff, the *Oceanic* with its two tall funnels and distinctive narrow profile could reach 21 knots.

The launch, on 14 January 1899, was an occasion of great rejoicing in Belfast. A stand had been put up on Queen's Island to accommodate 5,000 spectators, the money raised from the sale of tickets going to the Royal Victoria Hospital. There were visitors from Britain, America and Germany; special excursion trains had brought sightseers from stations as far apart as Cavan, Derry, Belturbet and Ballyroney; and estimates of the numbers present ranged from 25,000 to 150,000. The ship's hull had been painted white for the benefit of photographers and operators of the 'wonderful "living picture"

The sumptuous interior of *Oceanic II*, described at the time as 'a sybaritic ship', 'a Hotel Cecil afloat' equipped with lavatories of 'costly marble' – for first-class passengers only.
(Harland & Wolff)

Oceanic II: at the time of her launch on 14 January 1899, the biggest ship in the world and the first vessel to exceed in length Brunel's *Great Eastern*.
(Harland & Wolff)

apparatus'. The *Belfast News-Letter* described the scene:

Eleven o'clock approached, and the nervous tension of the operators became acute. . . an unduly adventurous and inquisitive boatman was escorted off the course by the ever vigilant harbour police. . . At twenty-seven minutes past eleven the final shots were fired, the workmen in the yard stood clear of the vessel, Mr A.M. Carlisle gave the signal for the launch, and cheering commenced. Then down came that great vessel, built for the accommodation of thousands of passengers, by thousands of the finest artisans in the world, at a cost of hundreds of thousands of pounds — the most wonderful illustration of the shipbuilder's art which the history of the world has furnished. She glided down the ways silently and gracefully, and with gradually increasing momentum, amid a grand volume of cheering, which even the discordant shrieks of thirty or forty syrens failed to drown. The ladies waved their handkerchiefs enthusiastically, none of the men were too unemotional or blasé to repress a joyful cheer, and the officers and crew on the deck astern raised their caps in acknowledgement. Her finely-rounded stern touched water in a few seconds, causing scarcely a splash, her propellers under the pressure of the Lagan began to revolve, and a swelling wave rolled to the sides of the vessel. One, two, three, seconds, and the Oceanic was afloat.

. . . The wave caused by the tremendous displacement just overtopped the level of the wharf, and the force of contact created a great shower of spray, which drenched dozens of the more adventurous onlookers — is it true that the Right Honourable W.J. Pirrie was one of their number? — stimulating some of them to flee incontinently. Many snapshots were doubtless abandoned, and the results obtained by others will as certainly be somewhat grotesque. But this was the uttermost extent of calamity.

The *Belfast News-Letter* celebrated the launch by printing this deathless verse:

She stirs!
She starts — she moves — she seems to feel
The thrill of life along her keel,
And spurning with her foot the ground,
With one exulting, joyous bound,
She leaps into the ocean's arms!
And lo! from the assembled crowd
There rose a shout, prolonged and loud,
That to the ocean seemed to say —
'Take her, O bridegroom, old and grey;
Take her to thy protecting arms,
With all her youth and all her charms!'

155

7
Years of Uncertainty
c.1900–1920

For Belfast the nineteenth century ended on a high note of prosperity and peace. Ugly sectarian rioting no longer stained the city's reputation; full employment prevailed in the mills, engineering works and shipyards; Protestant fear of Home Rule subsided as the Conservatives routed their opponents in the 'khaki' election of 1900; and the Catholic councillors seemed to be exerting a greater influence over the Corporation than before. In the years running up to the Great War citizens could boast that their city had the greatest shipyard, ropeworks, tobacco factory, linen spinning mill, dry dock and tea machinery works in the world, and that again – in 1910 and 1911 – Belfast had launched the world's biggest ship. The city's population rose from 349,180 in 1901 to 386,947 in 1911; even if this ten-year increase was down to 10.82%, the expansion of the built-up area did not slacken. If Dublin's population was equal to that of Belfast, the northern city's economic might was far greater. The French writer, Paul Dubois, expressed this opinion in 1907: '. . . with its red-bricked and smoke-blackened buildings after the American pattern, its factories and palaces, this workers' city resembles Liverpool or Glasgow rather than an Irish Town.' The Home Ruler, Stephen Gwynn, came to a similar conclusion in 1915: 'Belfast and the Ulster which is coming increasingly to centre about Belfast, is nearer to Scotland and more related to it than to Southern Ireland.'

Yet the constant boasts of Belfast's success and superiority had in these years a hint of strain in them; the very opulence of the City Hall, completed in 1906, seemed a little too self-conscious. For all the strength of their assertion, the rulers of Belfast were increasingly on the defensive. Mounting labour unrest threatened Unionist solidarity; the loss of the *Titanic* cast a shadow over the shipyards; and from 1910 it looked as if nothing less than open rebellion could prevent Westminster from breaking the Union. Only the outbreak of war in Europe postponed civil war in 1914 and thousands of the city's young men were to be slaughtered at the Somme in 1916 without even the consolation of victory. The Great War undermined the foundations of the city's prosperity, though few realised this at the time, and as Belfast prepared to be the capital of a province with its own Home Rule it was ravaged by blood-letting which exceeded even that of 1886.

'One saw. . . Orangeman march arm in arm beside his Nationalist fellow workman': the birth of a labour movement

Ireland was one of the last countries in western Europe to have an organised labour movement and even today the island remains very stony ground for the growth of socialism. Rural Ireland for decade after decade exported its discontent through emigration. Belfast, on the other hand, had emerged as the centre of the only great industrial area in the country, but there too an effective labour movement was slow in developing. The explanation in part is that the constant immigration of impoverished, unskilled and unassertive people from west of the Bann made it extremely difficult to unite the workers of Belfast to demand more from their employers. A more serious problem was that the working class remained deeply divided by sectarian and political differences.

There is an enduring myth that employers were solely responsible for maintaining these divisions. No doubt some employers welcomed the weakening influence of sectarian feeling on attempts to organise their employees. In many instances, however, it was the workers themselves who insisted on keeping certain trades and workplaces either exclusively Protestant or exclusively Catholic. For a long period in its history Belfast had been almost entirely Protestant. Most nineteenth-century immigrants were poor and unskilled, and the Catholics especially found themselves at a disadvantage in Belfast, where virtually every major employer was Protestant and where the comparatively well paid skilled trades were monopolised by Protestants. Bernard Hughes, the first notable Catholic employer in the town, expressed the frustration of his co-religionists when he said in evidence to the 1864 Commission of Inquiry:

There are few Catholic employers in the town and the others will not take Catholic apprentices, for the workers will not work with them as either apprentices or journeymen. Every trade has an Orange Lodge and their people know each other for they have signs and passwords, so that the Catholic population has no chance at all.

Recent research, by Peter Gibbon and Henry Patterson in particular, seems to indicate that in the shipbuilding and engineering industries the Orange Lodges were not primarily responsible for excluding Catholics from the skilled trades; instead the trades themselves − as in Britain − exercised their long-established right to select apprentices for their crafts. Almost inevitably those chosen were Protestant, and no serious attempt was made by either employers or governments to interfere with this method of recruitment. The 1901 Census showed that though 24% of the total population of Belfast were Catholic only a very small percentage were skilled workers. A high proportion of Catholics were in low-paid employment: one third of general labourers, 41% of dockers, and almost a half of flax spinners were Catholics; and even in the linen industry, characterised by low pay, the better paid skilled workers were mostly Protestant. The English socialist, Beatrice Webb, wrote that during a visit to Belfast in 1892 she spoke to

. . . hardfisted employers and groups of closely organised skilled craftsmen, many of them Scotch, veracious and cautious in their statements about their own conditions of employment and contemptuous and indifferent to the Catholic labourers and women who were earning miserable wages in the shipyards and factories of Belfast.

This observation implies that all low-paid workers in Belfast were Catholic; but as less than a quarter of adult male workers were skilled this cannot have been true. Protestants dominated the 'aristocracy of labour', but there were at least as many Protestants as Catholics who were unskilled and low paid. It was amongst the unskilled Protestants that the Orange Order had a vital role to

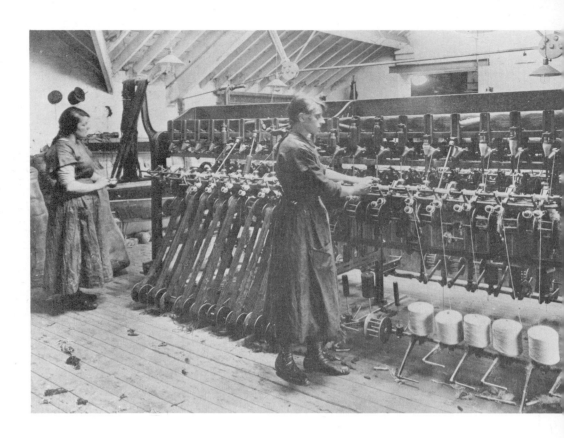

Flax spinners at Ireland's Mill, May Street, 1917; the lowest-paid textile employees in the UK, they suffered from rising living costs in the years preceding the First World War. (PRONI)

play; occupational Orange Lodges – such as the Belfast Paviors Purple Star, and the Belfast Stone Cutters – could be valuable in giving employment advantage to Protestants who otherwise had little job-bargaining power.

By the 1880s only the skilled artisans had been organised into trade unions and even these avoided coming into conflict with employers save in exceptional circumstances. The Belfast Trades Council, set up in 1881, was dominated by the smaller craft unions; the shipyard engineers, for example, were not represented until 1887. The Trades Council made no determined attempt to organise the unskilled and carefully avoided socialist politics. Members often spoke on Conservative Party platforms and its secretary, Alexander Bowman, was expelled when he stood as an independent labour candidate in East Belfast in 1885. It was not the Trades Council but British-based unions which began to organise the low-paid in Belfast. The Gasworkers had eight Belfast branches in 1891 and by 1896 the National Amalgamated Union of Labour had 2,000 members in the city. Attempts to bring female linen workers into unions failed completely. There was a new air of militancy, however, and, when linen-lappers went on strike in 1892 and the millowners over-reacted by locking out all their employees, a great demonstration was organised. The *Northern Whig* reported on 7 March:

Viewed merely as a spectacle, the demonstration was imposing. But when behind the pageantry, one saw the mighty cause of labour, represented not by any section of its patrons, but by every section of industry, beheld Orangeman march arm in arm beside his Nationalist fellow workman, heard Protestant and Roman Catholic bands play similar airs and saw no element of discord, it was evident that under all this outward show there lived a power that must be reckoned with.

The cause of labour still had a long way to go before it became mighty in

Belfast. The linen-lappers were dismissed by their employers and replaced by women and machines. A more impressive display of working-class strength was made when shipyard engineers went on strike in October 1895; 10,000 workers – many of them unskilled – were put out of work by the dispute and as the strike lasted until 1896 their condition soon became desperate. The *Northern Whig* reported in December:

That distress is only too prevalent in the city in consequence of the strike relentlessly forces itself upon one's observation daily. Knots of shivering workmen, tired probably of the hopeless search for work in which they have been engaged for weeks, are now to be seen gathered at the corner of nearly every principal street in the industrial districts.

With considerable difficulty two socialists, William Walker and John Murphy, persuaded the Trades Council to pay nearly 1,000 labourers, not members of any union, 5s a week; in doing so they did much to show the unskilled the advantages of joining trade unions. Change was slow, however, and the Trades Council remained in the control of trade union leaders hostile to socialism and indifferent to the plight of the low-paid.

The 1905 North Belfast by-election

In 1900 there were few signs that the first decade of the twentieth century was to be a time of exceptional hope for the cause of labour in Belfast. That year bonfires were lit in Catholic areas to celebrate British defeats in the Boer War and when Pretoria fell to the British in June, Protestant shipyard workers downed tools to parade through Belfast singing patriotic songs. There were sectarian disputes in the shipyards and Arthur Trew, leader of the Belfast Protestant Association, was convicted for his part in an attack on a Corpus Christi procession.

Belfast had already given a lead in Ireland in the organisation of labour. The Irish Trade Union Congress had been set up in 1894, and in 1899 half the affiliated trade unionists for the whole island were working in Belfast. In addition, the city had the largest group of labour councillors in the country, and it was there that the labour movement was to make its first attempt to win parliamentary representation. A split in the Orange Order in 1903 helped to make room for labour claims. In 1902 William Johnston of Ballykilbeg had died and, in the by-election for his South Belfast seat, Tom Sloan – the new leader of the Belfast Protestant Association and a strident working-class critic of Romanisation – stood against the official Conservative candidate. Sloan won the seat and was duly suspended from the Orange Order; in retaliation he founded the Independent Orange Order in July 1903 which soon had 55 lodges, 20 of them in Belfast.

The new Order was sympathetic to the labour movement and Sloan was the only Unionist MP to vote for the Miners' Eight Hour Bill. At the same time the Irish Parliamentary Party was in disarray; the reunion of the party in 1900 after the split over the Parnell divorce case seemed only to paper over the cracks. In any case, with the Conservatives comfortably in power at Westminster, there was no immediate prospect of obtaining Home Rule. As the Union was not apparently in danger the time seemed right for labour to seek a parliamentary seat in Belfast.

In 1900 the Labour Representation Committee – the forerunner of the Labour Party – was set up in Britain, and in 1903 delegates of 36 trade union

159

branches, members of the Independent Labour Party, the Belfast Ethical Society and the Clarion Fellowship met to establish the Belfast IRC; Keir Hardie and Ramsay MacDonald urged the meeting to prepare at once to win a seat for labour. North Belfast was quickly chosen as the most suitable constituency – in South Belfast most Protestant workers would be loyal to Sloan; in East Belfast Wolff was too formidable an opponent; and in West Belfast the margin between Unionists and Nationalists was too narrow. Robert Gageby and William Walker tied in a vote to choose the candidate. Walker, eventually selected, was a talented speaker and a socialist who had done much to organise linen workers. A severe recession in the winter of 1904–5, which left 19% of shipyard workers unemployed, helped to increase working-class discontent, and gave Walker the opportunity to address protest meetings of the unemployed.

When the sitting member for North Belfast, Sir James Haslett, died in 1905 the Conservatives chose Sir Daniel Dixon as their candidate for the by-election. Dixon was Lord Mayor of Belfast, a shipowner and timber merchant, a director of the Ulster Railway, and so hostile to the claims of labour that the Liberal Unionists and the *Belfast News-Letter* opposed his nomination – in short, he seemed the ideal opponent for Walker. Dixon's nomination brought Walker the energetic – if at times embarrassing – support of Sloan and the Independent Orange Order. There was even a chance that Joseph Devlin, the Nationalist MP for West Belfast known to be a champion of the underdog, would call on Catholic voters to poll for Walker. Could Walker win the backing of working people of both religions?

Dixon replied to this formidable opposition by declaring that Walker's election agent, Ramsay MacDonald, was sympathetic to Irish Home Rule. This, indeed, was true; Sloan's supporters insisted that Walker make his position clear. Walker declared that he was for the Union but that he was a new type of unionist who was 'determined that that union shall be beneficial to Ireland, that every advantage which can be obtained through the union shall be conferred upon the Irish people and that the Irish government shall be conducted not merely with efficacy but with economy'. Traditional unionists were reactionary and Home Rulers were reactionary; the international cause of labour was his cause as the *Belfast Labour Chronicle* proclaimed in July 1905:

Class ties are stronger than those of race and the workers of all lands and climes have a common class interest. They are all units in the army of labour and they ought therefore to forget their differences of race, language and colour and stand shoulder to shoulder in order to withstand the attack of their common foe capitalism.

Walker then agreed to answer a questionnaire presented to him by the Imperial Protestant Federation and his replies were published in the *Northern Whig*. MacDonald wrote in despair:

I was never more sick of an election than that at North Belfast and then the religious replies coming at the end of it knocked everything out of me. I am afraid that those answers of his will make it impossible to win the constituency.

This was true; the *Irish News* and Nationalist leaders made little comment on the election and it was estimated that 1,000 Catholic votes had been lost. Walker got 3,966 votes but Dixon, with 4,440 votes, won the seat.

It was not just the questionnaire which lost Walker the election. He had

been faced with the problem encountered since then by every labour candidate and by every candidate seeking both Catholic and Protestant votes in Belfast – was he for or against the Union? Walker's particular dilemma was that he was against Home Rule and in favour of linking the Irish labour movement with that in Britain; British labour overwhelmingly supported Irish Home Rule. From another point of view the vote for labour had been very impressive especially when it is remembered that most unskilled workers still had not got the vote. In the general election of 1906 there were indications that an unofficial alliance existed between Sloan, Walker and Devlin, and the Belfast Trades Council passed a resolution supporting all three candidates. Devlin described the three contests as 'a fight of the workers and toilers against intrigues, political machines and confiscation', and the chairman of one of his campaign meetings said that

their efforts would result in the blending of Orange and Green on Thursday next, and that it would be a three-leafed victory. They had a shamrock with the name of Devlin on it, and he trusted that next Friday morning it would bear the names – Devlin, Walker, Sloan (three cheers).

Sloan won by a margin of 800 votes, Devlin had a tiny majority of 16 votes, and while Walker was defeated again he increased his share of the vote; it seemed only a matter of time before he would win North Belfast. The following year, 1907, the cause of labour seemed to advance again in the most impressive strike Belfast had yet seen.

'As Belfast men and workers stand together': the 1907 Dock Strike

In January 1907 Jim Larkin came from Liverpool to Belfast as organiser of the National Union of Dock Labourers; it was to be here in Belfast that this tall and flamboyant champion of the underdog, conspicuous in his ten-gallon hat, was first to establish his reputation as the most electrifying Irish orator of his day and ultimately the most celebrated labour leader in Irish history. Though by 1900 Belfast had 57 unions with 19,000 members, the mass of the unskilled workers had yet to be organised. At the time of Larkin's arrival there were 3,100 carters at the Belfast quays; only a small number of the carters were members of any trade union. With the upturn of trade after the 1904–5 recession there was a new feeling of militancy amongst the low-paid: in 1906 flax spinners won an increase in their first strike for ten years and in the early months of 1907 engineering labourers, bakers, printers and coal-heavers – many not in trade unions – were in dispute with their employers. Larkin quickly won recruits and on 16 February the Glasgow *Forward* reported: 'The visit of Comrade Larkin. . . to organize the dockers is bearing good fruit, over 400 of them combining themselves together within the last three weeks.' Two months later all the carters and 2,900 of the dockers had joined Larkin's union. Most of the firms at the quays accepted the new union – an important exception was the Belfast Steamship Company at the York dock.

On Monday afternoon 6 May 1907 a small group of dockers went on strike at the York dock because they were asked to work with non-union men. Larkin persuaded the dockers to return but when they did next day they found their places filled by 50 men sent over from Liverpool by the employers' Shipping Federation; three days later another 100 'blacklegs' arrived. Thomas Gallaher, chairman of the Belfast Steamship Company, had

Big Jim Larkin inspires his audience with his pugnacious oratory in Queen's Square during the 1907 Dock Strike. (Belfast Central Library)

made up his mind to stamp out 'Larkinism', for he was also owner of the great tobacco works in York Street where many low-paid women and casually employed men had been organised by Larkin into a union. Larkin saw this struggle as an opportunity to win wage increases and new members by militant tactics; he referred to Gallaher as an 'obscene scoundrel' and said that 'although St Patrick was credited with banishing the snakes, there was one he forgot, and that was Gallaher – a man who valued neither country, God, nor creed'.

Wild words like these helped to unite employers and, at the same time, to spread the strike as other workers came out in sympathy. When the carters refused to move goods to the sheds of the firms in dispute with the dockers, the Master Carriers Association locked them out. Larkin exulted that he – a Catholic and a nationalist – was leading men who were Protestant Orangemen: the cross-channel docks in the dispute were manned by Protestants while the deep sea docks, where work was casual and irregular, were dominated by Catholics. Over the Twelfth of July holiday the coal merchants locked out their men having previously declared:

We have unanimously decided:
1. That no person representing any union or combination will, after this date, be recognized by any of us.
2. That we will exercise our right to employ and dismiss whom we choose and on whatever terms we choose. . .

By now Belfast had almost been brought to a standstill by the strike, and as Larkin regularly addressed meetings of up to 20,000 people from the Custom House Steps, employers called for action to curb the pickets. At this moment of crisis, men of the RIC in Belfast mutinied because they got no additional pay for their long hours of duty. The mutineers were transferred to country districts

162

while another 1,200 troops were brought into the city. To maintain solidarity the strike leaders called a great meeting for Sunday 10 August. Already the Independent Orange Order backed the strike and, to the delight of the meeting, Joe Devlin arrived to pledge his support for the 'cause of the workers'.

On 11 August mill-workers overturned two vans in Divis Street and showered stones on the troops and constabulary. As arrests were made the following day rioting flared up on the Falls Road and, after five hours of intense fighting, soldiers fired on the rioters, killing two. Order was restored next day when Catholic clergy, William Walker, and other strike leaders posted up handbills reading:

Not as Catholics or Protestants, as Nationalists or Unionists, but as Belfast men and workers stand together and don't be misled by the employers' game of dividing Catholic and Protestant.

George Askwith, the Board of Trade's most skilled arbitrator, arrived and sought out Larkin, as he later recalled: 'He was surprised to see us, but after intimating that the British Government and all connected with it might go to hell, launched into long exhortations of the woes of the carters and dockers and denunciations of the bloodthirsty employers, collectively and individually.' He did, however, agree to persuade the carters to make a settlement, 'and gave them lectures which no employer would have dared to utter'. The details of a wage increase obtained for the carters was announced at a great meeting in St Mary's Hall. Larkin asked Askwith:

'I wish you would pull my coat-tails if I say anything wrong.' There was no need for that precaution. In two minutes Mr Larkin had the men throwing up their caps and roaring applause.

The dockers were not so fortunate; their dispute had cost their union £7,000 and the general secretary, James Sexton, insisted on a settlement. The men returned to work in September with no pay rise though their union was given grudging recognition. The employers' attempt to set up a Protestant company union failed completely.

Some historians have seen this great struggle as a significant step taken towards religious reconciliation in Belfast and believe that the opportunity to detach workers away from their Nationalist and Unionist allegiance was lost. In the excitement of the strike, Protestants and Catholics had campaigned together, but it would take more than trade union militancy to entice them from their main political aspirations. Besides, events at Westminster were shortly to arouse the people of Belfast to passionate defence of, or opposition to, Home Rule.

'The prettiest villas that have been erected since Noah left the Ark'

The working classes of Belfast, in common with those in other major cities in Britain, suffered a severe decline in living standards in the years coming up to the First World War. The last thirty years of the nineteenth century had seen a dramatic fall in the cost of food: refrigerated ships – pioneered by Workman Clark – brought in cheap lamb and mutton from New Zealand; fenced in by barbed wire invented in Ulster, the American prairies yielded vast surpluses of corn and beef; and it was often in Harland & Wolff vessels that inexpensive

* P. G. Cleary, 'Spatial Expansion and Urban Ecological Change in Belfast 1861–1917' (see bibliog), p. 419.

grain and canned meat reached the ports of Britain. In these years, even the wages of flax workers, which had barely risen, increased their buying power by an estimated 200%. Now, in the Edwardian era, remembered for its glitter and ostentation, the whole trend was reversed as the gap between the rich and the poor yawned wide. Between 1895 and 1912 food prices increased by 29%, and in 1912 it was calculated that 59% of the unskilled worker's wage was spent on food. Little wonder then that the period was characterised by labour unrest as workers struggled for wage increases; only the best organised were able to prevent a fall in the purchasing power of their pay.

Nothing shows the decline in living standards in Belfast more graphically than the sudden fall in the number of new houses built for the working classes. Between 1901 and 1911 Belfast's housing stock increased by only 3.16% – in the best year, 1907, 1,303 houses were completed and yet this was only 28% of the number built in 1898. In the years 1912–17 only 2,319 new dwellings were put up; not since 1861 had the rate of building been so low. There was no shortage of houses offered for rent or for sale: 10,258 empty dwellings were listed in the city in 1901. Simply, skilled workers could not afford more than 5s, and unskilled workers more than 3s.6d. per week in rent, and builders could not afford to build for these low returns. The surplus stock was reduced to 4,921 by 1911 and by then builders who were not already bankrupt were concentrating on dwellings for the better-off. Just before the outbreak of war the Corporation subsidised slum clearance and new housing in Institution Place, John Street, Hamill Street and in Brown Square – a recognition that private enterprise could no longer be depended on to build for the poor.

Nevertheless, 11,000 houses were built in Belfast between 1900 and 1917. Only a tiny proportion were for the working classes, put up principally in the Donegall Road district and between North Queen Street and York Road. Nearly all the new building was for the middle classes in the suburbs and on the outskirts of the city; here land was comparatively cheap and houses could be larger and have more extensive gardens. As P.G. Cleary has observed:

The result was that although the numbers of houses constructed in this period were lower than those built in the two previous decades, the rate of physical expansion of the city was not initially seriously diminished. *

The development of middle-class suburbs was greatly assisted by the extension and electrification of the tramways. Indeed, the most ambitious project of the time was Sir Robert McConnell's Cliftonville Garden Colony which was designed for tram commuters; McConnell was a member of the Corporation's Tramways and Electricity Committee and it was no doubt due to him that the longest one-penny stage in Belfast in 1908 stopped at the entrance to Cliftonville Circus. The Cliftonville Garden Estates Company, set up as a subsidiary of McConnells in 1903, was inspired by the American street-car suburbs and Ebenezer Howard's garden city movement in England. The advertisements were enticing: 'It costs only a penny from the Junction, and you will see some of the prettiest villas that have been erected since Noah left the Ark. . . The beautiful panorama unfolded cannot be duplicated. . . Tennis Lawn for the Girls. Cricket Pitch for the Boys. Playgrounds for the children.' No two houses were to be exactly the same and W.J. Walshe's design provided for a pleasure-garden with a tea-house and bandstand, and three open gardens. The company promised to plant 100,000 shrubs, plants and

An electric tram on the eve of
the First World War at
Chichester Park on the Antrim
Road. Luxurious villas were
built at the limit of the
tram-lines in these years.
(Linen Hall Library)

trees and the streets were to be named Aster, Begonia, Daffodil, Hollyhock,
and Fern Gardens. Mortgages to 'suit the better class of artizan' were
available; even highly-paid workers, however, were unlikely to be able to
afford a deposit of £80 and weekly repayments of between 8 and 10 shillings a
week for a house costing £350, though a few were priced at £240. By 1911,
340 had bought houses on the site, but with incomes ranging between £200
and £500 a year they were clearly well-established members of the middle
classes. The company was forced to build more modest dwellings where it had
been planned to lay out the gardens, and the tea-house and bandstand were
never put up. Some of the luxurious villas of the original plan can still be seen
between Westland Road and Knutsford Drive.

McConnell also built detached houses at Ormiston, St James's Park and
Ravenhill Park. The Bloomfield Company and H. & J. Martin put up many
dwellings for the middle classes at Knock in these years; at Malone between
Cadogan Park and Balmoral Avenue; between the Antrim and Somerton
Roads, and generally between the Antrim and Shore Roads north of
Fortwilliam Park; at Ballygomartin; and at Bloomfield. Residential housing
expanded also at Stranmillis; in the Glen Road area at Norfolk Parade and
Divis Drive; along Ardenlee Avenue and Ravenhill Park, linking the Rosetta,
Ballynafeigh and Cregagh suburbs; and on the Upper Newtownards Road
connecting the exclusive housing at Knock and Belmont to the main built-up
region of East Belfast.

By 1914 even the demand for suburban homes was slackening. The First
World War eventually caused a shortage of timber, slates and labour and only
147 houses were completed in Belfast in 1917; even so, houses were difficult to
sell – the Bloomfield Company had to accept £350 for a new house in Martinez
Avenue in 1915 where seven years earlier they had sold an identical house for
£390. The building of residential suburbs pushed out the frontiers of the city to
such an extent that by the end of the First World War Belfast stretched for over
six miles from north to south and seven miles from east to west. Much of this
expansion was due to the modernisation of the tramways.

'Horse-Traction died last night in the city': electric trams, 5 December 1905

Belfast was one of the last major cities in the United Kingdom to have electric trams. An offer of £380,000 made by the Corporation's Tramways and Electricity Committee to buy out the BSTC was rejected in 1902. Finally, the Corporation sponsored a private Bill to take over the tramways which became law in August 1904. The BSTC claimed £392,000 in compensation, which was reduced by nine days arbitration in the courts to £307,500. Andrew Nance was a hard man to put down and he bounced back as head of the 'Belfast Corporation Tramways' in September 1904. The Corporation accepted a cheap tender by the local contractors, J.J. White & Company, who brought in experts and workmen from Britain. There was an immediate outcry from the labour movement; in October 1904 the Trades Council held a protest meeting of ratepayers in the Ulster Hall – the labour and nationalist councillors wanted the Corporation to do the work itself, using its own labour. It was a time of severe depression when there were over 10,000 unemployed in the city, William Walker declared at the meeting, and Edward McInnes criticised the contractors for 'flooding the overstocked labour market'. A demonstration at the Town Hall in Victoria Street was made the following year, and in its issue of 28 October the *Belfast Labour Chronicle* commented:

Belfastmen are determined not to allow their wives and children to be hungry while work they are perfectly capable of doing is handed over to middlemen and through them to the professional and peripatetic navvies and others who follow the contractors from district to district. The scene was a depressing one, for many of those who crowded the Town Hall and its approaches were skilled artisans to whom their present workshops are at present closed. Group after group thronged up the steps. . . to the evident consternation of Sir Samuel Black and those other fossilised corporation officials who had never before seen the citizens of Belfast when they were really in earnest.

The campaign failed and meanwhile the Falls Road Depot was extended to house all the new electric cars. A short section of the Falls Road near to the Depot was used for making trial runs and to instruct drivers how to operate the new electrical cars. Towards the end of 1905 the conversion to electric traction was complete and on Tuesday 5 December the new system was opened formally, as the *Northern Whig* reported next day:

Horse-Traction died last night in the city, having lagged superfluously on the scene for the past five years. . . the avidity with which the public greeted the new service proved how tired they were of the mid-Victorian methods to which, by the timidity and wrong-headedness of the Corporation of 1893, they were condemned.

A standard four-wheel, open-top car, No.66, was magnificently decorated and illuminated, and carried passengers for 6d each along all the routes, which began normal operations the following day. Electrification of 40 miles of track had cost £617,620 and, by January 1906, 233 new electric cars and 50 converted horse tramcars were in service. The longest penny stage was on the north side to the Cliftonville Garden Village and on the south side to the housing estate at Marlborough Park being developed by H. & J. Martin. The number of passenger trips increased from just over 30 million in 1905 to almost 43 million in 1906.

Nance built the Queen's Road tramway to the shipyards on Queen's Island; 80 tramcars ran every work day before 8 a.m. and between 5 and 7 p.m. to provide a service for the 14,000 Islandmen. While this new service was a striking success, another of Nance's projects was a signal failure. The Corporation acquired the Cavehill and Whitewell Tramway for £56,000 in 1911; 38 acres of woodland two miles north of the Chichester Park end of the line, assets of the company when purchased, were developed into a recreation ground for the city. Nance believed that the project would pay for itself and provide additional revenue for the Corporation tramways. Instead, the promenade and zoological gardens at 'Bellevue' (as Nance named it) cost over £30,000 to build in 1912 because it was necessary to shore up the unstable slopes with great buttresses of concrete. In addition, the foot of the Cave Hill was not a suitable place for a zoo and only the polar bears and penguins seem to have appreciated constant exposure to northerly and easterly winds. The over-ambitious Bellevue scheme was largely responsible for converting the tramways profit of £23,871 to a loss of £6,129; at a later date, however, a recreation project of this kind would have been considered money well spent.

'Dublin must look to its laurels'

> Gallants, this Thursday night will be our last,
> Then without fail we pack up for Belfast.

So cried Swift's strolling players, indicating how early the town became an essential haven for touring companies. The Imperial Colosseum Music Hall was built in Victoria Square in the 1860s; renamed Traver's Musical Lounge, then the Buffalo, and finally (completely refurbished in plush and gilt) the Empire, it became the city's most popular theatre for variety shows and melodramas. There Little Tich, Gertie Gitana, Marie Lloyd and – it is said – Charlie Chaplin performed before rapturous audiences, and at the Alexandra Theatre, on the corner of Durham Street and the Grosvenor Road, patrons gathered to hiss the villain in such melodramas as *Maria Marten, or The Murder in the Red Barn*. In December 1895 Belfast acquired a splendid theatre to match its new status as Ireland's largest city: the Grand Opera House was thus described by the *Northern Whig*:

The Glengall Street front has an imposing central façade, flanked with square towers, crowned with boldly moulded and domed minarets, the centre portion having a richly designed pediment finished at the top with a carved finial, from which an ornamental iron flambeau will cast a brilliant light at night, illuminating this and the adjoining street.

Frank Matcham's lavish interior, the *Belfast News-Letter* observed, created 'a most brilliant and charming Eastern effect'. The Grand Opera House opened with the pantomime 'Blue Beard'; perhaps feeling the effect of competition from the neighbouring Hippodrome theatre, it lowered its prices and became the Palace of Varieties between 1904 and 1909. Thereafter it became the Grand Opera House once more and attracted to its stage such celebrated performers as Sarah Bernhardt, Beerbohm Tree, and Forbes Robinson.

'Damn Yeats, we'll write our own plays!' Bulmer Hobson declared as he returned to Belfast after a visit to Dublin's Abbey Theatre. He and other Protestant intellectuals swept up by the Gaelic cultural revival were not

(Ulster Museum)

satisfied that the city should merely be the host to the best touring companies. They set up the Ulster Literary Theatre and its associated publication, *Ulad*, in 1904 and though the group had to swim hard against the prevailing anti-Home Rule tide it did more than any other to encourage indigenous creative talent. Struggling in almost constant penury, and never possessing a permanent home, the Ulster Literary Theatre was nevertheless the nursery of several accomplished actor-playwrights; when *The Drone* by Rutherford Mayne was staged in the Abbey in 1908, the *Irish Times* critic remarked: 'Dublin must look to its laurels, for in art, as in everything else, when Ulster makes up its mind to try, the rest of Ireland is hard put to beat it.' Gerald Macnamara's one act fantasy, *Thompson in Tir na nOg*, had its premier at the Grand Opera House in December 1912; Mayne recalled that the manager 'asked us not to let off too strongly in "Thompson" because he had been informed that there were certain men up there who had been told that this play made fun of a certain Order, and that they were all lined up with rivets and bolts in their pockets'. He need not have worried; the play was an instant success. George Shiels had his first play performed by the Ulster Literary Theatre though it was in the Abbey that he was to make his name. Helen Waddell's *The Spoiled Buddha* (1915) was a box-office flop, but she persevered as a writer and achieved distinction as a medievalist.

Forrest Reid contributed to *Ulad*, though cultural nationalism had no meaning for him. Brought up in 20 Mountcharles in the late 1870s and the 1880s, he never left Belfast for long, and from 1924 until his death in 1947 he lived at 13 Ormiston Crescent. This was Reid's Belfast – the comfortable suburbs so vividly evoked in his novels. A brief spell as a clerk with Musgrave & Co. left him with a fastidious distaste for commerce: the industrial heart of Belfast was to him dark and frightening and he felt no affinity with those who toiled with their hands in the city. His life-long obsession was the ecstasy and agony of youth, a theme most skilfully worked in *Following Darkness*, published in 1912 but rewritten and improved as *Peter Waring* in 1937. E.M. Forster described his Tom Barber trilogy as 'a unique chronicle of youth' and indeed, Forrest Reid was the first novelist from Belfast to win widespread recognition. So absorbed was he by what he himself described as 'some mysterious form of arrested development' that his novels give no indication of the sectarian bitterness and political turmoil of his time.

'A commercial cockpit'

On a visit to his native city in 1910 the businessman Sam Allen wrote that Belfast 'looks more Belfasty than ever. What an unattractive place it is!' The *Daily Mail* commented in July 1903 that Belfast was 'a commercial cockpit where sordid little struggles are continuously in process' and the painter Jack Yeats asserted that the religion of the city was that 'the man who sells his cow too cheap goes to hell'. Belfast – a parvenu by Dublin's standards – was bound, as a brash industrial city, to attract such uncomplimentary references. It is worth noting, besides, that the Yeats family of Sligo generally travelled to Belfast rather than to Dublin to lay in supplies of items which only a great city could provide, and it was in Belfast that Mr Allingham of Sligo had set up his five 'Hustler Shoe Stores' to sell cheap American boots.

The departure of propertied classes to live in the new suburbs left commerce in full control of the city centre. Belfast before the Great War had five large departmental stores, four of them built by local businessmen, two of which had branches in Britain – Robinson & Cleavers had three shops in London and one in Liverpool, and Anderson & McAuleys had branches in Brighton and Bournemouth. The enormous premises of the Belfast Co-operative Society in York Street were built in sections just before 1914. Chain-stores included not only 14 branches of the Co-op but also Tyler's 12 shoe shops, Duffin's 7 menswear shops, 6 Home & Colonial stores, and 4 shops owned by Thomas Lipton – the grocer who scandalised the Court by becoming a close personal friend of Edward VII. British firms found it profitable to set up in Belfast: they included Thorntons the waterproofs specialists; Lizars, opticians; Sawers, purveyors of high quality fish, meat and poultry; and two frozen meat retailers – James Nelson & Sons, with 18 branches, and the River Plate Company, with 12 branches. David Allen began his advertising business in Belfast, but his branch in London soon outgrew its parent. Messrs Cantrell & Cochrane sank artesian wells in Belfast to obtain pure crystal water for the manufacture of their aerated waters which sold all over the world. Sybil Gribbon, in her delightful survey of Belfast in 1911, found this 'irresistible gem' amongst the papers of the company:

The popping of Cantrell and Cochrane's corks is heard in the bungalows of the British cantonment in the great dependency in the Far East, and its sparkle is familiar to the Vice-Regal entourage up in the hot season refuge of the Anglo-Indians at Simla. Dons and seignorinas quaff this liquid boon in the tropical climes of South America; the West Indies welcome it as a treasure: Afric's 'sunny fountains' are out-rivalled in their very habitat by its gleam; the Antipodes have taken this gift of the Mother Empire with gratitude.*

There were new monuments to the sacred and the profane. When the Presbyterian congregation of the Fisherwick Church moved to a new building on the Malone Road, a new Church House and Assembly Hall were put up on the old site; the present building's exterior has been restored since it was gutted by a bomb in the mid-1970s. St Anne's Cathedral took more than 80 years to complete; on 9 October 1896 the Archbishop of Canterbury launched an appeal in the Ulster Hall for funds for a new cathedral and the fine old parish church was eventually demolished to make way for an uninspiring Gothic structure designed in the first place by Thomas Drew, son of the celebrated controversialist of Christ Church. In all, seven architects were called in before the Cathedral was finished.

It looked as if the churches, together with the business firms of Belfast, were following Napoleon's guiding principle in architecture: 'Whatever is big is beautiful.' Certainly the Technical College is one of the worst examples of architectural bad taste from this time; it was built on land which the Academical Institution was forced by debt to sell and it is difficult to disagree with Charles Brett's conclusion that 'it is the largest and most ornate cuckoo's egg ever laid in a songbird's nest'. Belfast had – until the bombing campaign of the 1970s – a fine collection of Victorian and Edwardian public houses: the best of these were the 'Morning Star' in Pottinger's Entry; the 'Beehive' on the Falls Road; the 'Elephant Bar' in Upper North Street; the 'Crown Bar' in Great Victoria Street; and the 'Stone Bar' in Church Lane, completed in 1905 – all but the last are still open today though they have been much altered. The very opulence of the Crown gin palace, built about 1885 by Patrick Flanagan of Banbridge, ensured that if the citizens of Belfast were going to sin they would sin in style; though, in the 1970s, its stained glass was shattered piece by piece

(From *The Industries of Ireland*)

* Sybil Gribbon, 'An Irish City: Belfast 1911', in Harkness and O'Dowd, *The Town in Ireland* (see bibliog), p. 208.

by successive blasts generally from the direction of the Europa hotel opposite, its interior was meticulously refurbished in 1981 by its present owners, the National Trust, in collaboration with Bass Ireland.

It was in the Edwardian period that Donegall Square was extensively rebuilt to become the hub of a great modern city. In 1902 the massive sandstone bulk of the Scottish Provident Institution was completed and the following year the Northern Bank was erected beside it in Donegall Square West; the Ocean Buildings consorted uneasily with remaining Georgian houses from 1902 in Donegall Square East; and the Scottish Temperance Buildings, complete with intriguing sculptures on the facade, were built in Donegall Square South in 1904. None of these buildings had great architectural merit. Oscar Wilde, in a lecture given in Belfast on New Year's Day 1884, said that Belfast did have 'one beautiful building. . . beautiful in colour, and very beautiful in design': this was Messrs Richardson Sons & Owden's linen warehouse at 1 Donegall Square North, designed by W.H. Lynn. The warehouse later became the headquarters of the Belfast Water Commissioners; the 'Water Office' lost its handsome chateau roof during the 1941 Blitz and it will undergo further alterations as the newly-acquired property of Marks & Spencer. Donegall Square was also given its centre-piece in this period – the City Hall.

The City Hall – water supply – public health

In 1871 the Corporation had built a fine red-brick Town Hall in Victoria Street but from its opening it was considered by many not sufficiently grand; as the *Irish Builder* observed the following year: 'The townspeople protested that it was not a public building not having a parapet.' When Belfast became a city in 1888, negotiations were made with the Countess of Shaftesbury for the site of the White Linen Hall, which had outlived its original purpose, and demolition began in 1896. The winner of the competition to select the design of the city's new administrative centre was the young London architect, Alfred Brumwell Thomas. Built by McLaughlin & Harvey, the City Hall cost £360,000, twice the original estimate; in part this was due to the insistence of labour and nationalist councillors that Corporation labourers – paid on average 3s a week above the going rate – be employed, and in part to the city fathers' determination that no expense be spared to proclaim Belfast's importance. Appalled by the building's expense, the Local Government Board at Dublin Castle ordered a special inquiry and the inspector, on being told that the foundation stone cost £500, asked sarcastically: 'It is a precious stone, I suppose?'

A great rectangle of Portland stone enclosing a central courtyard, with a dome 173 feet high, the City Hall certainly looks impressive and it is only in recent years that towering office blocks nearby have detracted from the effect it was designed to produce.

In retrospect, the greatest achievement of the Corporation in these years was not the erection of the City Hall but the provision of adequate supplies of pure water. From 1795 an elected committee of the Charitable Society, the 'Spring Water Commissioners', piped water from springs at Fountainville (in particular from the 'Bellows Spring' on the Lisburn Road opposite Wilmont Terrace) and later from a source in what is now Deramore Park. The water, piped through Stranmillis and the Botanic Gardens, was paid for by a rate which the 1800 Police Act empowered the Commissioners to levy. In 1840 these powers were transferred to the Belfast Water Commissioners (elected by those who paid the water rate), who began by building a reservoir at Carr's Glen. In 1865 all the reservoirs ran dry and the tap water turned green with algae; one glass was said to contain tens of thousands of insects, some of them an inch long. In the same year, just before the drought, the Commissioners obtained powers to build new reservoirs near Carrickfergus and in 1884 at Leathemstown and Stoneyford near Glenavy. The 'dams' at Woodburn, Lough Mourne, Stoneyford and Leathemstown were later to be highly prized by the city's trout anglers. By 1890, however, the city was using 9½ million gallons a day, twice the quantity used ten years earlier. It was in the Mourne Mountains that an adequate supply of water was found and in 1893 Parliament gave the Commissioners the right to the 9,000 acres of catchment area. In 1901 the first water from the Mournes – so pure that filtering was not needed – flowed by gravity alone through forty miles of pipe to Belfast. It was to take another thirty years before the great holding reservoir in the Silent Valley was completed.

The Corporation's record in improving public health was so strenuously questioned by opposition councillors that a Vice-Regal Commission was appointed in 1906 to make a full investigation. The Commission reported that the annual death rate from tuberculosis was more than double that of England and Wales, and worse than that of Dublin; that the death rate from typhoid was the worst in the United Kingdom; and that the sanitary state of much of Belfast was very poor as a 'result of inefficient sanitary administration extending over many years'. The overall death rate for the city, however, was no higher than in Manchester or Liverpool, and lower than in Dublin. Immediate action by the Corporation's Health Committee greatly reduced the deaths from typhoid; Purdysburn Fever Hospital, financed by the Corporation, opened in 1906 and five years later its medical superintendent reported that typhoid had almost been eliminated. The same vigour was not shown in combatting the scourge of tuberculosis.

Since its foundation in 1817 the General Hospital in Frederick Street had been outside the control of the Corporation; the strain caused by the epidemics of the famine years caused it to close temporarily for lack of funds in 1854; donations by the millowners, S.K. Mulholland and John Charters, paid for two additional wings in 1865; and in 1875 the hospital became by royal charter the Belfast Royal Hospital. In 1899 another charter renamed it the Royal Victoria Hospital and, guided by Lady Pirrie, a committee raised funds to build a more modern hospital on a site given by the Corporation on the Grosvenor Road. Opened by Edward VII in 1903, the Royal Victoria Hospital won praise for its modern system of ventilation (as was only proper since Davidsons and Harland & Wolff were world leaders in this field): powerful fans, each capable of drawing 10 million cubic feet of air per hour, drove air – washed through wet curtains of coarse rope and heated by steam pipes – to every ward without creating draughts. The Mater Infirmorum Hospital, set up by Bishop Dorrian in 1883, began in Bedeque House on the Crumlin Road; under the care of the Sisters of Mercy its prospectus declared:

This institution is established for the relief of the sick and dying poor, without distinction of creed and is supported by voluntary contributions. Aid is denied to no one, so far as the funds of the Institution allow. Sickness and destitution will ever be the only necessary passport to the Wards.

At first only 28 patients could be kept in the wards and in 1893 an appeal was launched to build an entirely new hospital nearby. It was opened by Sir Robert J. McConnell, the Lord Mayor, on 23 April 1900.

Voluntary effort and public enterprise had eradicated the most scandalous consequences of neglect and eased the growing pains of a burgeoning city. Certainly there were pockets of misery and deprivation remaining, but conditions of living were roughly comparable to those prevailing in the cities of similar size across the Irish Sea, and were much better than those in Dublin – heart-rendingly revealed there by the 1913 Lock Out and the government reports of 1914. The ability to maintain good living standards – adversely affected though they were by inflation – depended ultimately on the success of Belfast's commerce and industry, and on shipbuilding in particular.

'The wee yard'

> Terrible as an army with banners
> Through the dusk of a winter's eve,
> Over the bridge
> The thousands tramp. . .

Imposing though the sight was, the thousands crossing the Queen's Bridge twice a day made up only part of the army of men building ships in Belfast. By 1900 Workman Clark & Company had extended its yard on the north side of the river and, together with its yard on the south side and the Abercorn Engine Works, had ten building berths and two engine works. The affectionate term, 'the wee yard', had become singularly inappropriate for a shipbuilding business whose output that year was the sixth largest in the United Kingdom and whose reputation for excellence of design and quality of workmanship had become worldwide.

Charles E. Allen, son of the senior partner of the Allen Line, had been appointed engineering director of Workman Clark in 1891 and he did much to put the firm in the forefront of shipbuilding innovation. The launch of the 10,635-ton *Victorian* for the Allen Line in 1904 was an important moment in maritime history; the first turbine liner on the North Atlantic run, she proved the worth of high-pressure turbines for shipping. Workman Clark became renowned for specialist ships, refrigerated vessels in particular. The Houlder Company ordered a series of vessels for carrying frozen beef from South America to Britain; they included the *Urmston Grange* and the *Rippingham Grange*, completed by 1898 in time for use as troopships in the Boer War; and the *Drayton Grange* and *Oswestry Grange* in 1902, which also carried frozen meat from Australasia. The Shaw Savill & Albion Company ordered ships to carry frozen New Zealand mutton by the new route through the Panama Canal; the first was the *Matatua* in 1901, and the *Waimana*, completed in November 1911, was considered one of the world's finest refrigerated vessels. Workman Clark was a leading builder of fruit carriers; most of these vessels were for the United Fruit Company of Boston but two of the largest were the *Patuca* and *Patia*, launched just before the First World War, ordered by Elders & Fyffes for their West Indies banana trade. The Lamport & Holt Line had most of their combined passenger and cargo ships built by the 'wee yard', including the *Vandyck* (1911), the *Vauban* (1912) and the *Vestris* (1912) – high quality liners for the New York-River Plate run.

1909 was a particularly bad year for ship building and yet by the end of it

Islandmen pour out of Harland & Wolff at the end of the working day. The building (left, centre) is the firm's rather modest head office. In the background huge gantries stand over slip No. 2, from which the *Olympic* has just been launched, and slip No. 3, where the *Titanic* nears completion. (Welch Collection: Ulster Museum)

Workman Clark had launched 16 ships totalling over 88,000 tons. The following year the Clyde had to be specially dredged to take the *Aeneas*, the first of a trio of ships over 10,000 tons made for the Holt 'Blue Funnel' Line. The largest ship to leave the 'wee yard's' slips before the war was the *Ulysses*, over 14,000 tons gross and costing £250,000, built for the 'Blue Funnel's' Australian service. For all Workman Clark's achievement, however, the firm seemed but a pygmy compared with the giant of Harland & Wolff.

> . . . Splendid ships they build,
> More splendid far
> The hearts that dare conceive
> Such vastness and such power.
>
> Terrible as an army with banners,
> The legions of labour,
> The builders of ships,
> Tramp thro' the winter's eve.
>
> *from 'The Islandmen' by Richard Rowley*

173

'Gazing with undisguised awe at the leviathian': the *Olympic*

From the late autumn of 1908 a huge gantry, 228 feet above the slips, dominated the skyline of east Belfast; here Harland & Wolff prepared to build two immense ships on a scale never yet witnessed. The year before, Cunard had put into service the *Lusitania* and *Mauretania*, the largest and fastest vessels afloat, and now the White Star Line called on Belfast to provide the riposte to its rivals. Work began on the first ship, the *Olympic*, on 16 December 1608; by mid-February 1909 the flat keel and vertical keel plate were in position; and by April, the erection and riveting of the double bottom floors were well advanced. From the top of the gantry – where the city appeared to be spread out like a map below – huge cranes lifted tons of steel and carefully manoeuvred the frames into place. The after-end framing began in July and on 20 November the last frame was raised.

Now the central cantilever crane, the ten walking cranes, and twelve travelling cranes began to hoist the plates. Thousands of men crawled like ants over the skeleton; portable furnaces blazed all over the gantry; shipwrights, with the hottest and most dangerous job in the yard, wielded their hydraulic machines and drove three million rivets into the plates, filling the spaces between the rib frames. By the time the shell plating was finished in April 1910 the framing of the sister ship *Titanic* had risen up in the adjoining berth. That summer after the decks had been constructed, the joiners were fitting oak beams into the *Olympic*'s main dining saloon; on her sides men dangled, painting the keel in preparation for the launch on Thursday 20 October 1910. 'All roads led to the river front,' the *Belfast News-Letter* reported in its account of the launch next morning:

Queen's Road was thronged at an early hour with vehicular and pedestrian traffic, and when the yard was reached a good hour prior to the launch, admiring crowds were gazing with undisguised awe at the leviathan which reared her gigantic hull far above their heads. Underneath the bottom hundreds of workmen were busily engaged knocking away the props which served to support the ship. . . The men worked heartily; they 'chanted' and encouraged each other to fresh exertions as they swept away almost like dust the last barriers between the purely constructive work and the real mission of the graceful vessel which for almost two years had grown under their hands, plate by plate, deck after deck, until at length she Babel-like looked down with majesty upon her contemporaries. She was not built to fail; a higher destiny awaits her.

Lord Aberdeen, the Viceroy, and Lady Aberdeen had travelled up from Dublin by special train the previous morning and were joined by leading members of the Irish aristocracy, Miss Asquith, the Prime Minister's daughter, and J. Bruce Ismay of the White Star Line. White Star launching ceremonies were always simple in Belfast – no champagne was dashed against the sides and no christening took place:

Her nuptials were celebrated under conditions which the fairest bride might envy. . . At ten minutes to 11 o'clock two explosive rockets were fired and precisely at the hour fixed for the ship's departure another signal of a similar character heralded the great event. From the reserved stand Lord Pirrie cried 'Now'; the hydraulic pressure was released by Mr Charles Payne, and in the fractional part of a moment the huge mass was on its way, attaining a maximum speed of twelve and a half knots at one period. It was exactly 62 seconds from the first movement of the ship until she was wholly in the

THE WORLD'S BIGGEST SHIP.

The *Belfast News-Letter*
heralds the *Olympic*, launched
20 October 1910.
(Linen Hall Library)

water and about another 45 seconds sufficed to pull her up almost within her own
length. . . The north side of the river, the quays, and sheds were crowded with dense
masses of people who cheered themselves hoarse as the great event was consummated.

Once launched, the *Olympic* was moored at the new deep-water wharf to be
made ready for her maiden voyage. As before, the Harbour Commissioners
had anticipated development: after touring the principal British ports in 1900,
they obtained extensive new powers under the Belfast Harbour Act 1901 to
keep the port of Belfast to the fore; the Musgrave Channel, begun in 1899,
was completed in 1903; and in 1911 the Victoria Channel was deepened and
the Thompson graving dock completed just in time to receive the *Olympic*.
Late in 1910 and early in 1911 Harland & Wolff's 200-ton floating crane –
one of the largest in existence – hoisted the propelling machinery on board the
Olympic. On 1 April 1911 the great vessel slid into the Thompson dock – 886
feet long and 100 feet wide, it was the largest graving dock in the world.
Carpenters, decorators, and upholsterers put the finishing touches to the ship,
which for the first-class passengers was to be the last word in luxury – indeed,
luxury was put before speed for, as *The Shipbuilder* explained:

. . . high speed is a very costly requirement, not only owing to the great initial cost of
the propelling machinery and the heavy cost of fuel on service, but also on account of
the necessary fineness of the ship, which limits the earning power as regards cargo-
carrying and the extent of passenger accommodation.

First-class passengers could make use of the gymnasium, the squash court,
Turkish and electric baths, and electric lifts, all in the most opulent surroundings. On 31 May 1911 fitting-out was complete and the *Olympic*
steamed out of Belfast Lough: powered by two four-cylinder triple-expansion
engines combined with a low-pressure turbine, totalling 46,000 indicated
horse power, and 45,324 gross tons, she exceeded by more than 13,000 tons
her nearest rival the *Mauretania* and was by far the biggest ship ever launched.
It had been a remarkable achievement for Harland & Wolff, for at the same
time the firm had been completing two large White Star tenders; the *Maloja*,
shortly to be P & O's largest liner; the *Demosthenes* for the Aberdeen Line; the
Galway Castle for the Union-Castle Line; and sister ship to the *Olympic* – the
Titanic.

175

The *Titanic*, escorted by the Harland & Wolff tug *Herculaneum*, on her sea trials in Belfast Lough just before delivery to the White Star Line. There are few surviving photographs of this doomed liner. (Welch Collection: Ulster Museum)

The loss of the *Titanic*: 15 April 1912

A few hours before the *Olympic* left Belfast for the White Star's new 16-acre dock at Southampton, the *Titanic* had been launched. Though the great American financier, J. Pierpoint Morgan, had travelled specially from London for the event, Harland & Wolff had not even bothered to paint the *Titanic*'s hull white for the launch. The *Shipbuilder* published a special issue in the summer of 1911 to celebrate the building of these White Star giants; the few pages describing the *Titanic* seem to have been added as an afterthought, though she was 1,000 gross tons heavier than her sister. The departure of the *Titanic* for Southampton on 2 April 1912 merited brief, though fulsome, comment in the local newspapers. That day the *Belfast News-Letter* reported:

The new White Star liner Titanic, the largest vessel in the world, has now been completed. . . and at eleven o'clock this morning she will leave Belfast for Southampton. . . the decorations and equipment are on a scale of unprecedented magnificence and it is difficult to realise when standing in some of the spacious saloons or staterooms that one is really on board a ship and not in a large modern hotel. Special interest was manifested in the suite rooms for millionaires and other wealthy passengers. . .

On 10 April 1912 the *Titanic* left Southampton, called at Cherbourg and Queenstown (Cobh), and steamed across the Atlantic by the recognised northerly route. At 11.40 p.m. on 14 April she struck a huge iceberg a glancing blow, tearing a 300-foot gash in her hull and damaging five compartments; at 2.20 a.m. on 15 April the *Titanic* sank. As the *Belfast News-Letter* informed its readers on 17 April, 'her loss constitutes the most appalling shipping disaster in the history of the world'. Only 711 out of 2,201 passengers and crew were saved. The British inquiry, which began on 2 May, had some hard things to say: the *Titanic* had only 20 lifeboats and there had been no proper boat drill or boat muster; some boats had not been filled to capacity; the electronically operated double-cylinder watertight doors had not been enough to prevent water spilling over into other compartments; and not enough had been done to save the lives of third-class passengers – all first- and second-class children had been saved, but only 27 out of 79 third-class children survived, even though the lives of a third of the first-class adult male passengers had been saved.

It had not been Harland & Wolff but the *Shipbuilder* which claimed that the *Titanic* was 'virtually unsinkable'. Now a shadow had been cast over the reputation of Belfast and, in particular, over that of the White Star Line, Harland & Wolff's most valuable customer. It was not until after the First World War, however, that White Star's difficulties would affect the economy of Belfast. Meanwhile, for the Protestants of the city, there was another dark cloud on the horizon.

Defiance at Strandtown

On the very day people in Belfast were reading the first terrible details of the loss of the *Titanic,* the first important vote on the Third Irish Home Rule Bill had been taken amidst angry scenes in the House of Commons. It was a moment long awaited by the Nationalists of the Irish Party and long feared by the Unionists.

The Ulster opponents of Home Rule had been preparing for just such a crisis. Back in 1904 a group of southern unionists had proposed a very limited form of devolution; a group of Ulster MPs – horrified at this 'attempt to grant Home Rule on the sly' – decided 'to revive on a war footing for active work the various Ulster defence associations' and formed the Ulster Unionist Council on 30 March 1905. The Council, representing all loyalist groups in the north, banished the last remaining differences between Liberals and Conservatives in Ulster. The nucleus of the future Ulster Unionist Party, the Council would be on the point of rebellion in 1914, and the very heart of this resistance would be Belfast.

In 1906 the Liberals swept the Conservatives & Unionists out of office; with a huge majority they did not need the support of the Irish Party and though the new government was committed to Home Rule it was not high on the list of priorities. By 1910 the position in Westminster had changed dramatically: the Conservative majority in the House of Lords had repeatedly blocked Bills passed by large majorities in the Commons and had rejected Lloyd George's 'People's Budget' in 1909; it took two general elections in 1910 to force the Lords to capitulate. In 1911 the Parliament Act severely curbed the Lords' powers – from now on the Lords could only delay Bills from the Commons for a maximum of two years. Throughout this crisis the Irish Party had voted with the Liberals and since the elections of 1910 the Liberal Party and the

Conservative Party had been evenly matched in the Commons. Asquith's Liberal government could only stay in power with Nationalist support. Another Home Rule Bill was a certainty.

On 23 June 1911, 50,000 men from the Orange Lodges and Unionist Clubs assembled in the spacious gardens of 'Craigavon', the home of Captain James Craig in Strandtown. There, in east Belfast, they had come to meet their new leader, Sir Edward Carson. The cheering and singing crowd fell silent as Carson rose to speak:

With the help of God you and I joined together. . . will yet defeat the most nefarious conspiracy that has ever been hatched against a free people. . . We must be prepared the morning Home Rule passes, ourselves to become responsible for the government of the Protestant Province of Ulster.

The years remaining before the Great War were to show that Carson and his audience were in earnest. Carson was one of the most brilliant barristers of his day and had served in the previous Conservative government. A Dubliner, he was to earn the devoted support of the Protestants of Belfast; if in private he was moody and uncertain, in public his tall frame commanded respect and the grim set of his lower jaw seemed to show that he would be unyielding in his defence of the Union.

'James Craig did all the work and I got all the credit,' Carson once said with some justice. Son of a wealthy partner in Dunville's distilleries, Craig was no orator but he was the indispensable organising genius of the massive displays of loyalist solidarity. Carson led the Ulster Unionists because he wanted to maintain the Union for all of Ireland. Craig on the other hand was more realistic in seeking to maintain the Union for the sake of Ulster. For the moment their talents complemented each other and together they worked steadfastly to oppose Home Rule.

Churchill in Celtic Park

'We must not attach too much importance to these frothings of Sir Edward Carson,' Winston Churchill said in October 1911; 'I daresay when the worst comes to the worst we shall find that civil war evaporates in uncivil words.' A short time later Churchill learned something of the violent determination of Unionist feeling. He arrived in Belfast in February 1912 to be greeted by huge hostile crowds singing 'God Save the King' and jostling against his motor car. Denied the use of the Ulster Hall where a quarter of a century before his father had warned that Home Rule could come upon them 'as a thief in the night', Churchill was forced to speak in Celtic Park; there he addressed a disappointingly small Home Rule audience in a rain-sodden marquee. He left soon afterwards for the docks by a circuitous route and Unionist wits were not slow to say that he had left Belfast like a thief in the night.

Liberals and Nationalists not familiar with the north tended to regard the campaign against Home Rule as a 'gigantic game of bluff and blackmail', as John Redmond, the Irish Party leader, described it. Was it not true that only 17 out of 33 Ulster MPs were Unionist? Yet this was no last-ditch stand by the Ascendancy, though aristocrats were prominent in the movement. Belfast businessmen were at the core of the campaign and Protestant workers of Belfast were its most devoted adherents. Belfast was at the very heart of the argument against Home Rule – Belfast had thrived under the Union and it was from the Empire that it imported its fuel and raw materials and to the Empire that it sold its manufactured goods. Would not a Dublin parliament impose hurtful tariffs and try to take Ireland out of the Empire? Even when Lord Pirrie himself declared his support for Home Rule, his employees on the Queen's Island remained as fervent as ever in opposition to any attempt to tamper with the Union.

Religious antagonism was especially strong at a time when the Catholic Church was in the middle of a revival similar in character to the Protestant Revival of 1859. In 1908 the 'Ne Temere' decree promulgated by the Pope declared that marriages between Catholics and Protestants were null and void unless they had taken place in a Catholic church; in 1910 Belfast Protestants had been scandalised when Alexander McCann – encouraged by his priest, it was said – had left his Protestant wife and had taken his children with him; and in March 1912 the *Catholic Bulletin* declared that the 'time for action has arrived. . . To bring into the bosom of Holy Church the million of our separated brethren is a most attractive programme' – just what northern Protestants most feared in a Home Rule Ireland.

The danger of outright sectarian warfare in the city loomed large. Only by a series of massive displays of loyalist solidarity, the Ulster Unionist Council believed, could British sympathy be won and violence be avoided.

Covenant Day: 28 September 1912

> What answer from the North?
> One law, one Land, one Throne,
> If England drive us forth
> We shall not fall alone.

Kipling spoke true: the champions of Empire were rallying to Protestant Ulster, and on Easter Tuesday 1912 Andrew Bonar Law, the Conservative leader, was given a magnificent reception in Belfast. More than 100,000 marched past his platform at Balmoral in south Belfast; as a resolution against Home Rule was passed, the largest Union Jack ever woven was unfurled from a 90-foot flagstaff. Bonar Law assured his audience:

Once more you hold the pass, the pass for the Empire. . . The Government have erected by their Parliament Act a boom against you to shut you off from the help of the British people. You will burst that boom.

Later, in July, he committed his party to unconstitutional action when he said: 'I can imagine no length of resistance to which Ulster can go in which I shall not be prepared to support them.' Embittered by their humiliating defeats at the hands of the Liberals and divided on many issues, the Conservatives were at least united in their defence of the Empire. They threw themselves into a series of great public meetings which began in Enniskillen on 18 September 1912 and reached Belfast for the climax of the campaign on 28 September – Covenant Day.

That day the shipyards, mills and engineering works of Belfast were deserted and silent. In the morning, religious services were held in Protestant churches throughout the city. At the service attended by Carson the Presbyterian minister declared:

Sir Edward Carson.
(Radio Times Hulton Picture Library)

Ulster Day, 28 September 1912: thousands gather in Donegall Square, Donegall Place, and Royal Avenue to sign the Covenant, some in their own blood, in the City Hall from which this photograph was taken. (Radio Times Hulton Picture Library)

The Irish question is at bottom a war against Protestantism. It is an attempt to establish a Roman Catholic ascendancy in Ireland to begin the disintegration of the Empire by securing a second Parliament in Dublin. . . We are plain blunt men. We will not have Home Rule.

At midday the Ulster Unionist leaders made their way to the City Hall to sign the 'Solemn League and Covenant', to pledge themselves 'to stand by one another in defending for ourselves and our children our cherished position of equal citizenship in the United Kingdom and in using all means which may be found necessary to defeat the present conspiracy to set up a Home Rule Parliament in Ireland'. Carson was the first to sign.

When the leaders reappeared, the vast throng waiting in Donegall Square, Donegall Place, and down Royal Avenue as far as the eye could see, sang the National Anthem. Then the men were admitted to the City Hall to sign the Covenant; a half a mile of desks had been laid out to receive them, and 160 signed every minute. Some signed with their own blood. All over Ulster men were signing the Covenant and women separately signed their own declaration. Altogether 471,414 signed.

At the end of the day, Carson's carriage was drawn by supporters to the docks, where shipyard workers formed a guard of honour. There with what

180

little voice he had left, Carson assured the cheering crowds that 'If it be to fight I do not shrink!' and finished with the exhortation: 'Keep the old flag flying and No Surrender!' Captain Paisley welcomed him aboard the *Patriotic*, and as the ship put out to sea the bands played 'Come Back to Erin', fifty bonfires blazed on the hills and headlands surrounding Belfast Lough, searchlights scanned the water and salvoes of rockets leaped to the sky.

'The intensity of feeling was tremendous,' the *Belfast News-Letter* commented, 'but there was ever present a sense of individual responsibility swaying the people, bringing order and amenability out of what might otherwise have been chaos.' The Catholic and Nationalist minority in Belfast, too, had behaved with responsibility that day. A journalist with Home Rule sympathies, J.L. Garvin, no longer believed that this was a game of bluff and blackmail: '... no-one for a moment could have mistaken the concentrated will and courage of those people. They do not know what fear and flinching mean in this business, and they are not going to know.'

'I am off to Belfast. . . I go to my people'

Demonstrations alone could not stop Home Rule. Amid cries of 'Traitor!' and 'Resign!', and the rhythmical chanting of 'Civil war, civil war', Churchill attempted to steer the Home Rule Bill through the Commons. Before the end of 1912 the Bill passed through all its stages in the Commons and in January it went up to the Lords; there the hereditary peers rejected it by an overwhelming majority. But the power of the Lords had been curbed and the Bill was certain to become law before the end of 1914. Only unconstitutional action could stop Home Rule now. Guns were about to reappear in the streets of Belfast.

Throughout the final months of 1912 loyalists had been drilling all over Ulster. In January 1913 the Ulster Unionist Council united these paramilitary groups into one body, limited to 100,000 men who had signed the Covenant – the Ulster Volunteer Force. Recommended by Lord Roberts of Kandahar, General Sir George Richardson – who had led the British force during the Boxer Rising in China – was appointed commander. Richardson set up his headquarters in the Old Town Hall in Victoria Street and there he made meticulous arrangements to resist the introduction of Home Rule by force. Throughout 1913 the UVF grew rapidly and paraded openly; its commander divided the force into county divisions, regiments and battalions, and stockpiled food in case Ulster was blockaded by the Royal Navy. Meanwhile Carson and Craig made arrangements to make the City Hall the centre of a provisional government of 77 men; £1 million was pledged by loyalists to pay dependents if it came ot a fight.

At Westminster, in June 1912, T.G. Agar-Robartes had proposed the partition of Ireland as a compromise; 'I have never heard that Orange bitters will mix with Irish whiskey', he had said. Then, he had been howled down; now, early in 1914, the Liberals seriously considered the proposal and even persuaded Redmond to consider the idea of a temporary exclusion of Ulster counties for six years. 'We do not want sentence of death with a stay of execution for six years,' Carson told the Commons, 'I am off to Belfast.' At Euston less than an hour later he told reporters: 'I go to my people.'

Was Carson about to set up a provisional government in Belfast? Churchill – now First Lord of the Admiralty – ordered two light cruisers from Bantry Bay to Belfast Lough; seven battleships from the 3rd Battle Squadron off Spain to

A NATION OF FIRE-EATERS.
Peaceful Teuton. 'Himmel! They have all those armies! And the Fatherland has only one!' (*Punch*)

the Clyde; and eight destroyers from the Home Fleet at Plymouth to the same destination. Troops at the Curragh of Kildare were ordered north. Protestant Belfast prepared for a show-down; £20,000 had been set aside to form from the Belfast Volunteers a Special Service Force and by March 1914 a fully uniformed Special Service section was attached to each of Belfast's four regiments, ready to deal with any sudden emergency. In the Shankill, the Special Service Section of the West Belfast Regiment was raised by Captain F.P. Crozier, later prominent in the Anglo-Irish War. Richardson withdrew from the Old Town Hall to 'Craigavon' in Strandtown, ready for a last stand if necessary.

The expected blow did not fall. Officers of the cavalry at the Curragh refused to go to Ulster, and Asquith's Liberal government shrank from the task of disarming the UVF. It had been Asquith's last chance to do so. As news of the Curragh mutiny broke, Major Fred Crawford from Belfast was on the high seas with a huge cargo of arms. Only twelve knew of the arms-running; 'Crawford, I'll see you through this business, if I should have to go to prison for it,' Carson had said. At 10.30 p.m., while the authorities were searching a decoy coalboat in Belfast, the *Clydevalley* steamed into Larne with 80 tons of rifles and ammunition bought from Bruno Spiro in Germany. Within hours motor cars had distributed the weapons throughout Ulster. The Liberal government's nerve was now completely broken and even Redmond advised Asquith not to try to disarm the UVF. Meanwhile the nationalists themselves were beginning to arm. It looked as if nothing could prevent civil war.

'I see no hopes of peace'

'Personally I think the Orangeman with a rifle is a much less ridiculous figure than the nationalist without a rifle,' Patrick Pearse wrote in 1913, thus expressing the frustration of many nationalists who were becoming increasingly impatient at delays over Home Rule. Surely Home Rule was but a very limited form of devolution which would keep Ireland firmly within the Empire? Had not Cardinal Logue described the Bill as merely 'a skeleton on which to hang restrictions'? Home Rule had the approval of the majority in Ireland and the majority of elected representatives in Westminster: had the Ulster Unionists and their allies the right to stop it being implemented? 'The North Began' was the title given by Professor Eoin MacNeill to his article in the Gaelic League journal calling on supporters of Home Rule to arm themselves; by May 1914 MacNeill was President of 100,000 Irish Volunteers. Among the earliest and most enthusiastic recruits were Catholics in Belfast; the UVF was hardly in a position to criticise when they openly paraded and shouldered arms. It was in Belfast, where Unionists and Nationalists were separated only by invisible lines, that the danger of civil war was most acute.

'To me it is unthinkable, as it must be to you, that we should be brought to the brink of fratricidal strife upon issues so capable of adjustment as these you are now asked to consider, if handled in a spirit of generous compromise,' George V – that most conscientious of monarchs – said to leaders of the conflicting Irish parties called to a conference in Buckingham Palace. There was no spirit of generous compromise and the conference broke up on 24 July 1914; the same day Asquith told the Commons that Austria-Hungary had presented an ultimatum to Serbia. 'I see no hopes of peace,' Carson reflected gloomily; 'I see nothing at present but darkness and shadows. . . we shall have

FORE-ARMED.

Sir Edward Carson (on course of promenade on the quay, to Customs Officer Birrell). 'Capital idea this of stopping importation of arms. Now there's a dangerous character: you should search him. That's just the sort of bag he'd have a couple of howitzers concealed in'. (*Punch*)
Birrell was the Liberal Irish Chief Secretary and the 'dangerous character' is Redmond.

once more to assert the manhood of our race.' It was not to be in Ireland but in France that the manhood of Carson's loyalist race would be asserted.

Violence was increasingly seen as a respectable method of solving problems. In the spring and early summer of 1914, buildings in Belfast were attacked. Abbeylands, Major-General McCalmont's Whiteabbey home, was burned, the cost of destruction being £11,000; Orlands House, once the palace of the Catholic Bishop of Down and Connor, was burned down, with loss estimated at £20,000; the Tea House at Bellevue, Annadale Hall, and the pavilion of the Cavehill Bowling and Tennis Club were also set on fire. All had been the work of suffragettes and the constabulary found a home-made bomb in the gas oven of the Women's Social & Political Union's offices in University Street as material proof of further violent intentions.

Meanwhile, Harland & Wolff was having an exceptionally good year. Output was likely to be the highest on record; in the first twelve weeks alone 70,000 tons of shipping had left the ways – the 15,000 ton liner *Euripides* for George Thompson & Company, the 5,000 ton *Mississippi* – the first ocean-going diesel vessel – and the 48,157 ton *Britannic* for the White Star Line. Sister ship to the *Olympic*, the *Britannic* was the largest British-built ship, exceeded in size only by the Hamburg-built *Vaterland*. The *Britannic*, launched on 26 February, never was to reach her intended destination, America. On 1 August Germany declared war on Russia and on the same day arms were landed at Kilcoole, Co Wicklow, for the Irish Volunteers – Hamburg had supplied arms to both conflicting parties in Ireland. On 4 August Britain was at war with Germany. Two years later the *Britannic* met a violent end in the Aegean; by that time, thousands of the young men of Belfast had been killed on the Western Front.

'The one bright spot in the very dreadful situation'

'All officers, non-commissioned officers and men who are in the Ulster Volunteer Force. . . are requested to answer immediately his Majesty's call, as our first duty as loyal subjects is to the King': with this telegram Carson pulled his followers back from the brink of civil war. 'I say to the Government that they may tomorrow withdraw every one of their troops from Ireland,' Redmond had said on that emotional night of 3 August in the Commons; '. . . the armed Catholics in the South will be only too glad to join arms with the armed Protestant Ulstermen.' With evident relief the Foreign Secretary, Sir Edward Grey, said that 'the one bright spot in the very dreadful situation is Ireland'.

Protected from attack by the Royal Navy and out of range of German Zeppelins, the shipyards, mills and engineering shops of Belfast strove to meet the seemingly insatiable demands of the British war economy. For security reasons full details of the shipyards' output were not published but, as they attempted to replace the losses at sea, the workforce increased from 15,000 to 20,000, and Harland & Wolff was making Handley Page bombers in the last year of the war. The demand for linen rose so far as to raise the value of exports – which had been £9 million in 1904 – to £20 million in 1916. It was principally in the flax mills that Belfast's fairly small contribution to the munitions industry was made.

As a sample of Belfast's importance, in 1916 alone 192,958 head of cattle, 33,367 tons of grain, 121,700 tons of potatoes and fruit, 13,177 tons of rope

The (36th) Ulster Division parades past the front of the City Hall (right) in May 1915. Fourteen months later, thousands of these volunteers died at the Somme. (Hogg Collection: Ulster Museum)

and cord, 95,533 tons of linen and cotton, 41,454 tons of ores, 9,107 tons of aerated waters, 4,544 tons of tobacco, 17,546 tons of wines and spirits, and 173,777 tons of 'other articles' left the port of Belfast. Wartime inflation, however, ensured that living standards were maintained only by working extremely long hours to earn overtime pay. But it was in France that the citizens of Belfast paid most dearly during the war.

'There is not another Grosvenor Road fellow left but myself': the Somme, 1 July 1916

In the first hours of the morning of 1 July 1916 the men of the Ulster Division were already awake. Troops from the rear bivouacs moved to forward positions along dark communication trenches carefully marked by white tape. By 3 a.m. every man was ready. There were four-and-a-half hours to wait to zero.

'Our country and our Empire are in danger,' Carson had said to the Ulster Unionist Council on 3 September 1914; 'I say to our Volunteers without hesitation, go and help to save your country.' Almost intact, the UVF had been swept into the 36th (Ulster) Division; months of training followed at camps at Clandeboye, Ballykinler and Newtownards. Then, on 8 May 1915, the Division had been inspected at Malone and had marched through Belfast, its

184

main streets dressed in bunting and thronged with enthusiastic spectators. Now, in 1916, it was the anniversary of the Battle of the Boyne; many wore orange lilies and at least one sergeant draped his sash over his uniform. Here in Thiepval Wood men from Belfast prepared to go over the top in the battle of the Somme. As the sun rose into a clear sky the Allied artillery barrage reached a horrific climax. For six days the Allied guns had been firing; it was the heaviest bombardment so far in the history of the world. Private Robert Houston, from the Ormeau Road, had enlisted with the 8th Battalion Royal Irish Rifles; he remembered: 'We had to march all night to go to our trenches. Every man was carrying a 96 lb pack on his back and by the time we had dug ourselves in we were dog tired. But we had a right sup of dark rum on us too. I didn't take any myself but there were quite a few of the boys who had more than their fair share.' Charles Currie, a Catholic who had enlisted in what had been a temperance battalion of the Belfast UVF, recalled that he drank so many tots of rum that he remembered nothing of the start of the battle.

At 7.15 a.m., concealed by a smoke barrage and a lingering mist, the troops stepped out of their trenches and formed up in No Man's Land. At 7.30 a.m. the guns suddenly stopped firing to lengthen their range. Officers blew their whistles and the men advanced at a steady marching pace towards the German first line. Rifleman Edward Taylor of the West Belfast Volunteers recalled: 'Captain Gaffiken took out an orange handkerchief and, waving it around his head, shouted, "Come on, boys, this is the first of July!" "No Surrender!" roared the men.'

The massive bombardment had not knocked out the enemy machine-gun nests; Allied shells – far from destroying the German wire – had merely strewn jagged metal to impede the men's advance; and the very regularity of marching made the Ulstermen perfect targets. A wounded man lying in the mud shouted 'Give it hot for the Shankill Road!' and his comrades answered with a cheer. 'I was only 17 at the time,' Thomas Flanagan, a private in the 7th Battalion Royal Inniskilling Fusiliers, remembered. 'Muck, dirt, noise, horrifying noise, fear and everywhere the smell of death and the dead. . . it was just a barren scene of destruction.' 'All hell opened up when we went forward,' Private Houston recalled: 'It was like an earthquake with thousands of tons of TNT exploding all round. A right few of my mates got cut down that day. I suppose I was lucky.' He nevertheless lost both hands. James Thornberry, only fifteen when he joined the 1st Battalion Inniskilling Fusiliers in 1916, remembered: 'Mutilated bodies were strewn all around and at times I think I was more afraid of them than I was of the enemy.'

The attack of the Ulstermen north of the river Ancre was a disastrous failure: caught by crossfire in a deep ravine and trapped by impenetrable wire, they were forced to give up the front line they had captured. Opposite Thiepval Wood the Ulster Division advanced with astonishing speed, overwhelming the first, second, third and fourth lines; but their very success led to one of the most futile tragedies of the war. Just as victory seemed within their grasp the men were pounded by shell-fire from behind their own lines – the Ulstermen had arrived ten minutes earlier than it had been thought possible. Major Peacocke gathered the survivors into the Stuff and Schwaben redoubts and there they were assailed by machine-gun fire until nightfall when they gave up the territory which had been so dearly bought. That first day at the Somme 5,500 men of the Ulster Division had been killed or wounded. Four men – Private William McFadzean, Private Robert Quigg, Lieutenant Geoffrey Cather and

Captain Eric Bell — were awarded posthumous Victoria Crosses. The following day an English officer wrote this report:

I am not an Ulsterman, but yesterday, the 1st July, as I followed their amazing attack, I felt that I would rather be an Ulsterman than anything else in this world. My pen cannot describe adequately the hundreds of heroic acts that I witnessed. . . The Ulster Volunteer Force, from which the Division was made, has won a name which equals any in history. Their devotion deserves the gratitude of the British Empire.

The horror of that first day is poignantly illustrated by a letter, sent from the front by Private Herbert Beattie to his home in the Grosvenor Road:

Pte. H. Beattie
No. 11604 D Company
2nd Royal Inns Fus
5th Brigade 1st Army Corps
British Expeditionary Force

Dear Mother,

Just a few lines to let you know I am safe and thank God for it for had a ruf time of it in the charge we made Mother don't let on to V. Quinn mother or Archers mother that they must be killed wounded for they are missen of roll call, and tell Hugh that the fellow that youst to run along with E, Ferguson call Eddie Mallin he youst to have Pigens if Hugh dus not no him McKeown nows him tell them he was killed tell them that ther is not another grosvenor Rd fellow left but myself. Mother wee were tramping over the dead i think there is onley about 4 hundred left out of about 13 hundered, Mother you can let Alfred no some thing about Mother i have some Germans helmonts and sugases and i am sorey i could not send them home Mother if god spers me to get home safe i will have something ufal to tell you if hell is any wores i would not like to go to it Mothe let me here from you as soone as you can as i have got no word from you this fourt night dont forget to let me here from you soon.

This is all i can say at Present From you loving son Herbie.
Mother xxxxxxxxxxxxxxxxxxx

Father xxxxxxxxxxxxxx

show my Father this letter and tell him to writ

Mother x x x x x x

1916–1918

On 12 July 1916, when the clocks struck noon, all traffic in the streets of Belfast came to a halt. Trams stopped in their tracks and on the local railways the trains pulled up. Public courts adjourned and blinds were drawn. All work was suspended as the city remembered those who had fallen at the Somme. The Twelfth celebrations were voluntarily abandoned; instead citizens remembered the dead in deep silence as the *Belfast News-Letter* reported:

There was no outward manifestation of joy or grief, except for the display of the Union Jack from the windows or roofs of a large number of houses and business and industrial establishments, as well as at the Clifton Street Orange Hall (where during a

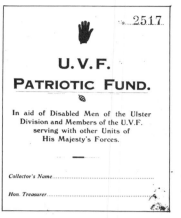

U.V.F.
PATRIOTIC FUND.

In aid of Disabled Men of the Ulster
Division and Members of the U.V.F.
serving with other Units of
His Majesty's Forces.

Collector's Name........................

Hon. Treasurer...........................

(H. Laird)

"seaʒan buiðe"

"THE SECRET OF ENGLANDS GREATNESS"

'Yellow John Bull': Dungannon
Clubs propaganda.
(Linen Hall Library)

portion of the day the emblem of the Empire floated at half-mast) but neither the Boyne nor Thiepval – the scene of the most glorious achievements in the present war – was forgotten in the sorrow-stricken city of Belfast.

As A.T.Q. Stewart has written, 'In the long streets of Belfast mothers looked out in dread for the red bicycles of the telegram boys. In house after house blinds were drawn down, until it seemed that every family in the city had been bereaved.' Strict censorship of the press and letters from the front kept the public ignorant of the full horrors of life in the trenches, the blunders of generals and the futility of much of the fighting – in a few misspelled lines Herbert Beattie had revealed more truth about the battle than the reports of all the Belfast newspapers put together. The Somme battle dragged on bloodily into November 1916 with nothing achieved, and the remnant of the Ulster Division fought elsewhere, notably at Messines, Langemarck, Cambrai and Passchendaele.

The Catholics of Belfast, too, had been fighting and dying. Some joined the Ulster Division while others were scattered through other Irish regiments which suffered terrible casualties on the Western Front and at Gallipoli. Though they had not been given a division of their own, those who had joined the volunteer movement to defend Home Rule shed blood – and in roughly the same prodigious quantity – fighting on the same side as the UVF. This sacrifice, however, did not heal the political divisions in the city. A small but determined group saw England's difficulty as Ireland's opportunity and Belfast was the home of the most zealous republicans in the country.

In the early years of the century Belfast had the most active cells of the Irish Republican Brotherhood in Ireland. At a time when the IRB was moribund in Dublin, Denis McCullough revitalised the separatist movement in the heart of Unionist territory. Disgusted by the slovenly manner in which he had been sworn into the IRB at the side door of Donnelly's public house on the Falls Road in 1901, McCullough weeded out of the movement those he considered faint-hearted – including his own father – and worked with unremitting zeal to enrol in the Brotherhood young men determined to fight for a republic. McCullough was joined by Bulmer Hobson – who had been educated at Friends' School, Lisburn, and who had founded the Protestant National Association – and together they launched the Dungannon Clubs to revive republican feeling. Like the United Irishmen before them, they soon had branches in other parts of the country. The clubs merged with other organisations in 1907 to form Sinn Fein – a title suggested by Edward Carson's republican cousin, Maire Butler. From Belfast they published a weekly paper, *The Republic*, which contained cartoons later reprinted as postcards. McCullough also attracted into his movement Sean MacDermott who had come to Belfast from Leitrim to find work. By 1914 the northern republicans virtually controlled the IRB: Hobson and MacDermott, with the help of another Ulsterman, Tom Clarke, ousted the leadership in Dublin and saw to it that McCullough became head of the IRB Supreme Council.

When the Great War began, these northern republicans decided to organise an uprising and the Easter Rebellion in Dublin in 1916 was largely the result of their planning; Hobson, however, made attempts to stop the rising when he realised that effective German aid was not forthcoming. The rising lacked widespread support but the events of 1916 were to have a profound effect on the future history of Belfast. The sacrifices of the UVF at the Somme had led

187

Asquith to conclude that the coercion of Ulster was 'absolutely unthinkable'. The 1916 insurrection may have been, in Adam Duffin's words, a 'comic opera founded on the Wolfe Tone fiasco a hundred years ago' but nationalist opinion began to move towards separatism. In their turn, Ulster Unionists no longer sought to stop Home Rule for the whole island but in Ulster only; southern Unionists were becoming reconciled to Home Rule and Adam Duffin wrote in disgust to his wife on 28 November 1917: 'the southern unionist lot. . . want to capitulate and make terms with the enemy lest a worse thing befall them. They are a cowardly crew and stupid to boot.'

On 11 November 1918 the First World War came to an end and a general election was called immediately. The Representation of the People Act 1918 more than doubled the Irish electorate and thousands of unskilled workers would be voting for the first time. In Belfast the number of seats was increased from four to nine. The election was a watershed in Irish history: Sinn Fein swept aside the Irish Parliamentary Party and 'Wee Joe' Devlin, returned for West Belfast, found himself the effective leader of a small rump of six Nationalist MPs. Yet the election was also a great victory for the Ulster Unionists who increased their representation at Westminster from 18 to 26 MPs. The Unionists had taken care to woo the newly-enfranchised by setting up the Ulster Unionist Labour Association in June 1918, and at a Workman Clark launching just before the election Carson told shipyard workers how grateful he was for their efforts while he had been First Lord of the Admiralty:

In the midst of it all the one great hope we had was that you would all do your duty. Not only did you do your duty but nothing pleased me more than when I heard that the men of Belfast beat the records all round. . . But for the efforts you made we should never have won and now that we have we ought to be grateful.

The Protestant workers – skilled and unskilled – had given their almost unanimous vote to Unionist candidates; that did not mean, however, that they were always the pliant tools of their employers, as the great strike of 1919 demonstrated.

The 44 Hour Strike 1919

Lloyd George, Prime Minister from 1916 to 1922, had done much in the last two years of the war to improve the living standards of the unskilled. In the Belfast shipyards a labourer's rate of pay had been 51% of a plater's and 54% of a fitter's; by July 1918 the rates had narrowed to 67% and 69%. Once the war was over the skilled sought a restoration of the pre-war differential in pay. Unionist leaders had given them lavish praise for their exertions during the war and the continuing prosperity of the yards increased their confidence; 28% of Clydeside shipyard workers were unemployed in the summer of 1918 but in Belfast the order books were full and 29,000 shipyardmen were kept busy. When the Engineering & Shipbuilding Trades Federation negotiated a national working week of 47 hours, the men in Belfast were infuriated – their unanimous demand had been for a 44 hour week.

This was a turbulent moment in labour history: in Russia the Bolsheviks were holding their own; in Germany and Italy revolutionary socialists were attempting to seize power; and Glasgow was paralysed by a general strike. By an overwhelming majority the shipyard men, the gas workers, and the electricity station workers voted to go on strike, and on 25 January 1919 a formidable struggle began. Strikers smashed the windows of shops still using gas light and electricity. The trams could not run, cinemas closed, the yards and engineering shops were silent, thousands of linen workers were put out of work, and by the end of the first week bread was running short in the city. Forty-four businesses were brought into the dispute, the Belfast Ropeworks were closed down, and, while pickets failed to stop the steam-powered linen mills altogether, great disruption followed. The *Belfast News-Letter*, reduced in size, believed that the strike was the work of 'Bolshevik agitators whose aim is to smash all the institutions of the country' and that the dispute 'will rejoice the heart of Sinn Fein and will play most powerfully into its hands'. The *Irish News* could make no comment as it was forced to cease publication altogether.

Lord Pirrie and the other employers demanded military intervention. The only prominent politician to support this demand was the Nationalist MP, Joe Devlin; Unionist leaders were loathe to alienate workers who had given them such a convincing vote in the general election. Brigadier-General Sir William Hacket Pain, Acting Police Commissioner for Belfast, was also reluctant to act against men he had helped to organise in the UVF before the war. Eventually, a stern rebuke from Dublin Castle and the arrival of the Commander-in-Chief of the army in Ireland led to intervention. At 6 a.m. on Saturday 14 February troops occupied the gasworks and electricity station; citizens were called on to volunteer to work the plants and by Sunday the trains were running again. The General Strike Committee assumed the strike was defeated but a mass meeting that Sunday in Custom House Square resolved to continue the dispute. However, only the yards and engineering works remained idle and by Thursday 19 February the strike had collapsed.

The 44 hour strike had not been the work of socialist agitators; leaders and rank and file were for the most part Protestant workers, unwavering in their support of the Union, who had been in search of better working conditions. Embittered by their defeat, they had an opportunity to show their resentment in the Corporation elections of 1920.

'A death-blow to the Unionist clique'?: the PR election of 1920

British governments often had used Ireland as a social laboratory for trying out new ideas: nineteenth-century examples include the police force, national schools and medical dispensaries. In 1919 Lloyd George's coalition government introduced the Local Government (Ireland) Bill which became law on 3 June; henceforth boroughs were to be divided into wards containing at least six councillors, each to be elected by proportional representation. The government's short-term aim was to give representation to minorities to find some middle ground between irreconcilable Unionists and irreconcilable Sinn Feiners. All the Ulster Unionists MPs voted against the Bill; Carson believed that voters would find the system elaborate and confusing.

Belfast Corporation, somewhat unwillingly, produced an acceptable scheme for turning the nine parliamentary constituencies into wards. It took three days to count the votes cast on 15 January 1920. Voters did not find the system unintelligible and the turnout was 65.7%, well above the usual. The results were not quite 'a death-blow to the Unionist clique', as the *Irish News* described them, but the Unionists were reduced from 52 to 29. The Nationalists won 5 seats and Sinn Fein another 5, but the striking feature of the elections was the success of the labour candidates: the Belfast Labour Party (founded in 1908) won 10 seats; independent Labour 3; and official Labour Unionists 6. In 1901, 55 out of 60 members of the Corporation had been upper middle-class while in 1920 there were 10 trade unionists – the largest single occupational group – and 19 working-class councillors altogether. British electoral reformers were particularly pleased that the new council very accurately reflected the wishes of the electorate and published a detailed analysis of the Belfast elections in an unsuccessful attempt to have PR adopted in Britain.

If PR was intended to weaken Sinn Fein in the rest of the country it failed completely; the separatists got a massive vote of confidence from the nationalist electorate. The local government election in Belfast was not the first step towards non-sectarian class politics. Loyalty to the cause of labour did not dent the attitudes of Belfast workers to the Union. War was raging now between armed republicans and the forces of the Crown and, as the conflict crept northwards, it became increasingly difficult for the leaders of the Belfast Labour Party to argue that the national issue was irrelevant. Belfast, indeed, was about to be engulfed by the worst sectarian violence yet seen in the city.

'The gates were smashed down with sledges': The expulsions 1920

'We in Ulster will tolerate no Sinn Fein – no Sinn Fein organisation, no Sinn Fein methods,' Carson said at 'The Field' at Finaghy on 12 July 1920. He warned the government: 'But we tell you this – that if, having offered you our help, you are yourselves unable to protect us from the machinations of Sinn Fein, and you won't take our help; well then, we tell you that we will take the matter into our own hands. We will reorganise. . .'

The 73 Sinn Fein MPs elected in 1918 took their seats not at Westminster but in their own assembly in Dublin, Dáil Eireann. There, on 21 January 1919, they had proclaimed the Irish Republic and, on the same day, the first shots of the Anglo-Irish War had been fired in Tipperary. In September 1919 the Dáil had been proclaimed illegal by the British government; any restraining influence Sinn Fein representatives might have had was now removed. Over much of the country British administration broke down and republican volunteers – the Irish Republican Army – engaged in a deadly guerrilla warfare with the security forces. From June 1920 the IRA extended their campaign into rural Ulster: for Belfast this was the beginning of more than two years of civil war.

On 21 July 1920, the first full day back at work after the 'Twelfth' holiday, notices were posted in the shipyards calling 'Protestant and Unionist' workers to attend a meeting at lunch time outside the gates of Workman Clark's south yard. It was the day of the funeral of Colonel Smyth, the RIC Divisional Commissioner from Banbridge, shot dead in Cork four days previously. At the meeting, speakers noted Sinn Fein's recent successes and referred to Carson's threat that loyalists would take action themselves if the offer of loyalist help was rejected by the goverment. The call to drive out 'disloyal' workers – Sinn Feiners and socialists – was enthusiastically supported. At the end of the meeting hundreds of apprentices and rivet boys from Workman Clark's marched into Harland & Wolff's yard and ordered out Catholics and socialists; some were kicked and beaten, others were pelted with rivets, and some were forced to swim for their lives, as one Catholic remembered:

190

Men armed with sledge-hammers and other weapons swooped down on Catholic workers in the shipyards and didn't give them a chance for their lives. . . The gates were smashed down with sledges, the vests and shirts of those at work were torn open to see if the men were wearing any Catholic emblems, and woe betide the man who was. One man was set upon, thrown into the dock, had to swim the Musgrave channel, and having been pelted with rivets, had to swim two or three miles, to emerge in streams of blood and rush to the police office in a nude state.

Amongst those driven out were Charles McKay, the Catholic who had led the General Strike Committee during the 44 hour dispute; the Labour councillor, James Baird; and John Hanna, a former master of an Orange Lodge. Catholics were expelled also from Barbours, Musgraves, Mackies, and the Sirocco Works. A committee headed by the Catholic bishop, Dr McRory, estimated that 10,000 men and 1,000 women had been expelled from their work. That first evening, trams carrying shipyard workers home were attacked as they passed the Short Strand. Intense rioting in east Belfast for the next three days led to the deaths of seven Catholics and six Protestants. By the end of 1922 more than 400 would have died violently in a city crippled by depression as it was striving to become the centre of a new provincial government.

Belfast in 1902: from M. J. Baddeley's *Guide, Ireland (Part I) Northern Counties.*

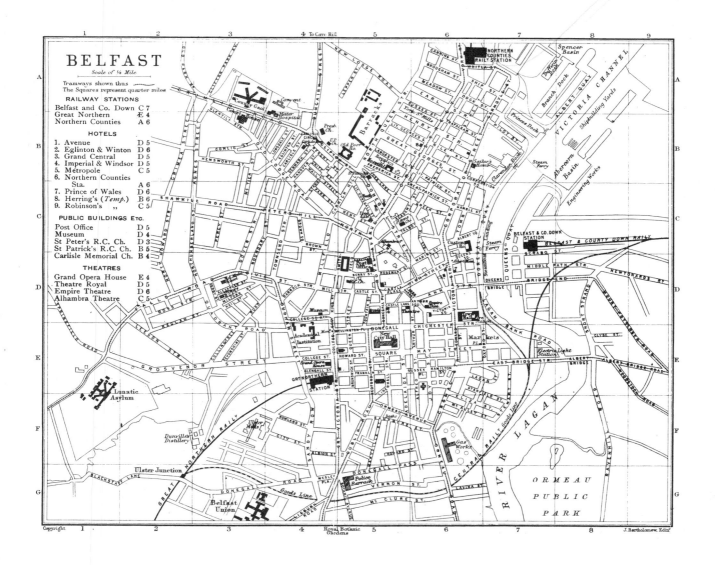

8
Years of Depression
c.1920–1939

Datsie-dotsie, miss the rope, you're outie-o,
If you'd've been, where I'd have been,
You wouldn't have been put outie-o,
All the money's scarce, people out of workie-o,
Datsie-dotsie, miss the rope, you're outie-o.
(Children's street rhyme)

On 2 December 1919 thousands of the unemployed gathered outside the City Hall to urge the Corporation to take action at a time when great distress was prevailing in the city. On their behalf Sam Kyle, Harry Midgley and Dawson Gordon met the Lord Mayor and urged him to implement the 1914 Act compelling councils to provide free school meals for necessitous children. The Lord Mayor replied dismissively that the extent of unemployment in Belfast was exaggerated and that it had been caused by the recent ironmoulders' strike.

The slump was not a temporary phenomenon – in Belfast, the Depression began early. In December 1919 there were 14,000 out of work in the city and by January 1922, when 27% of insured workers were unemployed, as many as 30,000 may have been idle in Belfast. The slump developed into a protracted depression as the traditional staple industries of the city continued to contract. For most people in Belfast these years were remembered as a time of poverty. Hugh Finnegan, a cattle dealer and butcher, recalls:

In the days of the great depression of the 1920s the popular and practical forms of transport were horses and drays. Farmers went down to the docks for their supplies of feeding stocks which usually came in 1½ cwt. bags. I used to go down Pilot Street, a long narrow street to dockland, and lolling against the walls were dozens of men awaiting a nod or a signal to come and assist. They would load the fourteen bags on my cart and when the job was completed they received the princely sum of one shilling – there was no quibbling, only competition for who would get the call.

Economic uncertainty combined with political turmoil to aggravate religious hatreds in the city. As Northern Ireland was brought to birth its capital was convulsed by community warfare brought to a new level of ferocity: between 1920 and 1922 Belfast seemed to resemble more closely the capitals of states created out of the wreck of the collapsed empires than the more stable cities of north-western Europe. Conflicting political aspirations prevented the early successes of the labour movement from being repeated and extended. Only the terrible effects of the Wall Street Crash brought workers of both religions together for a time in 1932. Desperately short of money, neither the government nor the Corporation could do much to provide relief; though the city's population rose from 386,947 in 1911 to 438,086 in 1937, the mass of the people had to press into dwellings built in the nineteenth century. At a Corporation meeting in April 1920 the Nationalist councillor, Oswald Jamison, claimed that 30,000 families were living in two-room accommodation. The extent of deprivation is illustrated by this children's parody of a popular hymn:

> There is a happy land far, far away
> Where they eat bread and jam three times a day.
> O, how we sweetly sing, dancing round the gravy ring,
> O, how we'd love to be far, far away.

On average one quarter of all insured workers were unemployed throughout the 1920s. Despite this, the working-class alliance of 1932 proved fragile, and sectarian conflict was renewed in the riots of 1935. David Kennedy recalled:

A wide street adjoining the Public Library in Royal Avenue gave space in those years for orators whose political spectrum ranged from pale pink to ultra-red. I remember one of them addressing a crowd:
'If you took all the Orange sashes and all the green sashes in Belfast and tied them round a ticket of loaves and threw them in the Lagan, the gulls, the common, ordinary sea-gulls, they'd go for the bread, but the other gulls – yous ones – yous'd go for the sashes every time.' *

* David Kennedy, 'Catholics in Northern Ireland 1926–39', in MacManus, *The years of the great test 1926–39* (see bibliog), p. 145.

'Fire, plunder and assault': Belfast under curfew, August–December 1920

The 'Troubles' which began in 1920 were partly economic in origin, unlike almost all previous rioting in the nineteenth century. The great expansion of shipbuilding and engineering during and immediately after the war had brought a significant number of Catholics into what had been exclusively Protestant trades; Alexander Boyd, independent labour councillor for St Anne's, was reported in the *Belfast News-Letter* of 2 August 1920 as saying:

At the beginning of the war orders poured into the shipyards and foundries and the labour which was required came largely from the South and West – men who did not do their duty in the trenches. They came to fill the places of those brave lads who went to the front and Belfast employers have not acted fairly to the ex-soldiers who were formerly in their employment.

Throughout 1919 the IRA had been fighting a guerrilla war with the British government in the south, and when the fighting spread to Ulster in 1920, the fiction that Catholics had not 'done their bit' presented Protestants in Belfast with the opportunity not only to strike a blow against republicanism but also to protect their jobs in the city. The violence became general throughout the city in August, and the Liberal and Labour press in Britain painted a dark picture of Protestant fury. 'The bloody harvest of Carsonism is being reaped in Belfast,' the *Daily Herald* commented. 'The gangs who have organised the reign of terror are the very people who protest they are afraid that *they* would, under even partial home rule, be persecuted and denied religious liberty.' The *Daily News* described the troubles of July and August as 'five weeks of ruthless persecution by boycott, fire, plunder and assault, culminating in a week's whole violence, probably unmatched outside the area of Russian or Polish pogroms'. The assassination of District Inspector O.R. Swanzy in Lisburn on Sunday 22 August had sparked off the worst week of conflict. Two days after the murder, St Matthew's Church in the Short Strand, and the 'Bone' – the Marrowbone, a Catholic area in north Belfast – came under Protestant attack. There had been 180 major fires in the last days of August causing damage estimated at just under £1 million; the *Daily Mail* reported that 400 families, mostly Catholics, had been driven from their homes; and by the end of the month 22 civilians had been killed in the city.

On 30 August 1920 the army erected sand-bagged emplacements and enforced a curfew in Belfast which was to remain in force until 1924; all trams were to stop and all places of entertainment were to close at 9.30 p.m., and every person within the county and city of Belfast was required to 'remain indoors between the hours of 10.30 p.m. and 5 a.m.'. The curfew did not stop the violence and another 23 people were killed in September 1920; though November and December were comparatively quiet the total of those who had died in Belfast over the year was 74 – 5 soldiers, 2 policemen, 35 Catholics and 32 Protestants. Meanwhile at Westminster the government was putting finishing touches to a measure designed to provide yet another solution to the Irish Question, and which would give the city of Belfast a new political role.

'An arrangement of fantastic complexity': Northern Ireland created, December 1920

In December 1920 Westminster finally agreed to give Ulster Home Rule, with Belfast housing its parliament. How was such an extraordinary outcome possible? The Home Rule Bill had been on the statute book since September 1914 and, in spite of the Anglo-Irish War still raging, its implementation could be delayed no longer. The Prime Minister, David Lloyd George, was a Liberal but his Conservative colleagues in the post-war coalition government had an overall majority in the Commons, including such unflinching Unionists as Bonar Law and Lord Birkenhead – even James Craig was a junior member of the government. The coercion of Ulster was inconceivable now, but Lloyd George did not give the Ulster Unionists exactly what they wanted. In what the historian A.J.P. Taylor has accurately described as 'an arrangement of fantastic complexity', the government gave a Home Rule parliament not only to Dublin but also to Belfast. By this Act 'for the better government of Ireland', Northern Ireland was composed of the six north-eastern counties with a local parliament in Belfast; representation for those six counties was to be reduced to 13 MPs at Westminster; and a Council of Ireland was to be set up 'with a view to the eventual establishment of a parliament for the whole of Ireland'.

Determined though they were never to accept an all-Ireland parliament, Ulster Unionists saw advantages in the new complex arrangement. A future Liberal or Labour government could seek Irish reunification and, as Charles Craig pointed out, 'without a parliament of our own constant attacks would be made upon us, and constant attempts would be made. . . to draw us into a Dublin parliament'. On 23 December 1920 the Government of Ireland Act received the royal assent; it was, in effect, to be the constitution of Northern Ireland for the next 50 years. Sinn Fein, representing the majority over the whole country, rejected the Act out of hand and were determined to make the Dáil the parliament of an Irish Republic. Thus it was that Belfast, which had led the long campaign against Home Rule, was now to be the capital of the only part of Ireland to get Home Rule.

'The Union Jack must sweep the polls': 24 May 1921

On 3 May 1921 Belfast officially became the capital of Northern Ireland. The Anglo-Irish War was at its height; business was deeply depressed in the city; and, though there were no major riots, an average of four sectarian killings had occurred every month since the beginning of the year.

Carson had failed to prevent the implementation of Home Rule and in any case he believed himself too ill to continue his leadership of the Ulster Unionists. Sir James Craig had been appointed Financial Secretary to the Admiralty and had expectations – justified or not – of high office at Westminster; in February he gave in to Ulster Unionist entreaties to become their leader and resigned from Lloyd George's coalition. Lady Craig recorded in her diary:

J. has his last day at the Admiralty, taking leave of his staff, and his last day at the House, giving up the keys of his locker, etc., and turning the card on the door of his room; also a long chat with the Prime Minister. When he joins us in the evening, we feel very mournful, and I have never seen him so depressed, as he is always so philosophical, and says one should never dwell on what is done with, but concentrate on the present and the future.

Harry Midgley.
(*Northern Ireland 1921–71*)

Craig did not brood for long on lost opportunities; he called elections for Empire Day, 24 May 1921, and immediately threw himself into the campaign. This was the first parliamentary election to be held in the United Kingdom under the system of proportional representation. Belfast was divided into four constituencies, North, South, East, West, each returning four members. Though there were three Labour candidates, the constitutional issue was the only one of significance. 'Rally round me,' Craig urged the voters, 'that I may shatter our enemies and their hopes of a republic flag. The Union Jack must sweep the polls.' The Nationalists, led by Joe Devlin, in their manifesto described partition as the greatest of all calamities that had befallen Ireland whose 'historic unity is to be violated with results disastrous to the peace and prosperity alike of the North and South' and declared that 'it is our fixed determination not to enter this North-East Ulster Parliament'. Sinn Fein, more ominously, stated that it was 'out to smash the Ulster Parliament and if it cannot be smashed in this election, it will have to be smashed otherwise'.

The election was bitter. The three Labour candidates in Belfast had little hope of making the social and economic plight of the city's poor a major issue; when they booked the Ulster Hall for a final rally on 17 May, loyalist shipyard workers barricaded the hall against them. 'Mass meeting of loyal shipyard workers who have captured Ulster Hall from Bolsheviks Baird, Midgley and Hanna request that you address them for a few minutes tonight,' telegraphed the men to Craig in London who replied: 'I am with them in spirit. Know they will do their part. I will do mine. Well done big and wee yards.'

'Your election,' James Baird said at the count, 'has been carried out under the worst intimidation and marked by wholesale personation.' Intimidation could not alone account for the overwhelming victory of the Ulster Unionists. In an 89% poll, 40 Unionists, 6 Sinn Feiners, and 6 Nationalists were elected. In Belfast the Unionists captured 15 out of 16 seats, not one Labour candidate was returned, and only one Nationalist — Joe Devlin — was elected. The Northern Ireland Parliament could now meet but it would only be Unionist MPs who would assemble in the City Hall, which the Corporation had proudly offered for its use.

'Stretch out the hand of forbearance': George V in Belfast

I could not have allowed myself to give to Ireland by deputy alone my earnest prayers and good wishes in the new era which opens with this ceremony, and I have therefore come in person, as the head of the Empire, to inaugurate this Parliament on Irish soil. . .

With these words King George V began his momentous speech to the Unionist MPs in the City Hall at the state opening of the Northern Ireland Parliament on 22 June 1921. The Anglo-Irish War was reaching a dreadful climax and only ten days before seven had died in renewed rioting in Belfast. Buckingham Palace had received numerous appeals urging the King not to risk his life by travelling to Belfast. In her diary Lady Craig showed how the demonstration of loyalty was combined with strict security:

Jun. 22. The great day. . . the King and Queen have the most wonderful reception, the decorations everywhere are extremely well done and even the little side streets that they will never be within miles of are draped with bunting and flags, and the pavement and lampposts painted red white and blue, really most touching, as a sign of their loyalty. . . J. goes to the docks of course to meet them and gets a great welcome from the enormous crowds everywhere along the route. They drive up High Street, and Donegall Place, to the City Hall. Luckily it was not very far, and precautions had been taken of every description, trusted men stationed in each house, and on every roof top, and the closest scrutiny of all in the houses, and of course in the streets too. Every alternate policeman faced the crowd but as there were troops in front, this was not specially apparent. The actual opening was the first of the functions. . .

The King's speech was clearly intended to reach far beyond the walls of the City Hall. With evident emotion he concluded:

I speak from a full heart when I pray that my coming to Ireland today may prove to be the first step towards an end of strife among her people, whatever their race or creed. In that hope, I appeal to all Irishmen to pause, to stretch out the hand of forbearance and conciliation, to forgive and forget. . .

Lady Craig continued her account of the day's events:

We then all went across to the Ulster Hall, where addresses were presented, Dolly Abercorn and I handing one to the Queen from the loyalist women of Ulster. After that there was an investiture, the scenes in the hall were unforgettable, as the people could not contain themselves, and cheered for several minutes, and broke into singing the National Anthem at a moment when it was not on the official programme. They finally left for the docks, J. and all the official people going with them, after a visit that was nothing but one huge success from first to last. When J. rejoined me at home again, he heaved the biggest sigh of relief imaginable, at having got them safely on the royal yacht again, after such a marvellous day without any *contretemps* to either of them. The King said to J. when he was saying goodbye in the yacht: 'I can't tell you how glad I am I came, but you know my entourage were very much against it.'

The King's entourage had reason to be anxious. June 1921 had been a bad

A crowd in flight during the bitter sectarian clashes of 1921: corner of York Street and Donegall Street, where the Art College now stands.
(*Northern Ireland 1921–71*)

month in Belfast, especially in the York Street area, the violence here being characterised not only by heavy use of firearms but also by the driving out of families from the mixed streets between the New Lodge Road and Tiger Bay. The UVF had been revived by Captain Sir Basil Brooke in Fermanagh, where Protestants formed a beleaguered minority, and members of the resurgent force had played a leading part in expelling Catholics from their jobs and homes in Belfast. In an attempt to discipline the loyalists, Westminster formed the Special Constabulary in October 1920. The hope that the 'Specials' would represent both communities was not realised and the formation of what was in effect a Protestant militia did nothing to reconcile Catholics to the new state.

The Specials were indeed to do much to defeat the IRA but when a number of them joined Protestant mobs in Belfast on 10 July, they came to be regarded as the enemies of the Catholic community as a whole. One coroner's jury commented: 'We think in the interests of peace the Special Constabulary should not be allowed into any locality occupied by people of an opposite denomination.' Fighting was particularly severe in east Belfast over the Twelfth holiday: during one week 16 Catholics and 7 Protestants had been killed and a great many homes – mostly Catholic – had been destroyed.

It was on 11 July that a truce agreed between the IRA and the British government had come into force – perhaps the King's appeal had been heard after all.

The 'Belfast Boycott' and the Anglo-Irish Treaty

'We have nothing in view except the welfare of the people,' Craig had said after the King's visit, but any magnanimous feelings were rapidly dispersed as discussions began in London between Lloyd George and Eamon de Valera, President of the Dáil. The Prime Minister seemed ready to make sacrifices at

197

Ulster's expense to obtain peace, and Craig had not been invited to these conferences to give his view. Never had Protestants felt so strongly that they had to look to their own defence, despite the presence of British troops. The British press, which gave graphic accounts of dispossessed Catholics in Belfast fleeing to safety, showed little sympathy for Northern Ireland's position. Meanwhile the Catholic minority in Ulster abstained from both local and central government institutions and the 'Belfast Boycott' – by which southern separatists refused to buy Belfast products and which had been sanctioned by the Dáil in August 1920 – continued, the Truce notwithstanding. The Belfast Boycott was more damaging than some historians have recognised; Belfast-made machinery, linen, whiskey and – above all – tobacco and cigarettes sold extensively in the south up to this. Gerry Moore, a bank official in the midlands at the time, recalled: 'The Belfast boys were the sharpest salesmen on the road – they could out-sell anyone. Then when the Boycott came in they disappeared like magic. There was neither sight nor sound of them.' The IRA gave force to the boycott by raiding freight trains and destroying Belfast goods in Dublin shops. Churchill recognised the real damage caused by the boycott when he later summed up his feelings:

It recognised and established real partition, spiritual and voluntary partition, before physical partition had been established. . . it did not secure the reinstatement of a single expelled Nationalist, nor the conversion of a single Unionist. It was merely a blind suicidal contribution to the general hate.

From 11 October 1921 a delegation from Dáil Eireann negotiated terms with the British government at Downing Street. Once again the Northern Ireland government was not invited to participate. Craig made many anxious trips to London and Lloyd George pressed him to make concessions. 'This may turn out to be a most historical meeting. I may have to resign,' Lloyd George threatened on one occasion, knowing that the Ulster Unionists had most to fear from a Labour-Liberal coalition. At 2.10 a.m., on 6 December 1921, the Anglo-Irish Treaty was signed in Downing Street, and its details were sent by special train and destroyer to Craig in Belfast. Craig was horrified: not only would the Irish Free State only have as much independence as the Dominion of Canada but the terms of Article XII provided also for a boundary commission which could tear lumps out of Northern Ireland, perhaps even the Mourne Mountains, the source of Belfast's water. The Ulster premier went immediately to London to protest. The Cabinet Secretary, Tom Jones, described the scene in a letter to Sir Maurice Hankey:

Sir James Craig was closeted with the P.M. . . . He then went off to his Doctor to be inoculated – I suppose against a Sinn Fein germ. Anyhow yesterday he charged the P.M. with a breach of faith. . . Carson, who I understood was in favour of the Boundary Commission, is very disgruntled at the position into which the P.M. has manoeuvred Ulster, and he did not turn up at the dinner at Sassoon's on December 7th, to celebrate the anniversary of the P.M.'s premiership, instead he wrote a nasty letter.

Even the *Daily Express*, normally sympathetic to the Ulster Unionists, commented that 'unless the Ulster cabinet abandons its uncompromising attitude it will be guilty of the greatest political crime in history'. The sense of Ulster Unionist isolation was complete. When he returned to Belfast Craig wrote the most bitter of his many letters to Lloyd George and threatened that Northern Ireland might 'find it necessary to call upon their friends and supporters – more especially the members of the Loyal Orange Institution – to come to their assistance by means of arms, ammunition and money. . . Loyalists may declare independence on their own behalf, seize the Customs and other Government Departments and set up an authority of their own.' Nationalists, too, were equally bitter in the north that their exclusion had been made permanent in Belfast – for Belfast would be the last place in Northern Ireland which a boundary commission would award to the Irish Free State. The clashing aspirations of the two communities in the city would make 1922 the bloodiest year so far.

'Like Uriah of the Bible I was being sent to the front line'

As the Treaty negotiations drew to a close, blood was flowing once more in Belfast. Control of law and order passed, on 22 November 1921, to the Northern Ireland government, more particularly to the Belfast solicitor and secretary of the Ulster Unionist Council, Richard Dawson Bates. Bates, Minister for Home Affairs in the Northern Ireland Cabinet, immediately set about the recruitment of more Special constables. If anything, disorder increased – mobs attacked the Short Strand and a bomb was thrown onto a tram carrying Protestant shipyard workers. Altogether 27 people were killed in sectarian fighting between 19 and 25 November and by the end of the year the death toll in the city for the previous twelve months had reached 109.

In the south, Sinn Fein was deeply divided over the Treaty; argument centred on the Irish Free State's continued membership of the Empire. In the Treaty debates in the Dáil not one deputy seems to have felt that the boundary commission would fail to bring major accessions of territory. Most assumed that Northern Ireland's economy would collapse. The IRA, restless from lack of action and opposed for the most part to the Treaty, launched a major offensive against Northern Ireland in January 1922. In Belfast there followed the worst violence in the city before the outbreak of the Troubles in 1969. Between 12 and 16 February, 31 people were killed in the city and there was shooting, rioting and house-burning almost every day. Robert McElborough, a gas worker in Belfast at this time, described in his memoirs what conditions were like in the Short Strand:

I was taken off the meter work and was told by the superintendent to keep the lamps in Seaforde Street and the Short Strand in repair. This area was one of the dangerous parts for shooting in the city. I asked why I was selected for this position and what had happened to the lamp maintenance man who did this district. I was told that this was a military order to keep this area lit up; I was issued with a permit and was told that I would have military protection if I applied to the officer in charge. I had the feeling that like Uriah of the Bible I was being sent to the front line.

The people living in this area did not want the streets lit as they said they were a target when on the streets, and felt more secure from bullets in the dark, but the military who were patrolling this area insisted that the lamps be lit. This was in 1922, and anyone who lived in the area remembers the cross-firing that was kept up day and night. No one would venture out and trams passed this area at full empty, or with passengers lying flat on the floor. . .

I can't tell how I got the cart into this area. I ran with it and got safely into Madrid Street and into Seaforde Street with rifles cracking overhead. When I arrived with the lamps and fittings I was surrounded by a number of men and women who told me to clear out. I had to explain my position as a workman. It was the women who carried the day in my favour, but I was told that every lamp and fitting that I fitted up would be smashed when the lights were lit, and I want to say here and now that during these winter months that I kept the lights repaired the people in this area never interfered with me. But there was times when I had to clear out, when someone who lived in the district had been shot by a sniper. It was the snipers on the roofs and back windows who were the danger. Anyone seen on the streets within the range of their gun was their target, and they found out later through the press what side he belonged to. I had seen men who were going to work shot dead as a reprisal for some other victim. My only dread was when I was standing on the ladder putting up a lamp, bullets that I suppose were meant for me went through the lamp reflector. I brought some of these lamps back to the workshops and my workmates had many discussions on my narrow escapes.

The situation in the city deteriorated further in March. Troops used machine guns against snipers in the Falls; men laying tram-lines on the Antrim Road came under fire; bombs were thrown into a crowd in Foundry Street and into the porch of St Matthew's Catholic Church; a bomb was thrown onto a tram passing the New Lodge Road; a B Special, Constable Vokes, was shot by British troops; and both sides perpetrated assassinations of frightful barbarity. Two examples are sufficient. Just after midnight on 29 March uniformed men, said to have been B Specials, broke into the home of Owen MacMahon, a Catholic publican who lived in Austin Road. Five members of the family were shot dead; only the youngest child, who hid under the table, survived. On 31 March a bomb was thrown into the kitchen of a home in Brown Street; Francis Donnelly – an Orangeman and a member of the Church of Ireland – had been reading his evening newspaper by the fire; he and his two daughters were severely wounded and his two boys – aged 12 and 2 years 10 months – died from their injuries; the attackers fired revolver shots at Donnelly's wife, who was nursing a baby, as they left.

Altogether 61 people died in Belfast in the violence of March 1922. Isolated Catholic and Protestant families were particularly vulnerable and intimidation, house-burning, rioting and assassination drew the lines between the two religions in the city more tautly than ever. Atrocity followed atrocity, counter-assassination followed almost every violent death, and large areas of Belfast were virtually at war. Historians have, until recently, concentrated their attention on the Irish Civil War in the south which had not yet begun. There were few episodes in that conflict, however, to equal in scale and ferocity those that occurred in Belfast in the spring and early summer of 1922.

'Is civilisation going to be allowed to exist?': March–December 1922

'Peace is today declared. . .' proclaimed the Craig–Collins Pact signed in London on 30 March 1922. Craig, for the Northern Ireland government, agreed to attract Catholics into the Special Constabulary and to reinstate Catholics expelled from the shipyards. Michael Collins, for the Provisional Government of the Irish Free State, agreed to act against IRA units operating from the south. 'How this was to be sorted out, I don't know,' commented General Sean MacEoin, and indeed it proved impossible to implement. Northern Catholics refused to apply to join the Specials and Craig made no real attempt to recover Catholics' jobs, though Westminster had given him £500,000 towards unemployment relief as an inducement. Most members of the Free State government were anxious to curb the lawlessness of the IRA, north and south, but it is now known that, after the Pact, Collins actually supplied rifles to northern IRA Units.

The Pact did not produce even a momentary lull in the violence in Belfast. On 1 April an RIC policeman was shot dead in Stanhope Street in Carrick Hill and next day police killed one man in Stanhope Street, another man in Park Street, and two men and a seven-year-old boy in Arnon Street. On 14 April an engine driver was shot dead at York Street station; on the 17th one Catholic and one Protestant were killed in fierce rioting in the Bone, and about 50 homes in Antigua and Saunderson Streets were burned; and on the 23rd a bomb was thrown at St Matthew's Church and one women was killed. The number killed in Belfast during the month of April was 36.

The government adopted drastic measures to restore order. In place of the RIC, the Royal Ulster Constabulary was set up on 5 April 1922 and by the summer there were 50,000 regular and part-time constables in the province — one for every six families in Northern Ireland. On 7 April 1922 the Civil Authorities (Special Powers) Bill became law, giving the Minister of Home Affairs authority to detain suspects and to set up courts of summary jurisdiction. George Hanna MP protested that the Bill was too complicated: there were, he said, 'nine sections of the Bill and thirty regulations. One section would have been sufficient: "The Home Secretary shall have the power to do whatever he likes, or let somebody else do whatever he likes for him". That is the whole Bill.' Robert Lynn, MP for West Belfast, argued in the debate on the Bill that 'the Government has not gone far enough. . . This is no time for indulging in legal hair-splitting.' The question at issue was simple, Lynn said: 'Is civilisation going to be allowed to exist, or is there going to be anarchy?'

On 18 May three Catholics were shot dead in Belfast and the following day three Protestants were murdered in a cooperage in Little Patrick Street. On 22 May, W.J. Twaddell, MP for West Belfast, was shot dead on the way to his outfitter's shop in central Belfast. The only MP to be assassinated in Northern Ireland until the murder of the Rev Robert Bradford in 1981, Twaddell had had an enthusiastic following on the Shankill Road; his murder led to the immediate imposition of internment on the same day. Two hundred were arrested on the first day, many being held in the Crumlin Road Gaol, and the curfew was extended. Rolls of barbed wire fenced off Ardoyne and the Bone. On that one day, 22 May, 14 people died in sectarian clashes. The burning of homes and business premises was worse than before, particularly as the IRA had decided on a campaign of setting fire to factories and houses owned by leading Unionists. Altogether 44 Catholics and 22 Protestants met with violent deaths in Belfast during the month of May.

Yet comparative peace returned to Belfast in the summer of 1922. In part this was due to the very severity of government action which pleased the city's loyalists. More important, the outbreak of civil war in the Irish Free State relieved the Northern Ireland government of pressure at a crucial moment. The IRA, opposed to the 1921 Treaty, had occupied major buildings in Dublin from April onwards. 'If we don't take action we will be considered the greatest poltroons in history,' said Arthur Griffith, premier of the Irish Free State. Action had to be taken after Sir Henry Wilson, military adviser to the Northern Ireland government, had been shot dead by the IRA in London on 22 June; on 28 June the National Army began to pound the Four Courts in Dublin with field-gun fire and the Irish Civil War had begun. IRA activists in Belfast who had not already been interned went south to fight on one side or the other. The Free State government used harsher measures than had been used in the north. Altogether 77 republicans were executed; one of the first – shot as reprisal for the murder of a Dáil deputy – was Joe McKelvey from Cyprus Street in Belfast.

In Belfast, 236 people had been killed in the first months of 1922 – more than in the widespread troubles in Germany in the same period. Between July 1920 and July 1922 the death roll for Belfast was 453 – 257 Catholics, 157 Protestants, 2 of unknown religion, and 37 members of the security forces. Catholic relief organisations estimated that between 8,700 and 11,000 Catholics had lost their jobs, that 23,000 Catholics had been forced out of their homes, and that about 500 Catholic-owned businesses had been destroyed. Nor had the dying and destruction come to a complete halt; 16 Catholics were killed in the late summer and autumn.

The arrest of members of the Ulster Protestant Association, responsible for the killings, helped to bring almost total peace back to Belfast by the beginning of 1923. Joe Devlin had used the word 'pogrom' to describe what Belfast Catholics suffered in these years. A pogrom is usually thought of as an attack on a defenceless ghetto; Protestants also had their ghettoes in Belfast and where these enclaves were isolated or formed salients they too had come under attack. Belfast had experienced a vicious sectarian war at a time of political turmoil, and yet the statistics speak for themselves: Catholics formed only a quarter of the city's population but had suffered more than half the deaths. Protestants argued that Catholics in the city were aiming for nothing less than the destruction of the state; Catholics replied that they had been denied the right to be in a state for which three-quarters of the citizens of Ireland had voted.

'The unemployed walking the streets'

The deep scars left by the Troubles might have healed in time had Belfast enjoyed a long period of prosperity after 1922. The boom years, however, did not return; 22.9% were unemployed in 1922 and for the rest of the decade around one fifth of all insured workers had no jobs. Belfast remained a great industrial and commercial city but her greatest firms – engineering, linen and shipbuilding – were always working below capacity, and output never reached the levels attained before and during the First World War.

Belfast's economic difficulties were not primarily due to partition or violence. The Troubles may have discouraged some new investment but the Irish Free State did not erect high tariff barriers against the United Kingdom until 1932. The real problem was that world trade conditions had changed: Belfast in these years was producing and attempting to sell goods of which there was a surplus abroad. The difficulties Belfast faced were almost identical to those experienced by Clydeside, Lancashire, the Tyne and other areas producing textiles and heavy engineering products. The new local parliament had been given almost no power to help under the Government of Ireland Act. Politicians at Westminster – who ultimately controlled Belfast's economic destiny – chose to give tariff protection only to new industries such as chemicals and motor car manufacture.

In 1925 the Chancellor of the Exchequer, Winston Churchill, returned the pound sterling to the 'Gold Standard'. The results were disastrous for Belfast:

the pound was overvalued by around 10% and the city's products became severely overpriced abroad. Significant recovery made in 1923 and 1924 was lost again. The numbers employed in the linen industry fell from 86,762 in 1924 to 70,421 in 1925 and unemployment in the industry rose from 9½% to 32%. Gone were the heady days during the war when over 163 million yards were exported annually; in the 1920s the average annual exports were 77 million yards. Worse still, the price almost collapsed; linen piece goods bringing in £100 in 1913 could fetch only £40 by 1927. In 1919 the Belfast shipyards launched 32 vessels, totalling 134,456 tons, and Workman Clark was second on the British list. In 1924, 15 ships totalling 71,956 tons left the slips; the 'economic consequences of Mr Churchill' (as Keynes put it) were an output of only 34,167 tons in 1925 and severe unemployment.

Belfast did not share in the world boom in the late 1920s – the 'roaring Twenties' were experienced elsewhere and had no meaning in the city. New industries – such as light engineering and motor car manufacture – helped to offset the decline of the staple industries in Britain; political turmoil and uncertainty may have kept them from coming to Belfast. In short, Belfast was the centre of the most disadvantaged industrial area in the United Kingdom. Unemployment was the scourge of these years and as many were out of work for extended periods they lost their eligibility for the 'b'roo' – the dole from the unemployment bureaux. Patrick Shea, working for the Ministry of Labour at this time, records in his autobiography:

The plague of the unemployed was NGSW; disallowance of benefit because the claimant was Not Genuinely Seeking Work. The onus of proof was on the applicant. Every six weeks he was required to produce proof that he was genuinely seeking work. This condition, which was very rigorously applied, sent the unemployed walking the streets to call at offices, shops, factories, warehouses and building sites asking for notes certifying that they had applied for employment but that there were no vacancies. . . it fell to me to interview a woman who had come to enquire about the rejection of her claim for benefit. She was a generously proportioned widow with the ready tongue of one who is not accustomed to being thwarted. Her employment record was such that her case was quite hopeless. . . I felt that I had handled a difficult situation rather well. She walked silently to the door, opened it and turning to the rows of silent men, now poring over their papers, she addressed the whole company. She spoke calmly and purposefully.

* Patrick Shea, *Voices and the sound of drums* (see bibliog), p. 117.

'During the war my husband made bombs. He spent four years making bombs. I wish to Jaysus I had one of them now.'

Corporation affairs

In June 1922 the Northern Ireland government followed up its victory over the IRA by putting forward a Bill to abolish proportional representation in local government elections. Though the opposition benches were still empty, the Bill did not go through without criticism. The Unionist MP for East Belfast, Thompson Donald, feared the permanent alienation of Catholics: 'I do contend that it gives minority representation. . . I think in all fairness the minority should have representation.' When the Bill passed through the Northern Ireland parliament, Westminster – for once – hesitated: was the spirit of the Government of Ireland Act being contravened? Lloyd George's disintegrating coalition had more serious worries, however, and the Bill received royal assent in September 1922.

The consequences for Belfast Corporation were far-reaching. The pre-1920 ward boundaries returned and so the elaborate gerrymandering of electoral boundaries, so evident west of the Bann, did not occur in Belfast. The effect of the abolition of PR, seen in the local elections of 1923, was to stultify political life in the city. The Labour Party's representation was cut from eleven councillors to two and the Unionists returned to the position they had held before 1920. The polarisation of the electorate during the Troubles was the principal cause of Labour's near collapse, but the first-past-the-post system probably made it more difficult for parties attempting to break out of the traditional moulds. In addition, the wards, being shaped like segments of cake, split the working class in the inner city by mixing it with the middle-class vote of the suburbs — an arrangement which had few parallels in British cities of similar size and character.

Labour had gained three more seats by 1925 but Belfast was not about to imitate other depressed urban areas in Britain by going over solidly to Labour. The Nationalists gained from the abolition of PR and recovered Falls and Smithfield wards — a further indication that the city was starkly divided into two irreconcilable political camps. Nevertheless, it must be recognised that under any democratic electoral system the Unionists were certain to maintain a comfortable majority in the City Hall — entrenched loyalties in both communities together with periodic threats to the Union — real or imagined — ensured that. It was natural therefore that the ruling group in the Belfast Corporation became uniquely entrenched, having little fear of being ousted.

In the inter-war period a clearly identifiable City Hall Unionist party emerged which could not only bring strong pressure to bear on the provincial government but also react indignantly against interference from the Northern Ireland parliament. To a remarkable extent this ruling élite was dominated by prosperous members of the business and professional classes — denounced later by some loyalists as 'the fur coat brigade'. The leading member of this ruling group was Sir Crawford McCullagh, first Chairman of the Housing Committee; though the Committee was condemned by an inquiry in 1926, McCullagh was elected Lord Mayor in 1931 — an office he held for sixteen years.

The City Hall Unionists could still show some of the constructive enterprise seen on pre-war days; the Corporation, for example, built the first municipal aerodrome in the United Kingdom, as Hugh Finnegan recalls:

Belfast's first municipal airport was on the Malone Road on the right hand side just past the 'Dub'. The Corporation bought a farm from Mr Archie Willis (who later married Miss Gallaher of Gallaher's Cigarettes). The airport was opened in 1924; as we had cattle beside Finaghy Road South I just had to look through the hedge to see the airport activities.

On the day of the opening, 30 April 1924, the Lord Mayor, Sir William Turner, was flown from Malone to Manchester. Later, alternative terminals were found at Aintree and Stranraer but the aerodrome at Malone was too waterlogged; the Air Ministry took over the service and transferred the Belfast terminal to Aldergrove.

The East Bridge Street electricity generating station, operating since 1898, could no longer meet the growing demand and in August 1923 the Harbour Power Station was opened. The Electricity Department's charges compared favourably with those in other British cities; 1,900 new domestic supplies were connected in 1927–9 and enough power was generated to supply Lisburn, Bangor and Holywood. By 1928 the Corporation Gas Department was producing 16½ million cubic feet of gas a day – more than the original Belfast Gas Light Company had produced in a year. The spiral-guided gasholder was the largest of its type in the world and almost the whole of the city's street lighting was still maintained by gas. Though the price paid by the consumer was perhaps the lowest in the UK, the Gas Department's profits were great enough to subsidise the rates, electricity, libraries, parks and public baths and to pay £294,632 towards the cost of building the City Hall.

Over £3 million was spent in the 1920s on reconstruction: the Malone Road, Falls Road, Shankill Road and other main thoroughfares were widened and resurfaced; in 1927 a bridge was built over the railway at Tate's Avenue; North Road Bridge was widened; a lock and a weir were made above the Albert Bridge; and three miles of roadway, together with sloped tree-lined banks, helped to make the lower Lagan slightly less offensive than before. This kind of expenditure appealed to the city fathers, but they remained passionately concerned to keep down the rates – it never occurred to them, for example, to reduce gas charges still further and money spent on social services was considered dangerously socialistic. Public health and Corporation housing were sadly neglected, though the city's record in eduation was rather better.

Progress in education

> Our wee school's a nice wee school,
> Made of bricks and plaster.
> The only thing that we don't like,
> Is our wee baldy master.
> He goes to the pub on Saturday night,
> He goes to Church on Sunday,
> To pray to God to give him strength
> To slaughter us on Monday.

'Sammy Ate your Orange!' was the meaningless phrase shouted at school attendance officers – with the letters SAO embroidered on their caps – as they sought out children supposed to be at school. School attendance for all children had been compulsory only since 1892; the Act brought Robert McElborough's career as a point shifter to an end though he continued to 'beak' on the Bog Meadows until caught by the attendance officer. His punishment was swift at Blackstaff National School:

The Master of this school put fear into every scholar. We were all boys and he certainly taught us, for he used his cane. . . I felt the weight of his cane when I got to school. He would make the strongest boy carry the defaulter on his back while he followed up with the cane: . .

In fact there is little evidence from the minutes that the Corporation's school attendance committee took its task very seriously. Under the old system, run by the National Commissioners of Education in Dublin, the city's elementary schools had been neglected and the Corporation had shown a marked reluctance to give help from the rates. A committee appointed to recommend

Schoolboys from St. Barnabas
Public Elementary School,
Duncairn Gardens, around
1930. (Henry V. Bell)

improvements, headed by R.J. Lynn, editor of the *Northern Whig* and
Unionist MP for West Belfast, estimated in its report in 1922 that about
12,000 children of school age in Belfast were without school accommodation.
Lord Londonderry's Education Act of 1923 envisaged striking improvements
by increasing grants and by making local education authorities responsible for
schools. Londonderry – who had a habit of emphasising points by striking his
ministerial table with his riding crop – declared that 'religious instruction in a
denominational sense there will not be. . .'

Though the 1923 Act refused to allow religious instruction in school hours
in the state schools, the Catholic managers would not transfer their buildings
to the control of the Belfast Education Committee, set up in October 1923.
The Catholic managers had declared in 1921 that 'the only satisfactory system
of education for Catholics is one wherein Catholic children are taught in
Catholic schools by Catholic teachers under Catholic auspices'. In the crucial
period when the 1923 Act was being framed, Catholics had refused to play any
part in the shaping of education policy and now their schools were worse off
than before – though teachers' salaries were paid, the government would cover
only 50% of the cost of cleaning, heating and lighting, and refused to
contribute to building costs. In 1923 there were 16,324 Catholics attending
schools but there were places for only 14,725, indicating an urgent need for
new buildings. Only the Christian Brothers' schools in the city agreed to accept
some government control in 1926, thereby gaining them an additional
£10,000 annually.

The Belfast Education Committee – consistently more progressive than
either the government or the Corporation as a whole – set out with genuine
determination to wipe out more than 90 years of neglect. Alderman James
Duff, the first chairman, was remembered by one of his officials as 'a real
dynamo supplying the energy to get local control off the ground. . . Ideas for
the development of the work of the Committee were inspired by him, and he
certainly kept the officers of the Committee on their toes.' The Committee
began by carrying out a detailed census of children and schools in the city. The
survey found that there were 59,370 of school age in Belfast but that there

were 64,064 children attending in all; 9,000 of these were either above or below school age, indicating that over 4,000 children of school age were not attending. Out of 195 elementary schools in the city only 6 could be classed as 'satisfactory' and only another 12 could 'be made satisfactory'; and, as the Committee reported in 1924:

. . . the great majority of the remainder would not be tolerated in any other part of the United Kingdom. There are about forty of these schools which are a direct menace to the health and physical development of the children and it is almost doubtful whether the children attending them would not be better in the street.

The first important task of the Director of Education, Major Rupert Stanley, was to close down as many of the delapidated buildings as possible. An easy solution was avoided: children under the school age of six were not put out, as their mothers were generally working in the linen mills. Work began on new elementary schools which were so well designed that today they look as if they were put up in the 1950s and not the 1920s. Their layout helped to prepare the way for better teaching for, as Norman McNeilly recalled:

* Norman McNeilly, *Exactly 50 years: the Belfast Education Authority and its work (1923–73)* (see bibliog), p. 12.

Anyone who can remember the old type school in the twenties and even the thirties, with perhaps five or six classes in a single room, will also remember the maze marching which had to take place to enable classes to change from one arrangement of positions on the schoolroom floor to a different distribution. This had to be done so that classes could change from desks, to standing areas, or to 'form-seat' areas, or to 'gallery areas'.*

Euston Street and Templemore Avenue were the first new schools, opened in 1926, and by 1929 Everton, Mountcollyer, Park Parade, Fane Street and Mersey Street were completed. In the first five years of the Committee's life about 50 of the worst schools were closed down; this meant that there was little perceptible improvement in accommodation. The Committee took over the School Medical Service from the Public Health Department and began to provide school meals for necessitous children in 1926: the food was served from the Tamar Street kitchen, with the help of Toc H, the St Vincent de Paul Society and the Shankill Road Mission.

Secondary schools continued with the minimum of interference; some free places had been provided by the Corporation before the war and now these were increased to fifty: thirty 'scholarships' for boys and twenty for girls. see the rapid expansion of places for academically able working-class children which occurred in Britain between the wars. Two who won these coveted city scholarships – J.C. Beckett and T.W. Moody – were to become renowned professors of Irish history. Five scholarships each year had been awarded for university places by the Corporation in 1913; no improvement on this figure was seen in the inter-war years.

Bible instruction

'PROTESTANTS AWAKE' proclaimed leaflets throughout the city in March 1925; the United Education Committee of the Protestant Churches – led by Rev William Corkey, manager of nine schools in the Shankill area – was denouncing the Education Committee's schools as godless. Duff defiantly countered that 'any clergyman who says that under the new education act the

Bible is thrown out of the schools is a man who has no right to wear the cloth'. The Ulster Teachers' Union, composed of Protestant teachers, passed a resolution condemning Corkey's campaign, the proposer denouncing 'discontented divines who were misleading people who could not think for themselves'. The United Education Committee's meeting in the Assembly Hall in Fisherwick Place on 5 March was impressive, however, and had the support of the Belfast County Orange Lodge. While his Minister of Education was immobilised by 'flu, Craig made concessions: a Bill was hastily passed to permit religious instruction and to allow management committees to appoint teachers. Londonderry resigned to take on what were for him more congenial opponents – his employees in the Durham coal mines.

The great majority of Protestant elementary schools – 73 by 1929 – now transferred to the control of the Belfast Education Committee. Still the 'discontented divines' were not satisfied and were determined to ensure that religious education in the local authority schools was 'Bible instruction'. Corkey and two other clergy confronted the Committee on 20 January 1928; the meeting was a bitter one. The clergy declared:

The Christian Churches when united are a much truer index of the public mind than any City Council. . . the Belfast Education Committee is setting up a dual system of education, one system for Roman Catholics, and another for those of any or no religion to which Protestants are compelled to conform. . .

The Belfast Education Committee replied: 'The comparison is not a very Christian one. We are unable to assume that the views of Christian Churches can only be voiced by clerics. . .'

Once more the Prime Minister gave way to the United Education Committee and Lord Charlemont, the new Minister of Education, prepared an amending Bill. The Belfast Education Committee urged the Minister not to increase clerical representation on management committees but was rapped over the knuckles by the Corporation for its pains on 28 April 1930. This was too much for Mrs Julia McMordie who resigned. This time the Catholic Church fought a strenuous campaign for more money; Dr Daniel Mageean, Bishop of Down and Connor, wrote to all churches in his diocese:

In view of the attack on Catholic interests in education by the Bill now before the parliament of the Six Counties. . . I would request the laity to join with the priest in praying that God may guide and help us in this hour of danger.

The Ulster Teachers' Union joined their colleagues in the Irish National Teachers' Organisation in opposing the Bill which nevertheless became law that year. The 1930 Education Act increased clerical representation on committees and specified Bible instruction during religious education lessons. 'Simple Bible teaching is based on the fundamental principle of Protestantism, the interpretation of sacred Scriptures by private judgement,' Dr Mageean observed, but he had scored a notable victory: henceforth Catholic schools would get 50% grants for school building and improvement.

The government did pay the entire cost of training both Catholic and Protestant teachers. In the 1920s the only teacher training college in the province was St Mary's until Stranmillis College was opened in 1929. When the Catholic Church refused to allow its trainees to go to Stranmillis – despite an offer of a separate hostel – the government arranged for Catholic men to

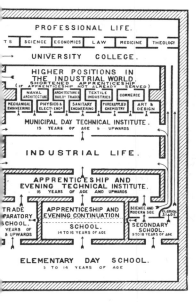

PROFESSIONAL LIFE.

How to climb the social and
economic ladder through
education. 'Diagram
illustrating the Correlation of
Education' from the *Souvenir of
the opening of the Municipal
Technical Institute* (College of
Technology) in 1907.

attend St Mary's in Middlesex. Craigavon eventually capitulated to a further
demand by the United Education Committee: in March 1932 three Protestant
clergy were invited to join the management committee of Stranmillis College.
The Ulster Teachers' Union protested at this 'abject surrender of the
government in acceding to the reactionary demands of the joint committee of
the Protestant Churches. . .'

Education did not suffer as much as most other public services in the city
during the depression of the 1930s. No year passed by without at least one new
school being opened – they included Glenwood and Strandtown (1930);
Linfield (1931); Seaview (1934); Avoniel (1935); Edenderry and Beechfield
(1936); and the Botanic and Model schools (1937-8). School inspectors noted
that schools transferred to the Committee were immediately improved
and several – including Lancaster Street, Porter's Memorial and Forth River –
were completely reconditioned. New sites were bought at Orangefield and
Glenard, and 56 unsuitable schools were closed. Four new Catholic schools
were opened in 1932: St Comgall's Boys' and Girls', and St Kevin's Boys' and
Girls'. The government ordered each County and County Borough to support
educational services by a shilling rate in 1934; the Corporation denounced this
as an 'income tax' and appealed to the Judicial Committee of the Privy
Council. The appeal failed, one of the Law Lords commenting: 'Income tax, if
I may say so, is a tax upon income.'

By 1939 the number of school places almost matched the numbers on the
rolls, though this was partly brought about by a fall in the birth rate. Despite its
signal failure to improve opportunities in secondary education, the Education
Committee had achieved much within the limits of its restricted budget.

Corporation housing: outstanding enterprise or dismal failure?

In 1929 the City Surveyor, R.B. Donald, claimed that the 'result of the
improvements to thoroughfares and the clearing away of old properties is that
Belfast can justly claim to be a City without slums'. Three years later the city's
Medical Officer of Health, Charles Thomson, referring to the expansion of the
suburbs, said that 'the rate of growth prevents the formation of slums as I
understand the term'. 'The outstanding enterprise of the Corporation since the
Great War was in connection with housing,' the Town Clerk commented in
the 1937 bicentenary edition of the *Belfast News-Letter*; 'It was a very
valuable contribution to the progress of the City at a difficult time.' No
comprehensive survey of Belfast's housing stock was taken in the inter-war
period to support these views and, indeed, there is much evidence to support
R.J. Lawrence's judgement that the Corporation's housing achievement
'cannot unfairly be described as derisory'.

House building had come to a virtual standstill during the war and as people
came in from the countryside to find work in the booming factories of Belfast
the problem of overcrowding became acute. The Corporation was extremely
reluctant to assume responsibility, but it had to respond to an Act of 1919
which compelled local authorities to draw up schemes for housing the working
classes. A 14-member Housing Committee, with Sir Crawford McCullagh as
chairman and T.E. McConnell – of the family of estate agents – as vice-
chairman, prepared a modest scheme and built 16 demonstration houses of
different types. The Northern Ireland government set out to mirror Britain's
social reforms step by step and its first Housing Act of 1923 imitated Neville

Chamberlain's policy of subsidising private builders. In 1924, however, Wheatley's Housing Act revolutionised housing policy by virtually making it a social service: councils were to build houses for renting and an upper limit was to be placed on those rents. Such a solution was certain to be expensive – could Belfast afford such a policy?

To the majority of Belfast Corporation councillors the Wheatley solution was quite unacceptable – an intolerable burden would be placed on ratepayers. Being a very big fish in a small pond, Belfast was in a strong position to influence the Northern Ireland government. The views of the Corporation generally counted for more than those of backbench and opposition MPs and of 16 amendments to housing bills between 1923 and 1936, 8 were promoted directly by the Corporation or by MPs on its behalf. Debates on housing in the Commons tended to centre on the city's problems though those of rural areas were almost as acute. The Corporation believed that private enterprise could cope adequately with the city's housing needs, provided subsidies were available, and the Minister of Finance was only too happy to agree. Thirteen Housing Acts regulated the subsidies – £60 per house in 1923, £100 in 1927, reduced to £25 in 1932 and withdrawn altogether in 1937.

The Housing Acts did give the Corporation new responsibilities but the performance of its Housing Committee was to show that the city fathers were barely fit to undertake these responsibilities. In March 1925 the auditor of the Ministry of Local Government protested that building contracts were not being put out to tender. Then, when independent accountants reported that the Corporation had been supplied with inferior timber and that £5,171 had been overpaid for building materials on the Whiterock Road site, the government asked Robert Dick Megaw to make a detailed inquiry. Megaw, reporting in October 1926, discovered irregularities on a wide scale – accounts had not been checked, inferior materials had been accepted, contracts had not been put out to tender and the city solicitor and members of the Housing Committee had a financial interest in the sites which had been chosen by consideration of 'profit to the vendor and not suitability for working-class housing'. One contractor had alleged that the Corporation paid 25% more than the market price for poor quality timber, and, out of one million bricks delivered by one firm, 66,000 had not been accounted for. Megaw noted the 'disinclination of everybody concerned' to help the inquiry and he found 'a feeling akin to fatalism as regards the chances of effecting any reform in the Corporation's management of its public duties'.* Eventually a private Bill was put through Parliament in 1930 to effect extensive financial and administration reforms, but the whole sorry episode had badly tarnished the Corporation's reputation.

Nevertheless, it was in the 1920s that most houses were built. Under the Subsidy Scheme, 913 kitchen houses and 88 parlour houses were completed, 333 of them at Whiterock, 209 at Donegall Avenue, and 205 at Seaview. Under a joint scheme with the government to provide unemployment relief the Corporation built 584 parlour houses and 518 kitchen houses at Ulsterville, Woodvale, Stranmillis, Donegall Road and Skegoniel. Under the Assisted Scheme – in which the government gave 25s for every £1 collected in rent – 363 parlour houses and 96 kitchen houses were erected at Wandsworth, Cherryvalley, Dundela and Rosebery Road. Both the Corporation and the government seemed satisfied that great progress had been made. 'To walk

* I. Budge and C. O'Leary, *Belfast: approach to crisis: a study of Belfast politics, 1613–1970* (see bibliog), p. 147.

along the roads on any of the Housing Estates in the time of summer,' the 1929 *Belfast Book* commented, 'is to see a sight which must gladden the heart of every lover of well-kept home gardens'; and the Junior Minister of Home Affairs, G.B. Hanna, believed these houses to be perfect for three or four children, a 'clean and tidy wife', and a father who 'does not want to go out either to a public house or to a Local Option meeting, he wants his "Evening Telegraph" – and after having patted the children on the head and said good night to them he sits down in that house which is his own or becoming so more and more every day.'

Indeed, most of these houses were very attractive, but the problem was that the average working-class family could not afford to buy or rent them. The houses at Cherryvalley and Wandsworth were difficult to let because they cost between 17s and 22s a week to rent, while the standard rent for parlour houses was 16s and for kitchen houses 13s. As prices and wages fell in the 1930s, rents for kitchen houses dropped to as low as 8s a week but this was still too high for working men earning around 30s a week – not to speak of those who had no work at all. The Housing Committee steadfastly refused to subsidise rents to a lower level; Dawson Bates, Minister of Home Affairs and MP for Victoria, remarked in 1932:

After all, builders are not philanthropists, and people are not prepared to invest their money in houses which are subject to restricting conditions of this kind.

The last large-scale building for 'artisans' in these years was in Glenard, Ardoyne, which reached completion in 1934–5. The houses were certainly built to a better standard than before the war: each had a 20-foot square garden in front, a kitchen, a larder and – in the outside yard – a toilet and coal store. But only a narrow passage separated the houses at the back, no bathrooms were provided, and the living space was little more than had been provided 50 years before. The houses were almost identical; still, they provided a desperately needed refuge for those driven out of Sailorstown in 1935.

Joe Devlin had called for 'a comprehensive housing scheme for the abolishing of all slums', and the Select Committee on Rents reported in 1931: 'The greatest need at the moment is for houses which can be let at low rents, i.e. not exceeding 6s a week'. Altogether 34,312 houses were put up in Northern Ireland in the inter-war years and of these only 2,600 were built by the Belfast Corporation. The complete failure to provide for the housing needs of the low-paid, particularly in the inner city, was not to be documented until 1944.

Public health

Failure to improve working-class housing, together with low income and unemployment, made it difficult to improve the public health of the city. The death rate in 1922–4 was 15.5 per 1,000 in Northern Ireland; 12.2 in England and Wales; 14.1 in Scotland; and 14.6 in the Irish Free State. The rate – which by 1936–8 had only fallen to 14.4 in Northern Ireland – was even higher in Belfast; for example, the infant mortality rate per 1,000 births averaged 97 in the city as against 77 for the province as a whole in 1934–8. The risk of mothers dying in childbirth actually increased in the inter-war period and the city had the highest death rate from tuberculosis in the British Isles.

A government commission, reporting in 1927, recommended a complete overhaul of the chaotic system of health services inherited by the province in 1921. Desperately attempting to find the money to keep unemployment benefits level with those in Britain, the government finally had to admit that it could not pay to implement the 153 recommendations made by the commission. Medical insurance was not introduced until 1930. Belfast did at least have a Public Health Department and its Medical Officer of Health, Dr Charles Thomson, believed that a good job was being done for the city. Dr Thomson, writing in the 1929 *Belfast Book*, described a typical Monday morning in Room 53 in the City Hall.

The Chief enters shortly after 9 a.m. A bell is rung and letters are brought to his desk. . . Not infrequently letters are received without the usual formality of a signature – one or two are signed 'Yours unanimously', a slight mistake for 'Yours anonymously'. We attend to them all. . . the Health Visitors are summoned at 9.35 a.m. to the Medical Officer's room. They are given the list of births which have been notified that morning; they visit the homes and teach many a little mother how to feed her baby through the helpless years of infancy, so that a sturdy Belfast lad may emerge from the chrysalis stage to take his share in carrying on the evolution of the City. . . There are all sorts and conditions on the telephone. Some want a dead cat removed from their back yard. . . Verily a soft answer turneth away wrath. Through in another room the colleague Medical Officer is sifting the day's notifications of Infectious Disease. . .

Dr Thomson's department, lacking specialist staff, was expected to do much, including inspection of food, milk, the abbatoir, and ships coming into port. One inspector was actually disguised as a dosser in the Common Lodging Houses keeping 'at least one eye open' for 'migrating "Ne'er do wells" who are lousy and who might "light up" the City if not watched'. As for venereal disease, Dr Thomson commented, the 'Public Health Department is at one with the theologians. People should keep a grip of themselves. . .' The Corporation, obsessed with keeping down the rates, would not pay for a more professional service and the government, unwilling or unable to raise taxes above the British level, could not increase its grants.

Dr T.F.S. Fulton, chief of the Education Committee's school medical service, was acutely aware of the city's shortcomings in public health. His annual reports became ever more despairing as he attempted to rouse public concern: in 1930 he made a plea for pre-school medical treatment as he had nearly 1,000 tubercular children on his books; in 1931 he called for compulsory medical inspection; in 1932 he noted that too many teachers 'are too lethargic to care" in 1933 he found a great many children suffering from malnutrition and anaemia; and in 1935 he reported that 20% of children got no medical or dental attention because of absence, or refusal by parents. Dr Fulton did what he could with inadequate staff; he increased medical inspections from 85,317 in 1924 to 204,218 in 1925 but he could allow only five minutes per child. He worked long hours in 112 Great Victoria Street (moving to the Old Town Hall in 1927) and opened branch clinics at the Mount and at 4 Carlisle Terrace.

Belfast did have the best hospitals in the province and probably in the island as a whole. Queen's University medical school was highly regarded and the British Medical Association held its 105th annual meeting in the city in 1937. The Royal Victoria Hospital acquired three additional wards in 1924 and Mrs Stanley Baldwin opened the 100-bed Royal Maternity Hospital in 1933. On the same site, a nurses' home and the Royal Belfast Hospital for Sick Children were built in these years. By 1935 the Jubilee Maternity Hospital has been completed at a cost of £53,000 and the Dufferin and Ava hospitals for children could accommodate 332 patients; the Union Infirmary's standards remained low due to lack of funds, however. The Workhouse Asylum was razed to the ground – deservedly – in 1927 and the mentally ill were treated at Purdysburn; here, alone of any institution in the province, some attempt was made to grade mental illnesses. The Purdysburn colony had a magnificent setting and the recreation hall there was equipped with 'a Cinematographic Installation'; patients could buy confectionery and tobacco in the Tuck Shop with tokens awarded for 'good conduct, etc'.

Efforts by hospitals to improve the health of citizens could easily be cancelled out by impoverished home surroundings and by the carelessness of neighbouring local authorities. Carrickfergus, Holywood and other towns poured untreated sewage into Belfast Lough; areas outside the city made no attempt to notify cases of infectious tuberculosis; and infected animals were constantly brought into the Corporation abbatoir from the countryside. Belfast did at least have a pure and abundant water supply. After delays, due in part to the fear that the Boundary Commission would award the Mourne area to the Irish Free State, the Silent Valley reservoir was finished in 1933. The project was a triumph of engineering skill and increased the supply of water to 21 million gallons a day – Silent Valley provided 11 million gallons, Woodburn 7½ million gallons, and Stoneyford 2½ million gallons for the city by 1939.

The Board of Guardians: 'Money given to the poor was wasted'

On 14 June 1926 hungry unemployed men gathered on the Shankill Road. There were almost 30,000 unemployed in Belfast and the city, with one third of the population of Northern Ireland, had half of the province's unemployed within its limits. As police drew their batons, Samuel Patterson of Wyndham Street addressed the crowd on behalf of the recently formed Unemployed Workers' Organisation:

Comrades and unemployed, we read in the Scriptures that the earth is the Lord's and the fullness thereof. We are here to bring to your notice the demonstration of the unemployed that is to take place tomorrow to the Poor Law Guardians. . . you were heroes when you were in the trenches. If you were still the same heroes, 300 of you could still go up to the workhouse, even though you have not the privilege of having a six-pounder behind you and take possession for a day. You could compel the dirty boss class to grant your demands. . . Here are the police coming. They are always on the alert when revolution is spoken of. Run like hell!

Charged with making a seditious speech, Patterson was sentenced to six months imprisonment the following day. The unemployed did indeed march on the workhouse on 15 June; led by bands, they walked from the City Hall to the Lisburn Road where a large force of police stopped them going through the gates. Only Jack Beattie and William McMullen, both Labour MPs and members of the Board of Guardians, were allowed to enter; there they obstructed the meeting when it refused to discuss Outdoor Relief, and they were then seized by the police and thrown out onto the pavement of the Lisburn Road.

Belfast had not joined in the General Strike of 1926 but as unemployment persisted and deepened after the return to the Gold Standard, unrest in the city mounted. Unemployment benefit – still theoretically related to insurance – soon ran out and those out of work were forced to turn to the Poor Law as the only official alternative to starvation. The Belfast Board of Guardians, composed of 34 members elected by ratepayers from local government wards and the greater Belfast area, still applied the old workhouse test with rigour. Recently moved from the Old Town Hall to Glengall Street, most of the Guardians were property owners with hopes of achieving greater political status in the City Hall or in the Northern Ireland Commons. As R.H. Wilson, the Clerk of the Union, noted in the 1929 *Belfast Book,* the Board 'has steadfastly resisted pressure from various sources to distribute outdoor relief to all able-bodied applicants and thereby has prevented many abuses'.

For a time after the setting up of the Northern Ireland state the Guardians had been prepared to give 'Outdoor Relief' as an alternative to the more expensive solution of keeping the destitute in the Belfast Workhouse. Applicants were carefully questioned by relieving officers; nothing could be given until savings had been exhausted; relief was in the form of groceries obtained by 'chits' from named shops and no account was taken of the need to pay for clothing, coal and rent; and the names of successful applicants were posted on gable walls. Such a system gave ample opportunity for rewarding political supporters and excluding political opponents, quite apart from the public humiliation involved. Permission to grant Outdoor Relief had been given under Section 13 of the 1898 Local Government Act, which stated that 'Such relief shall only be given after full enquiry into the circumstances of each case'. This last requirement and the reluctance to grant relief to able-bodied men caused deep resentment.

The demonstrations of 14 and 15 June 1926 were only two of many in these years; on the 19 January 1924, for example, 4,000 unemployed had demonstrated outside the Glengall Street headquarters. Belfast MPs, representing workers of both communities, joined forces in the Commons to castigate the Guardians; the most energetic were Jack Beattie, Joe Devlin, Tommy Henderson, William McMullen and Sam Kyle. The Unionist government preferred to avoid compelling the Guardians towards greater generosity but feared that their own supporters would be alienated. The exasperated J.H. Andrews wrote to Craig on 9 August 1928:

How they can call themselves the guardians of the poor I do not know as they approach the whole problem from the one viewpoint alone, namely, saving the ratepayers.

The Guardians were unmoved and seemed blind to the large-scale unemployment in the city. Andrews had made his protest after an unrewarding conference with the Guardians the day before; the minutes of that meeting record the views of the chairman, which do not seem to have been exceptional:

Faced with such sloth, fecklessness and iniquity, the Guardians' duty was to discourage idleness and to create a spirit of independence since much of the money given to the poor was wasted. . . He knew of betting shops in one street which did a roaring business amongst the poor. . . These people would make an effort to find work if they found they could not get relief.

Lily Coleman, Chairman of the Belfast Board of Guardians 1928–9, and celebrated for her remark, about Outdoor Relief applicants with large families, that there was 'no poverty under the blankets'. (Linen Hall Library/*Belfast Book 1929*)

Another member noted with distaste that 'about 60% of the applicants are Roman Catholics from a particular quarter of the City'. Mrs Lily Coleman, elected to the chair in 1928, became celebrated for her remark, referring to large families, that there was no poverty under the blankets.

Meanwhile around 200 charities gave some form of relief in Belfast. These included the Shankill Road Mission and Toc H, but by far the most important organisation was the St Vincent de Paul Society which rivalled the Guardians in the relief provided. On average the Society spent £12,150 a year and until 1932 gave Outdoor Relief to a greater number than were assisted by the Poor Law; in 1928, for example, St Vincent de Paul helped 11,801 compared with 997 given relief by the Board of Guardians. Twenty 'conferences' or parish units collected money and organised volunteer help; free meals were served every day to the destitute; second-hand clothing was given out; and a factory was set up to make disinfectants and put together bundles of firewood to sell cheaply to the poor.

In 1928 at Westminster Neville Chamberlain overhauled local government and swept away the Boards of Guardians. In Belfast the Poor Law was to remain in force for another twenty years. By now, however, the Guardians had not only alienated the Catholic community but had also antagonised the Corporation and the government. Before the end of October 1928 a Bill was put through to force the Guardians to continue to provide and, indeed, to increase Outdoor Relief – the government did not implement the new English system where payments were made in cash and of right, partly out of fear of the expense involved and partly to avoid alienating faithful party supporters in the city. Protesting that the Poor Relief (Exceptional Distress) Act was prescribed, undemocratic and unfair', the Guardians were slow to carry out their statutory duty. Tommy Henderson had insisted that the names of those relieved would no longer be pasted up and Joe Devlin supported the measure:

. . . in the back lanes of our cities there are crowded dens of men and women who, through no fault of their own, are not insured and are suffering from starvation. It is only the least proud of them who go to the workhouse or ask for Outdoor Relief.

In November 1929 a delegation of four Protestant clergy congratulated the Guardians for their stand against this 'wastrel class' and called on them 'to cut off grants to parasites'. Nevertheless, by then relief schemes were underway. Applicants accepted had to work for their grocery chits and unemployment insurance stamps were not paid. The road resurfacing scheme was begun in April 1929 and by the end of September 325 able-bodied men had been given work. James Dennison remembers:

The conditions were very bad in Belfast and they brought in a scheme, Outdoor Relief. The men didn't get paid; they got chits for groceries and that sort of thing and they worked on jobs in the various streets. They had a big stone crusher and they dug up the cobblestones, crushed the cobblestones down to size and mixed that with sand and cement. Then they concreted all the roadways. And some of the men were in a very bad way. I can remember one occasion they were doing round the front of our house in Posnett Street and my mother happened to go out to the door and this man was sitting on the footpath and two or three other men round him. So she wanted to know what was wrong and the foreman said that this man hadn't had food from the previous day. So my mother brought him in and made him a meal. Conditions were very, very bad.

The Great Crash and its consequences: 'Conditions will become tragically worse...'

During September and most of October 1929 the Wall Street stock market wavered, moving gently downwards. Then on 23 October security prices crumbled in a wave of frenzied selling. 'The fundamental business of the country,' said President Hoover, 'is on a sound and prosperous basis.' He was wrong: in less than a month the securities listed on the New York Stock Exchange lost $26 billion – more than 40% – of their face value. 'We have now passed the worst,' Hoover announced in May 1930; America had not passed the worst and in 1931 financial panic swept Europe and even the Bank of England was forced to close its doors. The Great Crash wiped out savings and confidence alike, and brought in its wake the Great Depression during which for years on end families were without work and without hope.

Heavily dependent on a limited range of exports, Belfast was particularly vulnerable. As world trade contracted and as foreign governments raised import controls to prohibitive levels to protect their ailing economies, the numbers out of work in the city rose alarmingly. For Belfast, the Depression continued remorselessly throughout the Thirties. By 1932, the number of unemployed in the province was 76,000 – 28% of insured workers; of these, no less than 45,000 were in Belfast. The numbers out of work fell only slightly thereafter until they shot up to a peak in 1938 – a year when the rate for the province exceeded even that of Wales. The real figures were higher as many out of those who had exhausted the dole were struck off the register and no longer included in the figures. It can be estimated that between one quarter and one third of adult males in the city were unemployed throughout the Depression.

In 1927 the White Star Line had joined the Royal Mail group, after a quarter of a century under American control; with new financial strength the Line shortly afterwards placed an order with Harland & Wolff for a giant 1,000-foot quadruple-screw liner. The keel was laid in 1928 and it was calculated that at around 60,000 tons the completed vessel – to be named *Oceanic III* – would be the largest ship in the world. Now the onset of the slump killed the project and the ship was never finished.

It was some compensation that White Star instead signed contracts for two smaller ships – the *Britannic* and *Georgic* – which were nevertheless the largest motor liners in Britain. Fitted with Burmeister & Wain 10-cylinder diesel engines, these sister ships – the only motorships ever owned by the White Star Line – gave faithful service as troopships during the Second World War. Once the *Georgic* had been launched in 1931, grass began to grow on the slips; Harland & Wolff did not launch a single ship in either 1932 or 1933. By December 1932 unemployment in shipbuilding and engineering was an alarming 64.5%. The world crisis was too much for Workman Clark: after the delivery of the tanker *Acavus* in January 1935 the 'wee yard' had no more orders and was forced to close down. The *Acavus* had borne the yard number 536, an indication of the firm's output since 1879.

The impact of the Depression was most severe on countries exporting raw materials and food: these included the principal markets for Belfast linen – America, Argentina, Australia and Canada. In times of distress a luxury item such as linen was one of the first to go as buyers turned to cheaper cotton and rayon. As states slapped prohibitive tariffs on imports there followed a near

The linen mills remained the
biggest employers of labour in
these years. Kennedy's Factory,
Cupar Street: Lily (seated, centre
foreground) and Minnie Gawley
(end of second row, far right)
began as 'half-timers' early in
the Great War, and lived for
most of their lives at 50
Brookmount Street in the
Shankill. Photograph taken
about 1920. (Cynthia Wilson)

collapse of linen output in 1930. Smaller firms went to the wall and one third
of workers in the industry became unemployed; employment in linen which
had been 86,762 in 1924 was steadily reduced to 61,000 in 1935.

The formation of the National Government at Westminster in 1931 and the
decision to abandon the Gold Standard brought some recovery, for the fall in
the value of sterling made linen exports more competitively priced. The
recovery was slight, however, and not enough to compensate for the loss of
men's jobs in other industries. Besides, profits and wages were kept down by
low prices: 170 million yards produced in 1924 had been sold for £10½
million but 142 million yards in 1932 only brought in £5 million. The
desperate position to which many were brought in the city is illustrated by a
report in the *Belfast News-Letter* of 11 October 1932: a man arrested for
breaking the windows of Anderson & McAuley's store told the court: 'I broke
the windows because I was hungry. Jail is the only place where I can get food.'

The same newspaper commented in its editorial on 2 October 1932:

The problem of distressed unemployed is forcing itself or being forced upon the
attention of the community generally. Winter approaches, the church clergy, heads of
church missions, lay social workers and others state that at no time within their
experience were there such poverty and need as exist at present. We are told that those
on Outdoor Relief are on the verge of starvation; unless something is done and done
quickly, conditions will become tragically worse. . .

217

'What about the 78,000 unemployed who are starving?': 1932

Despite the growing crisis the government had not found it necessary to interrupt the summer recess. Friday 30 September 1932 was an important day for the provincial parliament: for the last time the MPs were sitting in the City Hall before moving to the new parliament buildings at Stormont. Pursuant to Standing Order No. 85, Members were informed of a long list of papers presented to parliament including the Parasitic Mange (N.I.) Order, the Anthrax (N.I.) Order, the Foreign Animals (N.I.) Order, and the Importation of Wrapping Materials (N.I.) Order. In the name of the Prime Minister, Notice of Motion was given:

That the cordial thanks of this House be extended to the Lord Mayor and Corporation of Belfast for their kindness in granting the use of the City Hall for this meeting of the House of Commons of Northern Ireland. . .

The Prime Minister, Lord Craigavon, rose to speak to the motion. This was too much for the Hon. Member for Pottinger, Jack Beattie: he seized the Mace and shouted out that his motion had been unaccountably refused, a motion to bring 'to your notice the serious position of the unemployment in Northern Ireland – the serious menace which faces the people in the Division which I have the honour to represent'. Uproar followed as Beattie refused to withdraw and as Tommy Henderson, Independent Unionist for Shankill, joined forces with his anti-partitionist Labour colleague and poured a torrent of invective at the ministerial benches:

We have not met for four months and we are going to adjourn for another two months; in the meantime the starving people of Northern Ireland are to continue starving. [Mr Speaker *rose*] The unemployed will have to beg in the streets. I condemn the way the Government have treated the unemployed; it is a disgrace to civilisation [Mr Speaker: 'Order, order'].

Beattie again held the Mace, crying out: 'I am going to put this out of action. . . The House indulges in hypocrisy while there are starving thousands outside.' He then wrested the Mace from the Serjeant-at-Arms, advanced towards the Speaker, and threw it upon the floor. Henderson continued to roar out above the tumult:

What about the 78,000 unemployed who are starving?

The demand for Outdoor Relief had been rising alarmingly – on 31 January 1931, relief had been given to 272 men and women (giving aid to 1,137 people when dependants were included); by 2 January 1932, 884 were being relieved (4,008 including dependants); and by 10 September 1932 the number of cases had jumped to 2,612, affecting 11,983 in all. These people were 'out of benefit', that is, no longer eligible for the dole from the 'b'roo'. Provided the stringent means test had been passed successfully, applicants got the following each week: 24s for the largest families, 16s for a couple with two children, 8s for a married couple, 3s.6d. for a single man, and single women got nothing at all. Little wonder, then, that the following resolution was adopted by the Presbyterian Churches in Belfast:

We, the members of the Presbytery of Belfast, are deeply concerned about the widespread distress in our city, due to unemployment and the exhaustion in many cases of unemployment benefit. We are of opinion that as a rule the grants that are being made to those who are entirely dependent on outdoor relief are inadequate to provide the barest necessities of life.

The Rev. J.N. Spence, of the Belfast Central Mission, pointed out that in 17 large British cities the average rate 'is £4.4s.0d and in Belfast rather less than £2.10s.0d per head, whilst the Poor Rate is also greatly lower. . . it is only true to say that Belfast has a smaller rate per head of population than any British city of comparable size'.

The prevailing distress brought together – very briefly – working-class people of both communities in the city in common protest. A small group of delegates to the Belfast Trades Council, led by Tommy Geehan and Betty Sinclair, organised the Outdoor Relief workers and on Monday 3 October, 600 went on strike demanding increased payments; that evening 60,000 from all over Belfast – led by bands playing 'Yes, we have no bananas' – marched from Frederick Street Labour Exchange to a torch-lit rally at the Custom House steps. The following day a deputation from the Unemployed Workers' Committee met the Guardians; the workers told the Guardians that they could give 'hundreds and hundreds of names who are absolutely destitute in the city. They are begging and borrowing like worms.' 7,000 had accompanied the delegation to the Workhouse. On 5 October police were in conflict with rioting crowds in Protestant and Catholic areas; as J.J. Kelly recalled:

When Orangemen and Catholics, the lines of starvation already etched in their hollow cheeks, gripped hands and declared emotionally, 'Never again will they divide us', there was consternation in the ranks of the professional politicans. Trouble was brewing in the city. . .

'Are youse goin' to let them down?': the ODR riots, October 1932

On 10 October 1932 the Unemployed Workers' Committee planned a great protest demonstration for the following day. As there had been rioting in many areas for almost a week, the government banned all marches under the Special Powers Act. Instead of a march, there was a violent conflict between the unemployed and the police on Tuesday 11 October, as the *Belfast Telegraph* reported:

Serious disorder broke out in the Albert Street area of the Falls this afternoon. The police had been mercilessly stoned, and finally compelled to fire to restore order. The rowdy element obtained control for a while and ugly scenes were witnessed. These included:-
Barricades on Falls Road;
Smashing of tramcar windows;
Burning of watchmen's huts;
Wrecking of road-mending equipment;
Attempt to loot shops;
Smashing of windows in National Bank, New Northern Mills, and some shops and public houses. . . Shots rang out and the police were compelled to reply to the fire. . . Constables wearing bandoliers filled with bullets and with rifles at the ready were speedily jumping out of caged cars. Other constables with revolvers in hand peered cautiously round the street corner as the hail of stones came out of Albert Street. Batons were useless and the police were compelled to fire. . .

The Times gave a prominent place to the rioting in its edition the following morning:

It was in a fight between police and civilians in the Killingtree district tonight that the man was shot dead. He was Samuel Baxter, and is stated to have been merely a looker-on.

'Killingtree' should have been 'Cullingtree', but otherwise the report was accurate – the rioting had claimed a life. Meanwhile, as J.J. Kelly remembered:

On the Shankill Road crowds of growling men lounged about – waiting. The police stood around too. It was early in the afternoon. Suddenly a big red-faced woman ran to the crowds of men and in quick, terse language told them that the unemployed and the police were in conflict on the Falls Road – one man was killed and others were wounded – and the fighting was still going on. 'Are youse goin' to let them down?' she almost shrieked. 'No, by heavens, we are not,' they roared back, and in a twinkling a veritable orgy of destruction had begun. . . Flames appeared. 'Here are the peelers,' shouted some as an armoured car appeared. There was a rattle of gunfire. Pandemonium broke loose. . .*

* J. J. Campbell, 'Between the Wars', in Beckett and Glasscock, *Belfast: origin and growth of an industrial city* (see bibliog), p. 151.

At Agnes Street a watchman's hut was set on fire and a barrage of planks was put across the road, before it too was set alight. The police were driven back into Northumberland Street, as the *Belfast Telegraph* reported:

The policemen were forced to retreat to either side of the street, and with backs to the wall proceeded to empty their revolvers over the heads of the crowd which bear a retreat.
Meanwhile the London *Times* correspondent was watching another confrontation in east Belfast:

In the Newtownards Road district where dense crowds of strikers congregated, an attempt was made to form up in procession. . . At Templemore Avenue an attack was made by a crowd armed with stones on an isolated party of police. They drew their batons, but things were looking very ugly when police reinforcements in a caged car appeared on the scene.

The *Belfast Telegraph* described what followed:

As the crowd continued to advance an order was given: 'Draw – Ready – Charge!' Men in the crowd went down like nine-pins, and the rest fled helter skelter in the direction of the Albertbridge Road. In a few moments that end of the thoroughfare was clear, save for a few encumbent men here and there. . .

That night the government imposed a curfew but the violence continued. There was fierce rioting in the York Street area the following evening when police opened fire with rifles on crowds of looters. John Kennan, of Leeson Street, was shot dead and the list of wounded filled the newspaper columns. Both the Corporation and the government were determined to coerce the Guardians and on 13 October the Board were summoned to meet the Cabinet at Stormont. Substantial increases in relief were announced next day and Tommy Geehan declared: 'A glorious victory has been achieved'. On Saturday 15 October the British Trade Union leader, Tom Mann, led the funeral procession of Samuel Baxter – certainly the most impressive demonstration of working-class solidarity the city has ever seen.

'You got everything cheap. . . mind you, you'd have to work brave and hard'

Even in the depths of the Depression the majority of insured workers in Belfast nevertheless remained in employment. Some firms in the city actually defied the economic trends and increased their business. Both tea and tobacco help to depress the appetite and it is not surprising therefore that Davidsons and Gallahers prospered during the hungry Thirties. Davidson's Sirocco Works continued to supply 70% of the world's tea machinery and Gallahers raised its exports from 4,000 tons of tobacco and cigarettes in 1930 to 10,000 tons in 1936. Still the largest independent tobacco factory in the world, paying £5 million annually in duty and employing 3,200 people, Gallahers owed its success to the efficient application of modern technology. J.G. Michaels, the firm's managing director described the manufacture of cigarettes in the York Street factory in 1937:

Members of the medical profession will be impressed with the scrupulous measures to ensure the purity of the products. From the leaf-conditioning room the 'raw material' is skilfully stripped by the nimble fingers of the girls who remove every particle of stem. Next the stripped leaves are fed into cutting machines whose great guillotine knives of razor-edge keenness rise and fall at a speed of 500 a minute. Each machine consumes 600 lbs of tobacco an hour and as the great flakes fall they are sucked away into a series of great cyclones and whirled and tossed about under strong suction which eliminates the dust. Every particle of foreign matter is trapped and eddied away, and the strands of perfect tobacco fall in golden cascades into skips ready for the most amazing of all the many intriguing machines in the great building – the cigarette maker. One could watch for hours the endless stream of cigarettes pouring from these machines like the flow of a waterfall. Ribbons of cigarettes race along as though imbued with the spirit of the chase. . .*

* R. Marshall, *The book of Belfast: compiled for the 105th meeting, in 1937, of the British Medical Association* (see bibliog), p. 122.

Other businesses retained their reputation and trade. The Belfast Ropeworks, employing 4,000 people and covering 40 acres, produced 13,000 tons in 1936, exporting 1,500 tons of rope, 10,000 tons of cordage and 800 tons of twine. Belfast milled 100,000 tons of the 125,000 tons of wheat imported into the province in 1936, the largest firms being Neills, Andrews, and White, Tomkins and Courage. The Ormeau Bakery was the only bakery in Ireland to be awarded the silver seal of the Institute of Hygiene.

Linen, despite its misfortunes, remained the biggest employer of labour in the city. The York Street Flax Spinning Company had 63,000 spindles and 1,000 power looms, and employed 5,000 workers; the guide to the works concluded: 'One comes away feeling that there is at least one British manufacturing house which does not appear to stand in great need of our present King's historic exhortation to "Wake Up".'*In 1937 advertisements for William Ewart's mill proclaimed that it produced 2 million yards of cloth a month from its looms and enough thread from its spindles to go 'round the globe in 90 minutes'. In the *Belfast News-Letter* bicentenary supplement of 1 September 1937, Alfred S. Moore indicated the extent of the industry's production:

* *A visit to the works of York Street Flax Spinning Co. Ltd. Belfast* (Belfast, n.d.), p. 35.

Visualise a great white highway one quarter mile broad extending down Ireland from the Giant's Causeway to Mizen Head in Cork – 300 miles – and you can grasp the magnitude of the Ulster linen annual output. In fact, its extent would cover Belfast's whole city area (21 square miles) thrice over.

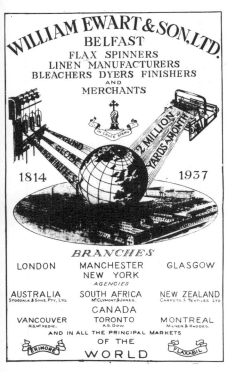

WILLIAM EWART & SON, LTD.
BELFAST
FLAX SPINNERS
LINEN MANUFACTURERS
BLEACHERS DYERS FINISHERS
AND
MERCHANTS

IN CRUCE SPERO

1814   1937

2 MILLION YARDS A MONTH

BRANCHES

LONDON   MANCHESTER   GLASGOW
          NEW YORK
              AGENCIES

AUSTRALIA   SOUTH AFRICA   NEW ZEALAND
Stoddale & Sons, Pty, Ltd.   McClymont & Jones.   Carpets & Textiles Ltd

          CANADA

VANCOUVER   TORONTO   MONTREAL
R.G.McKEDIE.   A.S. Dow   Milner & Rhodes.

AND IN ALL THE PRINCIPAL MARKETS
          OF THE
          WORLD

ERIMORE   FLAXABIL

Wages in the linen mills remained low, and right into the 1960s flax dust and water about the feet endangered the health of workers. Yet, as one Belfast doffer told Betty Messenger:

I tell you, in the mill you got a good laugh. And you were harashed – you were really harashed – but you got a good laugh, and your pay was goin' on.

Not only did the camaraderie of the mills help to compensate for the harsh conditions of work, but also wages bought more in the 1930s than before due to the rapid fall in commodity prices – after all, those who suffered most in the Depression were the peoples of colonial states and other underdeveloped lands. Dances at the 'Orpheus' were popular at 1s.6d and the warmth and excitement of the cinema could be enjoyed for the price of two 2lb jam jars. Bella O'Hara certainly has happy memories of this time:

Well the old times was the best where you got everything cheap. You got a pound of sausages for 4d, so you did, you got a quarter of pound of steak for a 1d. Mind you, you'd have to work brave and hard, and you'd to go in your bare feet at 6.30 in the morning and that's the God's truth.
You could have got a halfpenny of tea, and you got a halfpenny of sugar, up in McCroan's, up Lancaster Street, 6 o'clock in the morning, and I used to say, 'Give us a bap, give us a halfpenny of tea and a halfpenny of sugar'. Well that was as good as what you are getting now for what you're paying. And you'd have got lovely bacon cuttings – I'd have called them 'kilties' garters' – 4d a pound, with potatoes, it was a really good feed, it was grand. And then you'd a bit of bread and butter, a bit of margarine, it would have done ye rightly for your supper. You had to do it. Over in the wee chemist I used to say 'Give us tuppence of the treacle'. We put treacle on the bread and eat it like jam. It was lovely. It kept you all right too, it kept your bowels right. . .

'See Belfast, devout and profane and hard'

The picture house gave the people of Belfast a more complete opportunity to escape the poverty which limited the lives of so many than had ever been available to previous generations. By 1925 there were eleven silent-picture houses in west Belfast alone: these included the Clonard (1912) built on the site of Horner's Foundry opposite the Falls Library; the Picturedrome (1913) at the corner of Northumberland Street and the Shankill Road; the West End (1914) at the junction of Carlow Street and the Shankill Road; the Gaiety (1917) in North Street; and the Sandro (1920) which – a sign of the times, perhaps – replaced the Emmanuel Mission Hall in Sandy Row. These survived to become 'talkies' in the 1930s; until then silent films caused problems for those who could not read and one woman told Rose Sullivan 'that in order to derive the maximum entertainment from the films, she had to pay the admission fee for someone to go along and read the titles for her'.*A penny earned by running messages gave many a child a glimpse into an enthralling fantasy world and many a harassed mother timely relief on Saturday afternoons, as Maureen Smyth remembers from her childhood visits to the Clonard penny matinée:

The tickets were flat metal squares with a hole in the centre and the attendant threaded these squares onto a piece of stout cord, as he let the children in. . . it used to be pandemonium before the house darkened. Boys were yelling, fighting, hitting each

* Rose Sullivan, 'The Silent Picture Houses of West Belfast', in Heatley, *Outline Annual 1975* (see bibliog), p. 33.

"Ormo" HANDKERCHIEFS
are acknowledged to be amongst the best
of their kind that Belfast produces.

The above picture by an Irish Artist gives
some idea of the wealth of talent at the disposal
of the manufacturers in matters of design.

Mc.BRIDE & WILLIAMS LTD
Ormeau Avenue
BELFAST

'Weavers' by William Conor
(1881–1968), Belfast's best-
loved artist. (Ulster Folk
Museum)

* Maureen Smyth,
'Reminiscences of "The Penny
Matinee"', in Heatley, *Outline
Annual 1975* (see bibliog), p. 44.

other with their caps, crawling under the seats and nipping legs, at which the girls would scream and shriek. . . we used to stamp our feet on the floor and chant 'hurry up, hurry up', and this chant continued until – blessed moment – the lights dimmed, the operator's box lit up and the first numbers and marks flashed across the screen to indicate that the pictures were about to start. A lone pianist would tinkle the piano keys – and we were off. *

Live theatre catering for popular audiences found it difficult to compete with the cinema. The Hippodrome and Alexandra theatres became picture houses, though the Empire struggled on to become the home of the Belfast Repertory Theatre Company, founded by Richard Hayward in 1929. The Repertory's most original playwright was Tom Carnduff; his first play, *Workers*, staged at the Abbey in October 1932, was criticised for its weak technique but, the *Irish Times* critic concluded, 'for an out-of-work shipyard employee, who has had no previous experience of the stage, it is rather a remarkable achievement'.

In the period of rapid growth Belfast had not been a flourishing centre for the creative arts; it was in the years of uncertainty and decline that the city was to shake off its reputation for being a cultural waste-land. John Lavery was the first citizen to win international fame as an artist: born at 47 North Queen Street in 1856, he began his career hand-tinting photographs; he exhibited at the Paris Salon in 1883 and settled soon after in London as a highly successful portrait painter; after serving as a war artist, he was knighted in 1919; and before he died in 1941 he had been created a freeman of both Belfast and Dublin. He returned to his native city, where he painted a fine triptych in St

Patrick's Church, Donegall Street, in 1919, and presented thirty pictures to the Belfast Museum when it moved to Stranmillis in 1929.

Paul Henry, son of the minister of Great Victoria Street Baptist Church, left the Broadway Damask Company to become the best-known painter of the rugged scenery of the far west. His contemporary, William Conor, preferred the urban landscape of his native Belfast. Though he was appointed official war-artist in both world wars, Conor's unique talent – seen particularly in his lively street scenes and gentle sketches of women and children – was not given full recognition until after his death in 1968.

The finest poet to have been born in Belfast, Louis MacNeice (1907–63) adopted an uncharacteristically harsh tone when writing about the city and its inhabitants. His mother pined for her Connemara homeland, his father outraged his parishioners by refusing to sign the Covenant, and he himself was distanced from his fellow-citizens by his English public-school education and his contempt for narrow sectarianism. In 'Valediction' (1937) he wrote:

> See Belfast, devout and profane and hard,
> Built on reclaimed mud, hammers playing in the shipyard,
> Time punched with holes like a steel sheet, time
> Hardening the faces, veneering with a grey and speckled rime
> The faces under the shawls and caps:
> This was my mother-city, these my paps.
> Country of callous lava cooled to stone,
> Of minute sodden haycocks, of ship-sirens' moan,
> Of falling intonations – I would call you to book. . .

Born in Belfast in 1909, W.R. Rodgers abandoned the Presbyterian ministry to castigate his city's narrowness in compelling, energetic verse. He had more affection than MacNeice, however, for his people and their liking for 'spiky consonants in speech'. In a poem to conclude an unfinished book he was editing with MacNeice, he wrote:

> The apple blushed for me below Bellevue,
> Lagan was my Jordan, Connswater
> My washpot, and over Belfast
> I cast out my shoe.

C.S. Lewis (1898–1963), born at 47 Dundela Avenue, chafed only gently against the puritanism of his comfortable childhood in Belfast. The city and its people barely touched his writings but he does recount in his autobiography that he and his brother wrote stories of 'Animal-Land' when his family moved to 76 Circular Road – it is tempting to speculate that these formed the nucleus of his delightful novel for children, *The Lion, the Witch, and the Wardrobe*.

'Visible proof of the permanence of our institutions': opening of Stormont, 1932

The extent of co-operation between the working classes of both religions in 1932 can easily be exaggerated and romanticised. There had been minor sectarian riots in Belfast in 1931 and Catholics returning from the Eucharistic Congress in Dublin in 1932 were stoned as they emerged from Great Victoria Street station. Nationalists had virtually deserted the provincial parliament

The opening of the Northern Ireland parliament buildings at Stormont by the Prince of Wales (later Edward VIII) in November 1932. Designed by Sir Arnold Thornley and faced in Portland stone, it stands on a plinth of unpolished Mourne granite about five miles east of the city centre.

when Craig – created Lord Craigavon in 1927 – abolished PR in Northern Ireland parliamentary elections in 1929. Joe Devlin and his colleagues ignored the celebrations in November 1932 when the Prince of Wales opened Stormont; indeed the Prince, according to St John Ervine, performed the ceremony 'with an unsmiling face and glum and sulky looks', though he enjoyed playing a Lambeg drum in Hillsborough later in the day.

The completion of Stormont – a fine neo-classical structure in a magnificent setting on the Upper Newtownards Road – was, in the words of Hugh Pollock, 'the outward and visible proof of the permanence of our institutions; that for all time we are bound indissolubly to the British crown'. This very permanence left Catholics in the city feeling more abandoned than ever. In the wake of the 1932 riots, Unionists and Nationalists did suffer some reverses in the 1933 Stormont election; Harry Midgley – a Protestant and a known critic of clericalism – won Dock (a largely Catholic constituency) for Labour and Jack Beattie – a Protestant anti-partitionist Labour candidate – won Pottinger with the help of Catholic and Protestant votes.

There were times when the battle lines were not tautly drawn. When, on 18 January 1934, Joe Devlin died, a thousand Unionists stood in silent tribute at the annual gathering of the Ulster Unionist Labour Association; Sir Crawford

McCullagh, Dawson Bates, Andrews and Pollock attended the funeral; and Craigavon wrote: 'I have never entertained anything but admiration for his personal character. . . no bitterness ever tainted his private life.'

Devlin's successor as Nationalist leader, T.J. Campbell, was less willing to compromise with his opponents. Perhaps fearful that their supporters would go over to Labour or loyalist splinter parties, Unionist leaders made little effort to restrain sectarian feeling in their public statements. In November 1934 Craigavon gave his notorious description of Stormont as a 'Protestant Parliament for a Protestant People'. Catholic leaders, too, made irresponsible pronouncements; Cardinal MacRory, at one time Bishop of Down and Connor, had declared in December 1931: 'The Protestant Church in Ireland — and the same is true of the Protestant Church anywhere else — is not only not the rightful representative of the early Irish Church, but it is not even a part of the Church of Christ.'

How easily sectarian passion could be aroused was to be tragically demonstrated in the Belfast riots of 1935.

'Forget the things that are behind. Forget the unhappy past': 1935

The Depression in Belfast was unrelenting — this was no temporary down-swing in the economy like that which had followed the post-war boom. As the bitter quest for work continued, sectarian hatreds were easily brought to the surface. In 1935, feelings ran high when Protestants triumphantly celebrated King George V's Jubilee; a Catholic was shot dead in his shop in Great George's Street and rioting flared up in east Belfast as the Catholic church in Willowfield neared completion. In the disturbances in May and June 1935, 26 were injured and at least 40 homes were damaged. Fearing trouble on the Twelfth of July, the Ministry of Home Affairs banned all parades from 18 June. 'You may be perfectly certain that on the Twelfth of July the Orangemen will be marching throughout Northern Ireland,' was the defiant response of Sir Joseph Davison, the Orange Grand Master, and during an acrimonious debate at Stormont on 10 July, Tommy Henderson said:

I take very strong exception to the conduct of the Minister of Home Affairs in putting a ban on the loyal inhabitants of Northern Ireland. The Prime Minister has said that this is a Protestant Parliament for a Protestant people. On every platform in the country the Government have prated about their loyalty.

Lord Craigavon was abroad on one of his numerous tours of the Commonwealth and in his absence Dawson Bates lifted the ban. The Rt Rev Dr MacNeice, Church of Ireland Bishop of Down and father of the poet Louis MacNeice, feared trouble and made this appeal on the eve of the celebrations:

Forget the things that are behind. Forget the unhappy past. Forget the story of the old feuds, the old animosities, the old triumphs, the old humiliations.

There were no disturbances as the Orangemen paraded on the Twelfth of July but at the Belmont 'Field' Davison referred directly to the Bishop's appeal:

While I give this right rev. gentleman all due respect for his high ideals and while I strongly desire and advocate peace I presume to ask: . . . Are we to forget that the flag of Empire is described as a foreign flag and our beloved King insulted by Mr De

The funeral of W. G. Baird, son of the founder of the *Belfast Telegraph,* in October 1934. The cortège is passing the *Telegraph* offices in Royal Avenue. (M. B. Browne)

Valera? Are we to forget that the aim of these people is to establish an all-Ireland Roman Catholic State, in which Protestantism will be crushed out of existence? But, above all, are we to forget the heroic achievements of our forefathers, who defended the beleaguered City of Derry and shed their blood at Enniskillen and on the other battlefields against the Papal forces of James?. . . (Cries of 'No' and cheers).
[*Belfast News-Letter,* 13 July 1935].

Henry S. Kennedy saw no sign of trouble as the Orangemen returned to the city centre:

I walked from the city centre along Royal Avenue to go on duty at 7 o'clock in the newspaper office where I was employed. Abreast of me was an Orange procession, its vivid banners and bright sashes filling the drab street with unaccustomed colour, the air loud as the skirl of the pipes, the blare of the brass and the lilt of the flutes came in

227

successive waves of tuneful music. . . As I reached the corner of Donegall Street, the procession was swinging around into that street as solemn, as serious, as heavy footed as ever. This, I thought, was not the material from which trouble was made. You might as readily expect disorder from a procession of bishops.

But looking ahead into York Street he saw that the trams had stopped; trouble had not been avoided after all.

Riot at Lancaster Street: 12 July 1935

As the last two or three lodges approached Lancaster Street shots rang out, and at once the Orangemen broke ranks and turned into Lancaster Street, only to be greeted with a volley of stones from over the roofs of the houses.

The *Belfast News-Letter* clearly believed that the procession had been fired upon. The *Irish News* offered a different explanation: the Protestants had made an unprovoked attack rushing 'up into Lancaster Street smashing windows on both sides as far as Pentland Street, deacon poles and stones being the weapons used. The Catholics rallied, and seizing stones drove the invading mob back into York Street. . .' The *Belfast Telegraph* headline ran: 'Grave Disorder in Belfast. Unprovoked Attack on the Orange Procession'.

Later, after careful and detailed investigation, Henry Kennedy decided that all the newspapers had failed to give an accurate explanation for the start of the conflict: he concluded that neither side had planned to make an attack on the other but that a drunken Protestant had struck a Catholic bystander talking to a policeman; Orangemen had left the parade to help the Protestant; a Catholic assumed that a major attack had begun and fired a revolver, killing a Protestant; and that Orangemen, assuming that an unprovoked attack had been made on their parade, had invaded Lancaster Street to vent their fury. 'I was satisfied,' Kennedy wrote, '. . . that the danger to the city was not so much in the existence of groups of murderous gunmen but in a situation where two hostile parties reacted so violently to an offence or an imagined offence.' Whatever its origin, the rioting that followed was severe and the *Northern Whig* described it as 'the worst night of disorder since 1921–22'. Kennedy recalled:

I remember a man out in front firing a revolver repeatedly in the direction of Lancaster Street. It looked so harmless in action, the reports of the shots so faint, the small puffs of smoke so innocent that it was incredible that this was an instrument of death. . . At another stage when an attacking party had again entered Lancaster Street and again been driven out there came over the roof tops a shower of heavy stones. To my quickened senses those stones seemed to fall in slow motion, and I marked one particularly big one falling, as I thought, just past the head of a man running along the middle of York Street. But he fell and lay crumpled up and quite still. One moment he was running and the next he was lying on the ground. Again came the queer illusion that it was part of a child's game.

The historian A.T.Q. Stewart remembers:

I have the most vivid memory of the day, the first clear coherent memory I have – etched on my young mind by terror. The city being as usual quiet and dead on the holiday, my mother and aunt decided to take me to the Zoo on the Antrim Road. When we came out, the trams were not running and we were far from base. Then we

---

> **BATTLE OF YORK STREET AS SEEN FROM TRAM**
>
> *Seething Mob Hurling Stones And Firing Revolver Shots*

228

began to hear gunfire from the city centre. My mother and aunt began to run, lifting me by both arms. They were perfectly calm and silent but their apprehension transmitted itself to me like an electric current. I couldn't understand what was wrong. It was when the steady machine-gun fire was heard that the women lifted me up. Meanwhile my uncle, who had elected to stay at home with my father, jumped into his car and went to find us – a needle in a haystack. He found us, miraculously, in Manor Street, of all places! I used to tell my students before 1969 that I had heard the last machine-gun fired in Belfast. They were derisively incredulous. After 1969 it wasn't necessary.*

* From a note to the author.

Animosities nurtured over the centuries welled up once more as the two communities clashed repeatedly, sweeping the armed constabulary aside. As the *Belfast News-Letter* reported the following morning: 'The police were powerless to enforce their requests that the marchers should desist and proceed along another route. In one instance, policemen were thrust forcibly to one side, and were threatened by deacon poles.' Later that evening, the *Irish News* reported, 'For over two hours battle raged between the opposing forces, and scenes that almost beggar description were enacted. Armoured cars, firing machine-guns, while police, armed with rifles or revolvers, fired upon gunmen and stone-throwers at all points, but from the corner of Donegall Street to the middle of York Street the fighting raged uninterruptedly for two hours.'

That night two civilians were killed, 35 civilians and 3 policemen were wounded, 14 houses were set on fire and 47 other dwellings were wrecked. Troops were called in and a curfew was imposed, but the rioting continued unabated the next evening. As *The Times* correspondent reported:

The trouble on Saturday night arose shortly before 10 o'clock, the curfew hour. A Protestant band marched down to Nelson Street, taking a wreath for one of their comrades, Edward Withers, who was shot dead on Friday night in the disturbances after the attack on the Orange procession. The band played 'The Dead March' and 'Onward, Christian Soldiers', and it is alleged that several shots were fired. A large crowd had followed the band, and they got completely out of hand. They rushed into North Ann Street, and before the police could prevent them they smashed all the windows of houses occupied by Roman Catholics. They also invaded Earl Street and North Thomas Street and continued their orgy of destruction. . .

Two more people were killed and more than 50 persons were treated in hospital for gunshot wounds and injuries from stones and other missiles – ambulances from all over the city could not cope and the authorities had to press taxis into service.

'It is all so wanton and so meaningless'

Night after night the violence continued, though troops attempted to separate the mobs by stringing out rolls of barbed wire. Soldiers with fixed bayonets were posted at these collapsible wire entanglements and at other danger points; police patrolled the whole York Street area on foot, in tenders, and in cage cars; and Whippet cars, with their Vickers guns at the ready, were stationed at strategic points throughout the city. On Sunday 22 July a concerted effort was made by church leaders and the city fathers to restore peace. Crawford McCullagh, responding to representations made by trade union leaders and all the churches, called on citizens 'to absent themselves from all assemblages in the streets and public places, not using or encouraging the use of language liable to cause offence to others. . .' Dr MacNeice was busy forming peace committees while the Catholic Bishop, Dr Mageean, issued this pastoral:

I ask you to crush all bitterness out of your hearts; do it for the love of God and love of our Divine Redeemer. Give offence to no man. Avoid all occasions of arousing animosity. Assist, when you can, in the maintenance of order. . .

It was nearly the end of August before the rioting ceased by which time 13 had been killed – 8 Protestants and 5 Catholics. At an inquest on riot victims the City Corner made this impassioned appeal:

It is all so wanton and so meaningless. No good of any kind can be achieved by it. It makes one wonder why any portion of our citizens in an age of education and civilisation such as we at present live in, should become so savage and destructive, and so heartless. Party passion is a very inflammable commodity. Bigotry is the curse of peace and goodwill. The poor people who commit these riots are easily led and influenced. . . There would be less bigotry if there was less public speechmaking of a kind by so called leaders of public opinion. . . It is not good Protestantism to preach a gospel of hate and enmity towards those who differ from us in religion and politics.

The balance of deaths had been on the Protestant side but the Catholics had suffered most. Most of the wounded were Catholic and 514 Catholic families were driven out of the York Street area; some fled to refugee centres in the Falls Road and others squatted in houses nearing completion in Ardoyne. Ardoyne, the *Irish News* commented on 19 July, 'is one of the few places in the city where sanity reigns, and where Protestant and Catholic live in mutual trust and confidence'. The exodus of Catholic families from the Dock area led to the mingling of people of both denominations in north-west Belfast, but the two communities did not merge completely and in 1969 and 1971 isolated families here were to find themselves terribly vulnerable when sectarian conflict erupted once again.

'The mobs on both sides broke loose,' said the Church of Ireland Dean of Belfast; 'To describe the shootings and evictions as a one-sided pogrom is absurdly unjust.' Broadly speaking this was true but the Nationalist leader, T.J. Campbell, was right to point out that over 2,000 Catholics and only a handful of Protestants had been driven from their homes and that 95% of the £21,669 compensation for destruction to property was paid out to Catholics. At the request of Campbell and Dr Mageean, over 100 MPs at Westminster called for an inquiry but Baldwin refused saying that 'for fundamental constitutional reasons the possibility of holding an inquiry by the Imperial Government is completely ruled out'.

At Stormont, Craigavon also refused an inquiry but he did urge caution: '. . . I hope all Members of the House will, in view of what has happened, realise that an ill-spoken word, even in this House, may possibly cause further trouble, which I am sure everybody desires to avoid. (Hon. Members: Hear, hear).' For a time political leaders were more restrained in their public pronouncements and, though fringe groups continued to attempt to foment sectarian passion, Craigavon's conciliatory gestures to the minority were noticeable enough to attract this denunciation from the Amalgamated Protestant Associations and Leagues of Ulster:

Craigavon is always speaking about 'step by step' with Britain, but he is not only a step behind, but he is hundreds of miles behind. He is step by step with Rome day and daily.

The bitter memories of the 1935 riots were not forgotten. Jim McConville, a child when his family moved from Spamount Street to the Falls for safety, recalled later:

For us children at that time 'the Troubles' were incomprehensible, but we knew who the enemy was – or thought we did. On one occasion, the Catholic mother of one of my playmates was startled out of her wits when her wee son, with three or four others, came charging up the hall in terror, screaming:
'The Fenians are coming, the Fenians are coming!'

'A snap election on an unreal issue': 1938

> De Valery had a canary up the leg of his drawers
> And when it got down it sat on the ground
> And whistled 'The Protestant Boys'.

De Valera, in power since 1932, had been waging an 'economic war' with Britain (which further reduced Belfast's exports of manufactures to the South) and in 1937 had drawn up a new constitution laying claim to the six northern counties. On the morning of 12 January 1938 Craigavon read the newspapers in bed, as was his custom, and learned that the question of partition would be raised at a conference to be held in London. According to Lady Craigavon, the Prime Minister was unusually quiet while dressing and just as breakfast was finishing he told her he had decided to challenge de Valera by calling a general election. The campaign was low-key in rural areas, but in Belfast the election was bitterly fought and the signal for renewed turbulence.

'Vote Loyalist by Voting Progressive Unionist. God Save the King', election posters proclaimed all over the city; W.J. Stewart, MP for South Belfast, had become increasingly critical of the Unionist Party, and what he considered to be its unadventurous economic policies, and had recently launched the Progressive Unionist Party. 'Let There be Straight and Upright Dealing. Vote Loyalist Against the Wreckers'; Craigavon seized this opportunity to brand the breakaway Unionists as 'wreckers' during critical negotiations in London between de Valera and Neville Chamberlain. It was not in the loyalist camp, however, that the divisions were most serious. In the previous election Harry Midgley had been elected for Labour in Dock, a predominantly Catholic constituency, and now he was standing for re-election. Outspoken in his support for the beleaguered Spanish Republic, Midgley was challenged by the Nationalist, James Collins, who openly backed Franco's armed rebellion. Night after night there were violent clashes in the constituency. On 1 February, as the *Irish News* reported next morning:

Shouts of 'Up Franco', 'Remember Spain', 'We Want Franco', the singing of 'A Soldier's Song', and prolonged booing greeted Ald. Harry Midgley, Labour candidate in Dock, when he attempted to hold meetings in Hardinge Street and Annadale Street, and the meetings had to be abandoned. Fists and umbrellas were waved threateningly at the brake in which were Ald. Midgley and his supporters. . .

The next evening Midgley was forced to abandon a meeting at McCleery Street, off York Street, and on 3 February, after his lorry had been rushed by a

(Irish News)

CRIES OF "UP FRANCO"
T ELECTION MEETING
ALDERMAN MIDGLEY HOWLED DOWN

Exciting Scene In Dock Constituency

LABOUR SPEAKERS REFUSED HEARING

hostile crowd in Pilot Street, he moved on to Dock Street, there to denounce General Franco as 'a monstrosity' and 'a killer of babies'. Midgley also had harsh words for Franco's apologist in Belfast, the Rev Dr Ryan, who told the press: 'He classes me with dictatorial clerics and mercenary politicians; he pleasantly describes me as one who supported assassination, outrage and persecution. . .'

Collins had his own problems when republicans wrecked his meeting in St Mary's Hall on 7 February. As the *Irish News* reported: 'Republicans sang "The Soldier's Song" and Nationalist supporters, rising from their chairs sang "A Nation Once Again", while children screamed with fright. In the confusion chairs were overturned and added to the general turmoil. The scenes continued for nearly an hour, when the police, who were summoned, arrived. . .' Collins did get peace for long enough to declare: 'The Central-Falls-Dock Nationalist Axis athwart in Belfast will be something to set before Mr. Chamberlain at his next talks with Mr. De Valera'.

On 9 February, as voters went to the polls they read that Franco had routed the Reds at Teruel and that unemployment in the province had risen by 9,314 over the previous month. It was not the new high record figures of those out of work which dominated election day. For the *Belfast News-Letter* the 'Vital Question which People Must Answer' was 'Do the people of Ulster wish to remain citizens of the United Kingdom or to become citizens of an All-Ireland Republic?' It was a violent day: in Oldpark armed men burned a Unionist car; Nationalist cars were stoned and wrecked in Falls, where twenty windows were broken and five people were injured after a police baton charge in Slate Street; Republican and Nationalist women fought in the streets and tore each other's hair; and for the B Specials it was a day of full alert.

Not a single Progressive Unionist was returned and J. Maynard Sinclair's Unionist majority over W.J. Stewart in Cromac was 3,500; Dawson Bates easily fended off the Progressive Unionist and Labour candidates in Victoria; the Unionists held Oldpark despite a big Labour vote; and in Falls the Nationalist, Richard Byrne, retained his seat. In Dock not only was Midgley bottom of the poll, but the Unionists captured the seat; Midgley declared defiantly: 'I have preserved my soul, my independence, and my character, and I will never bow to any dictatorship, theological or otherwise.' Jack Beattie, after a stormy campaign in Pottinger, was now the sole Labour MP for Belfast, and even he had been expelled from the party for his anti-partitionist views. Tommy Henderson narrowly won in Shankill. Tears ran down his cheeks as the result was announced, and a supporter vaulted the table to kiss him; he was carried shoulder high from the City Hall to the Shankill where the people sang, 'Tommy's Up the River with yer Ya! Ya! Ya!' and 'Our Tommy can birl his leg', and someone shouted 'They'll have to go to Chicago for gunmen to beat you, Tommy!'

'He is the one politician who can win an election without leaving his fireside,' the *Daily Express* had said of Craigavon on 13 January, and, indeed, a severe bout of 'flu did confine the Prime Minister to his fireside throughout the campaign. Not only had he routed the 'wreckers', but he had also brought off a Unionist triumph equalled only by that of 1921. *The Times* commented on the Unionists' success:

A snap election on an unreal issue has given them complete victory. . . Whether it was worth while to advance the date of the election in order to prove what has been self-evident since Parnell's day is another matter.

Little change seemed in prospect for either the politics or the economy of Belfast. Yet in this year, when the Depression was at its deepest, Westminster promised important help with social services expenditure and contracts began to come in as the re-armament programme developed. But with the first steps towards economic recovery came another threat of insecurity – greater than was realised in Belfast at the time – the threat of total war.

Poster for the fiftieth anniversary (October 1982) of the Outdoor Relief campaign, incorporating a contemporary issue of the *Daily Worker*. (WEA: North Belfast Workshop)

9
Years of War and Change
c.1939–1945

The great Depression had struck hard at the city's vulnerable economy. More and more businesses laid off workers or closed down altogether, and, in the spreading atmosphere of economic insecurity, political attitudes had hardened, and intensified political hatreds had broken to the surface in renewed blood-letting and destruction. The government and the Corporation, both teetering on the edge of bankruptcy, had been unable to finance adequate schemes to relieve the misery. In the winter of 1938, it was estimated that 36% of the city's population were living in conditions of 'absolute poverty'.* The 1930s in Belfast were empty years, years of disillusionment, when plans to improve the citizens' quality of life had been abandoned and when hopes for permanent peace in the city had seemed to vanish forever.

* A. Beacham, *Survey of living conditions in a representative working-class area in Belfast* (see bibliog), p. 11.

The day Britain declared war on Germany, Craigavon said at Stormont, 'we here today are in a state of war and we are prepared, with the rest of the United Kingdom and Empire, to face all the responsibilities which that imposes on the Ulster people'. The politicians stressed the need for sacrifice, but for the people of Belfast, the coming of the war brought new hope to those who had known no future but the dole from the 'b'roo'. As in the Great War, Belfast could expect to be far from the reach of the enemy and yet to prosper greatly from war contracts. Citizens would even be safe from the threat of conscription for, despite repeated appeals by Craigavon and his successor, Andrews, the Westminster government had no intention of repeating the abortive attempt of the spring of 1918, when united nationalist opposition rendered the Irish Military Service Act unenforceable.

The fall of France and the Low Countries in the summer of 1940 suddenly gave Belfast an international strategic importance it had not hitherto possessed and, at the same time, put the city in peril of attack from the air. The 1941 Blitz gave Belfast its first direct experience of total war and shattered the complacency of the authorities by laying bare the neglect of the two previous decades. If these years of war brought death and injury to many citizens and razed large areas of the city, they were also a time of positive change when suffering and later full employment blurred social and communal divisions, and decisive steps were taken to effect a permanent improvement in the condition of the people.

Belfast an arsenal

'The bomber will always get through,' Baldwin had once remarked gloomily at Westminster; this was universally believed in official circles and it seemed sensible therefore to manufacture vital war materials as far as possible outside the expected range of enemy air attack. British re-armament began at the close of 1935 – earlier than is generally recognised – and it was in 1936 that Belfast, with its spare engineering capacity, its reputation for technical ingenuity, and its large pool of skilled labour was chosen as a major centre for aircraft production.

Already the Belfast Harbour Commissioners, with their customary foresight, had obtained parliamentary permission to build a large aerodrome at Sydenham. Short Bros of Rochester were persuaded, with the help of government money, to join with Harland & Wolff in setting up an aircraft factory on Queen's Island adjacent to the proposed airport; in May 1936 a new limited company, Short & Harland, was launched and only a month later some 1,000 piles were being driven into reclaimed land to provide firm foundations for the factory. Production – organised on a 'flow' system as in large car factories – began even before the buildings were finished; in an assembly shop in the neighbouring shipyard fuselage sections were being made meanwhile; and by the end of 1937, 6,000 people were on Shorts payroll striving to meet the government order for 50 Bristol Bombay twin-engined transports and 150 Hereford bombers. Mrs Neville Chamberlain opened Belfast Harbour Airport in March 1938 and, as a result, Shorts had 370 acres of reclaimed land available for test flights. A Flying Training School was set up at Sydenham; lectures were given in the Donegall Chambers, and at night instructors (Hugh Falkus, later famous as a Battle of Britain ace and a naturalist, was one of them) flew Demon aircraft to give practice to army searchlight batteries. The first Bristol Bombay was delivered in April 1939 and by 3 September 11 Bombays and 4 Herefords had been built.

The pace of production stepped up after Britain's declaration of war on Germany; 44 aircraft had been delivered to the RAF by the end of 1939. Meanwhile the four-engined Stirling – the first of the heavy bombers – was being secretly developed at Sydenham; Empire flying boats were hoisted ashore by Harland & Wolff's giant floating crane and converted for war service; and here Sunderland flying boats were made with the sheltered Belfast Lough providing ideal water for test flights. By the end of 1940 Shorts had built, tested, and delivered 206 aircraft.

Though they lacked facilities for building the largest warships, the Belfast shipyards had, by the outbreak of war, launched the 10,000-ton cruiser HMS *Belfast,* and work was well under way on the 28,000-ton aircraft carrier HMS *Formidable,* and on destroyers, corvettes and other smaller warships. In great secrecy a new ordnance factory was built by Harland & Wolff in 1938–9, anti-aircraft shells were made by James Mackie and Sons, and the Sirocco Works made ventilators for munition stores. In the first seven months of 1939 Northern Ireland received government contracts worth more than £6 million for equipment such as battle dress, service dress, bedding, and electrical wiring. Nearly all of these contracts went to Belfast; the most terrible conflict the world had experienced had begun and yet, for the moment, the economic future of the city seemed secure.

These hopes were not immediately realised. Shortage of raw materials and the dislocation caused by transfer to wartime production hampered efforts to mobilise fully the labour of the city. Unemployment actually rose every month until February 1940. Neither the government nor the Corporation – both mainly composed of elderly men who had little understanding of the modern blitzkrieg – took seriously the potential danger to the civilian population of the

Issued by the Northern Ireland Ministry of Commerce in December 1940. (PRONI)

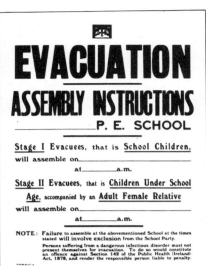

Poster announcing the first official evacuation scheme. (From *Exactly Fifty Years* by Norman McNeilly)

city. There was some feverish activity in September 1939 when sand-bag shelters were put up in the grounds of the City Hall, trenches were dug in the Harbour estate and in city parks, and gas masks were assembled in the Ulster Hall. Volunteers enlisted as fire brigade reservists, and joined rescue parties and demolition squads. A complete black-out of the city was ordered by the Ministry of Home Affairs.

This early enthusiasm rapidly evaporated. The Air Raids Precautions Act of 1938 was belatedly and tepidly enforced. The Corporation clearly believed it was a needless extravagance to build an adequate number of shelters for the citizens. Attempts to evacuate children were half-hearted. Before the war it was planned to evacuate 70,000 children; it was not until July 1940 that a scheme was adopted to take 17,000 out of Belfast. Very few children turned up and more than half of those evacuated had returned by the spring of 1941. So lacking was the Corporation in any real sense of urgency that vital pipe fittings for fire-fighting appliances and building materials for shelters were not available when Hitler turned his forces westward. The consequences of this neglect were horribly revealed in the spring of 1941.

'Are not such men the King's enemies?'

'We are King's Men and we shall be with you to the end,' Craigavon said in a broadcast to the British people early in 1940. Not all were King's Men. On the day war was declared a soldier was severely wounded by IRA snipers in Alliance Parade, and six armed men stripped a Territorial soldier of his uniform in East Bridge Street. 'Are not such men the King's enemies? Could any punishment be too great for such men?' Craigavon asked in Stormont the following day. About 60 men were interned and kept in Crumlin Road goal or held on board the *Al Rawdah*, a hulk anchored off Killyleagh. Enough IRA activists in Belfast remained at large to distribute issues of *War News*, burn gas masks, and broadcast anti-British propaganda from a transmitter never found by the RUC. In December 1939 Sean McCaughey, a Belfast sheet-metal worker, returned from internment in the south to become the commanding officer of the IRA 'Northern Command'. For a time the IRA was more active in Belfast than in Dublin, but McCaughey was drawn into a sordid witch-hunt against his southern superior, Sean Hayes. Some information about British military installations in Ulster was passed on to German agents in the south, who never got the opportunity to transmit what they learned. Its strength sapped by arrests in the north and almost extinguished in the south by ruthless repression, the IRA was never more than an irritating nuisance to the Stormont government. Perhaps the main consequence of its actions was that the government, in exaggerating the danger from the 'fifth column', underestimated the vulnerability of Belfast to German air attack.

'The period of the next moon. . . may well bring our turn'

In the spring of 1940 the vortex of total war swung westwards and as the shattered remains of the British army gathered on the Dunkirk beaches, Churchill remarked gloomily in his map room that the only properly armed and disciplined force left in the United Kingdom was the Ulster Special Constabulary. When the Chiefs of Staff recommended that equipment for the defence of Belfast should be doubled, neither fighter aircraft nor ack-ack guns were available. Suddenly and unexpectedly, as the Battle of Britain was being

236

Issued by the Ministry of Public Security, Stormont Castle. (PRONI)

fought, Belfast found itself with a crucial role to play in the struggle against Germany. In the Western Approaches U-boats wreaked havoc on British shipping which was forced to take an unaccustomed route northwards around the coasts of Ulster. 'All had to come in around Northern Ireland,' Churchill said later. 'Here by the grace of God, Ulster stood a faithful sentinel.'

Ansons flew out from Sydenham, Aldergrove and Newtownards in all weathers, but their elusive targets continued to inflict devastating losses. John Kelly Ltd and the Head Line, Ulster's principal shipping firms, incurred more than half their total wartime losses in the first half of 1941. Admiral Raeder reported to Hitler: 'The main operational area at present is the western part of the North Channel and the waters west of Scotland. It is very remunerative.' Meanwhile unemployment melted away as Belfast firms strove to meet their contracts.

'I have heard speeches about Ulster pulling her weight but they have never carried conviction,' Edmond Warnock said at Stormont after resigning as Parliamentary Secretary to the Ministry of Home Affairs in September 1940. He condemned the Prime Minister for staying in office 'until the hand of God removes him'. On 24 November 1940 Craigavon died at his home in Belfast and was replaced by John Andrews; one of the ablest ministers since the founding of Northern Ireland, he took office when Ulster was in the greatest danger. British cities had already suffered major air raids – could Belfast, now a vital arsenal, be attacked by German bombers? Evidently the Chiefs of Staff thought so, for in October 1940 they agreed to send more fighter aircraft to Sydenham, Aldergrove and Nutt's Corner.

Even so, Belfast remained the most unprotected major city in the United Kingdom. On 24 March 1941, J.C. MacDermott, the Minister of Public Security in Northern Ireland, expressed his anxiety in a letter to Andrews; anti-aircraft cover was less than half the approved strength in Belfast, the city did not possess a single searchlight, and no other town in the province had any defence at all. He concluded: 'Up to now, we have escaped attack. So had Clydeside until recently. Clydeside got its blitz during the period of the last moon. There are certain technical reasons which probably give us some ground for thinking that at present the enemy could not easily reach Belfast *in force* except during a period of moonlight. The period of the next moon from, say, the 7th to the 16th of April, may well bring our turn.'

On the night of 7–8 April six German bombers raided Belfast, and completely destroyed the 4½-acre Harland & Wolff fuselage factory, reduced a major timber yard to ashes, and delivered damaging blows to the docks. Compared with the horrifying raid on Coventry the previous November, the attack was a small one. The people of Belfast, however, now knew that their city was vulnerable after all.

The Blitz: April 1941

On the evening of 15 April nearly two hundred bombers – Junkers, Heinkels and Dorniers – protected by Messerschmitt fighters, flew over Cardigan Bay and dropped height as they reached the coast of Co Down. As anti-aircraft gunners took post and the Hurricane crews obeyed the order to scramble, the bombers reached Belfast, and dropped hundreds of flares to light their targets. 'They made the moon look dull – like a slice of turnip,' Joseph Tomelty recalled. Then incendiaries, high-explosive bombs, and parachute mines

The Blitz 15–16 April 1941. The ruins of High Street, photographed from Castle Place. (*Belfast Telegraph*)

began to rain down. John Carlin remembered:

The sirens sounded once again, and as their terrible wail rose and fell so did the sickening feeling of terror in my young stomach. Suddenly the sky was lit up by flares dropped from the German planes. The noise of anti-aircraft guns filled the night air. My mother gathered the two of us children under her arms and we ran to a farm-house nearby. As we were running, pieces of exploding shells fell round us. I shall never forget the terror in my mother's voice as she pounded the farmhouse door: 'Let us in! For God's sake let us in!'

Mistaking the Cavehill Road waterworks for the Lagan river, it is thought, the Germans concentrated their assault on the north of the city. All around the city anti-aircraft guns attempted to strike back at the bombers above. Joseph Tomelty recalls: 'Searcher bullets whizzed through the air to shatter the lights of the flares. The anti-aircraft guns were woof-woofing. There were deep, far-away rumblings, like the noise of the drums on the Twelfth.' Even the guns of HMS *Furious*, under repair at the docks, added their fire to the barrage. Then, at 1.45 a.m., a single bomb, landing at the corner of Oxford Street and East Bridge Street, destroyed the telephone service connections and left the city almost defenceless – all contact was lost with Britain, and the anti-aircraft guns fell silent for fear of shooting down the Hurricane fighters, now left without orders. York Street spinning factory, the largest of its kind in Europe, fell, killing over 30 instantaneously, obliterating 42 houses in Sussex Street and demolishing 21 houses in Vere Street. Over 60 were killed when a bomb fell near a shelter in Percy Street; all the wardens of Clifton Street, just returned from a dance at the Ulster Hall where Delia Murphy had been singing, were killed; and in one house in Ballynure Street 16 died, 9 from one family. By the time the 'all clear' sounded at 5 a.m. on 16 April, 203 metric tons of blast bombs, time-bombs and parachute bombs, and 800 fire-bomb canisters had fallen on the city.

238

Norddeutsche Ausgabe
126. Ausg. / 54. Jahrg. / Einzelpreis 20 Pf.

Norddeutsche Ausgabe
Berlin, Dienstag, 6. Mai 1941

VÖLKISCHER BEOBACHTER

Kampfblatt der nationalsozialistischen Bewegung
Großdeutschlands

Starke Kampffliegerverbände bombardierten Belfast

Angriffe auf Rüstungswerke und Hafenanlagen auch in England
Ein Zerstörer und vier Handelsschiffe versenkt

Berlin, 5. Mai.

Das Oberkommando der Wehrmacht gibt bekannt:

Starke deutsche Kampffliegerverbände führten in der letzten Nacht einen wirksamen Angriff gegen den wichtigen Umschlaghafen Belfast in Nordirland. Gewaltige Explosionen, viele Großbrände, vor allem in Anlagen der Flugzeugindustrie sowie in der Vickers-Armstrong-Werft wurden beobachtet. Vier im Hafen liegende Schiffe gerieten in Brand.

Andere Kampffliegerverbände bombardierten die Werften der britischen Kriegsmarine und Ernährungsbetriebe in Barrow in Furneß, der britischen Westküste und erzielten in den zum Teil von den Angriffen der obigen Nacht noch brennenden kriegswichtigen Anlagen des Werfts-Gebietes neue Volltreffer. Weitere Luftangriffe richteten sich gegen Rüstungswerke bei Hartlepool sowie gegen die Hafenanlagen von Ipswich und Plymouth.

Im Seegebiet um England verloren Kampffliegerverbände vier Handelsschiffe mit zusammen 21 000 BRT, sowie einen Zerstörer. Sie beschädigten durch Bombenwurf fünf weitere große Handelsschiffe schwer.

Bei einem Tagesangriff leichter Kampffliegergruppen gegen den Flugplatz Manston in Südostengland wurden mehrere Flugzeuge am Boden zerstört und Brände in Unterkünften und Betriebswerkstätten hervorgerufen.

In Nordafrika wurden britische Gegenangriffe vor Tobruk schon beim Ansatz durch Artilleriefeuer zerschlagen.

Die Kriegsmarine hält mit der Donauflotte minenfreie Schiffahrtswege auf der Donau offen.

Kampfhandlungen des Feindes fanden über dem Reichsgebiet weder bei Tage noch bei Nacht statt.

Dem Wort des Führers folgte die Tat
„Heftige und anhaltende Angriffe"

Das britische Luftfahrtministerium gibt schwere Schäden zu
Sorgen um die Seeverbindungen

A German newspaper report of the air-raid on Belfast on 4–5 May 1941. The account is accurate, apart from Harland & Wolff being confused with Vickers-Armstrong. *(British Museum)*

Translation:

STRONG AIR FIGHTER UNITS BOMB BELFAST

Also attacks on munitions factories and docks in England. A destroyer and four trading vessels sunk.

Berlin, 5 May: The High Command of the Armed Forces announces:

Strong German bomber formations last night carried out an effective attack on the important port of Belfast in Northern Ireland. Violent explosions and many large and extensive fires were observed, especially in the factories of the air-armaments industry, as well as in the Vickers-Armstrong shipyard. Four ships lying in the harbour were set on fire.. . .

* Douglas Carson, 'The Belfast Blitz', broadcast on 22 November 1973 in the *Modern Irish History: people and events* series (BBC Radio Ulster)

Firemen toiled in an almost hopeless attempt to control the fires, and the fire brigades of Dublin, Dun Laoghaire, Drogheda and Dundalk sped northwards to Belfast's aid.

In an admirable gesture of solidarity the Lord Mayor of Dublin, Alfie Byrne, rode in one of his city's fire engines all the way to Belfast. 'It was very cold, and I nearly froze driving that open engine to Belfast,'* a southern fireman remembered. 'I had to sit on my hands to keep them from getting numb. There were no landmarks on the way up; we reached our destination by following the telephone lines. . . The fires in Belfast were the worst I ever saw in my life. The whole area was in ruins and there were human bodies and dead animals lying all over the place – the worst thing I ever saw in my life.' A shipyard worker saw rats 'marching up the road like an army, leaving all the shops and engine works'. Over 700 died, 1,500 more were injured, 1,600 houses were destroyed completely and over 28,000 dwellings were damaged severely.

Jim McConville recalls:

As we crossed the Shankill and approached the Old Lodge Road the devastation became apparent. Denmark Street had been badly hit, the Lower Crumlin was a shambles and along the Antrim Road every third house gave evidence of the pounding the area had received. We reached the old Lyceum Cinema, turned down Stratheden Street and soon saw what was left of the aunt's house – a gap where the door had been, another for the window and inside a pile of bricks and rubble. We rooted around, hopelessly, to see if anything could be salvaged. I found the frame of the Singer treadle sewing machine, tried to wrench it free but hurriedly withdrew my hand as the still hot metal seared my flesh. Down the hill of the New Lodge Road we tramped, and pulled up in horror when we saw the remnants of the York Street Mill. It was as if a great hand had sliced down at an angle, cutting it in two.

Professor John Blake, the official historian, concluded: 'No other city in the

United Kingdom, save London, had lost so many of her citizens in one night's raid. No other city, except Liverpool, ever did.'

One hundred and fifty bodies were taken for identification to St George's Market and as many were laid out on the white-tiled bottom of the Falls Road Baths. Joseph Tomelty remembers: 'I went down to the Baths. Only a few weeks ago I'd gone swimming here, kicking my feet in fifty yards of green water. Now, today, it was dry, and its white-tiled floor covered with the bodies of the dead. Bodies of the poor they were, of the homeless poor, lying in their own shabby blankets. . .' The Falls Road escaped attack, as Jim McConville recalls: 'People afterwards attributed this to the fact that God was a Catholic, and these same people brought forward the clinching proof that not one Catholic Church had suffered.' Rumours circulated in Protestant areas that Catholics had helped to guide German bombers by shining torches from the roof-tops.

Many families travelled by the Great Northern Railway to Dublin. Andy Fagan, then a member of the Red Cross in Dublin, recalled: 'They arrived down with literally nothing and the problem was where we were going to put them. In the end we made dorms by hanging up sheets of canvas in Mespil Hall, Baggotrath Church Hall, and the St John's Ambulance Hall in Strand Street.'

The Blitz: May 1941

Before the defences of Belfast could be strengthened, the Germans returned. The moon was so bright that no flares were needed when the 200 bombers began to fly over the city around midnight on 4 May 1941. This time the Luftwaffe had no difficulty dropping oil-bombs and parachute mines on the very heart of industrial Belfast. The shipyards were devastated, causing a 45% loss on shipbuilding construction. Three corvettes nearing completion were destroyed and the transport ship *Fair Head* sank at her moorings. The flight shed, stores and runways of Shorts' aircraft factory were badly hit. The Harbour Power Station and York Street Railway station were reduced almost to rubble. To people taking refuge on the Cave Hill, it looked as if the city below had become an inferno; for firemen the battle against the flames was almost impossible since the principal water mains had been fractured and the fire-hoses could not reach the river water when the tide went out.

In Germany, it was accurately reported: 'In view of the ideal bombing conditions and the large conflagrations observed, the raid can be considered a success.' Since the targets this time were industrial rather than residential, and citizens took greater care not to expose themselves to danger, the casualties were much lower than in the previous raid – 150 killed and 157 badly injured – but the damage to the war effort was greater. The production of Stirling bombers were seriously delayed; it was over a year before night work could resume in the aircraft factory; and it took six months to bring the shipyards back into full production.

Many cities in Britain had suffered, or were to suffer, as severely as Belfast during the Blitz; in some respects, however, Belfast's plight was unique. The protection provided for the people was lower than that given in any other city of the United Kingdom of comparable size and as a result the number killed was exceptionally high. Also, since Belfast was the only large urbanised area in Northern Ireland, it proved almost impossible to accommodate those who had been made homeless. Altogether, 56,000 houses had been severely damaged and 15,000 citizens had no homes whatever after the raids. After the first raid 40,000 had to be put up in rest centres and 70,000 provided with daily meals in emergency feeding centres. A mass exodus to the countryside followed the Blitz but the provincial towns – despite the spontaneous generosity many city people found in them – could only take in a small proportion of those who sought refuge. Officially 49,000 evacuated from Belfast, though it is certain this figure is too low.

It is estimated that for several weeks 10,000 slept in ditches and fields outside Belfast; it was a mercy that not only did the weather keep fine but also that the Germans never again returned in force.

Jim McConville remembers:

The exodus began around 10 p.m. Hundreds went as far as the Falls Park; thousands felt safer another mile out of the city. Parents and children 'well happed up' against the cold night air would sit around on folding stools, or lie on ground sheets; some could and would sleep; most of us talked, joked and bantered as only the Belfast working man can; someone would light a cigarette and immediately from all around would come: 'Put out that match! Do you want Jerry to see us?!'

'I broke down after the things I saw. I broke down when I saw lying dead men I had been reared beside,' Tommy Henderson said bitterly at Stormont, and, looking angrily towards the ministerial benches, he asked:

Will the Right Hon. Member come with me to the hills and to Divis mountain? Will he go to the barns and sheughs throughout Northern Ireland to see the people of Belfast, some of them lying on damp ground? The Catholics and Protestants are going up there

The Blitz 15–16 April 1941. People salvage what they can from Sunningdale Park, north Belfast. These houses were close to the Cavehill Waterworks, which the Luftwaffe appears to have mistaken for the docks and Harbour Estate, possibly because Mr. Kemp, the manager of Harland & Wolff, put up a dense smoke-screen as the bombers approached. *(Belfast Telegraph)*

mixed and they are talking to one another. They are sleeping in the same sheugh, below the same tree or in the same barn. They all say the same thing, that the government is no good.

'This nightly journey "up the road" to the safety of the countryside, and return in the early hours of the morning helped intensify the feeling of togetherness that had grown up as the war progressed,' wrote Jim McConville. 'People came to know neighbours who until that time had remained relative strangers. New friendships were forged; old acquaintances and long-time neighbours were seen in a new light; kindness and a helping hand appeared from the most unexpected quarters.'

The city in commission

The air raids exposed the ineptitude of both the government and the Corporation. Many had died unnecessarily because the authorities had been too mean to build enough shelters, too complacent to see that the fire services were properly equipped and too slack in preparing for the evacuation of people from the city. The consequences of decades of neglect were revealed as pale hungry children lined up to be deloused and as adults, old before their time, joined the food lines in the emergency centres. In addition, the air raids put people out of work; in the shipbuilding, engineering, and aircraft industries in the city, unemployment rose from 1,700 in April 1941 to 5,800 in May and, in the linen industry, unemployment was as bad as it had been in the darkest years of the Depression.

Never was the prestige of the Corporation so low. The report of an inquiry in June 1941 into the administration of Whiteabbey Sanatorium indicated that years of undisturbed power had led to incompetence and corruption. It concluded that the Corporation Tuberculosis Committee had tried to force the purchase of a site for the sanatorium 'without any regard to its obvious unsuitability and extravagant price'. The Stormont government put the city into commission: that is, it appointed three commissioners under the Minister of Home Affairs for a 3½-year period to make all appointments, purchases and contracts, and to set the level of rates and municipal taxes. The government did not save itself from criticism by taking this action, however, and in December 1941 the hitherto safe Unionist seat of Willowfield was lost in a by-election to the Labour candidate unseated at Dock in 1938, Harry Midgley. Andrews was becoming increasingly unpopular and was forced by his own colleagues to resign on 30 April 1943.

A new prosperity

Sir Basil Brooke, who had led the successful cabinet revolt, became Prime Minister at an opportune time. Northern Ireland was ready at last to make a full contribution to Allied victory. By now the damage inflicted on the Harbour Estate had been largely repaired, the 'Atlantic Gap' (where before U-boats could strike without fear of counter-attack) had been filled with the aid of Sunderlands and long-range Liberators from Lough Erne and Ballykelly, and the convoys came in with ever-increasing security.

Unemployment fell as the city's industries worked to full capacity. At Harland & Wolff the numbers employed rose from 9,100 in 1939 to 20,600 in 1945, with 150 ships, totalling over 500,000 tons, launched during the period;

10,000 field guns were manufactured by the firm, and from August 1939 to November 1943, 550 tanks were made, after which the workforce concentrated on the production of fleet carriers for the Far East war. The Sirocco Works produced grenades, gun-mountings and radar equipment; Mackies specialised in the manufacture of armour-piercing shells; smaller businesses supplied a bewildering variety of munitions and components. Air-raid damage and shortage of certain raw materials, however, ensured that unemployment was never completely eradicated; during 1942–4 it rarely fell below 15,000 The linen industry suffered violent fluctuations in spite of the mounting demand for uniforms, tenting, parachutes and flying suits.

In case of further attacks from the air, Shorts dispersed as many of its processes as possible across the city and its neighbourhood. Fuselages and components were made at the King's Hall, Balmoral; women assembled undercarriage and fuselage parts at Mackies; a linen mill at Lambeg converted to the manufacture of tail planes, flaps, fins and rudders; sheetmetal pressings were made at Hawlmark, Newtownards; and aircraft wings were produced at Long Kesh and in a Largymore furniture factory. Creighton's garage on the Lisburn Road, Brown's garage on the Albertbridge Road, a temporary hangar at Dunmurry, and several farm outbuildings on the fringe of the city were pressed into service as makeshift stores. In August 1944 a delegation from the Ministry of Aircraft Production reported that Shorts were employing 10,500 people and that 150 Herefords, 50 Bombays, 78 Sunderlands and 865 Stirlings had been made in addition to the completion of numerous repairs and conversions. The bulk of Shorts' output was used to inflict on German cities devastation immeasurably more extensive than that suffered by Belfast in 1941.

Shortages and hardships notwithstanding, the people of Belfast now experienced a prosperity they had never known before. Income per head, which was only just above one half of that in Britain before the war, now rose to three-quarters of the greatly increased income per head in Britain during the war. It was a precarious prosperity, however, dependent on the stimulus of war. Perhaps the first visible sign of this prosperity was that working people repainted their kitchen houses; many doors in east Belfast, it was said, appeared in a uniform battleship grey.

Jim McConville recalls:

Not only was there the opportunity of a good weekly wage; as usual the 'fly men' were up to all the dodges and the prime example of this was the Yard. The biggest dodge was getting someone to 'throw in your board'. Many of the workers would be prepared to take a chance and put in the boards (the modern equivalent is the time-card) of two or three of their workmates and these same workmates would spend the day elsewhere. . . I remember going to the Classic Cinema one summer afternoon. . . I followed the usherette down the aisle unable to see anything but the screen and herself silhouetted against it. I wondered why she showed me to a seat so far into the body of the hall, but, becoming quickly engrossed in the film thought no more about it until a particularly dramatic moment arrived in the film. The heroine, wakened from her sleep and aware of a prowler in her darkened bedroom, called out 'who's there?' in a quavering voice. I must have jumped about six inches out of my seat when from all around me thundered the reply 'IT's SKIBOO!' During the interval I discovered that the hall was filled with Yard men. . .*

Classic Cinema.
(From the brochure for formal opening, 1923)

* J. McConville, '1935 and All That' (unpublished memoirs).

'A faithful sentinel'

Welcomed by the Governor, the Duke of Abercorn, and the Prime Minister, still then J.M. Andrews, the first American contingent arrived in Belfast on the morning of 26 January 1942. 'Operation Magnet' had begun; for a short time the United States forces made Northern Ireland their principal base for an assault on Hitler's Europe. By the end of 1943 there were 100,000 American troops in the province. In 1944 they moved to England to prepare for the D-Day landings and Belfast's contribution was largely confined thereafter to what its factories could produce.

The brief American incursion brought in Hershey bars for the children and augmented audiences for the theatres. Formed partly from a company of actors stranded in Dublin at the outbreak of war, the Savoy Players were on stage at the Grand Opera House six nights a week for six years. After seeing the performance of their 200th play, an American journalist wrote:

I have seen many plays in London, Los Angeles, and New York. In no city or theatre have I seen players so warmly received, night after night, week after week. *

* Sam Hanna Bell, *The theatre in Ulster* (see bibliog), p. 59.

The war gave a welcome stimulus to the Group Theatre, formed from amateur and semi-professional drama societies and launched with a performance of Louis Walsh's *The Auction at Killybuck* in St Mary's Hall on Boxing Night 1938. Unlike the Ulster Literary Theatre, the Group found a permanent home – in the Ulster Minor Hall, leased from the Belfast Corporation. Harold Goldblatt and James Mageean provided professional direction and management, and from the moment it opened at its new venue in March 1940, the theatre attracted capacity audiences; *Boyd's Shop* was the most popular play of all for, as Sam Hanna Bell observed, 'some quality in St John Ervine's play reminded men and women of homely virtues reported missing if not dead in those sombre early days and black nights of the War'.*

* *op cit.*, p. 70.

The earlier inaction and ineptitude of the Stormont government, and the proved corruption of some members of the City Hall Unionists, were partly forgotten as citizens saw improvement in their security and prosperity. More confident and apparently more competent than his more liberal predecessor, Andrews, Brooke enjoyed wide support, not least because the distinguished Allied commander, Field Marshal Alan Brooke, made the Prime Minister's family name famous across the world. Brooke also came close to extinguishing the IRA in Belfast. Stimulated by the American presence, the IRA launched a new campaign. Six volunteers were captured in Cawnpore Street after an RUC constable had been killed; all six were condemned to death but the sentences of all but one were commuted.

Belfast was placed under curfew and once again the RUC patrolled the streets in armoured cars and 'cage' lorries. Sixty armed attacks were reported in the final months of 1942 but these only led to further arrests. Either sentenced or interned, the most determined activists were held in Crumlin Road gaol. Four internees had escaped in May 1941. Four sentenced IRA men escaped over the gaol's wall in January 1943; two of them, Hugh McAteer and Jimmy Steele, made a spectacular appearance at the Falls Road Broadway Cinema on Holy Saturday. While the staff was held at gunpoint, the audience was forced to participate in an Easter commemoration for 'the dead who died for Ireland'. Steele and McAteer were subsequently recaptured, nevertheless, and the steady attrition of arrests reduced the IRA in Belfast to a few hunted men seeking refuge rather than action. By hangings, street gun-fights and incarceration in bleak camps, the de Valera government had shattered its former associates north and south. Gerry Boland, Eire's Minister for Justice, claimed with much truth that the IRA was dead. That Belfast was entirely free from IRA activity by the end of the war was in large measure due to the unwavering repression administered by the Dublin government.

'Here, by the grace of God, Ulster stood a faithful sentinel'; Churchill was at pains to acknowledge Northern Ireland's contribution. In a letter to Andrews, still Unionist leader if no longer Prime Minister, he wrote: 'But for the loyalty of Northern Ireland and its devotion to what has now become the cause of thirty governments or nations, we should have been confronted with slavery and death. . .' Catholics and Protestants alike felt proud when General Eisenhower saluted them from the steps of the City Hall. Particularly after the fall of France, Belfast's geographical position and industrial capacity gave the city a vital, if unforeseen, role to play in the Second World War. The war had revealed the extent of economic, social and educational deprivation in the city; energetic attempts would be made to deal with that deprivation immediately after the war. In addition, the horrors of the Blitz, by throwing together people from both communities, had reduced sectarian animosity in the city to its lowest level since the founding of Northern Ireland.

The Blitz 15–16 April 1941. The devastation as seen from North Street, looking down Bridge Street, into High Street. (*Belfast Telegraph*)

10
Years of Hope
c.1945–1968

At noon on 8 May 1945 the Ulster United Prayer Movement held a victory thanksgiving service in the grounds of the City Hall and soon afterwards a huge crowd of citizens and servicemen filled Donegall Square as the city echoed to the sound of church bells, ship sirens and factory hooters in celebration of the capitulation of Germany. Then a great hush fell as Churchill's broadcast was relayed from the City Hall. At the conclusion of the speech some servicemen in the City YMCA rose to their feet and sang the Doxology. The Lord Mayor, Sir Crawford McCullagh, told the crowds in Donegall Square they had much for which to thank Almighty God, Who had given them victory. He concluded:

We must not forget that we are still at war, and that much remains to be done before the world is at peace. We must not slack. Celebrate the victory and go back to work.

For the people of Belfast, however, VE Day was the end of the war as far as they were concerned. Bustling crowds surged through the main streets of the city and in Protestant districts kerbs and air-raid shelters were painted in loyal colours. The City YMCA, which had served 3¼ million meals and given sleeping accommodation to 330,000 during the war, provided 4,000 free meals that day. That evening, as the *Belfast Telegraph* reported,

For the first time in six years the City Hall was flood-lit. As the illumination was switched on at 10.40 p.m. there was a tremendous cheer from thousands of people, among them many Allied Service men, who were much impressed by the majesty of the building silhouetted against the darkening sky. The Albert Memorial was also flood-lit, and here also large and excited crowds assembled. Huge bonfires blazed in many parts of the city and around them bands of young people danced in jubilant mood right into the early hours of the morning.

Dozens of effigies of Hitler were burned on lamp standards. On the Shore Road a bugle band led a procession of youngsters in the midst of whom was carried an effigy of the Führer, wearing his swastika and hanging from the gallows.

For the citizens of Belfast the Second World War had been far more harrowing than the First. Now the sense of optimism and hope seemed stronger than in 1918; to a large extent this was justified, for the city was about to enjoy the longest period of peace and prosperity in its history. It is true that the era of Belfast's greatness had long passed and that the closing of the York Street Mill in 1951 marked the return of economic weakness so apparent in the inter-war years. Westminster, however, came increasingly to the rescue despite

246

an extreme reluctance to become involved in Stormont's political affairs. The 'imperial contribution' became a legal fiction as successive British governments underwrote the cost of aid to industry and welfare services which brought a more dramatic improvement in the living standards of Belfast people than probably in any British city of comparable size.

For the first time the population of the city fell; numbers living in Belfast, which had risen from 438,086 in 1937 to 443,671 in 1951, dropped by 6.2% to 416,094 by 1961. This, however, not only demonstrated the increasing artificiality of the city boundary but also was a reflection of the growing prosperity and mobility of citizens who moved out to burgeoning suburbs. So successful was O'Neill's government in attracting new firms to the Belfast area that by the end of the period economists were proclaiming that the problem of unemployment was solved in the city, if not in the province as a whole.

The IRA campaign of the Fifties had little effect on Belfast, and the 1964 Divis Street riots and the sectarian shootings of 1966 were widely publicised because they were so exceptional. Nevertheless, there were ominous signs for the future: the Stormont election of 1949 showed how little progress had been made in improving community relations in the city; pockets of high unemployment and wretchedly poor housing were dangerously concentrated in Catholic working-class areas of Belfast; and improved education and the mass media encouraged discontent. It could be argued that post-war governments in London and Belfast had planted dragon's teeth which were later to spring up as armed men.

A gentle ripple: the post-war elections

Anxious to demonstrate the loyalty of the Ulster majority before the British electorate went to the polls, Brooke called a general election for the Stormont parliament for 15 June 1945. The *Belfast News-Letter* believed that 'the Constitutional question emerges as the governing issue' and certainly in rural Ulster the election would be fought along traditional lines. Nevertheless, the war years had seen a steady growth in the confidence, solidarity and militancy of the labour movement and in Belfast there seemed a real hope that there would be a significant shift in the voters' usual loyalties. Some speculated that labour would control a majority of the city's constituencies.

The fear expressed by the Marquis of Donegall that the government was 'hanging on by its eye-lashes and could be put out of office at any time' proved to be completely unfounded. With 37 seats the Unionists were as impregnable as ever; still, in Belfast itself labour candidates had done well considering that the different parties had split each other's votes in several constituencies — Beattie was elected as Independent Labour MP for Pottinger; Midgley won Willowfield for Commonwealth Labour; Harry Diamond as a Socialist Republican ousted the Nationalist in Falls; the Labour Party won Dock, Oldpark, and (in a by-election in 1946) Belfast Central; and the redoubtable Tommy Henderson, elected again as an Independent Unionist for Shankill, was arguably as much a labour MP as the others.

In the Westminster election three weeks later Beattie took West Belfast again and the other three city seats were won by Unionists. In Britain the Labour Party won the most overwhelming victory in its history; with a margin of 180 seats over the opposition it had a clear mandate to implement its radical programme which ultimately would do much to transform the lives of the people of Belfast. However much they admired Churchill, the British electorate preferred to entrust to Attlee the task of post-war construction.

In 1946 democracy returned to Belfast's municipal government when the statutory period of commission rule came to an end. The Elections and Franchise (NI) Act 1946 laid down that half the aldermen and all the councillors would have to stand for re-election every third year. In the Corporation elections of that year the Labour Party increased its representation from 4 to 8 seats; Independent Labour won 3 seats in Falls; and the Nationalists were reduced to 4 councillors for Smithfield. The Unionist majority remained massive, however, and if there was a tidal wave sweeping Labour to power in Britain, it had petered out to a gentle ripple by the time it had reached Belfast.

'The work will have to begin immediately': a quiet revolution

On 2 June 1941, the Right Rev J.B. Woodburn, the retiring Moderator of the Presbyterian Assembly, had given this warning in his sermon:

After the big Blitz of a few weeks ago I was inexpressibly shocked by the sight of people I saw walking in the streets. I have been working 19 years in Belfast and I never saw the like of them before — wretched people, very undersized and underfed down-and-out-looking men and women. They had been bombed out of their homes and were wandering the streets. Is it creditable to us that there should be such people in a Christian country?. . . We have got to see that there is more talk of justice; we have got to see it enacted, and the work will have to begin immediately. If something is not done now to remedy this rank inequality there will be a revolution after the war. . .

The plight of the city's poor had been revealed as thousands had sought refuge in the countryside after the air raids. The 1946 Report on Health and Local Government Administration remarked that 'the shock to householders who granted them sanctuary was second only to the shock they had received on learning of the disaster which had befallen Belfast'.

There was a revolution after the war, but not of the kind feared by Dr Woodburn; it was a quiet revolution originating in Westminster which did much to prevent barricades being built in the streets in these years. In 1942 Beveridge had sketched out his ground plan of a welfare state for Britain, and after 1945 one welfare measure followed another at Westminster, vigorously opposed though they were by Unionist MPs there. Yet Bills which had been criticised stage by stage by Unionists in London were shortly afterwards proposed with enthusiasm by government ministers at Stormont. The main explanation for this apparent contradiction was that Britain was prepared to pay most of the very large sums needed to finance welfare legislation in Northern Ireland. Lavish aid from Westminster was about to sweep away many of the consequences of decades of neglect. In 1946 it was agreed that, provided parity of taxation was maintained, Northern Ireland would enjoy the same standards of social services as those prevailing in the rest of the United Kingdom. The people of Belfast, who had lived under the shadow of the Poor Law long after it had been dismantled in Britain, were about to enjoy a more striking improvement in their material welfare than in any previous period in the century.

Post-war housing

A crash programme of house building seemed to be Belfast's most urgent need

Rowland Street in the 1950s. 'Let us enter Sandy-row. This locality is not unknown to fame. . .' Houses described by Rev W.M. O'Hanlon in 1853 were still inhabited in the latter half of the twentieth century.

Houses from Rowland Street have been carefully reconstructed at the Ulster Folk Museum.

in 1945. Though it observed that housing in the city compared favourably with towns of similar size and character in England, the Carnwath Report of 1941 pointed out that 'some of the houses were mere hovels, with the people living in indescribable filth and squalor' and that others had 'damp mouldering walls, many of them bulging, ricketty stairs, broken floors, crumbling ceilings. . .' Then the Blitz destroyed 3,200 houses in Belfast and damaged another 53,000. A survey of housing in the city was made in 1943; as the city welfare officer, Lucius O'Brien, recalled: 'The results were pretty shocking and we sent the report to Mr Harry Midgley who was then Minister of Security. It seems that it aroused great feeling in the Cabinet.' The government ordered the first comprehensive survey of housing in the province, and the results were published in 1944.

This 'Interim Report' of 1944 showed that 48,000 houses damaged in the air raids had been repaired by Belfast Corporation; 74,590 houses in the city were fit or repairable; 23,479 were overcrowded; and 'inhabited totally unfit' houses numbered 4,537. Overcrowded and totally unfit houses were 26.8% of the total in Belfast and 23,591 houses were needed immediately. The problem was acute in the inner city – 65.9% of houses in Smithfield and 53.6% in Court were classed as overcrowded and/or totally unfit. 60% of citizens lived in 'the poorer districts of Belfast' where there was an average of 60 dwellings per acre. The problem was so severe that exceptional measures would have to be taken, and the report recommended a housing commission to supplement the work of the local authorities.

William Grant, the Minister of Health and Local Government, incorporated several of these recommendations in his Housing Act of 1945. The Housing Trust was set up with power to borrow from the government to build houses and to pay back the capital with interest over 60 years; beyond this state assistance, the Trust had to pay its own way and fix its rents in relation to the cost of construction. Lucius O'Brien, the first chairman of the Trust, recalled:

On February 14th 1945, the very day the act was finally passed, vacant premises were handed over to us in Donegall Square South. Without furniture or even a telephone and two civil servants on loan the only staff, the five of us started from there to set the Trust in action. . . Our first deal was with some builders who agreed to finish off for us an estate at Graymount on the Shore Road, which they had had to leave half completed when war broke out.

By early 1946 the first Housing Trust estates were going up at Cregagh, Finaghy and Andersonstown, but its statutory duty to fix its rents to cover the cost of building ensured that it would not provide housing for those most in need. In 1946–7 the rents were fixed at fourteen shillings a week; O'Brien said later: 'This was a great shock and disappointment to us. The 14s. seemed a lot in those days and was much higher than we had hoped for.' There was no shortage of applicants, however, and those capable of paying the rents did to some extent relieve the housing pressure for those who remained in the inner city. Meanwhile the Stormont government subsidised privately-built housing at £48 a dwelling (the subsidy was only £10 in Britain) and Belfast Corporation's 'Hustle the Houses' Committee pressed ahead with its own schemes: houses were put up on Blitz sites and prefabricated bungalows were built at Beechmount, Shore Crescent, Annadale Embankment, upper Malone and elsewhere.

The progress made was not sufficient, however. Speaking to a motion proposed by Bob Getgood at Stormont, condemning the failure to house homeless people, Frank Hanna, MP for Belfast Central, said that he foresaw 'some terrible trouble in Belfast; the Government's sitting on a keg of gunpowder, and when the trouble arises they will not be able to say that they have not been warned'. Grant replied that Belfast Corporation had selected sites for 1,925 new permanent houses and 1,000 prefabricated temporary bungalows and that the Housing Trust had sites for 2,802 houses outside the city boundary. When in January 1944 Councillor A. Cleland, chairman of the Corporation Housing Committee, announced that contracts had been placed for the forthcoming year to build 1,063 houses and 800 aluminium houses, it was pointed out that there were 23,000 applicants on the Corporation's housing list; Councillor R. Hill said that there were 2,000 marriages each year in the city and he believed that by 1951 there would still be 23,000 applicants.

The problem of slum housing in the inner city had not been tackled comprehensively. The average density of persons per room in Belfast had hardly changed since before the war – in 1937 it was 0.88 and in 1951 it was 0.86. Overcrowding was still very severe in several wards in 1951: 30.1% in Smithfield, 20.7% in Court, 20% in Dock and 19.8% in Falls lived at a density of more than two persons per room. In Dock, for example, 242 families occupied one room each and 544 occupied two rooms each (135 of these 'households' were composed of 5 or more persons).

Nevertheless new housing brought significant change to the shape of Belfast. Between 1926 and 1951 the built-up area of Belfast nearly doubled and from 1945 to 1954, 11,000 dwellings were built in and around Belfast, 6,500 by the Housing Trust and the Corporation. Because of the application of more stringent standards in public housing and the need of private housing to avoid ostentation to attract the subsidy, the distinction between the two became blurred in the new estates. Suburbs in the north reached Whitewell, pushed through the Carnmoney Gap and joined with Glengormley; in the south, housing separated by the Bog Meadows spread out and fused at

Finaghy; and in the south-east, estates lapped against the Castlereagh Hills and were reaching the Dundonald Gap. Councillor Cleland warned in January 1949:

Unless steps are taken to extend the City boundary – and taken early – we shall be without building land and be unable to plan any further building beyond the present programme...

Nearly three quarters of the land surface of Belfast Borough was built over and for the first time the city was running out of building sites. The radical re-thinking which was to lead to the controversial Matthew 'Stop Line' had begun.

A new health service

The Blitz had revealed to public gaze, in a way that cold statistics could not, the appallingly low standards of health in Belfast; those in rural areas who had thrown open their homes to evacuees were horrified to find so many children from the city infested with lice and wasting away from tuberculosis. Tuberculosis was responsible for almost half the deaths in the age group 15–25. Infant mortality was higher in 1940 than it had been twenty years before and the maternal mortality rate was the highest in Britain or Ireland. Belfast Corporation appealed to the government for help in January 1941 as the state grant for maternity and child welfare was only 21% of local authority expenditure when the law permitted a grant of 50%.

In September 1941 the Corporation invited Dr T. Carnwath, former deputy Chief Medical Officer of the English Ministry of Health, to report on the state of the city's health. Carnwath found that the administration of Belfast's health services was chaotic, as responsibility was divided between the Poor Law medical service, the government, and the Corporation. Another inquiry reported in 1944; one member of the Select Committee said: 'Some of the evidence was so bad that we had to stop it and ask the Minister of Home Affairs to take action.'

Brooke set up a new Ministry of Health and Local Government in 1944 and asked William Grant, a former shipyard worker, to be the first Minister. Energetic action was taken but it was not until Britain had introduced her national health service that the Unionist government outlined its own scheme for a comprehensive medical service. In one field – tuberculosis – Stormont was not prepared to wait for a lead from Britain; in 1941 the Tuberculosis Authority was set up with a mission to find affected victims, treat them, and eventually to extirpate the disease altogether. A special section was established to wage an unrelenting war on the most killing variety of tuberculosis, Koch's bacillus. The Authority's campaign was so determined and effective that the death rate was reduced by 1954 to the same level as that in England and Wales. So well had the authority done its work that it was dissolved in 1959. The south followed the north's lead and from 1948 Dr Noel Browne, the Inter-Party Minister for Health, set out to combat Ireland's most dangerous killer disease with unique vigour. The 32-county drive to eliminate this scourge could be said to have been the most heartening step forward made in these years.

In July 1948 the National Health Service, open to all, totally free and almost completely comprehensive, came into operation in Britain. In the same year an almost identical act passed through Stormont; because of cruel neglect in the past, the impact of this new service was more profoundly felt in Belfast than in any city in Britain. The dispensary system, the separate hospital administrations, and the power of the two Belfast Poor Law Commissioners were swept away and the Northern Ireland General Health Services Board was brought into being to provide general medical services for the whole province. All the hospitals in the city came under the control of the Hospitals Authority, with the exception of the Mater Hospital.

The improvement in the service provided for the citizens of Belfast was striking. On 30 September 1948 the Belfast Board of Guardians was formally abolished and the Workhouse infirmary became the Belfast City Hospital 1,245 of the 1,748 inmates were in the infirmary at the time; the remainder stayed on in the other workhouse buildings, now described as a welfare hostel. Eventually all the Workhouse was given to the City Hospital but many older people in Belfast continued to fear hospitalisation as, to them, it still meant 'going to the workhouse'. A Central Laboratory, a Radiotherapy Centre, and a Blood Transfusion Service were set up in the city, and chairs in Mental Health and Dentistry were established in Queen's University. Outpatient departments in Belfast increased from 46 to 85 between 1948 and 1959; Wakehurst House, a new geriatric unit of 200 beds, was built; an experimental ward unit was opened at Musgrave Park; an Institute of Clinical Science opened to service the teaching hospitals of the city; and construction had begun on a new hospital at Dundonald in 1959. Deaths in childbirth fell to the same level as for England and Wales by 1954, and by the 1960s the mortality rates for the province as a whole were the lowest in both Britain and Ireland.

In Britain, the 1947 Health Act included a clause stating that 'where the character and associations of any hospital transferred. . . are such as to link it with a particular religious denomination regard shall be had in the making of appointments to the Board of Management to the preservation of the character and associations of the hospital'. This clause was left out of the 1948 Act in Northern Ireland, and as a result the Mater Hospital refused to come in under the Hospitals Authority. Unlike similar hospitals in England, the Mater was not allowed to claim for payment for its outpatient services. Staying out of the state system, the Mater attempted to finance itself by 'YP' football pools, though it continued its free service to people of all creeds, the great majority of whom paid national insurance. If the new health service helped to promote contentment and reconciliation in the city, the Mater Hospital issue did much to undo the beneficial effects. It was not until 1968 that the Hospital could claim for the free services it provided and not until 1971 that state grants became available.

Educational reconstruction

Much of Belfast's education system was literally blown apart during the air raids of 1941 – bombs destroyed 18 schools and the Education Committee's Central Kitchen in Tamar Street, and damaged the Carlisle Clinic and 34 other schools. Before that, the decision to raise the school-leaving age in September 1939 had been suspended and all school construction had stopped in 1940. After the Blitz almost 30,000 children and more than half of Belfast's teachers were evacuated, causing a 10% drop in attendance. And yet the war gave education a better reputation in the city: the chief billeting officer for the whole city was a school teacher, all plans for evacuation were left to teachers, and teachers had been highly resourceful in organising Belfast schools to take in up to 15,000 homeless people.

Dr Stuart Hawnt, appointed Director of Education in December 1941, ensured that improvements requested by the government were quickly applied. Prompted by Dr Carnwath's report, the Education Committee provided milk to necessitous children from October 1942 and a general school meals service from January 1943. The meagre 50 scholarships to grammar schools in the city was increased to 200 a year by 1945. The Chief School Medical Officer – moved from the Old Town Hall to Arthur Street – was given an assistant; the Committee took over Graymount Open Air School for children suffering from chest complaints and 'general delicacy'; Edenderry Nursery School was acquired; and Grosvenor High School was opened in January 1945.

It was in 1944 that the British education system was revolutionised by the Butler Act: primary education was to end at the age of 11, and free and compulsory secondary education was to be provided by three types of school – grammar, secondary, and technical. In June 1944 the Presbyterian General Assembly in Belfast resolved:

The General Assembly is convinced that any less a measure of reform in Northern Ireland than that now secured for England would be disastrous to the well-being of the people of Northern Ireland.

The newly-appointed Stormont Minister of Education, Lt-Col Samuel Hall-Thompson, put forward his White Paper, 'Educational Reconstruction in Northern Ireland', in December 1944. Its basic aim was to apply the benefits of the British reorganisation to Ulster.

Three long and rancorous years were to pass before the main elements of the Butler Act were applied to Belfast.

'I feel there has been a betrayal of Protestantism': the 1947 Education Act

'One aim of the White Paper is further to ostracise the Catholic voluntary schools,' T.J. Campbell declared at Stormont, and in his 1945 Lenten Pastoral Dr Mageean, the Catholic Bishop of Down and Connor, said that Hall-Thompson's scheme would 'establish a colossal system of state controlled education'. The Minister of Education proposed to increase capital grants to voluntary (mainly Catholic) schools from 50% to 65% and to provide milk and meals for necessitous children, and books to these schools free of charge. Far from being satisfied by these proposals, Catholic leaders condemned them as putting their schools under great pressure to join the state system, particularly as reorganisation would involve a huge increase in expenditure. Besides, they argued, state schools would remain Protestant schools eligible for 100% capital grants – Catholic schools were discriminated against.

It was Protestant opposition to the government's proposals, however, which caused Hall-Thompson most trouble when his Education Bill was published in 28 September 1946. The Bill intended to scrap the 1930 Act's insistence on Bible instruction, seeking only compulsory collective worship and religious instruction in state schools, and it also provided a conscience clause for teachers not wishing to give religious instruction. Just as the Catholic Church wanted to maintain complete control over its schools and yet receive 100% capital grants, so many Protestants sought the retention of an unmistakeable Protestant ethos in the state schools.

'There are no sacrifices we will not make, in order that our Protestant form of inheritance will be made secure,' declared the Dean of Belfast at an angry protest meeting in the Wellington Hall on 8 November 1946. Two days later Hall-Thompson was howled down, at a meeting of the Ulster Women's Unionist Council in Glengall Street, when he said that 'in the State schools the religious instruction must be undenominational'. So great was the uproar that Lady Clark asked to be excused from the chair. At another protest meeting on 13 November, held in St Jude's church hall, Professor Robert Corkey (brother of Rev William Corkey) asserted that state schools would be thrown open to 'Jews, Agnostics, Roman Catholics and Atheists'. When some of the audience interrupted Corkey with cries of 'Nonsense!' and 'Tommy-rot!' others called for their expulsion, declaring: 'We don't want Communists here.'

The debates at Stormont on the Education Bill in December 1946 were exceptionally bitter. 'I feel there has been a betrayal of Protestantism,' said Herbert Quin, Unionist MP for Queen's University; nevertheless, Hall-Thompson persuaded first the cabinet and then a majority at Stormont to support him and in 1947 his Bill became law. It was a notable defeat for traditionalists but they were to have their revenge in 1949. Hall-Thompson proposed to pay Catholic teachers' insurance and superannuation; the Prime Minister attended a protest meeting of the Grand Orange Lodge in Sandy Row Orange Hall and agreed to amend his Minister's scheme. Hall-Thompson resigned and was replaced by Harry Midgley, who had been his most vituperative critic in 1946. Midgley's constant denunciation of the Catholic Church, and willingness to serve as a cabinet minister during the war, had earned him respect in loyalist circles and in 1947 he had joined the Unionist Party; he did not, however, attempt to undo Hall-Thompson's work. Throughout the long acrimonious dispute little had been said on whether or not the reorganisation proposed was the best educational solution. During the 1946 debate Lord Glentoran had remarked ruefully: 'The trouble about us here in Ulster is that we get excited by religion and drink.'

Progress in Secondary and Further Education

Meanwhile the salaried officials of the education authority in Belfast kept their heads down during the controversy. Spending rose rapidly and by 1947 had reached £300,000, the equivalent of a two shilling rate. It took two years for the Education Committee to devise a scheme which would put the 120 provisions of the 1947 Act into effect. The principal task was to convert the Public Elementary School system into a new primary and secondary system. Pupils would leave primary school at 11 years old; selected by a qualifying examination, the most able 20% would proceed to grammar school and the remaining 80% were to go on to an 'intermediate' secondary school. The Education Committee divided the city into 12 districts, each with its nursery, primary, and secondary provision. Catholic managers grouped their parishes to form five areas, with a boys' intermediate school and a girls' intermediate school in each area, in addition to a Christian Brothers' intermediate school and a girls' intermediate school to be run by the Sisters of Mercy.

At first there were not enough free grammar school places for those who had qualified. Grosvenor High School, opened in January 1945, was the Education Committee's only grammar school and so temporary buildings had to be put up quickly at Ashfield and Carolan Road. The traditional grammar schools successfully resisted direct control and preserved their identity largely intact. All continued to charge fees and to take in a proportion of pupils who had not passed the qualifying test; yet all – including even Campbell College – obtained direct grants from the state and were not therefore 'public schools' in the British sense. By 1959 there were only 1,898 pupils attending the Education Committee's three grammar schools: Annadale (1950), Carolan (1958), and Grosvenor (which moved to the Orangefield site in 1959). The middle classes of Belfast preferred to pay supplementary fees for their sons and daughters at the direct grant schools and as a result the 1947 Act did less to break down social barriers than had been originally expected.

The only possible way of providing enough secondary school places in time to cope with the war-time 'bulge' in births was to convert former public elementary schools – such as Edenderry, Glenwood, Linfield and Park Parade – into secondary intermediate schools. It was not until 1952 that the first purpose-built intermediate school was completed and most of the remainder were put up in the middle and late 1950s; in 1957–8, for example, Ballygomartin Boys', Everton Boys' and Orangefield Boys' intermediate schools were built and opened. For a time, classes in these city schools were very large and it proved difficult to implement a more liberal approach to teaching recommended in government reports. The Belfast Education Committee made an early attempt to make its secondary system comprehensive, but the Director's request for permission to provide 'suitable courses of secondary education for all ranges of ability' was turned down by the Ministry of Education in March 1953. The Committee long resisted the 1947 Act's insistence on separate technical schools; eventually technical courses were provided in four intermediate schools.

The 1947 Act called for further education provision. The Stanhope Street Further Education Centre opened in December 1948, with classes formed from day-release students sent by the GPO. The Juvenile Instruction Centre at Felden House, Whitehouse, started classes for school leavers in 1953 (David Bleakley was the first principal); it moved to the Jaffe school on the Cliftonville Road in 1958 where it was popularly known as the 'b'roo school' as it was primarily concerned to provide for unemployed boys. Adult classes in Danube Street Working Men's Club supplemented the work of the WEA and the expanding College of Technology. The Rupert Stanley College was opened on 27 May 1965 by Major Rupert Stanley, Belfast's first Director of Education. By then the Belfast Education Authority was spending £3 million a year on education.

Though great progress had been made in the education system in the city, many of the hopes of those who sought full equality of opportunity had been dashed. Above all, little had been done to break down the sectarian barriers in Belfast's schools – the Catholic voluntary schools were determined to stay outside the system and, though many Catholics attended the more prestigious Protestant grammar schools, the local authority schools in effect remained Protestant schools. It was only – quietly and unobtrusively – in the growing further education sector that young people of all creeds were being educated together.

Cultural revival

Sam Hanna Bell

The 1947 Education Act helped to create a more appreciative audience for the work of writers and artists who had reached maturity before its implementation. The expansion of higher education drew into the city a talented new generation and by the end of the period Belfast had become one of the liveliest centres for the creative arts in these islands.

The sense of cultural disruption and personal displacement felt by people from isolated rural communities forced to move into the city formed the central theme of Michael McLaverty's novels and short stories; in *Call My Brother Back* in particular, Belfast, tainted by the ever-present menace of bigotry and violence, offered no escape. *December Bride*, Sam Hanna Bell's moving and sensitive first novel was a reminder that the Ulster countryside was equally stifling and brutal; his later fiction has Belfast as its setting. Bell, like several other writers in the post-war years, did not at first receive the recognition he deserved. It was Brian Moore who finally dispelled the widely-held belief that Belfast was a cultural backwater; born in Clifton Street the son of a surgeon, he became the only novelist from the city with a truly international reputation. Unlike earlier writers such as St John Ervine who were proud of the city's economic achievement, Moore painted a very unflattering picture of Belfast. In *Judith Hearne* and *The Emperor of Ice-Cream*, Moore vilified his native city for its grim, grey bleakness, its pathetic down-trodden people, its narrow inept politicians and the suffocating atmosphere of religious bigotry and sexual prudery. Maurice Leitch confronted sectarianism with skill, particularly in his novel *Poor Lazurus*, and both he and Moore confirmed the low opinion they had of Belfast by showing it their heels. Janet McNeill portrayed a very different Belfast in her novels *As Strangers Here* and *The Maiden Dinosaur*: a cool, controlled, ironic stylist, she scrutinised the limited and limiting world of the middle-class and middle-aged Protestants of the northern suburbs.

In the eye and ear of several poets, Belfast remained an ugly city, its citizens culturally and materially deprived, aggressive and brutal. John Hewitt, while he condemned his 'creed-haunted, God forsaken race,' was the most articulate poetic voice of the Northern Protestant experience. His retirement to Belfast, after fifteen years as Art Director of the Herbert Gallery in Coventry, has been astonishingly vigorous, with a new collection of poetry appearing almost annually. Roy McFadden's legal training is evident in his poetry, where he can judge a character or situation with a precise phrase or image, deflate pretension and yet preserve compassion and humour. Hewitt's and McFadden's work did much to inspire a younger generation of writers at Queen's University; here Laurence Lerner taught in the English Department and Philip Larkin worked in the library, but it was Philip Hobsbaum who was the real catalyst. 'When Hobsbaum arrived in Belfast,' Seamus Heaney wrote later, 'he moved disparate elements into a single action. He emanated energy, generosity, belief in the community, trust in the parochial, the inept, the unprinted.' Thus given confidence to write, Heaney at once won critical acclaim for *Death of a Naturalist* (1966), a collection of poems inspired principally by his childhood on a farm in Co Derry. Derek Mahon wrote with disturbing power, though in such poems as 'Glengormley' and 'Teaching in Belfast' he clearly found his native city colourless and enervating. The picaresque ballads of James Simmons contrasted sharply with Michael

Longley's finely constructed gentle and reflective poetry.

Meanwhile, the Group Theatre continued to encourage new talent: between 1940 and 1955 nearly fifty plays had their performance on its stage. Its very success led to the loss of its best actors (including Colin Blakeley, Stephen Boyd, J.G. Devlin, James Ellis, Harold Goldblatt, Denys Hawthorne and Harry Towb) who achieved wider fame in films, television, and the London theatres. It was in the Group that Joseph Tomelty, Jack Loudan and Gerald McLarnon established themselves as playwrights. In 1957 the Group Theatre accepted *Over the Bridge* by Sam Thompson; shortly afterwards, the management lost its nerve and decided not to stage the play, declaring that they were 'determined not to mount any play which would offend or affront the religious or political beliefs or sensibilities of the man in the street. . .' It was the end of the Group as a centre for serious drama and thereafter it became the 'Home of Ulster Comedy' presided over by that most versatile caricaturist of the Belfast character, James Young. Thompson's play had its first performance at the Empire in January 1960, a devastating reminder of the hatreds still lurking just below Belfast's surface in these quiet years. The Empire closed down the following year and it was left to amateur groups, such as the Circle Theatre and the Lyric Theatre to provide a stage for local writers. The Lyric, set up in 1951, soon became the most vibrant centre for the dramatic arts in Ulster though its theatre (with seating for only fifty and a stage measuring fifteen feet by twelve) was for many years a converted back room of the Derryvolgie Avenue home of its founders, Mary and Pearse O'Malley.

The Chapel Gate Election: 10 February 1949

On 7 September 1948 Eire's premier, John A. Costello, announced that his state would become a Republic. Would the next step be for the British government to allow this Republic to exercise its constitutional claims over Northern Ireland? On 28 October Attlee gave the assurance that 'no change should be made in the constitutional status of Northern Ireland without Northern Ireland's free agreement'. Consequently Brooke called a general election to demonstrate once more that Ulster was British. The election, especially in Belfast, was a bitter one.

In the rural areas the election was as likely as not to be a sectarian head-count but in Belfast the real question was whether or not the Unionists could recover the ground lost to labour in 1945. It would be extremely difficult for the Northern Ireland Labour Party to argue now that the constitutional issue was irrelevant, yet it tried. When canvassing in the Oldpark, Bob Getgood was asked 'What about the Border?'; his reply, that voters should refer to his party's manifesto, was not likely to inspire confidence.

Meanwhile, on 27 January 1949, southern political parties met in the Dublin Mansion House and agreed to establish 'an anti-partition fund to be created by subscriptions and the holding of a national collection in all parishes on Sunday next'. The issue of the *Belfast Telegraph* for 31 January (which also announced that Harold Wilson was removing the rationing on suits and costumes) had the banner headline: 'The Chapel Gate Collections. Dublin. Limerick. Donnybrook lead. . .'

And so the northern election was quickly dubbed 'the chapel gate election', and loyalists were furious that southern financial aid was being given to anti-partitionist candidates. Jack Beattie, who accepted money from the fund, had his election meeting in Templemore Avenue broken up and was shouted down in Madrid Street; he sent a telegram of protest to Downing Street: 'Stoned by official Unionist mobs and denied the right of free speech in my election campaign to-night. Armed Stormont police took no action. . .' The following night his Unionist opponent in Pottinger, Dr Sam Rodgers, said:

It is a strange thing to see a big six-footer like him going to a wee man like Mr Attlee to seek protection. Why does he not do his crying to Mr Costello, the man he really supports? (Cheers)

It was the most violent moment of sectarian bitterness since 1938. Opposition candidates in Cromac and Dock were also stoned and mobs struggled with each other every evening in the darkness. Anti-partitionists can hardly have been pleased to read the *Belfast Telegraph* headline of 3 February: 'Cars from Dublin to help the Pro-Eire Men'.

'We stand for the Crown and the Union Jack. We will not submerge ourselves in a republic. We are King's men and will never quit,' Brooke said, and Hall-Thompson rode round his constituency like William of Orange on a white horse and brandished a blackthorn stick presented by Carson's son.

The Unionists eliminated the Northern Ireland Labour Party, which lost its three Belfast seats to them. Beattie was defeated in Pottinger and the only surviving labour MPs were two anti-partitionists; for the first time all opposition MPs at Stormont were Catholic.

The most serious casualty in the election was the modest advance in reconciliation in Belfast made during the war and immediately after. Labour would no longer straddle the constitutional question; NILP at its conference on 8 April agreed to 'maintain unbroken the connection between Great Britain and Northern Ireland. . .' and anti-partitionist labour supporters banded together under the Irish Labour Party. In the Corporation elections in May, 6 wards went to the Unionists without opposition, NILP lost all but one of its 8 seats, and the Irish Labour Party won 3 seats in Smithfield and all 4 seats in Falls. In the 1950 Westminster election Beattie lost his West Belfast seat to Rev Godfrey Macmanaway in a bitter sectarian contest; however, Macmanaway, as a clergyman of the Established Church, was disqualified by a Privy Council ruling and eventually in October 1957 Beattie recovered West Belfast by the tiny margin of 25 votes.

The *Princess Victoria* disaster: 31 January 1953

On the morning of 31 January 1953 the mail vessel *Princess Victoria* nosed its way out of Stranraer into a violent gale, with winds gusting up to 120 m.p.h. As Fusilier Walter Baker said afterwards: 'The *Princess Victoria* took a terrific beating from the mountainous seas as soon as she left Loch Ryan. Finally, one very high wave burst open the ramp doors at the stern used for loading vehicles, and the water poured in. The ship took a list and then we realised that we were in a serious position.' The time was 10.34 a.m. and the vessel was four miles north-west of Corsewall; her radio officer immediately sent out an SOS. As the *Belfast News-Letter* of 2 February recorded:

Helplessly she floundered at the mercy of the gale, which bore her steadily away from the Scottish coast down the Irish Sea. . . Stewardesses helped to shepherd women and children together, and wrapped them in blankets while the crew assisted passengers along the decks lashed by stinging spray. . . The position was hopeless. At 1.15 p.m.

came the signal 'We are preparing to abandon ship'.

Robert Harper, who played outside left for Linfield Football Club, recalled:

A girl in the uniform of the WRNS tripped and lost her hold. She fell away from us and into another compartment. We formed a chain by linking hands and dragged her back. . . I was thrown out of the lifeboat and was swept on to the side again and pulled in by other survivors.

Steadily taking in the sea and buffeted by the unabating wind, the *Princess Victoria* capsized. James Kerr, of Serpetine Road, told a reporter afterwards:

'I never saw a crowd of people so calm in an emergency. . . The other lifeboat was swept across her keel and overturned, and that was the last we saw of any of the passengers. . . On a raft which passed us were a woman and child, and later we sighted a baby in the water with a life-jacket.

At 1.25 p.m., four miles from the Copelands, the *Princess Victoria* sank; her master, Captain James Ferguson, went down, one hand held stiffly in salute. 128 people perished in the disaster. Among the 45 bodies landed at Belfast were those of Major Maynard Sinclair, MP for Cromac and Minister of Finance, and Sir Walter Smiles, MP for North Down. Many other Belfast people had died in the icy seas, for the Larne–Stranraer ferry was the shortest and cheapest route between the city and Britain. The storm had been one of the worst in living memory: 125 died that weekend in England and in Holland the dykes had been swept away. An inquiry reported on 26 November 1953 that, nevertheless, the owners had been negligent and that the immediate cause was the 'inadequacy of the stern doors, which yielded to the stress of the seas, thus permitting the influx of water into the car space'.

> Imagine a congregation of mornings rainbowed
> With planned and paid-for futures, liquidated
> There in the roaming sea; and pleasantnesses,
> Quiet attachments like dogs, pictures and books and tables,
> The tobacconist's at the corner, the paperboy:
> Serene suburban forevers uprooted and tossed
> Into barking distances, whose waves,
> Running like wolves, lope to the leaping kill.
> *from* 'Elegy for the Dead of *The Princess Victoria*' by Roy McFadden

'Activity at the Queen's Island continues at a very high level'

On 8 October 1951 the shipbuilding correspondent of the *Belfast Telegraph*, after reporting that Harland & Wolff had won an order from the Alfred Holt Line for a cargo-liner – the eighth since the war for the firm – wrote a general account of work in progress:

Activity at the Queen's Island continues at a very high level. Already the yards have launched eight ships of more than 100,000 tons, and at least two more are likely to reach the water before the end of the year. Sixteen slipways are now occupied and preparations are being made for the laying of keels in the remaining two. One of the ships concerned is the 28,000 ton passenger liner for the Peninsular and Orient Steam Navigation Co. Ltd. and the other is expected to be an oil tanker of 32,000 tons d.w. for the British Tanker Co. Ltd. Both the Abercorn and Victoria Yards are fully engaged. . .

Seven cargo liners were on the slips in the Abercorn and Victoria Yards; two refrigerated motorships for the Shaw Savill Line were being built in the Queen's Yard; four oil tankers were rising up in the Musgrave Yard, including the 28,000-ton *British Skill*; the previous Saturday the Union Castle liner *Rhodesia Castle* had left Belfast and a sister ship was being built; and Harland & Wolff had orders for fifteen other vessels. Later that month, on 30 October, the largest vessel in the Royal Navy, the aircraft carrier *Eagle*, left Belfast. By the end of the year 13 ships, totalling 155,388 tons gross, had been launched from Queen's Island, including the *Juan Peron*, the world's largest whale factory ship. 21,000 men had been kept fully employed and marine machinery of 114,595 i.h.p. had been sold.

The stimulus of war had been entirely responsible for the revival of Belfast's economy since 1939, and the UK, with the help of Marshall Aid, had been able to avoid a repetition of the sharp slump which had followed the First World War. For several years after 1945 the demand for goods was greater than the supply and Belfast's businesses – efficient and inefficient – were able to maintain a high level of production. As shipping companies strove to replace wartime losses so Harland & Wolff regularly launched over 100,000 tons a year. Could this level be maintained? This warning was given by the *Belfast Telegraph* on 3 January 1952:

The Harland & Wolff Building Dock on the East Twin, at the time of its completion in the late 1960s the biggest graving dock/dry dock in the world. It was designed for the building and repair of super tankers.

In the future British shipbuilders may be faced with intense competition from Germany and Japan. Allied controls on shipbuilding in Germany were lifted in April, and strenuous efforts are being made to restore the industry in that country to its former prosperity. Japan may eventually be an even more formidable rival than Germany, because she is able to draw upon large reserves of cheap labour. . .

A year later the firm's managing director, Dr Denis Rebbeck, referred to 'very deadly competition' and said: 'I would not be in the least surprised if this year Germany does not head the output for the world and that is a dangerous signal.'

Belfast did lead the UK yards in output that year, and throughout the 1950s Queen's Island remained the largest shipbuilding unit in the world with an output of more than 100,000 tons a year. By 1959 the works covered 300 acres, employed 20,000 workers, and could boast that on 24 occasions since their foundation they had headed the returns of tonnage output of ship-building firms throughout the world.

On 16 March 1960 the people of Belfast gathered – as they had done so many times before – to witness a launching. There were 10,000 ticket holders in the Musgrave Yard alone. Dame Pattie Menzies, wife of the Australian Prime Minister, was welcomed at the launching platform by Sir Frederick Rebbeck, Lord Wakehurst, and the RUC band playing 'Waltzing Matilda', to perform the ceremony of breaking a bottle of Australian red wine on the bows. As the 45,000 ton P & O liner *Canberra* entered the Lough, some 20,000 spectators cheered vociferously.

Few realised that this was the last great launching of its kind in Belfast. The success of air transport left only the luxury cruise market for the great passenger liners. After the completion of the *Canberra* there was serious unemployment amongst shipyard workers and the workforce fell to around

13,000 as competition from foreign builders increased and world shipping freight rates fell.

A programme of modernisation began in the Musgrave Yard in 1958; two shops were made into one berth to build tankers of the largest size and a fabrication shop of 55,000 square feet was built, serviced by gantries for twin-fillet and multi-power welding of steel and aluminium, and covered by 60- and 30-ton cranes on separate levels in each bay. All machines were repositioned to introduce line-flow production methods in the preparation shop. Harland & Wolff was now ready to meet the growing demand for huge tankers, and contracts were won in the 1960s for the largest vessels ever to leave the slips in Queen's Island: these included *Methane Progress,* capable of carrying 12,000 of liquid methane, and absorbing 1,200 tons of aluminium alloy in its construction; the *Texaco Maracaibo* and the *Rimfonn,* both at the times of their launching the largest tankers ever built in the UK; and the oil tanker *Myrina,* 192,250 tons and 1,050 feet long – the largest vessel ever built in Europe when she was launched in 1967.

Despite their size, tankers did not require the elaborate and luxurious accommodation for passengers for which Harland & Wolff had been famous. The workforce at the Yard had fallen to around 10,000 by 1970 and the overall importance of shipbuilding to the economy of Belfast had greatly diminished.

Linen: boom and decline

When Hitler's Panzer units swept first into Belgium and France, and then into Soviet Russia, they were cutting off Belfast's main supply source of flax. Linen tow yarn leaped in price from 9s. to 35s. a bundle and by the end of the war 150,000 acres of Ireland were being used to grow a domestic flax supply. After 1945 Belgium and France once again became the principal source (Russia, which had grown nearly 70% of the world's flax between the wars, ceased to export after 1950) and government price controls helped to prevent violent fluctuations in the output of the Belfast mills. Indeed, in the post-war years, the only limit on output seemed to be shortage of raw material. It was a seller's market until 1949, when there was a brief set-back, and then production resumed at an even higher level.

Throughout 1951 Belfast newspapers printed photographs of the York Street Mill rising from the ground which had been bombed ten years before; the rebuilding reflected the confidence of the industry that linen had a great future in the city as prices soared to their 1921 levels at the onset of the Korean War. Then came a sudden collapse, and employment fell by 50% between July 1951 and July 1952. Two of the three great linen mills in Belfast – York Street (with 1,000 looms and 60,000 spindles) and Brookfield (1,400 looms and 35,000 spindles) – closed down altogether, and the third – Ewarts – survived only by greatly reducing output.

Other textiles were affected by this slump, but they later recovered and expanded while linen did not. During the post-war years, while supplies of flax had been restricted, rayon had taken over much of linen's traditional garment trade. In the 1950s and 1960s nylon, terylene and other synthetic fibres dominated the textile market. The spread of dry-cleaning was discouraging for linen as wool, cotton and synthetics could be made to resist solvents more effectively; in addition laundering became more expensive and the use of

Old and new: photograph from Albert Street/Durham Street looking northwards. In the foreground the premises of Durham Street Weaving Company and the decayed and congested nineteenth-century housing of the lower Falls; left, background, the twin spires of St. Peter's Pro-Cathedral; and a Liebherr crane, right background, stands beside the Divis Flats complex, nearing completion,
(Linen Hall Library)

modern detergents was damaging to linen. Damask tablecloths went out of fashion, and warmer homes and cars led clothes manufacturers to use lighter linings and consumers to buy cotton or synthetic underwear instead of cambric.

One by one famous Belfast linen firms closed down; there had been 200 linen businesses (most of them in the city) in Ireland earlier in the century and by 1980 there were only 20. The great warehouses in Bedford Street closed and were converted either into offices or into tailoring premises notorious for the low wages paid. It was in Bedford Street, however, that I last saw an authentic linen worker's wedding celebration in the early 1970s, similar to a memory recorded by Betty Messenger:

When anybody was gettin' married, they carried on terrible. They tied your sleeves at the bottom and filled it full of rove bobbins. And the day you were stoppin' your work they wheeled you out in a handcart. . . on the Falls Road, singin' songs and makin' a fool of ye, in an old hat and all. But you had to enjoy the joke.

Industrial strengths and weaknesses

By the mid-1960s only 10% of industrial employment in Belfast was being provided by linen and shipbuilding. The report by K.S. Isles and Norman Cuthbert, *An economic survey of Northern Ireland,* had been published in 1957; it was the most penetrating and comprehensive study of its kind so far and its erudition still impresses the reader today. Isles and Cuthbert noted the continued preponderance of Belfast in the province's economy: '. . . the outstanding characteristic of location of the industrial population in Northern Ireland, now as in the past, is its high degree of concentration in the Belfast area.' 60% of insured industrial workers were in the Belfast area while the next most important centre – Derry – only contained 5.9% of such workers in the province; altogether 75% of industrial workers were insured at exchanges within 25 miles of Belfast. In addition, Belfast was the strongest part of Ulster's economy for, according to the report, 'the essential difference is that Belfast enjoys a greater diversity of industry than the rest of the province'.

Nevertheless, Isles and Cuthbert had some hard things to say. Belfast shared with the rest of Ulster many serious economic weaknesses – the city was remote from the rest of the British economy; natural resources were meagre and, apart from agriculture, there was a dearth of raw material and fuel for industry; most finished goods had only a small provincial market; and, above all, the range of industries which could prosper was restricted by the high cost of fuel and cross-channel transport. Indeed, Isles and Cuthbert effectively exposed a coal ring in Belfast; an unreasonable freight charge of 15s.5d. per ton, for example, was added to the 63s. the coal cost in Scotland.'The price may also be excessive because of the exercise of monopoly power in fixing the freight rates for the cross-channel shipment,' they concluded and recommended investigation by the Monopolies Commission.

No matter how the sale of coal was improved, Belfast's location reduced the city's competitiveness except in a narrow range of firms where fuel and transport costs were relatively unimportant in relation to total costs. In shipbuilding, for example, a high proportion of the cost of production was labour and the finished products could transport themselves. High quality precision engineering – at Shorts and Mackies, for example – had developed rapidly in Belfast since the war and seemed to be the kind of employment which the city should seek in the future. Was the government doing enough? At a time when unemployment in Britain was negligible, Northern Ireland had unemployment rates varying from 10.4% in 1952, to 6.4% in 1956, to 9.3% in 1958. The percentages were lower in Belfast than in other industrial centres such as Strabane and Derry, but there was nevertheless a problem of constant unemployment in the city, especially amongst unskilled men, and this, concluded Isles and Cuthbert, was 'no mere passing phase but a persistent problem'.

In addition, wage rates were rapidly catching up with those in Britain. Unskilled workers had lower wages than those in comparable cities in Britain though the margin was decreasing; in 1954 building labourers earned £6.13s.10d. a week in Belfast and £6.19s.4d. in Glasgow. Skilled workers tended to earn more per week than their counterparts across the Irish Sea; fitters and turners had £7.8s.4d. in Belfast and £7.4s.11½d. in Glasgow. The shipbuilding wage rates were standardised throughout the UK, and increasingly national wage agreements would ensure that workers in Belfast would be paid the same as their counterparts in Britain. Economists predicted that such agreements would reduce Belfast's competitiveness as the city's industries had to bear the added costs of expensive fuel and transport. If unemployment was not to increase, output per worker would have to be higher in the city than the UK average or substantial government aid would have to be given.

Almost all of the increase in industrial employment between 1948 and the late 1950s was the result of government help; yet the assistance given by such legislation as the Industries Development Act of 1945 and the Re-equipment of Industry Act of 1951 was unadventurous. Critics pointed out that not enough was being done to attract new industries, and referred to the success of enticements offered to foreign investers in the Irish Republic. In the 1960s, however, the Northern Ireland government adopted more imaginative policies and these were to transform the character of the city's economy.

'We must do more. We intend to do more': the Wilson Plan

In the 1958 Stormont election the Northern Ireland Labour Party made a striking recovery by winning four seats in Belfast. Pottinger and Oldpark had been represented by Labour before but the loss of Woodvale to Billy Boyd and Victoria to David Bleakley was a serious blow to the Unionist Party. Rising unemployment clearly had played an important part in the election, and it was significant that both Boyd and Bleakley had been shipyard workers, for unemployment at Queen's Island was severe. Giving unwavering support to the Union, the four NILP members formed an official opposition and sharply criticised the government's inactivity in promoting industrial recovery, especially in Belfast. Much of the electorate was impressed for in the 1962 Stormont election the four NILP MPs retained their seats with greatly increased majorities.

In October 1962 a group of senior civil servants — the Hall Committee — painted a gloomy picture of the province's economic prospects and, by implication at any rate, criticised the government's lack of energy and imagination. When Desmond Boal, Unionist MP for the Shankill, voted with the Labour opposition the Prime Minister — Lord Brookeborough — was forced by his own party to retire in March 1963. His successor was Captain Terence O'Neill. Minister of Finance since 1956, O'Neill was more aware than most of his colleagues of the economic difficulties of Northern Ireland; on 29 November 1962 he had addressed the Pottinger Unionist Association:

We have held the line while old industries have faltered. But it is not enough. We must do more. We intend to do more.

Now, as Prime Minister, O'Neill could see that the government did more. He accepted that the staple industries — shipbuilding, linen and heavy engineering — were likely to continue their decline and believed, as recommended in the Wilson Plan of December 1964, that the only answer was to make a major drive to attract new industry from Britain and abroad. The Wilson Plan in turn had accepted the principal recommendations of Professor Sir Robert Matthew, who had been commissioned in 1960 to prepare a survey and plan for the Belfast region; these were published in 1964. In brief, the government decided that an attempt should be made to spread industrial development beyond Belfast: a new city was to be created in the Lurgan-Portadown area; seven other growth centres were to be developed; the Matthew 'Stop Line' was to mark the limits of Belfast beyond which the city should not grow; four motorways and a ring road round Belfast were to be built; and a second university was to be set up at Coleraine in preference to expanding Queen's University. Altogether the scheme was estimated to cost £450 million and was designed to make the province more attractive to outside industrialists than development areas in Britain and at least as enticing as the

Whitaker plans in the Irish Republic, where 234 new foreign firms had established themselves between 1959 and 1965.

Economic transformation

Members of Belfast Corporation had grave reservations about the Wilson Plan and the Matthew 'Stop Line' in particular; many believed that foreign enterprises would be happiest in the Belfast area and that the restriction on the growth of the city was unnatural. Nevertheless the inducements offered to outside firms were bound to create new employment for the people of Belfast. By 1965 William Jenkins, the Lord Mayor of Belfast, was able to write in the city's industrial handbook:

Although the level of unemployment has given cause for concern a recent marked upsurge in the large employing industries, together with the impact of new industries established under the Government's policy of providing factory premises and giving liberal financial assistance, has resulted in a lessening of the concern and there are obvious signs of prosperity ahead.

It was difficult to disagree with this conclusion. The most striking developments were on the fringes of the city in the new industrial estates where the erection of factories was balanced by the integration with them of housing, shopping centres, schools, churches and recreation facilities. Groups of factories at Castlereagh, Dunmurry, Whitehouse, Carnmoney and Monkstown flanked planned residential areas. Firms such as British Oxygen, ICL (makers of data preparation equipment), BVC (the Goblin 'Teasmade' was its best-known product), and the Hughes Tool Company brought a new air of prosperity to Castlereagh, for example, and much of east Belfast besides. Other firms to set up on the periphery of the city included Autolite (a Ford subsidiary) and Grundig at Dunmurry, and Michelin at the impressive industrial complex at Mallusk.

It was no longer essential for industry — and light engineering in particular — to cluster round the port of Belfast, and electric power liberated factories from the need for coal easily transported from the docks. Many of the newly-established firms — such as Bridgeport in Lisburn and Courtaulds at Carrickfergus — were well beyond the frontiers of the city and yet they provided much valuable employment for people living in Belfast. Within the city boundary itself the development of new industry was not significant but the new firms in the Belfast conurbation were providing work for 20,000 by 1967.

The new factories did much to compensate for the continued slow decline of the traditional industries in the city. Yet some of the established businesses prospered and expanded in these years. James Mackie & Son, the only large firm making the full range of textile machinery, remained one of the most important firms of its kind in the world and soon established mastery in the making of machines for the synthetic fibre industry. By the end of the 1960s Mackies were employing 6,000 people and were producing a wider range and a greater volume of machines than all the textile engineering businesses together in their nineteenth-century heyday. Musgraves had had a substantial export business in dust-collection equipment, power-station fans, and structural steelwork, but closed down in 1965. Davidson's Sirocco Works, however, remained one of the principal engineering firms in Belfast; the firm

was noted for its large air pre-heaters for their power-station fans and for producing some of the largest fans in the world for mine ventilation. Like Mackies, the Sirocco Works exported most of their output. The Belfast Ropeworks, with 25 acres of production space, remained the largest cordage factory in the world, and Gallahers continued to prosper as part of an international combine.

Shorts at the peak of war-time production had employed 10,500 people, and had prospered so well after 1945 – with the help of government orders – that by the 1960s the aircraft factory was the second largest employer in Northern Ireland. Immediately after the war Short & Harland concentrated on converting Halifax bombers, Sunderlands and Junkers (captured from the Germans) to civilian passenger aircraft and even made thousands of ten-gallon milk cans to meet a desperate post-war shortage. The success of Vickers Armstrong prevented Shorts from becoming the major manufacturer of military aircraft but the demand for passenger flying boats remained strong: the first Solent was named in May 1949 by Princess Elizabeth and the first Sealand was sold to Christian & Missionary Alliance of New York for use in Indonesia. Shorts developed the first tail-less aircraft, the Sherpa, in 1951 and pioneered the vertical take-off SC 1 in 1955.

Under sub-contract, more than 100 Canberras were built and the Britannia was enlarged to become a freighter, the Belfast – the largest aircraft of its type; the Belfast was not a commercial success and the RAF bought only ten. More important was Shorts' involvement in making twin-jet Fokker passenger airliners and Skyvan light aircraft. The Skyvan was the real success of the 1960s and by 1967 orders for 67 had been won for these versatile light freighters. In addition to its 1 million square feet of production floor space at Queen's Island, Shorts had two modern factories at Castlereagh producing close-range anti-aircraft missiles; by 1965 these Seacat missiles had been ordered by eight foreign navies.

By the late 1960s Belfast seemed to have achieved a healthy diversity in its economy; in addition to the products mentioned above, businesses large and small in the city produced such items as felt roofing, fertilisers and agricultural chemicals, travel bags, hospital equipment and telescopic boat-hooks. That Belfast port handled 70% of the province's trade and imports and exports valued at £450 million in 1965 was in part due to the Harbour Commissioners' programme of reconstruction. The Sinclair wharf for general foreign trade was completed in 1958; in 1959 a 200-ton cantilever crane was installed at Stormont wharf (a new deep-water wharf on the west-side of Victoria Channel which was itself widened and deepened between 1958 and 1963); and altogether improvements by 1966 had cost £9 million. Esso established a depot, and the BP oil refinery opened in 1964, its burning waste gases soon becoming a familiar beacon at night. Link Line Ltd started a container service to Liverpool from Spencer Dock A and then from Belfast quay in 1959, and shortly afterwards another service began to Heysham.

In 1967, 100,000 people were employed in manufacturing in the Belfast conurbation. This figure is lower than that for Belfast's Edwardian high noon but total employment in the city had risen from 150,000 in 1901 to 250,000 in 1967 mainly as a result of the expansion of office, administrative, and service work. In 1967, for example, there were 22,000 central and local government servants whereas in 1901 there had been only 5,000 in the Belfast area. In 1966–7 unemployment in the city was down to around 3%, less than half the rate for the rest of the province, and there was a shortage of female and skilled labour. Much of the progress had been due to generous aid from Westminster, cunningly masked by byzantine financial arrangements between Stormont and Whitehall. This was a time of cheap energy and burgeoning world trade and the strictures of the Isles and Cuthbert report were forgotten. Yet Belfast remained abnormally dependent on prosperity abroad and when that prosperity evaporated a decade later much of the economic structure of these years collapsed like a pack of cards.

The Matthew 'Stop Line'

In 1944 the Interim Housing Report pointed out that 'if some of the poorer districts of Belfast, where over 60% of the people live and where there is an average of 60 dwellings per acre, were to be developed at, say, twenty dwellings to the acre, only one third of the present population could be rehoused in these areas in two-storey dwellings.' The Committee recommended the erection of flats as the slums were cleared and added:

In mentioning this point the Committee are fully aware of the fact that Belfast people have no experience of flats and may not be anxious to have any. The alternatives are to travel long distances to work with concomitant expense and reduction in leisure time or to be housed near one's work in flats.

The Corporation, which from 1956 was responsible for slum clearance as well as the erection of new houses, built 11,600 dwellings in 30 development areas between 1944 and 1968 but preferred not to put up flats. Unity Flats, built at the bottom of the Shankill to rehouse Catholics in the Carrick Hill area, and Divis Flats in the Catholic Lower Falls, were exceptions to the Council's usual policy. The Housing Trust did build flats but preferred to blend them with more traditional dwellings. At Belvoir, for example, towering blocks of flats, maisonettes, terraces and three-sided courts were designed to create a pleasing variety and a minimum disturbance to the countryside. James Cairncross, the Trust's chief technical officer, said in October 1965 that Belvoir 'is a beautiful site and we are exploiting it by putting up two blocks of multi-storey flats. This saves a lot of open space.' However, Stanley Anderson, the Trust's Housing Officer, pointed out that at an average cost of £3,000 per living unit, flats were 50% more expensive than traditional two-storey dwellings and, he observed: 'High flats can be very solitary places. . . In all my visits I have only twice met anyone in the lifts. . .'

Only a massive programme of building of high-rise flats could have prevented the population of the inner city falling in these years. Rightly, this solution was not sought and so, as houses were put up to more stringent standards, the only direction in which the population could go was outwards. Belfast Corporation applied for an extension of the borough boundary in 1947 but this application was rejected. The government was advised repeatedly to limit Belfast's growth. For example:

The present geographical distribution of industry is unevenly balanced as between Belfast and the rest of the Province and new industries should be attracted, where possible, to provincial towns rather than Belfast.

(Planning Advisory Board 1944)

268

With the unfortunate development of English cities in mind, we lay particular stress on the importance of regulating and limiting the outward growth of Belfast. . . we strongly recommend that what is commonly known as a 'Green Belt' should be established.

(Planning Commission 1945)

* F. W. Boal, 'Belfast and its future development', in Beckett and Glasscock, *Belfast: origin and growth of an industrial city* (see biblio), pp. 173–4.

The concentration of population and industry in Belfast is out of balance with that in the rest of the Province. . . we consider that all practicable steps should be taken to preserve what remains of the green belt. . .

(Planning Commission 1951)*

By 1960 it had become increasingly difficult to define Belfast. Geographers, such as Emrys Jones and F.W. Boal, recognised not one Belfast but several. First there was the Inner City marked on maps by the boundary of Belfast County Borough but little else. Here the population had fallen from 444,000 in 1951 to 400,000 in 1961 and the average number of persons per house had dropped from 4 to 3½ in the same period.

The second Belfast was the Fringe which extended out to the limit of continuous building and took in Dondonald, Andersonstown, Dunmurry, Glengormley, Newtownabbey and even Lisburn and Holywood; here there were 85,000 people in 1939, 120,000 in 1951, 180,000 in 1961 and 220,000 by 1966. The Inner City and Fringe together had a population of more than 600,000 by 1966, a net gain of around 100,000 since 1945.

The third Belfast was what Jones and Boal called the Regional City, an area extending out from the City Hall, taking in farms and parks to a limit of about 25 miles, held together by a network of roads – an area with a population of 950,000 in 1966. The expansion of the Fringe and Regional City had been helped by the rise in car ownership: in 1951 there was one car to every 33 people in Belfast Borough, in 1961 one to every 12, and by 1965 one car to every 8.

By the beginning of the 1960s the Stormont government had arrived at the conclusion that, with the spread of large estates on the suburbs of the city, Belfast would become so large that it would develop into a sprawling mass, filling the Lagan Valley to Lisburn and beyond. In 1962 Sir Robert Matthew and his team produced a plan for the Regional City which the Government decided to implement. The Matthew Plan had three main features: a Stop Line was to be drawn around the city and no new building could take place outside this line; new towns were to be created at Antrim and Lurgan-Portadown (Craigavon) and people were to be encouraged, and indeed paid, to move to them; and a number of small towns around Belfast such as Bangor and Newtownards were to be designated as growth centres and people were to be paid to move to them also.

Members of Belfast Corporation viewed the Stop Line – particularly when the Wilson Plan was published in 1964 – with mounting alarm. Belfast Borough seemed condemned to inevitable decay: industry would be encouraged to go far beyond the city; house prices in the inner city would be pushed up artificially; and, above all, the Corporation would be denied the right to levy rates on prosperous householders and businesses in the Fringe. The Corporation's position was weak because it did not have a fully-fledged planning department to argue its case until 1965. The most effective criticism of the Regional Plan to build Craigavon and to impose a brake on the growth of Belfast came in a 7,000 word statement in August 1964 made by the head of the design team, Geoffrey Copcutt:

I think we should cut our losses. . . the prosperity of the province is at present keyed to Belfast, and it is likely than any brake on the expansion of the port and city will produce, not consolidation, but decline. . . It is optimistic to restrict the one proven growth point in an increasingly competitive world, on the assumption that potential industrial customers can be steered elsewhere for charitable purposes. To the Ministry of Commerce, with the immediate and continuing objective of stimulating job opportunity in Northern Ireland, its single greatest asset in this work is Belfast, which combines domestic, social, cultural, educational and industrial facilities to a degree unparalleled in the rest of the province.

In addition, Copcutt pointed out that the level of unemployment in the city was still a cause for concern. In its issue of 15 August the *Belfast Telegraph* ran the banner headline: 'I WON'T BE INFLUENCED BY COPCUTT STATEMENT,' SAYS CRAIG. William Craig, the Minister of Home Affairs, went ahead with the Regional Plan with the full support of O'Neill's cabinet, and the Corporation accepted the Stop Line with a bad grace. The immediate effect of the Matthew Plan was to stop most building on suburban sites around Belfast and the city's redevelopment programme slowed down further as people refused to move to the new towns. Sites such as Benview, Moyard, Turf Lodge and Black-mountain – the only greenfield building areas available within the Stop Line – were developed at very high density, thus piling up trouble for the future. The housing shortage within the city became so acute that permission was granted to build new suburban estates at Ballybeen, Ballyduff, New Mossley, Glencairn and Twinbrook in the late 1960s and early 1970s. By then problems far greater than those posed by the Stop Line had erupted.

The Divis Street riots: September 1964

On 1 August 1964 Belfast newspapers carried lurid accounts of a concert given by the Rolling Stones in the Ulster Hall the night before. The previous November, when the Beatles had appeared at the ABC cinema, Belfast's teenage population had broken out 'in almost unbelievable scenes of mass-hysteria'. Now the disorder greeting Mick Jagger and his group 'made the Beatles look like Old Time Music Hall', according to the *Belfast Telegraph* report, which continued:

The fans were fainting like nine-pins. They were screaming, hysterical and some of them troublesome. Some had to be strapped to stretchers. And were they the riff raff of Ulster teenage society? Not at all. They were well-brought-up grammar school girls – nearly a hundred fainted during the madhouse performance. . .

The reporter commended the more restrained response of the young people of Ballymena who when faced with the Rolling Stones had a 'fainting rate of only one per minute'.

Such reports seemed to indicate that Belfast was little different from other major cities in western Europe. Many believed that the city was putting behind it the turmoil of the past. Sectarian tension seemed to ebb after the 1949 election. On 2 July 1955 a car blew up in the grounds of Stormont and the driver, Brendan O'Boyle, was killed; O'Boyle had been attempting to blow up the Stormont telephone exchange. The incident appeared to be an isolated one and in February 1956 the Catholic bishops declared it to be a mortal sin to be a member of an illegal organisation. The biggest IRA offensive since 1922 was launched in December 1956, but this 'Operation Harvest' was essentially a rural campaign and Belfast was almost completely unaffected – the IRA command clearly realised that it had insufficient support in the city to go on the offensive there. With the help of internment in the Irish Republic the campaign failed and the IRA ordered its volunteers to dump arms on 26 February 1962.

The success of the Northern Ireland Labour Party – particularly in Woodvale and Victoria – in 1958 and 1962 would not have been possible if Protestants in Belfast had feared that the constitution was in danger. O'Neill made friendly gestures to the Catholic minority and, in August 1964, gave official recognition to the Northern Committee of the Irish Congress of Trade Unions. Yet in that same year came a clear indication that Belfast was not just like any other major western Europe city and that the old community tensions had not been eradicated.

On the evening of Monday 28 September 1964 men of the RUC set out to remove an Irish tricolour flag from the Republican Party's headquarters in Divis Street. A Westminster election campaign was in full swing and the Unionist candidate for West Belfast had sent this telegram to the Minister of Home Affairs:

Remove tricolour in Divis Street which is aimed to provoke and insult loyalists of Belfast. James Kilfedder.

The Minister, Brian McConnell, had decided to act after a meeting with senior police officers that morning and he had the authority to do so under the 1954 Flags and Emblems Act; at the same time, under the 1961 Public Order Act, he confined a loyalist protest march – organised by Rev Ian Paisley, leader of the Free Presbyterian Church – to an area away from Divis Street. At least 2,000 Republican supporters that evening attempted to bar the way of the police; the RUC returned with armoured cars and heavily armed reinforcements; and, running the gauntlet of showers of stones and bottles, the police broke down the doors of the Republican Party's headquarters with crowbars and seized the flag. Liam McMillan, the Republican candidate, declared that unless the flag was returned another would be put in its place on Wednesday.

That Wednesday evening the rioting was intense: police were driven back by a barrage of stones, scrap metal and bottles; some petrol bombs were thrown; a Corporation trolley-bus burned furiously; armoured cars looked menacing in the narrow dark streets and, with their headlights and searchlights, picked out the dense mass of struggling rioters and police; water cannon – in use for the first time in more than 40 years – sprayed the crowds somewhat ineffectively; and throughout there was a cacophony of wailing sirens, yells, shouted party songs, and the crash of breaking glass.

The author – irresponsibly and out of idle curiosity – was there to see what was happening but was prevented from giving a further eyewitness account by being knocked insensible for the first and only time in his life. British people were now able to watch on their television screens an updated re-enactment of communal conflict which had blighted Belfast for more than a century.

Yet the rioting was quickly over and had no immediate sequel. O'Neill went

'We both share the same rivers, the same mountains, and some of the same problems.' Captain Terence O'Neill, Prime Minister of Northern Ireland, with Sean Lemass, Taoiseach of the Irish Republic: Stormont 14 January 1965.
(Belfast News-Letter)

out of his way to conciliate the Catholic minority by, for example, visiting Catholic schools and having talks with Cardinal Conway (who was the first Belfast Catholic to reach such high office in the Church). Meanwhile Anglo-Irish trade talks led to a trade agreement in 1960 and by 1965 preparations were being made to set up a United Kingdom-Irish Republic free trade area. In secret, O'Neill prepared to carry out what was perhaps the most daring stroke of his career: an invitation to Sean Lemass, Taoiseach of the Republic of Ireland, to come to Stormont.

'I shall get into terrible trouble for this': Lemass at Stormont

On the night of 13–14 January 1965 gale force winds, gusting to 80 miles per hour and accompanied by torrential rain, swept Belfast. At the height of the storm the outward bound Glasgow steamer *Royal Ulsterman* struck an oil tanker berthed at the Sydenham oil refinery and St Brendan's Church in Connsbrook Avenue collapsed. That night the Prime Minister, Captain O'Neill, lay awake for other reasons: he had invited the Republic's premier, Sean Lemass, to visit Belfast next day. 'Welcome to the North,' O'Neill said as Lemass stepped out of his Mercedes shortly after noon. There was no reply.

In the lavatory of Stormont House Lemass broke his silence: 'I shall get into terrible trouble for this.' Over a splendid lunch the Taoiseach became more relaxed and garrulous. Ken Whitaker, who had done as much as O'Neill to set up the meeting, remembers: 'Our hosts thought the occasion worthy of champagne. The atmosphere was most friendly. I imagine Dr Paisley's worst fears would be confirmed if I were to say that the red wine we drank was Châteauneuf de Pape!' It was not until 1 p.m. that O'Neill informed his cabinet colleagues and the press that Lemass was making an official visit. Barry White was amongst the excited group of pressmen who had raced to Stormont; he recalls:

272

There wasn't a single discordant note about the whole ceremony; everybody was smiling, and it was a very relaxed historic occasion, with a lot of very loud laughter. O'Neill had quite a reputation for a loud raucous laugh, and this was bellowing out drowning most of the chit-chat going on, and then they disappeared inside Stormont Castle for talks.

Brian Faulkner was the only northern minister who had met Lemass before: '. . . the first thing Lemass said to me was "I hear you had a great day with the Westmeaths a few weeks ago." I said, "That's right indeed, I didn't realise you knew." "Ah," he said, "the boys told me." He said, "Have you had a day with Charlie lately?"' Faulkner's regular hunting with the Taoiseach's son-in-law and Minister for Agriculture, Charles Haughey, helped to break the ice between members of the Northern Ireland cabinet and the southern visitors. After discussions on possible north–south economic co-operation Lemass then departed for Dublin; O'Neill was interviewed by Alan Reid for television and said:

We both share the same rivers, the same mountains, and some of the same problems, and therefore I think it is reasonable that the two premiers should meet and discuss matters of mutual interest, and that is actually what we did today.

No immediate hostile reaction greeted the O'Neill–Lemass meeting and the people of Belfast seemed to turn their televisions over contentedly to the next episode of 'Crossroads'. Later that evening as usual small queues formed outside the city cinemas – *Gunfight at the OK Corral* was showing at the Forum, *The Big Country* at the Broadway, and *Carry on Cleo* at the ABC – and Lemass arrived in Dublin to say to waiting reporters: 'I think I can say a road block has been removed.'

Sunday swings

O'Neill had alienated several of his colleagues by springing the news of the Taoiseach's visit on them at such short notice, but he appeared to win the whole-hearted support of the Protestant electorate in the Stormont election of November 1965. Billy Boyd and David Bleakley lost their seats at Woodvale and Victoria, and the NILP vote fell in every constituency the party contested. The fall in NILP support was not – as in 1949 – because the Union was in danger but because O'Neill had in effect adopted much of the programme of economic reform and reconciliation put forward by the labour opposition.

The Northern Ireland Labour Party had lost support for another reason. In 1959 the widow of Sir Daniel Dixon presented Dixon Park to the Corporation on the understanding that any swings put up for children there would be available on Sundays. This large and beautiful estate four miles south of Belfast could not be refused and it immediately became popular with children who could reach it. Opposition councillors contrasted the free swings of Lady Dixon Park on Sundays with the chained swings of the city play centres. Official support for traditional sabbatarianism was a unique feature of the city quickly noticed by visitors. Early in 1964 NILP had adopted the following policy: 'Labour will support the opening of children's playgrounds and recreational facilities on Sunday for those who wish to use them.'

In October the Education Committee, headed by Hilda Hawnt, re-commended – by a majority of one – the opening of play centres on Sundays but, on 2 November, the city council turned down the recommendation by 27 to 25. Two NILP councillors had voted against the recommendation and another abstained. The two who had voted against were expelled from the party but were readmitted ten days later. Charles Brett, chairman of the party the previous year, recalled:

. . . the public did not forget about it: the party had lost credit both with Catholic and Protestant voters: the trend towards the acceptance of Labour as a non-sectarian alternative was reversed, and at the following general election, in November 1965, the party suffered a crushing defeat. . .*

* C. E. B. Brett, *Long shadows cast before* (see bibliog), p. 87.

The Lagan Bridge controversy

'There are many things to praise here in Belfast,' wrote 'I.M.D.', a Scottish visitor, in the *Belfast Telegraph* on 2 February 1949. 'I would like to mention the excellent transport service, whose speed and comfort make travelling a pleasure.' She continued:

My first sight of an 'Island' tram, however, with its human cargo clinging on for grim death, as many on the outside as in the tram, was a wondrous sight. How did they manage to stick on and not get crushed to death? How did the conductor ever collect all the fares?

During the war, tram traffic had been exceptionally heavy and the air raids had inflicted much damage – the Salisbury Avenue depot received a direct hit, lines were torn up in the city centre, and many vehicles were put out of action. The scene described by 'I.M.D.' was soon to disappear: trolleybuses were first introduced on the Falls Road in 1938 and had the war not intervened all trams would have been replaced by 1944. Trams disappeared on the Donegall Road and Cliftonville routes in 1947; further abandonments in 1951 included Oldpark, Stranmillis, Malone and York Road; and the last trams – the 'Island' trams – ran for the last time on Saturday 27 February 1954 when twelve Chamberlain cars left Ardoyne for a ceremonial run to the Queen's Road terminus. The quiet and pollution-free trolleybuses ran until the early 1960s though omnibuses had been used increasingly from their first introduction on the Cavehill route on 4 October 1926.

'Their problem is to get rid of 2,500,000 square setts,' ran a *Belfast Telegraph* headline on 8 October 1951, with this report underneath:

It all began some time ago when the Corporation decided to resurface several of the city's thoroughfares with asphalt. As workmen tore up large sections of the Antrim, Donegall, Ormeau and Upper Newtownards Roads, hundreds of tons of square setts accumulated. Before the present programme is completed the figure will have risen to 20,000 tons, or around 2,500,000 square setts.

Another major improvement was the construction of a new bridge over the Lagan, alongside the Queen's Bridge, between 1963 and 1965. Among the names suggested were 'Churchill', 'Lagan', and 'Somme'. The City Hall Unionist Party met on 14 February 1966 and by a margin of three or four votes chose 'Carson' as the name for the new bridge. The Opposition denounced the decision and the Governor, Lord Erskine, telephoned the Town Clerk to say that 'he was perturbed at the effect on Her Majesty of possible controversy over the name of the bridge'. Some Unionists changed their minds and got the

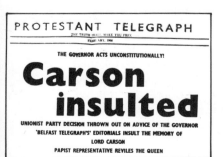

PROTESTANT TELEGRAPH
THE TRUTH SHALL MAKE YOU FREE
FEBRUARY, 1966

THE GOVERNOR ACTS UNCONSTITUTIONALLY!

Carson insulted

UNIONIST PARTY DECISION THROWN OUT ON ADVICE OF THE GOVERNOR
'BELFAST TELEGRAPH'S' EDITORIALS INSULT THE MEMORY OF
LORD CARSON
PAPIST REPRESENTATIVE REVILES THE QUEEN

Aerial view of Belfast 1960, looking northwards. This photograph captures the inner city before Sailorstown and other nineteenth-century streets were cleared. The lack of recreation space, apart from Ormeau Park (right foreground), is striking. The gasometer (centre foreground) was the largest of its kind in the world. (Aero Films Ltd)

support of republican councillors for an alternative name, 'Queen Elizabeth Bridge'. The chairman of the Improvements Committee, Charles McCullough, resigned, but this was the name given when Queen Elizabeth II opened the bridge in person the following year.

'Let us shed the burdens of traditional grievances'

As the Queen drove up Great Victoria Street on 4 July 1967 a concrete block was thrown from a building under construction and hit the bonnet of the royal car. It was a sharp reminder to the Westminster government that – despite outward appearances – Belfast was not just like any other British city.

At the time there appeared to be ample evidence that prosperity was slowly eroding the lines of communal division in the city. Many of the new firms employed workers of all religions; in the more prosperous housing estates there appeared to be some religious mixing; young people seemed to be united by a common enthusiasm for popular culture; and Captain O'Neill committed himself to reconciliation, saying on 8 April 1966:

If we cannot be united in all things, let us at least be united in working together – in a Christian spirit – to create better opportunities for our children, whether they come from the Falls Road or from Finaghy... let us shed the burdens of traditional grievances and ancient resentments. There is much we can do together. It must and – God willing – it *will* be done.

In retrospect, historians can find signals warning of Belfast's violent future. Catholics waited with growing impatience for the Prime Minister to convert his declared intentions into positive reform. Many loyalists were certain that O'Neill was endangering the constitution by holding out the prospect of change to the minority: such Protestants turned increasingly to the founder and Moderator of the Free Presbyterian Church, Rev Ian R.K. Paisley. Paisley had attracted wide attention by his strident denunciation of the ecumenical movement and his protests against the visits of southern politicians to Belfast; his Martyrs' Memorial Church on the Ravenhill Road attracted impressive congregations at a time when attendance in other Protestant churches in the city was declining; his *Protestant Telegraph* tirelessly vilified the Prime Minister; and his blend of populist loyalism, fervent mission-hall fundamentalism, and pugnacious oratory made a deep appeal to those Protestant workers – in east Belfast in particular – who viewed O'Neill's patrician liberal Unionism with mounting disgust.

Feelings ran high in Belfast in 1966, the fiftieth anniversary of both the Easter Rising and the battle of the Somme. A petrol bomb was thrown into the Unionist Party Headquarters in Glengall Street on 18 February; a Molotov cocktail bomb was hurled into a Catholic school on the Falls Road two days later; a petrol bomb was thrown at Holy Cross Primary School on the Crumlin Road on 6 April; trouble was narrowly avoided during the Easter Rising celebrations in west Belfast; an elderly woman was killed in a petrol-bomb attack on a public house on 7 May; and John Scullion, a Catholic, was shot and mortally wounded in Clonard Street on 27 May.

When Paisley led a march on 6 June through Cromac Square, in the Catholic Markets area, there was rioting which rivalled in intensity that of two years before. Arrested for his part in dusturbances at the Presbyterian General Assembly later in the day, Paisley refused to be bound over and was jailed for three months. On 27 June three Catholics were shot in Malvern Street on the Shankill Road and one, Peter Ward, died of his wounds. In December, O'Neill said that the violence of the year 'had inhibited our progress and disfigured our reputation throughout the English-speaking world'. 1967, apart from incidents during the royal visit, was the last quiet year the city was to enjoy to the time of writing.

11
Years of Violence and Decline
c.1968–1982

Holy Mary, Mother of God,
Pray for me and Tommy Todd,
I'm a Fenian and he's a Prod,
Holy Mary, Mother of God.
(Children's street rhyme)

Belfast began as a foreign town: it was an English-Scot protestant establishment to which the native population only slowly and gradually moved. Consequent growth maintained the protestant ascendancy, and Irish people were looked upon almost as immigrants. They had an alien tongue, a different religion, a lower socio-economic position, and they were by no means integrated with the new culture. They occupied, in addition to their traditional sector in the south-west, the zone of transition and decay.

With these words Emrys Jones concluded his survey of religious distribution in his *Social geography of Belfast,* published in 1960. By looking carefully at the 1951 census returns, district by district, Jones revealed how little real integration had occurred in the twentieth century. Though he found that segregation decreased with every rise in social ranking, it remained almost as prevalent as it had been after the displacement of population in the 1920–22 troubles in the industrial areas of the city. There were only two broad sects of any significance in Belfast. Differences between Protestant sects, once significant, had become politically unimportant: Presbyterians were the strongest religious denomination, accounting for 30.4% of the city's population in 1951; members of the Church of Ireland (significantly – and perhaps surprisingly – lower than the Presbyterians in social status) accounted for 29.7%; Methodists accounted for 7.8%; and other Protestant sects – such as the Brethren, Baptists and Congregationalists – made up no more than 1½% of the population. In 1926 the Catholic population had reached its lowest recorded proportion, 23%, but by 1951 it had recovered to 25.9%. There were only 1,140 Jews, 44 Moslems, 17 Hindus and 14 Sikhs; in 1951 only 'a minute percentage' either belonged to non-Christian sects or had not stated any religious allegiance. Whether or not the citizens of Belfast regularly practised their religion, the vast majority unhesitatingly felt themselves either to be Protestant or Catholic. It was amongst the working classes that segregation was most complete, especially in Ballymacarrett and the Falls-Shankill region of West Belfast.

In 1968 F.W. Boal, of the Queen's University Department of Geography, published an academic paper with the formidable title, 'Territoriality on the Shankill-Falls Divide, Belfast'. Little did he know how topical his study was to become and how closely its findings would be examined by politicians, civil servants, army commanders and research students across the world in the years that followed. The Falls-Shankill divide had been identified previously by Emrys Jones as the most segregated area of Belfast, by Estyn Evans as the 'sharpest junction between districts', and by Frankfort Moore as 'the seismic area of the city — that part in which streaks of disagreement lie in parallel lines. . .'

The particular zone studied by F.W. Boal lay between the Shankill and Springfield Roads and astride the Shankill and the Falls, covering 41 acres and containing nearly 5,000 people — in reality two distinct areas, Clonard (98% Catholic) and part of the Shankill (99% Protestant). Interviewing a 10% random sample of the 1967 electoral register, F.W. Boal and his assistants demonstrated how sharply the two adjacent communities were divided: of 197 married couples interviewed, only one pair had crossed the tribal barrier in choosing their mate; football supporters expressed not so much the competitive spirit of sport as a partisan statement of political allegiance in their choice of team — Linfield in their true-blue colours were favoured by 74% in the Shankill while Glasgow Celtic in their green strip were supported by 73% in Clonard; that *no* supporter crossed this sporting barrier indicates that football prowess was not the only criterion; the two communities even received most of their news from separate sources; the *Irish News* was read by 84% in Clonard while the Shankill preferred the *Belfast News Letter* and the popular English dailies, only 3% of those interviewed there finding the *Irish News* acceptable. The main exception to the general pattern of segregation was that many from Clonard did their shopping on the Shankill Road — a trade quickly lost when the Troubles returned in 1969. In addition, the *Belfast Telegraph* had a uniform readership, giving that paper 'an important role as a potential integrator operating across the religious community boundary'. Nevertheless the statistics, maps and diagrams revealed a division so rigid that the study's conclusion seemed almost superfluous: 'The cumulative evidence indicates the presence of two very distinctive territories.' These two territories met only in one narrow mixed area — Cupar Street. It was to be here that violence was to break out with renewed ferocity in 1969.

The conflict this time was to be so long-lasting that Belfast became the most continuously disturbed major city in Europe since the ending of the Second World War. Soldiers of the same British Army which took position in the Shankill-Falls divide in August 1969 would in 1982 still be carrying maps akin to those first drawn by F.W. Boal. By then, however, small but important alterations had been made on those maps: well-known landmarks, familiar buildings and even whole streets had disappeared. The alterations indicated 13 years of violence, destruction and decline — a decline hastened by conflict but primarily the result of inner-city decay and the accumulating effects of an economic depression which had reached the dimensions of a major crisis by 1982.

'Augean stables of corruption'

It was in the International Hotel, in Donegall Square South, that the Northern Ireland Civil Rights Association was formed in 1967. Yet the initiative for launching the Civil Rights movement had come principally from west of the Bann and not from Belfast; it was from Derry and rural councils that the most irrefutable evidence of local government boundary manipulation, unjust housing allocation and job discrimination was generally drawn. The unrest emerged out of a dispute over how Northern Ireland as a whole was run and how the Catholic minority across Ulster was treated, dissatisfaction crystallising into a simple slogan, 'One Man, One Vote', expressing a single issue – that in council elections only ratepayers could vote. The leaders of this campaign pinned unreasonably high hopes of radical change on achieving universal suffrage, while the Unionist government seemed to give credibility to those hopes by the obstinacy with which they opposed it. As marches and counter-marches, demonstrations and counter-demonstrations merged into attack, counter-attack, riot and murder the very existence of a semi-autonomous province was once more called into question.

To examine in detail the origin of the present troubles requires a survey of the whole history of Northern Ireland, which is beyond the scope of this book. Apart from the fact that it was the centre of the provincial government and bureaucracy, Belfast must, nevertheless, have had special importance because of its sheer size and because the violence there was to be more severe than anywhere else in the province. The charge that ward boundaries were blatantly gerrymandered does not stick in Belfast; when PR in local government elections was abolished in 1922, the city simply returned to the electoral divisions drawn before the First World War – ward boundaries which had been approved by Nationalist MPs at Westminster. Catholics in Belfast were no more unfairly represented in local government than were – for example – Conservative supporters in Ebbw Vale or Labour supporters in Hampshire. The real problem was that the anti-partitionist opposition had no prospect of controlling the city's affairs, no matter what democratic electoral system was applied – had it been able to do so loyalists would have regarded the Union as being irreparably undermined.

The divisions in the city were not created by the setting up of the Northern Ireland regime but emerged over centuries of previous history. Provincial autonomy from 1921 onwards brought no profound change in the running of the Corporation; that, in part, was the problem – extensive changes in the operation and responsibilities of local authorities in Britain were not in general applied to Belfast. The dead hand of the Local Government Act of 1898 remained to blight local politics long after it had lapsed from the statute book. Then, a Conservative government had smashed the landlords' corrupt monopoly of power in local affairs to replace it by more democratic control. In Belfast, where the authority of landlords had been swept away long before, the 1898 Act was important not for what it did but for what it failed to do: it did not ensure that jobs and contracts were given out by merit and open competition alone. 'As the Act did not provide for competitive entrance examinations,' Joseph Lee has written,[*] 'appointments were virtually by favouritism only, and non-canvassing automatically disqualified. It later took the Free State years to clean out the augean stables of corruption and confusion that flourished under it.' In fact the augean stables were never cleaned out completely in the South and it is likely that favouritism in appointments in Belfast never reached the depths plumbed by many local authorities in the Republic. In Belfast, however, the system of patronage which had emerged in the nineteenth century continued and developed after 1921. The problem here was that most of the patronage remained permanently with the City Hall Unionists; it cannot have been educational advantage alone which ensured

* J. Lee, *The modernisation of Irish Society 1848–1918* (Gill and Macmillan, 1973), p. 128.

* D. H. Akenson, *Education and enmity* (see bibliog), p. 35.

that 681 out of 714 Corporation paid officials were Protestant in 1922 and that the salaries of the Protestant employees amounted to £17,223 compared with £637 for those of the Catholic employees.*

Despite a more professional approach and more open competition for some contracts and jobs, patronage increased as local government spending rose after the Second World War. Polarised local politics ensured the continued domination of the City Hall Unionists, though Independent Unionist and NILP gains caused some alarm. Politics in Catholic areas of Belfast had been highly confused since 1945. In some constituencies, such as Cromac and Falls, anti-partitionist labels had been bewildering after the rejection of the Nationalists. In others, such as Pottinger, Central, Dock and Oldpark, Catholic voters appeared to have supported NILP until the Sunday Swings controversy.

What is certain is that opposition councillors played the game of favouritism and patronage with as much enthusiasm as the Unionists. A newly-elected councillor was liable to be asked what binmen he wanted to appoint; if he refused to appoint, he was likely to be told that his share of jobs would be distributed evenly amongst the other 59 councillors. Contracts, houses and even the most insignificant jobs were therefore given out as favours to supporters of all parties represented. It was perhaps just as well in some respects that the Corporation's housing record was so poor and that most of the new dwellings in the city were built and allocated by the Housing Trust, which operated a fair points system. It is possible that patronage eased community tensions for a time especially as Catholics benefited roughly in proportion to their numbers in the city. This overlooks the certainty that Catholics in Belfast were in most urgent need of rehousing, as the 1944 Interim Report and later surveys revealed. Unemployment, too, was most acute in Catholic estates. In 1972, when male unemployment in the Belfast urban area was 8.2%, the rate was 33.3% in Ballymurphy–New Barnsley, 23.7% in Dock, 20.4% in Whiterock, and 19.7% in the Lower Falls; had F.W. Boal, P. Doherty and D.G. Pringle compiled these figures in 1968 it is unlikely that the pattern revealed would have been very different.

Every major city in the United Kingdom had areas of high unemployment and severe deprivation – social and economic inequalities alone did not create the turbulence in Belfast from 1969 onwards. Such inequalities, however, must have intensified resentment in a city lacking a basic political consensus and bedevilled by sectarian animosity. Discrimination in employment was a natural product of a divided community and Catholics and Protestants discriminated with equal zeal; for historic reasons (the Protestant domination of skilled trades, for example) Catholics were bound to be at a disadvantage in this game. The traditional employers were Protestant in the main and not all the multinational firms established in the urban area were able to resist labour pressure to favour one religion or the other. Though Harland & Wolff was adjacent to the Catholic Short Strand it employed only 400 Catholics out of a total workforce of 10,000 in 1970, and though the Sirocco Works and Mackie's Foundry were sited in Catholic districts the number of Catholics employed there was insignificant. Similarly, because most public houses in the city were owned by Catholics, most bar staff were Catholic.

The Cameron Inquiry was to conclude that rising prosperity and greater educational opportunity brought a significant expansion of the Catholic middle class, but it seems likely that this judgement needs some qualification.

Taking the twentieth century as a whole, the growth seems to have been at both ends of the scale: in 1911 only 5% of Catholics were in professional or managerial occupations, while in 1971 the percentage had increased to 12%, but the percentage in unskilled work had likewise increased from 20% to 25%.

The Civil Rights movement was at first most active outside Belfast, and the first big march was held at Coalisland in August 1968. It was, however, the march in Derry on 5 October 1968 which brought the attention of the world to affairs in Northern Ireland. Until millions of viewers saw pictures of police in conflicts with demonstrators flashing across their television screens, few had taken any interest in the province.

In Belfast the campaign for civil rights had been launched by a group of undergraduates and postgraduates who had been drafting detailed proposals for reform for several years. A Joint Action Committee organised a march of about 3,000 people to the City Hall on 9 October 1968; their way barred by counter-demonstrators, they sat down in Linenhall Street and resolved to form the People's Democracy, which was launched formally two days later. Many of the earliest members of the PD feared that direct action would be provocative and counter-productive; the activists were not to be restrained, however, and on 24 October a group of them occupied the Great Hall in Stormont for three hours. On 1 January 1969 Michael Farrell led a PD march from Belfast to Derry, news of which dominated the mass media, after the marchers had been attacked at Burntollet.

'Enough is enough,' O'Neill said on television on 5 January. 'We have heard sufficient for now about civil rights; let us hear a little about civic responsibility.' The influence of television can hardly be overestimated at this stage and the Prime Minister's Ascendancy voice and style compounded his difficulties in winning hearts and minds. O'Neill's position was an exceedingly unhappy one – he had done little to satisfy those who sought change and at the same time a growing number of Unionists were turning against him because he appeared too conciliatory. The Stormont general election of 14 February 1969 witnessed the break-up of traditional Unionism in the confusion of pro-O'Neill and anti-O'Neill Official and Unofficial Unionist candidates. Internal opposition against O'Neill built up to such an extent that he resigned as Prime Minister on 28 April 1969, despite a strenuous campaign by the *Belfast Telegraph* to rally support for him. 'I have tried to break the chains of ancient hatreds. I have been unable to realise during my period of office all that I had sought to achieve,' he said in his resignation speech.

Under the new Prime Minister, James Chichester-Clark, community hatreds intensified in Belfast as it was announced that universal suffrage would be introduced in time for the next local government elections. There was serious rioting directed against the police on the Crumlin Road, in Hooker Street, and in Ardoyne in May and June 1969. On 12 August the Apprentice Boys marched in Derry and the fierce and protracted struggle between the police and the people of the Bogside began. Two days later the scene shifted dramatically to Belfast.

August 1969

On Thursday 14 August tension steadily increased in several parts of Belfast. The police, who had been under virtual siege in Hastings Street barracks the

He got elected. (Election hand-bill)

The unthinkable: loyalists in furious conflict with the Royal Ulster Constabulary and the British Army on the Shankill Road. That night, Saturday 11 October 1969, Constable Victor Arbuckle was mortally wounded – the first policeman to be killed in the present Troubles. (Pacemaker)

previous night, were strained and fearful. For three days conflict had raged in the Bogside and that afternoon the RUC had been withdrawn from riot duty there to make way for troops from HMS *Sea Eagle*. News came in that a man had been shot dead in Armagh – the first violent death of the present Troubles. Angry Protestants were gathering in the Shankill and the Specials had been called out. That evening the apparent victory of the people of the Bogside brought out Catholic youths in strength in front of the Divis Flats. Police armoured personnel carriers, failing to disperse the rioters, merely became targets for volleys of stones and petrol bombs. As darkness fell police and Special constables on foot attempted to close in from the side streets, and behind them Protestants mobilised.

Suddenly shots rang out, from which side it will never be known for certain. Within minutes gunfire became general. Police Shorlands – armoured cars made on Queen's Island – fired bursts of heavy-calibre bullets from their Browning machine guns; many shots hit the Divis Flats and there a nine-year-old boy was killed as he took refuge in a back room. Protestants surged down the narrow streets interconnecting the Shankill and the Falls, tossing petrol bombs into houses as they went, and as they emerged into Divis Street the mobs clashed repeatedly. Allegations that the Specials, fully-armed part-time policemen, all of them Protestants, had lent their support to the Shankill mob inflamed opinion on both sides. There was furious fighting, too, at Ardoyne. Shots could still be heard as the dawn came on Friday 15 August. Including those who later died of their wounds, six men had been killed in Belfast; at least twelve factories had been destroyed; and over 100 houses had been wrecked and another 300 damaged by petrol bombs.

It had been largely Catholics who had lost their homes and they crowded into church halls in the heart of the Falls with what belongings they had been able to take with them. Some took the train at Great Victoria Street for Dublin. Isolated Protestant and Catholic families moved out to make their way hurriedly to relatives and friends. Huge barricades sprang up, particularly in the Falls: telegraph poles, trees, thousands of paving stones, vans, trucks, cars and 60 Corporation buses were used to construct them. That Friday afternoon, two British Army battalions were sent into the Falls Road where residents, preferring them to armed police, plied the soldiers with cups of tea. Not enough troops had been brought in to prevent further violence that night: virtually all the houses in Bombay Street in Clonard were destroyed; other houses in Brookfield Street were set on fire; and a Protestant rioter was killed in Ardoyne. The scale of the conflict can be seen from the Scarman Tribunal report which stated that 1,820 families fled their homes during and following this rioting; 1,505 of these families were Catholic, making up more than 3% of all Catholic households in Belfast.

By sending troops for active duty into the streets of Belfast, the British government had made one of the most crucial military decisions since Suez. For their part, citizens found that their city had become a war zone; soldiers first blocked off streets with knife-rests and concertina wire; later, sensitive areas were separated more permanently by walls of corrugated iron bristling with barbed wire. This 'peace line' notwithstanding, violence was to continue in Belfast not just for week after week but for year after year.

'Outright communal hostility': 1969–71

On Friday 10 October 1969 the report of the Hunt Commission of Inquiry into policing the province was published. For activists on the Shankill Road this was too much — the previous month the Cameron Report had upheld Catholic charges of discrimination and now not only were the RUC to be deprived of their arms on normal duty but also the B Specials were to be disbanded. On Saturday around 10 p.m. about 3,000 loyalists advanced down the Shankill towards the Catholic Unity Flats. When police attempting to halt them were fired upon, and a constable was killed and another was wounded, the 3rd Battalion the Light Infantry moved in. In intensity the conflict almost matched that of 14 August as the troops came under protracted rifle and automatic fire, not to speak of showers of petrol bombs; yet the army fired only 26 shots, killing two rioters with cool deliberation. In the days that followed extensive arms searches were carried out and barricades removed. As barricades in Catholic areas of the city had been dismantled by consent some weeks before, relative calm returned for the remainder of the year.

1970 began with hopeful signs for the future. Catholics were the first recruits for the new reserve force, the Ulster Defence Regiment; the Alliance Party was formed in the spring, unionist but dedicated to reform and reconciliation; and in August a party was created to give the minority one voice, the Social Democratic and Labour Party. But as relations between the British Army and Protestants improved, a new military force appeared: the Provisional IRA. The Provisionals had arisen primarily because of dissatisfaction at the failure of the traditional IRA to fight effectively in August 1969. The Provisionals went into action for the first time in June 1970, during savage rioting in east Belfast when another six lives were lost. On 3 July 1970,

One of the first barricades to be erected in Belfast in August 1969. Corner of Leeson Street and the Falls Road. (Henry V. Bell)

after an arms find in Balkan Street, General Freeland declared a curfew in the Lower Falls and maintained it for the next 35 hours. A house-to-house search produced over a hundred handguns, but the government in Westminster later acknowledged that the curfew was counter-productive. Three civilians had been shot dead and another had been run down by an army vehicle. The *Sunday Times* 'Insight' team concluded:

3-5 July 1970 did convert what was perhaps only an increasingly sullen Catholic acceptance of the Army into outright communal hostility... In the months that followed, recruitment to the Provisionals was dizzily fast: the movement grew from fewer than a hundred activists in May-June to nearly 800 by December.*

* *Sunday Times* 'Insight' team, *Ulster* (Penguin, 1972), p. 221.

That summer the Provisionals launched a bombing campaign, clearly with the aim of creating sufficient dislocation to force Britain to withdraw from Northern Ireland. Targets in July and August included the Elsinore Hotel, the Northern Bank in High Street, the homes of Rev Martin Smyth and Lord Justice Curran, and an electricity sub-station. By 15 September 1970 there had been 100 explosions but 70% of these were in the west of the province: this was merely a foretaste of what was to come. Violent incidents increased steadily for the rest of 1970 and reached a new pitch of intensity in 1971. On 6 February the Provisionals killed the first British soldier in Ulster since 1922 on the New Lodge Road and when three young Scottish soldiers were lured to their deaths on 10 March, loyalists demonstrated to call for the introduction of internment.

Flight: internment and population movement

Chichester-Clark resigned on 20 March 1971 with the intention, he said, of drawing Westminster's attention to the deteriorating situation in the province. His successor, Brian Faulkner, had long sought the premiership and his supporters and opponents alike expected him to take more vigorous action against the IRA. The difficulty for the government and security forces was that their enemy was largely unseen and, unless caught red-handed, could melt back unnoticed into their communities. The bombing campaign intensified with hardly a day passing without an explosion somewhere in the city. One of the worst incidents occured on 25 May when a suitcase of gelignite was thrown into the reception area of the Springfield Road RUC/Army Command Post; 22 were injured, including a two-year-old child whose skull was fractured, and a sergeant of the Parachute Regiment was killed as he attempted to protect children. The Hannahstown transformer was destroyed on 18 June at a cost of £1½ million. As incident followed incident the Stormont government's resolve to intern suspects was stiffened. The internment operation began at 4.15 a.m. on Monday 9 August 1971.

The British Army had a list of 452 men to be arrested; 342 were picked up; 116 were released after 48 hours; and the rest were held either in Crumlin Road jail or on the converted troopship *Maidstone* moored at the Belfast docks. Internment did not even achieve the government's short-term aim of arresting the most active men in the IRA. Police and army intelligence was clearly out of date; most of those taken were members of the Official IRA; no real attempt was made to arrest Protestant men of violence; and several of those held were merely non-violent critics of Faulkner's government.

Terrible violence followed. That day two soldiers and ten civilians were killed; Catholics fled from their homes in streets near the Crumlin Road; and Protestant families fled from Ardoyne, some setting fire to about 100 houses evacuated as they moved out. Rioting and shooting continued almost without ceasing into the next morning. Tuesday 10 August 1971 was the most violent day in Belfast since 1969: 11 people were killed in the city, including Father Hugh Mullan, shot while administering the last rites to an injured man at Ballymurphy. About 240 houses at Farringdon Gardens, Velsheda Park and Cranbrook Park in Ardoyne were destroyed by fire, and by Thursday 12 August over 7,000 refugees from Belfast were reported to have arrived in army camps in the Irish Republic.

It is beyond the scope of this chapter to examine in detail the rights and wrongs, and the effectiveness or otherwise, of the imposition of internment. What is certain is that internment had a direct and long-lasting impact on the development of the city and on the distribution of the population in particular. Michael Poole had submitted his report on 'residential displacement' occurring in 1969 to the Scarman Tribunal on 15 May 1971; this showed that in August 1969 there was a direct confrontation across the territorial boundaries between solidly segregated areas, and that population movement was concentrated in the inner city, making segregation even more rigid than before. In 1971 Richard Black, Francis Pinter and Bob Ovary made a detailed study of residential displacement in the first three weeks following the introduction of internment. 'The total number of movements for which we could account for both origin and destination was 2,100,' they concluded in their report (entitled *Flight*) though they added that 'new information is still coming in'. The report explained further:

. . . the nature of the movement of population this August has differed greatly from the major upheaval which unsettled the Belfast community in August 1969. . . On this occasion the Army 'Peace Line' dividing the strongly segregated areas appears to have been effective at least in preventing further significant dislocation of population, and the major upheaval has transferred to the mixed areas which were formerly thought to serve as 'buffer zones' guaranteeing stability.

This re-sorting of mixed areas into segregated areas (foreshadowed by the New Barnsley/Moyard evacuation of Protestants in 1969) is an extremely ominous development and shows no sign of being arrested in the immediate future. . .

In this three-week period more than one in every hundred families in Belfast was forced to move; intimidation, fear of intimidation, and destruction of their homes were the reasons given for moving. Only a few families (in the Falls-Springfield area) did not mention intimidation but left to get away from constant street gun-battles. An uncounted number of families had wrecked or set their own homes on fire as they left, to prevent 'the other side' moving in.

2% of the 45,000 Catholic households in the city were displaced: they moved principally from New Ardoyne, Ballysillan and Monkstown in the north; from the Springfield Road, the Donegall Road area, and Roden Street in the west; and from Bryson Street, Mountpottinger and the Ballybeen and Tullycarnet estates in the east. About 0.5% of the 135,000 Protestant households in Belfast were displaced: they moved principally from the Farringdon-Cranbrook Streets of New Ardoyne, the Ballynure streets of the Oldpark, and the New Lodge in the north; from the Grosvenor Road end of Roden Street-Lanark Street, and Merkland Street in the west; from Suffolk and Lenadoon in the south-west; and from Bryson Street in the east. Altogether 60% of the movements were made by Catholic families and 40% by Protestant families. The hopeful development of mixed housing in the post-war years had collapsed completely in all but the solid middle-class residential areas of the city. Protestant families dispersed widely throughout Belfast, but mainly to the new housing estates such as Monkstown and Ballybeen beyond the city boundary, while Catholics crowded into the older housing of north Belfast, the Falls, and the newer Andersonstown estates. Henceforth it would be even easier than it had been before for young people to grow up in self-sufficient communities without regularly meeting others of a different religious background.

Whole areas of the city were inflamed throughout the month of August 1971. Thirty-five people had been killed, most of them in Belfast; 26,000 families were refusing to pay rents and rates in protest against internment; Belfast Corporation Transport announced that it had lost £135,000 in August due to the Troubles; and every night the city reverberated to sharp sounds of rifle and automatic fire, and windows rattled with the shock waves of distant explosions. Internment had failed to weaken the Provisionals and, indeed, as details were revealed of the disorientation and sensory deprivation to which internees were subjected, recruitment increased.

From August to the end of 1971 it seemed that the Provisionals were making a concerted attempt to destroy the commercial life of the city, though it is more likely that the primary aim was to force political change. Victorian buildings, near to the end of their life span, collapsed easily and burned fiercely but the glass of new office blocks could be replaced. The campaign inflicted costly damage and stretched the security forces to the limit but, even when carried on over several years, did not cause devastation equal to that brought about by the 1941 Blitz. Inevitably, innocent victims lost their lives, causing revulsion amongst those who sympathised with the Provisionals' political aims; examples include a bomb at the Electricity Board's offices on the Malone Road

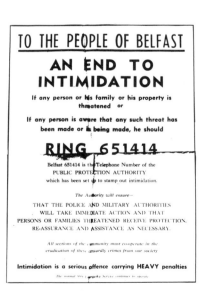

Issued by the Northern Ireland government.

Billy Blease, created Lord Blease of Cromac in July 1978, seen here with Vic Feather, former General Secretary of the TUC, who was raised to the peerage at the same time. Blease won government recognition for the Northern Committee of the Irish Congress of Trade Unions in August 1964 and worked unceasingly, but with limited success, to keep sectarianism out of the trade union movement.

on 25 August which killed one person and maimed sixteen others, and an explosion at the Four Step Inn on the Shankill Road which killed two and injured twenty on 29 September.

An acute water shortage in Belfast was worsened by the exceptional demands made on the fire brigades, and more than a million gallons were lost when the water pumping station supplying Whiterock and Ballymurphy was blown up on 8 October. The violence showed no sign of abating as 1971 drew to a close. The explosion in McGurk's public house in North Queen Street on 4 December was perhaps the most horrific single incident of the Troubles. Fifteen people were killed; by the light of arc-lamps surgeons treated the injured in the open; gas escaping from fractured pipes flamed in the rubble as all through the night the dead and mutilated were uncovered brick by brick; and rescue operations were hampered as nearby the army came under fire and rival crowds fought in the darkness. The bomb had probably been placed by loyalist paramilitaries. On 6 December a factory warehouse on the Dublin Road burned so fiercely after a Provisional bomb attack that the adjoining Salvation Army Citadel collapsed, killing a woman officer. On 11 December an explosion at a Shankill furniture store killed two children and two adults; the surgeon who certified the deaths of the children recalled the scene in the mortuary: 'I remember standing there with two policemen. And we cried our eyes out.'

The prospects for 1972 looked bleak indeed.

The fall of Stormont and the power-sharing Executive

When, during a demonstration on Sunday 30 January 1972, 13 people were shot dead by soldiers of the 1st Parachute Regiment in Derry, the furious reaction of the minority quickly spilled over into Belfast. The Provisionals' bombing campaign now reached its peak. The Abercorn restaurant was bombed when it was crowded with shoppers on Saturday 4 March. Janet Bereen and Anne Owens had been sitting almost on top of the bomb when it exploded. They were killed. Four people – Rosaleen and Jennifer McNern, Irene Arnold, and Jimmy Stewart – lost both legs. Rosaleen McNern's right arm was ripped off as well; Mrs Arnold lost an eye. At least 136 people were

Meanwhile, some citizens were projecting another image of Belfast across the world: Mary Peters won the gold medal for the Pentathlon at the 1972 Munich Olympics. Other celebrities include: Heather Harper, the opera singer; George Best, the footballer; James Galway, the flautist; and Alex 'Hurricane' Higgins, the snooker champion. (Rowel Friers: *Ireland's Saturday Night*)

injured. On 20 March an explosion in Donegall Street killed two policemen and four civilians.

In the desperate situation, Westminster invoked the 1920 Government of Ireland Act and sought direct control of security. Brian Faulkner and his government resigned rather than approve this demand. On 24 March Edward Heath, the British Prime Minister, announced the suspension of the Stormont government. After just over fifty years of life the Northern Ireland parliament had effectively come to an end.

Much of Belfast closed down on 28 March, the day of the last sitting of the provincial parliament. A huge column of loyalists marched with their bands to Stormont to hear Brian Faulkner and William Craig — now the leader of Vanguard, a large paramilitary force — address them from the balcony. William Whitelaw arrived as Secretary of State for Northern Ireland to face the most intractable problems: barricades were being thrown up in Protestant areas; sectarian assassinations spread fear across the city; and, as so many lived in dread of a knock on the door, more people again moved their homes. Assassination was the weapon principally employed by loyalist paramilitaries, while the Provisionals brought out their guns in July in a dispute over houses in Lenadoon and were responsible for the worst incident of the month — 'Bloody Friday'. On a beautiful afternoon on 21 July, twenty-six bombs were set off in Belfast: seven people were killed at Oxford Street Bus Station, another four died in the Cavehill Road shopping centre, and 130 had to be treated for injuries, many extremely severe. Troops faced no resistance when they swept away barricades in Catholic areas on 31 July, but the Provisionals remained strong and on 25 September bombed the new Russell Court Hotel: damage was estimated at £2 million. Assassinations continued to exact a terrible toll; forty people, most of them in Belfast, were murdered in the last four months of 1972.

In 1973 Westminster made a concerted effort to find some sort of political solution. Proportional representation was tried for the first time since 1922 in the new district council elections held on 30 May 1973. The results for Belfast were: Unionists 25; Alliance 8; SDLP 7; Democratic Unionists 2; Republican Clubs 2; NILP 2; Independent Unionists 2; United Loyalists 2; Vanguard 1. The proliferation of parties could not disguise the fact that the middle ground in the city was depressingly narrow. These local elections were in effect a dress rehearsal for the Assembly elections on 28 June 1973; the Assembly was to replace the Northern Ireland parliament with an executive of 12 to be appointed by the Secretary of State from elected representatives. It was Westminster's hope that a government representing both communities would be created. Belfast was divided into four six-seat constituencies, and 9 Official Unionists, 4 Alliance, 3 SDLP, 3 Unionists, 3 Democratic Unionists, 1 Independent Unionist and 1 NILP candidate were elected in the city.

The numerous and unstable loyalist groupings both in Belfast and in the province as a whole made Whitelaw's task exceedingly difficult and it was not until 22 November 1973 that the formation of an executive could be announced. Brian Faulkner was appointed Chief Executive and Gerry Fitt his deputy; former political opponents now sat down together and for the first time — and, so far, the last time — in the history of Northern Ireland a government representing both communities was formed. A conference between the British and Irish governments followed at Sunningdale Civil Service College in Berkshire between 6 and 9 December 1973; here it was

Gerry Fitt.
(Rowel Friers: *Irish Times*)

agreed that eventual unification of Ireland should only take place with the consent of the majority in Northern Ireland and that a Council of Ireland should be set up primarily to promote north–south economic cooperation.

This apparent reconciliation was not reflected in the streets of Belfast. Thomas Niedermayer, managing director of Grundig, was kidnapped on 27 December 1973, never to be seen alive again; a man was killed in cross-fire at Ormeau on 1 January 1974, the day when the power-sharing Executive officially took up duty; bombs inflicted extensive damage in Upper North Street on 2 January; a man was shot dead at the doorway of his home in east Belfast on 5 January; and, in short, there were daily reports of yet another violent death, yet another explosion or yet another item to add to the depressing catalogue of bitter communal unrest in the city.

When on 22 January 1974 the Assembly met for the first time at Stormont, anti-power-sharing loyalist members disrupted proceedings for more than an hour until the RUC forcibly removed 18 of them. Already, on 4 January, the Unionist Council had rejected the Sunningdale agreement and the prospects for power-sharing looked gloomier still when Whitelaw was replaced by Francis Pym and a Westminster general election was called for 28 February. 'Dublin is only a Sunningdale away' the posters of the United Ulster Unionist Council – the coalition of loyalist parties opposed to power-sharing – proclaimed; the UUUC won 11 out of the 12 Ulster seats, three of them in Belfast. More than half the electorate had voted for the UUUC – in effect, a vote of no confidence in power-sharing. Supporters of the UUUC marched in triumph to Stormont on 9 March 1974 and proclaimed their intention of bringing down the Executive; it soon became clear that they meant what they said.

'The shutdown is on, it's complete, it's irrecoverable. . .': the UWC strike 14–27 May 1974

On Tuesday 14 May 1974 the Assembly rejected a motion condemning the Sunningdale agreement by 44 votes to 28. At 6.08 p.m. Harry Murray and Bob Pagels, representing the Ulster Workers' Council, informed the press at Stormont that a strike would begin in protest at the motion's defeat. After stating that electricity output would be reduced from 725 megawatts to 400, Murray concluded:

It is a grave responsibility but it is not ours. It is Brian Faulkner's. He and his friends are ignoring the wishes of 400,000 people who voted against them in the General Election and in doing so they must take the responsibility for this strike. [*]

* R. Fisk, *The point of no return* (see bibliog), p. 19.

Tracing its origins back to groups of loyalist workers in the shipyards from 1969 onwards, the UWC by 1974 had become a 21-man committee drawn from Harland & Wolff, Mackies, Gallahers, the Sirocco Works, the Castlereagh industrial estate, the Post Office, and Ballylumford power station. In union with loyalist paramilitaries, the UWC, uncertain of the support of UUUC politicians, called the strike without waiting for their approval. On 15 May most firms in the city reported to the Belfast Chamber of Commerce that 90% of their employees had turned up for work. The first day of the strike had gone badly for its organisers; that afternoon at the Vanguard headquarters in Hawthornden Road the UWC decided to call on businesses throughout the city to demand their closure. Faulkner's Executive and the Westminster government's representatives — Merlyn Rees, the Secretary of State, and Stanley Orme, the Minister of State — seem to have underestimated the effectiveness of what Tommy Lyttle of the paramilitary Ulster Defence Association described as 'intimidation – but intimidation without violence. . .' Already in April 1974 the number of violent deaths in the province since 1969 had reached 1,000 – more than 620 of them being in the Belfast area – and in the first two weeks of May there had been 11 killings and 13 explosions in the city. Now the UWC was to reduce Belfast to a state of near paralysis.

By Saturday 18 May the city was experiencing power blackouts lasting up to six hours at a time. Tilley lamps hissed on the counters of large department stores in the city centre; dairies and bakeries had been forced to shut down; and the major industries of Belfast could no longer operate. On Sunday night the UWC ordered the erection of almost a hundred road blocks encircling the inner city and the following morning gangs of youths hijacked lorries and cars to seal off main routes to the city centre; only Andersonstown, south Belfast and the Falls were not cut off from the rest of Ulster. The RUC and the British Army believed it best to maintain a 'low profile' and left the barricades alone. Many citizens continued to make their way to work on foot, and by two-wheeled transport. Nevertheless, when Len Murray, General Secretary of the TUC, attempted to lead a return to work at Harland & Wolff on Tuesday 21 May only 200 were prepared to follow him. As Robert Fisk reported in *The Times* the following day:

From almost the first moment that one drives past the hijacked lorries, and the men in black leather guarding them, the realisation dawns that most of the Protestants behind the barricades are supporting the strike. The Government's carefully nurtured belief that 'loyalists' are staying away from work only because of intimidation seems to be farther from reality each day. . .

Lieut-General Sir Frank King, GOC Northern Ireland, now had 17,500 troops in the province under his command; to use his men to break the strike, he believed, would be disastrous. 'If you get a very large section of the population which is bent on a particular course,' he said, 'then it is a difficult thing to stop them.' Yet on 24 May Harry Murray said: 'We wouldn't oppose our own British Army. This is the army that I joined up in 1939-45. How could I oppose the British Army?' On the evening of Saturday 25 May the Prime Minister, Harold Wilson, made a controversial broadcast; if it was intended to weaken support for the strike then it failed. Wilson described the strikers as 'people who spend their lives sponging on Westminster and British democracy and then systematically assault democratic methods'. Supporters of the power-sharing Executive were aghast: nothing was better calculated to unite loyalists behind the UWC than Wilson's refusal to recognise them as people with full rights as United Kingdom citizens.

At 5 a.m. on Monday 27 May, troops took over the principal petrol stations in Belfast. In response, the UWC ordered a reduction in electricity to 10% of capacity and a withdrawal of workers in essential services. At 9.30 a.m. that morning Hugo Patterson, the official spokesman for the Northern Ireland Electricity Service, was interviewed for the BBC by Barry Cowan:

Patterson: Let's be clear about this; this shutdown is on, it's complete, it's irrecoverable. I don't think there's any going back on this one now.
Cowan: In other words, as of two minutes ago, nine-thirty, the complete shut-

* R. Fisk, *The point of no return*, (see bibliog), p. 140.

down of power in Northern Ireland has begun and cannot be stopped.
Patterson: . . . you're right. . . We are past the point of no return.*

Patterson, whose pessimistic voice could be heard on the air almost every hour throughout the strike, had long predicted a complete breakdown, though there is evidence that the UWC regarded a total shutdown as detrimental to their cause. Faulkner, unable to persuade his SDLP allies even to negotiate with the strikers, resigned at 1.20 p.m. that Monday and, now that the Executive had fallen, a loyalist demonstration at Stormont became a massive victory rally. Brian Garrett, chairman of NILP, went to Hawthornden Road to implore the UWC to order a return to work; there he found power workers and loyalist politicians singing 'O God, our help in ages past' by candlelight. One of the most effective general strikes in Europe since 1945 had come to an end.

'Special social need'

Morale had been remarkably high in almost all parts of Belfast during the UWC strike. Loyalists opposed to power-sharing were elated with the prospect of victory while republicans had rising expectations of British withdrawal from Ulster – indeed, Provisional IRA action almost ceased in the city and there seems to have been a general belief held by republicans that the strikers inadvertently were doing their work for them. Meanwhile churches, voluntary groups and relief organisations had thrown themselves into the task of providing social services where the official services were paralysed by the strike. In Catholic areas the Central Citizens Defence Committee and the Central Co-ordinating Committee for Relief – with hard-won experience going back to 1969 – were able to give aid with efficient speed. The South Belfast Community Association, an amalgamation of eighteen community groups in the area, was active from the start of the strike; it reported later that 'the operation demonstrated clearly the strength of community spirit throughout the area, the level of community concern, the willingness and urgency with which community groups were ready to rally around and tackle problems and ensure that hardship would be minimised.'

Operating a 24-hour service, agencies all over the city stored food, bottled gas, paraffin and other essentials, and attempted to organise transport for those most in need. For example, in an estate of 500 households, two meetings were held on 26 May; 400 women attended the one at 4 p.m. and 500 men were present at the other at 5 p.m. The following evening a public meeting in a small Catholic community in central Belfast attracted an attendance of 800 people. Louis Boyle observed:

* Louis Boyle, 'The UWC Strike: May 1974', in Darby and Williamson, *Violence and the social services in Northern Ireland* (see biblio), p. 160.

Few areas were left uncovered; never before had so much community activity been seen in Belfast; public meetings when held were packed, volunteers were numerous and it seemed in some areas that everyone was involved in some way.*

Voluntary action had been swift and effective in response to an unprecedented crisis; it was the local authority and government agencies, however, which had to cope with the more enduring problem of social need in the city. When violence erupted in 1969 the social services in the Belfast urban area were run by the welfare departments of Co Antrim, Co Down and Belfast Corporation. The Antrim welfare department acted decisively by opening an emergency office in Andersonstown; its senior staff lived in the area and co-ordinated a special team of social workers to distribute cash, bedding, food and fuel to needy families. Belfast, in contrast, did not provide an exceptional service until forced to do so by the government. The whole of the greater Belfast area was more logically administered when the Eastern Health and Social Services Board was set up in October 1973. The biggest of the five districts in the EHSSB is North and West Belfast, containing a population of nearly a quarter of a million: this area contained and still contains some of the worst poverty in the United Kingdom. Peter Townsend's monumental study, *Poverty in the United Kingdom*, published in 1979 but based on research carried out ten years earlier, was the first of its kind to include Northern Ireland. Townsend made a detailed survey of Smithfield and St George's wards, comparing them with deprived areas in Glasgow, Salford and Neath. He concluded:

With the exception of Neath, the percentage found to be in poverty or on the margins of poverty by the State's standard was high being 38 for selected areas of Salford, 48 for Glasgow Shettleton, and 50 for Belfast. The figure for the UK as a whole was 28.

A succession of inquiries established that extensive parts of Belfast suffered deprivation rarely matched in cities across the Irish Sea. Several government departments worked together from 1974 to study poverty in the Belfast urban area; their report, 'Belfast Areas of Special Social Need' (1977), identified the main areas of deprivation:

... the geographical distribution suggests two major need syndromes. One is characterised by unemployment, low incomes and overcrowded housing resulting from large family size. This has a West Belfast distribution. The other is an inner city syndrome, distinguished by sub-standard housing, poor physical environment, low incomes, lack of skills and concentrations of persons with different forms of physical handicap whether associated with age or health.

The study group applied 39 indicators of social need, including un-employment, overcrowding, educational level and deaths from bronchitis. The 18 wards defined as Areas of Special Social Need contained 25% of the city's population but 48% of the adult male unemployed, 62% of the long term unemployed, 51% of children in care, 40% of the educationally subnormal, and 45% of juvenile delinquents in the urban area. There was an alarmingly close connection between deaths from bronchitis and houses lacking basic amenities. Many of the wards identified were in the North and West Belfast district of the EHSSB; here there had been 50 killings in 1976 alone. Persistent violence increased the hardships endured by the people in the area – public service workers often refused to work there, bus services were often called off, and sleep was frequently broken by the noise of shots, explosions and rioting. The EHSSB was reluctant to admit that these districts had special problems arising out of the Troubles; an official report in 1975 failed to mention paramilitaries and dismissed the violence in two lines in a 3,000 word document.

The 1978 Belfast Household Survey was carried out by the Housing Executive in an attempt to provide information not available due to the cancellation of the 1976 Census. It showed that 77,000 people – 19% of the city's population – had left Belfast between 1971 and 1978, that 75% of households in the inner wards lacked four basic amenities, that 42% of all households in 1978 had a weekly income of below £40 each, and that unemployment (then 9% for the city as a whole) was exceptionally high in the following Ward and District Council Areas: Clonard 22.2%; Court 20.2%; Falls 29.3%; Grosvenor 27.8%; Milltown 21.3%; New Lodge 24%; Whiterock 35.3%.

The acute problems of Whiterock, and the housing estate of Ballymurphy in particular, were examined in 1979 by a sub-group of the Belfast Areas of Special Social Need working party. It reported that in Ballymurphy 51% of heads of households earned less than £40 per week, that 48.7% were unemployed and that the average household size was 6.5 persons (compared with 3.0 in the Belfast urban area). 39% of heads of households were aged between 15 and 39, indicating that demand for employment would remain high for many years to come. The whole Whiterock area contained 3% of the urban population but less than 1% of the city's total employment opportunities. Indeed, west Belfast in all had 33% of the urban area's population but only 17% of the city's job opportunities. In 1980 the Child Poverty Action Group interviewed over 1,000 families in Turf Lodge, New Lodge, Tully-carnet and Ballymacarrett, and came to the conclusion that about two thirds of the families there lived on or near the poverty line. Poverty was particularly severe amongst pensioners, single parents and the unemployed, and about half those interviewed appeared to be entitled to, but were not claiming, at least one state benefit – Townsend had found that there were 12% eligible for but not claiming supplementary benefit in Northern Ireland compared with the UK average of 5%.

In short, not only was Belfast sharply divided by religion and politics but also by living standards. One group of citizens enjoyed incomes, houses and other amenities equivalent to those in Britain, while the other group suffered deprivation on a scale seen in few other areas of the European Economic Community and made all the more galling by contrast with the consumer paradise portrayed in mass advertising.

It was in housing that the distinction between the haves and have-nots was most clearly seen.

Housing: 'an emergency situation requiring emergency procedures'

Despite the achievement of attracting new industries to Belfast and its environs in the 1960s, little real progress had been made then in solving the city's formidable housing problem. The rate of house building by the Corporation, the Housing Trust and subsidised private builders had been sufficient only to keep pace with the increase in the number of new households. In 1962 the City Architect had reported that the Corporation had built only 350 flats and houses over the previous year and that 58,700 new dwellings would be required over the next 20 years.

The Corporation's poor house-building record was due only in part to the apparent immobility of the City Hall Unionists and a determination to keep down the rates. The government had turned down requests for an extension of the city boundary and yet there was only enough land for about a quarter of the new dwellings needed within that boundary. On 3 January 1964 Sir Cecil McKee, as reported in the *Belfast Telegraph*, declared that Belfast councillors did not see why 'they should have to spend ratepayers' money on building outside the boundary' when the rates would be paid to other local authorities. Neighbouring councils were themselves not keen to assume responsibility for Belfast's overspill population, and it was partly in an attempt to resolve this question that Matthew had been asked to produce a regional plan for the city. The Matthew Stop Line and the urban motorway scheme, far from solving the housing problem, merely created an atmosphere of uncertainty and encouraged further delay.

Violence increased Belfast's housing difficulties; 3,570 families moved as a direct result of the Troubles in the summer of 1969 and a further 2,100 households were forced to move in August 1971. Between 1969 and 1976 25,000 houses were destroyed or damaged by explosions in the city. As families fled from troubled streets their abandoned homes were often broken up and vandalised; by the end of April 1975 there were 9,000 houses in Belfast irreparably damaged or bricked up. Belfast Corporation brought in an emergency housing scheme to rehouse those made homeless in 1969 but by then the Stormont and Westminster governments had decided to take housing out of the hands of local authorities altogether. The Northern Ireland Housing Executive was set up as the sole housing agency for the whole province; on 10 October 1969 the following communiqué was issued:

... the governments have concluded that this is an emergency situation requiring emergency procedures... they have, therefore, decided reluctantly that local authorities are not geared – and cannot be geared – to handle such a task and that the best hope for success lies in the creation of a single-purpose, efficient and streamlined central housing authority. . .*

* Susan Kennedy and Derek Birrell, 'Housing', in Darby and Williamson, *Violence and the social services in Northern Ireland* (see bibliog), p. 100.

The Housing Executive took over responsibility for the building, management and allocation of all public housing from local authorities, the Housing Trust and development commissions. The new agency did not begin to operate until October 1971 and meanwhile the Corporation ran down its house-building programme still further.

Immense problems faced the Housing Executive from the outset. During 1971–2 there were 22,000 tenants in the public sector on rent and rates strike as part of the civil disobedience campaign in protest at the introduction of internment, and there were still over 17,000 refusing such payments in 1973. In 1972–3 there were 14,000 houses in Belfast damaged by explosions; over 5,000 dwellings were affected by squatting by March 1973; contractors often refused to tender for the most troubled areas in west Belfast; many building sites were easy targets for theft and vandalism; skilled workers and technicians were in short supply; and workmen were understandably reluctant to go into disturbed parts of the city. 18% of the Housing Executive's employees resigned in 1972–3; this high turnover of staff aggravated the agency's problems of centralising housing control. Finally, having created a great bureaucratic machine, the Westminster governments showed a growing reluctance to pay for the building of the new dwellings Belfast so desperately needed. Unfit houses were being demolished faster than new dwellings were being built and in 1973 the Housing Executive put up only 435 houses in Belfast.

When in the summer of 1974 the Housing Executive completed its first comprehensive survey of existing housing conditions in the province, the findings for Belfast revealed the huge size of the city's housing problem. The

New houses in Bombay Street, replacing those burned in the riots of August 1969. (Ulster Museum)

figures for Northern Ireland as a whole were bad enough – 19.6% of the total dwelling stock was statutorily unfit compared with 7.3% in England and Wales. In the Belfast urban area at least half the houses required repairs of £250 or more, and 24.2% of all dwellings – 29,750 out of a total stock of 123,120 – were statutorily unfit. Even more alarming was the revelation that in Area 'A' (the inner city west of the Lagan) half the houses, excluding bricked-up houses, caravans and shacks, were classed as unfit. In this area 34.3% dwellings had no wash-hand basin, 32.4% had no inside toilet, 29.8% were without a fixed bath in a bathroom and 23.2% had been built before 1870. The black picture painted by the 1974 survey led the Housing Executive to mark out Housing Action Areas in the city with a programme designed to prevent houses on the fringes of redevelopment areas deteriorating any further. In particular, grants were made available to improve older houses (75% rising to 90% in cases of special hardship) and housing associations were encouraged to take part in the task of rehabilitation. Vast areas of Belfast were to be controlled by the Housing Executive making it, in the words of a government minister, 'the largest slum landlord in Europe'.

Meanwhile, the Westminster government was being forced to reconsider the whole question of how best to develop Belfast and the area surrounding it. For many, the planners' dreams on paper were becoming a nightmare when implemented.

The planning that went awry

By the 1960s Belfast's dependence on coal had been replaced by a dependence on cheap oil. The city's gasworks converted to naphtha; from 1962 the power stations burned oil; steam-powered linen mills gave way to synthetic fibre plants powered by electricity and using oil by-products as raw material; diesel replaced steam on the railways, which were reduced from 640 to 210 miles between 1945 and 1981; and the last trolleybus ran in Belfast in 1968, leaving the streets clear for the free-ranging diesel buses. Its complete conquest delayed by the Depression between the world wars, the internal conbustion engine – which Dunlop and Ferguson had done so much to adapt to road transport – was now supreme. The number of motor cars on the province's roads had leapt from 33,500 in 1945 to 350,000 in 1979 and commercial vehicles had quintupled in the same period. Industry was no longer tied to easy access to the Belfast docks for coal supplies; it was free to roam almost where it willed, freed by the ability to connect in with the nearest available power line.

It was in this time of cheap energy, economic expansion and optimism that the Matthew Plan and the Belfast Urban Motorway had been conceived. These schemes, which were designed to affect the lives of so many citizens, had already been implemented in part when the Troubles began in 1969. The Ministry of Development and Belfast Corporation jointly employed the firms of Travers Morgan and the Building Design Partnership as consultants. That the urban motorway would cut a swathe through densely packed and ageing dwellings in Sandy Row, the lower Falls and the lower Shankill was welcomed by the planners, for, as Matthew stated:

A down-at-heel atmosphere is the worst enemy of industrial progress. . . the delapidated towns, the slums and congestion of central Belfast – all these are liabilities that the economy of the country cannot afford in this critical stage of its history.

The Building Design Partnership estimated that 74,500 new homes would be needed in the Belfast urban area by 1981 but that there were sites for only 47,500 dwellings within the Stop Line; 27,000 families, therefore, would have to move to the new growth centres. Few in power thought to ask the opinion of the people who were to have their homes demolished and be sent out beyond the city boundary. The road-building programme was well advanced by 1969 and by then two major motorways reached out from Belfast, gashing through rich agricultural land. The effect of the new road system was dramatically revealed in Belfast's dockland – there a tight-knit community was broken up, most of the terraced housing of Sailorstown was demolished and its population rehoused in North Queen Street or dispersed to the growth centres. As docker-poet John Campbell wrote:

> In Sailorstown a motorway
>   sprawls where once tough men held sway,
> Where happy children used to play
>   . . . in Sailorstown. [*]

* John Campbell, *Saturday night in York Street* (Blackstaff Press, 1982), p. 4.

The urban motorway – the estimate of its cost was put at £10 million in 1961 and raised to £300 million by 1973 – would engulf 300 acres of land on which stood 7,000 homes; 5,700 of these were scheduled for demolition but the remaining 1,300 were sound dwellings which would have to be pulled down to meet the demands of motor transport. Inner-city blight spread more rapidly as property owners let buildings decay in the projected path of the motorway. Then the plans began to go awry: paramilitaries threatened to take direct action to stop the scheme; contractors proved unwilling to face the hostility of enraged residents; the Belfast Urban Study Group at Queen's University called on the government to abandon the Travers Morgan road plans; and the Sandy Row Redevelopment Association, the Shankill Redevelopment Association, and the umbrella Greater West Belfast Community Association mobilised opinion in opposition to the road. At its first full meeting the Belfast City Council, set up to replace the dissolved Belfast Corporation, called on the government to reconsider its plans. The grandiose scheme was abandoned and only the first leg of the motorway was to go ahead; it is scheduled for completion in 1983–4.

'It will be the mid-1990s before the renewal problem, as presently defined, will be solved'

The Housing Executive had the unenviable task of implementing the redevelopment plans envisaged by Matthew and the Building Design Partnership. As with the urban motorway, so schemes for demolishing old dwellings and rehousing the displaced families had to be modified partly as a result of popular resistance. In the Shankill, for example, blight had been given 14 years to spread in the period between the time when the plans were first mooted and when the area was finally vested in January 1974. Only a small number of those families displaced could be rehoused in the same area; competition for completed dwellings was intense and made more difficult by squatting. Blocks of flats, four to six storeys high, were built with their backs to the Shankill Road to act as noise barriers to the urban motorway. Already popular opposition had led to the abandonment of plans for 15-storey flats. A joint study by the University of Surrey and the Shankill Community Council in September 1974 found that in blocks of flats in Upper Townsend Street,

difficulties included the noise from people walking up the stairs, the worry about fire, the fact of not having a 'proper' front door. . . lifts so rarely work. . . There are those who are not well and find climbing the stairs very hard. . . many of the small children hardly ever get out as their mothers are afraid to let them down the stairs on their own.

In addition, the very design of these 'Weetabix' blocks helped to destroy the sense of community in the area. In his moving study, *The rape and plunder of the Shankill*, Ron Weiner records one resident's feeling of loss:

It was a grand road to live on. In fact it was one of the best roads for shopping and kindness and people were so friendly and happy. What a pity to watch it just dying away fast. It would break your heart because we loved this road. To me the old Shankill was heaven.

Aware of the failure of high-rise dwellings in British cities, the Housing Executive returned to more traditional designs; 1,200 modern purpose-built homes had been demolished by 1982, an unlettable block of flats had been sold to the private sector and another block had been offered for sale. Under the banner headline, 'The 1,200 Homes Nobody Wants,' the *Belfast Telegraph* of 15 April 1982 reported that there were 1,132 vacant properties in Belfast, 'the majority being difficult-to-let property in Highfield, Glencairn, Blackmountain, Eglinton flats – which have been put up for sale – and acquired properties in the mid-Shankill area'. The new low-rise housing, however, combined traditional and varied styles with modern amenities; the Housing Executive buildings at Cromac, Bridge-End, Sandy Row and the bottom of the Oldpark rightly drew admiring comment from both outside experts and those who lived in them.

If high-rise flats were unacceptable, then strict modern standards made it impossible to rehouse every family within each area where unfit dwellings had been demolished. For many the solution was to move to the growth centres, though generous resettlement grants were unable to prevent Craigavon being anything but an extremely expensive failure. The whole problem of finding suitable sites was greatly increased by the political and sectarian strife in Belfast. Hopes that polarisation of the two communities in the new estates could be avoided were quickly dashed. People felt secure only when they were surrounded by others of their own religion and Harry Simpson, the Housing Executive's first Director General, observed: 'I don't think it is possible for us, because of our ideas, to try to force people into living where they don't feel safe.' As the Community Relations Commission pointed out in 1974: 'The basic problem is not a lack of compassion, but a lack of housing in areas where victims of intimidation are prepared to live.' Many estates in the suburbs and growth centres were exclusively Protestant in composition, but Catholics — apart from those who could afford to buy houses in the mixed middle-class suburbs — tended to feel safe only in west Belfast. The waiting list for west Belfast became, and remains, immensely long. The only merciful solution was to breech the Matthew Stop Line; Poleglass was marked as the site to relieve the pressure, despite objections from some loyalist politicians. When Poleglass is completed, residential Belfast will be connected in a broad band with Lisburn; 368 houses had been finished by July 1982 and the second stage, to be known as the Stewartstown Neighbourhood, was launched with the aim of providing another 1,150 homes.

Much had been achieved but the task ahead remained formidable. A second House Condition Survey was carried out in 1979: 2,500 new houses had been built since 1974, 13,000 unfit dwellings had been demolished, and altogether the dwelling stock had fallen from 123,120 to 112,681. In other words, demolition of old housing was faster than the building of new homes within the city boundary. 41% of the total dwelling stock still required action; when faced with cuts in public expenditure Charles Brett, Chairman of the Housing Executive, declared on 16 October 1980:

The figures for overcrowding in Belfast are just double those in Manchester, one of the worst housed cities in England. The proportion of houses lacking at least one amenity is just double too. Over two-thirds of the pointed applicants on the Belfast waiting lists are in genuine and urgent need of rehousing. . . Over the past year, the Board of the Executive has searched with increasing desperation for additional sources of funds. . .

Rising costs pushed rents above the level which many tenants could afford to pay, particularly as inflation and economic difficulties increased the number of people living in or around the poverty level, especially between 1980 and 1982. In 'Belfast Housing', a paper prepared for a Housing Executive in-service conference in March 1982, Frank O'Connor pointed out that the waiting list in Belfast was 10,500 and concluded:

If the pattern of the five year survey is maintained then it will be the mid-1990s before

Rev. Ian Paisley keeps a lonely vigil at the gates of Stormont parliament buildings during the loyalist strike of May 1977. Though the strike was largely a failure, Paisley's political fortunes rapidly recovered and in the European election of June 1979 he won just under 30% of first preference votes, 8% ahead of the Official Unionist Party vote for two candidates. (Pacemaker)

the renewal problem, as presently defined, will be solved.

Failure to find a solution: 1974–82

Attempts to tackle Belfast's housing problem and to devise better social and economic strategies were affected by the continuing violence in two contradictory ways. On the one hand, the protracted disruption of large areas of the city interrupted the implementation of improvement schemes and discouraged new industrial investment. On the other hand, world-wide publicity given to the conflict impelled Westminster to spend greater sums of money than before in striving to repair the neglect of the past. Belfast's problems were examined more professionally and more intensively than those of any other city of comparable size in the EEC – indeed, public servants are apt to remark that such investigation is the fastest growing industry in the city. Meanwhile, the search for solutions in the political field continued.

The collapse of the power-sharing Executive in 1974 ensured that direct rule from London would continue for the time being. In an attempt to reduce the level of violence the Labour government pulled the army out of some sensitive areas and the RUC was asked to take its place; inconclusive negotiations were made with the Provisional IRA; and it was decided to end special category status for detainees. In a new search for a resolution of the Ulster question the government held elections for a Constitutional Convention on 1 May 1975 (the seventh poll in Northern Ireland in little more than two years); out of 24 city seats the UUUC coalition won 13, Alliance 4, SDLP 3, the Unionist Party of Northern Ireland (Faulkner's Unionists) 2, NILP 1, and Independent Loyalists 1. As the UUUC held 47 out of 78 seats there was no hope of another power-sharing formula being accepted. Merlyn Rees, the Secretary of State for Northern Ireland, rejected the Convention Report which recommended a return to simple majority rule and by 1976 all hope of a political settlement for

* Alf McCreary, *Survivors* (Century Books, 1976), pp. 177–8.

the foreseeable failure had disappeared.

Meanwhile murders, bombings, and other violent incidents continued to disfigure the life of the city. To give but one example, in April 1975 twelve-year-old Tony Meli was cruelly wounded by an explosion in his parents' café. His father described what happened:

. . . I saw Tony lying among the glass and the blood and the debris. His right forearm had been blown off and he was rubbing his eyes with the stump, and crying. . . He had lost a forearm, his eye had gone and the other one was threatened. He had a terrible hole in his chest, his lung was badly damaged, he had lost three fingers on his left hand and his face was scarred. The blue plastic radio had been packed with nails and when it was switched on the explosives inside detonated and hurled the nails in all directions, mostly into Tony. He was in the operating theatre for nine hours, and not just a couple but literally teams of doctors and other specialists worked on him. . .*

In the summer of 1976, at a time when there seemed to be some abatement of violence, the Provisional IRA murdered Christopher Ewart-Biggs, the new British Ambassador to the Republic of Ireland — never had the prospect of future reconciliation seemed so distant.

In August 1976 Mrs Anne Maguire was walking near her home at Finaghy with her four children when a car crashed into them; Mrs Maguire was badly injured and three of her children were killed. The driver, a member of the Provisional IRA, had just been shot dead at the wheel of the car in a gun battle with the British Army. Next day Mrs Maguire's sister, Mairead Corrigan, and Mrs Betty Williams, who had witnessed the tragedy, founded the Peace People. For many years teachers, community workers, and groups such as Women Together and Protestant And Catholic Encounter had been working hard to promote reconciliation in the city, but this new peace movement captured the imagination of Belfast citizens to an extent that others previously had not. The world applauded when in a march through the Shankill, residents warmly shook hands with nuns and Catholic priests. In torrential rain the Peace People marched up the Falls to a more hostile reception; the author was in the procession and was struck by the contrast between the middle-class marchers in his section (in other sections the working classes were well represented), well protected by expensive coats from the downpour, while those who hurled abuse and stones through the delapidated lower Falls were drenched, inadequately protected by cheap anoraks. Certainly the Peace People's analysis of the conflict was simplistic and the solutions offered often arcane and unrealistic, but the recognition they won abroad was deserved. They found it impossible, however, to sustain widespread support in Belfast — they were prophets with least honour in their own city.

The conflict continued but the Provisionals now directed their offensive principally against the security forces thus creating a more peaceful atmosphere for ordinary citizens. Loyalists in the city were turning increasingly to the Rev Ian Paisley for leadership, and it was he who launched another strike — to demand tougher security measures — in May 1977. The new Secretary of State, Roy Mason, responded more rapidly than his predecessor, however, and the 'stoppage' failed. Mason was energetic in his attempts to help the Belfast economy and it was under him that a deal with John De Lorean was made in August 1978 which seemed to show a real determination to tackle unemployment blackspots in the city. Lord Melchett proved to be the most popular British minister since direct rule had begun, showing unexampled energy in visiting schools, calling conferences and establishing good relations with community groups; the new leisure centres in the city were largely his creation. Don Concannon also earned a deserved reputation for zeal in promoting improvement in the inner city. Revelations of mistreatment of prisoners at Castlereagh tarnished Mason's record, however. The Provisional IRA launched a new bombing campaign at Christmas 1977 and many small stores in the city were destroyed by fire bombs. The worst incidents occurred early in 1978 and in February a bomb killed 12 people at the La Mon hotel in east Belfast, bringing considerable revulsion against the Provisionals in Catholic housing estates.

As the life of the Labour government drew to a close in 1979, sporadic fire bombing continued. In April, for example, the Motor Taxation Office in Ormeau Avenue was destroyed; the author's colleagues and students, housed in an upper storey, escaped immolation by a perilous 3½ minutes. In the May general election the Democratic Unionist Party, founded by the Rev Ian Paisley and Desmond Boal in September 1971, made two striking gains in Belfast at the expense of the Official Unionist Party: Johnny McQuade won North Belfast and Peter Robinson beat the sitting member, William Craig, in East Belfast by a margin of 54 votes.

Those who thought Paisley's star had been descending since the failure of

Continuing unrest: rioting in Castle Street following a demonstration against the Queen's visit to the province during the Silver Jubilee celebrations, August 1977. (Pacemaker)

The funeral of Bobby Sands on 7 May 1981. Elected MP for Fermanagh – South Tyrone on 9 April 1981, Sands died on hunger strike on 5 May 1981. Owen Carron, who won the seat shortly afterwards, helps to support the coffin. (Pacemaker)

THREATS

If you know anything about terrorist activities – threats, murders, or explosives – please speak <u>now</u> to the CONFIDENTIAL TELEPHONE

BELFAST 652155

* Review team, *Economic and industrial strategy for Northern Ireland* (HMSO, 1976), p. 66.

the 1977 loyalist strike were given a further jolt on 7 June when, in the elections for the European parliament, he got 170,688 votes – more than twice the number obtained by his nearest loyalist rival, John Taylor. No longer was Paisley's support confined to the workers of east Belfast and the people of Ballymena. Humphrey Atkins headed the new Conservative administration at Stormont; even if Belfast had become a more peaceful city by the autumn of 1979, the murders of Airey Neave and Lord Mountbatten, and the killing of 18 soldiers at Warrenpoint, gave every indication that Ulster society was as divided as it ever had been and that the Secretary of State's attempts to find an acceptable political solution were doomed to failure.

In 1980 the 'dirty protest' was gathering strength at the Maze Prison following the withdrawal of privileges which had accompanied political status. This became better known as the 'H-Block' protest in 1981; Bobby Sands began his hunger strike on 7 March, was elected MP for Fermanagh-South Tyrone on 9 April, and died on the sixty-sixth day of his fast on 5 May 1981. Feelings in many parts of the city were now running very high but the Westminster government refused to make concessions to what it considered to be blackmail; it was not until 3 October 1981, after ten men had starved themselves to death, that Provisional Sinn Fein announced the end of the hunger strike.

On 14 November the Rev Robert Bradford, MP for South Belfast, and the caretaker of the building in Finaghy where he regularly met his constituents, were assassinated. Paisley organised a protest demonstration at the City Hall and in Belfast, as in the province as a whole, political polarisation was so complete that plans for 'rolling devolution' devised by the new Secretary of State, Jim Prior, seemed to lack any real hope of being widely accepted.

From recession to crisis

The Northern Ireland economy is in serious difficulty and, if no measures are taken, the outlook is grim. Unemployment is 10% and, on present policies, it is unlikely to

216 days of protest in the Maze

A chronology of how the hunger strike progressed over 216 days and 10 deaths

March 1—on the fifth anniversary of the withdrawal of special status, hunger strike is started by Bobby Sands, previously officer commanding the IRA at the Maze.

April 9 — Fernmanagh - South Tyrone byelection. Labour's spokesman on Northern Ireland Mr Don Concannon tells Commons: "A vote for Mr Sands is a vote of a Provo." More than 30,000 people—about 6 per cent of Northern Ireland's Catholic population—elect Mr Sands as MP.

April 24—European Commission for Human Rights sends four-man delegation to Belfast in an abortive attempt to resolve the dispute.

April 29—Pope's personal secretary flies to Belfast in another abortive mediation attempt.

May 5—Sands dies on 66th day of his fast.

May 7 — Sands's funeral is attended by 50,000 people—in population terms equivalent to well over one million in Britain.

May 8— ᵗʰᵉ ⁱˢʰ ᵒ

Guardian: 5 October 1981

fall below that level, whatever upturn there may be in the national economy. . .*

With these words W.G.H. Quigley and his review team summarised the economic condition of the province in their report of 1976. What had happened to the promise of the 1960s when industrial production, especially in the Belfast area, had grown much faster in Northern Ireland than in the UK as a whole and only a little more slowly than in West Germany?

Though it is difficult to quantify, political turbulence must have had a most damaging impact on Belfast's attraction as a suitable city for new manufacturing investment. Financial compensation for destruction caused by the conflict could not make up entirely for the havoc wrought. When Grundig closed down its Dunmurry plant in October 1980, one of the reasons given by the management for doing so was the existence of 'disturbances of a political nature'. In general, however, it was not so much that multi-national firms wanted to leave the region but more that prospective investors were deflected elsewhere by the violence. Writing in the *Cambridge Journal of Economics*, Bob Rowthorn estimated that 24,000 jobs had been lost due to the conflict; this, surely, was no more than an informed guess. Nevertheless, output in the Irish Republic rose by 50% in the 1970s when the Ulster economy suffered repeated setbacks – in the 1960s growth in the North and South had been developing at an almost equal rate and the Republic's better performance in the following decade cannot have been due solely to lavish borrowing and superior inducements held out to multi-national firms.

There are reasons for believing that the city's economy would have run into grave difficulties by the mid-1970s even if the most perfect peace had prevailed. The closing of the Belfast Ropeworks and of the Rolls-Royce factory at Dundonald early in this period indicated dangers ahead. That such a large and long-established firm as the Ropeworks could go out of business was a reminder that Belfast's indigenous industries were still in decline even when world trade was buoyant. The decay of the city's staple industries had been so rapid that expansion in manufacturing output in the 1960s had not had a great impact on employment; by 1970 about 65,000 new industrial jobs had been created with the help of government money, mostly in the Belfast region, and yet total manufacturing employment in the province was only 180,000 as compared with 185,000 in 1956. The closure of the Rolls-Royce plant indicated that when parent firms ran into difficulties they naturally shut down their outlying operations first. In addition, the arrival of new firms coincided with the shifting of labour-intensive industries to less developed areas while computers and electronics began to revolutionise methods of production in the most advanced regions. In time, factories in the Belfast area had to adopt some of this advanced but labour-saving technology to remain competitive. Indeed, Belfast helped to pioneer a relatively simple technical development which led to the loss of jobs – roll-on/roll-off containers at the docks replaced time-consuming and expensive labour. As Larne has short sea routes, it proved the most suitable port for this unitised freight, and Belfast began to lose its dominant position in the province's trade.

In 1973–4, the oil crisis dealt a severe blow to the Belfast region. By then Belfast had become more dependent on cheap oil than perhaps any other city of similar size in Britain. Now, far from the commercial hub of the EEC, the city had to cope with rising transport costs for both its imported raw materials and its exported finished goods. The Belfast area had become a world centre of

303

synthetic fibre production, consuming prodigious quantities of oil in the manufacturing process; now, almost at the stroke of an OPEC pen, the whole industry (facing in addition Far Eastern and American competition) became unprofitable. Inducements offered to outside firms remained generous but by this time other states, faced with recession, were holding out equally tempting grants and Belfast lost the special attraction for industrialists it had once had.

In 1979 the economy of the western world, and that of the UK in particular, took a downward plunge, and by the second quarter of 1980 this depression was leaving a trail of devastation in Belfast. Between 1979 and the autumn of 1981 no less than 110 substantial manufacturing firms in the province closed down. In the past Belfast had been more immune to the worst effects of economic downturns than other parts of Ulster, but now the number of businesses collapsing both inside the city boundary and just beyond it caused widespread alarm. In 1979 closures in the Belfast area included Belfast Cables; Electro Photonics; Peter Pan Bakeries; Antrim Crystal; Gordon & Flack; and the May Street Handkerchief Works. In 1980 the largest firms to shut down were Courtaulds, Larne; Hill & Craig; John Sherrard; Albion Ltd; Ulidia Factory; Beecham Foods; Rosebank Weaving; Walker Caledon; Lombard Manufacturing; Watson Malcolmson; Filtrona; Magee Clothing; Carrington Printers; and Grundig.

Economic decline had become a major crisis.

'The factory resembled a well kept graveyard'

The De Lorean sports car factory in Belfast officially closed yesterday and the funeral, such as it was, passed off uneventfully. The obsequies were performed by the 1,500 workers and the Department of Health and Social Security who kept open two social security offices on the Bank Holiday, so the workers could sign on the dole. The factory resembled a well kept graveyard. . . The presses, huge extractor fans, ovens and jigs were silent; about 1,000 cars sat motionless on the assembly line, vainly waiting for the engineers and fitters to transform them into status symbols for American roads. The tragedy attendant on all funerals was in the pride with which Mr Brendan Mackin, a shop steward and the former De Lorean production foreman, guided me through the factory. As he demonstrated a gull-wing door, it squeaked and he said: 'Don't be put off by the noise: it's just the new hinges'. On the driver's seat a quality control inspector's note lay discarded. . .

With this account, published in the *Guardian* on 1 June 1982, David Beresford described the end of the most energetic attempt to bring industrial regeneration to west Belfast. Not long after it had been launched in 1978, the De Lorean factory had had to face a slump in the American automobile market, and the company had lurched from one financial crisis to another. Though Westminster had made around £80 million available to the firm, De Lorean was probably under-capitalised – after all it had cost about £500 million to put British Leyland's Mini Metro on the road. On 24 May 1982 the official receiver announced his failure to keep the company in being.

The feeling of gloom which had followed the closure of British Enkalon in Antrim on 15 July 1981 was now intensified by the shutdown of De Lorean. Some firms were entirely unaffected by the depression, but most which survived were forced to lay off part of their work force. On 19 January 1982 Shorts announced that they would pay off another 650 workers, in addition to the 300 redundancies and early retirements disclosed in October 1981. Harland & Wolff had been saved in 1975 only by a government grant of £50 million; the shipyard made losses of £43 million in 1979 and £32 million in 1980, and Westminster provided another £42½ million subsidy in July 1980. In 1982 a £29 million order was secured for a 170,000-ton British Steel bulk carrier – an order which according to the company's chairman, Dr Vivian Wadsworth, was 'in the nick of time' and had prevented the loss of 800 jobs. 'One swallow does not make a summer and one ship does not make Harland & Wolff,' warned a spokesman for the workers, Jimmy Blair.

A paper prepared by the Research Department of the Irish Congress of Trade Unions in October 1981 showed that most of the leading firms in the Belfast area had reduced the size of their workforce since 1976; among them were: Harland & Wolff (9,300 to 7,000); Gallahers (2,525 to 2,002); the Sirocco Works (900 to 700); Goblin BSR (375 to 320); Blackstaff Holdings (480 to 197); and Mackies (3,700 to 3,200). In one of these firms, the author was told, the employee who hands out the redundancy notes is known as 'the Angel of Death' and men laid off have been seen to shed tears openly.

The economic crisis coincided with the implementation of new policies by Margaret Thatcher's Conservative administration. As cuts in public expenditure began to have effect, the construction industry quickly ran into acute difficulties. Before this, government spending on capital projects had been exceptionally high by UK standards; between 1979 and the autumn of 1981 unemployment amongst those previously employed in construction rose by over 75%, reducing employment in the industry to the lowest level recorded since the Second World War. For the first time since 1945 service employment, which had grown every year without exception, dropped in 1981. On paper the reduction in government spending did not appear severe, but as the purchasing power of the pound sterling continued to fall, the effect was to magnify the economic crisis affecting Belfast. It was not even necessary for the government to make public servants redundant – refusal to take on new staff or to replace those who retired in itself blighted the prospects of those entering the labour market for the first time.

Not even news of the horrific effects of IRA car bombs in London, which killed or mortally wounded ten soldiers, could push details of unemployment statistics off the front page of the *Belfast Telegraph* on 20 July 1982. A total of 21.1% of the insured working population of the province was unemployed; the figure for the Belfast area was 17.8% but since this region includes Lisburn, Bangor, Carrickfergus, Larne and other places normally possessing low unemployment rates, the percentage for Belfast alone was certainly about the regional average.

The changing face of Belfast

For the ordinary citizens of Belfast the most dangerous and disruptive period of the Troubles had been between 1969 and 1974, when street violence and intimidation had been followed by a sustained bombing campaign, then a spate of sectarian assassinations, and finally the loyalist strike. Thereafter the conflict became primarily a struggle between the security forces and the paramilitaries, and slowly and cautiously people began to return in greater numbers to the city centre.

Belfast by then bore many marks of the preceding struggle but the city's ability to adjust and recuperate had been remarkable. Electricity and water supplies were quickly restored after bomb attacks on installations and though

by 1976 the Post Office had suffered frequent raids on its sub-offices, the loss
of 175 of its vehicles, and the destruction of 29 telephone exchanges, it was
rare indeed for the city's daily post not to be delivered. Between 1969 and the
middle of 1975, 200 buses had been burned or otherwise wrecked in Belfast
but despite the murder of ten employees on duty and frequent disruption on
some routes, the service kept going. Private enterprise played its part; Belfast
Corporation Transport had been handed over to the private sector and the
new Citybus found itself facing spirited competition from two 'black taxi'
services, one on the Falls and the other on the Shankill, serving a predominantly working-class clientèle at prices sufficiently profitable to themselves but still undercutting bus fares which were amongst the highest in
Europe. These taxis appear to have been controlled to a certain extent by
paramilitaries; certainly protection money was paid by the operators, and
indeed by the proprietors of many drinking and gambling establishments in
the city. Though all three of the city's railway stations were destroyed by fire
and bomb, the trains kept running and new stations were built at East Bridge
Street and Botanic Avenue. The Troubles did help to precipitate the closure of
the economically ailing cross-channel ferry services to Heysham and Ard-
rossan by destroying the tourist trade but air services continued without
interruption, though at the cost of making Aldergrove the most closely
defended airport in Europe.

The appearance of the city centre had been altered considerably by
incendiary and bomb attacks. Between 1971 and 1973 three fires caused a loss
of around £1 million each and the destruction of most of the Belfast Co-
operative Society's department store in York Street caused damage estimated
to be £10 million. The most famous hotels, such as the Grand Central and the

Midland, closed down; the Russell Court Hotel on the Lisburn Road was so severely damaged by a bomb in its underground car park that it was forced to shut down only weeks after it had opened, though its shell still stands; the Europa Hotel, completed on the eve of the Troubles, was attacked more often than any other hotel, but survived as the principal haven for journalists reporting the conflict. By the middle of 1975 over 400 public houses in the province, more than half of them in Belfast, had been damaged or destroyed; while some were rebuilt, many familiar bars disappeared forever, and for a time illegal drinking clubs proliferated.

The gaps left by Victorian buildings bombed or pulled down in the city centre were in general filled by ugly office blocks. There had been some element of planning in the building of central Belfast in the late eighteenth century and again in the nineteenth century; now all attempts to produce a pleasing overall effect seem to have been abandoned. The new skyscraper in the City Hospital grounds – costing over £50 million and yet to be opened and named – is the most imposing of Belfast's recent structures; the Northern Bank in Donegall Square West is perhaps the least tasteless of the office blocks; but, overall, the large modern buildings around the city centre create a soulless atmosphere.

From 1975 onwards the life of central Belfast showed signs of revival. New stores – such as Marks & Spencer, Boots, Penneys, and Dunnes – replaced those which had been lost, though suburban supermarkets at, for example, Glengormley, Dunmurry, and even as far away as Bangor, Lisburn and Newtownards, permanently captured trade lost in the city centre. Because of the high level of city-centre bombings, the main shopping area had been enclosed since 1972 by metal security barriers; all pedestrians were searched by uniformed security men and women, and virtually all vehicles were excluded. The traffic-free environment produced by this extraordinary system, which continues to the time of writing, was further enhanced from 1976 by the creation of well-designed pedestrian precincts. 'Spruce-up' schemes did something to mask the spreading decay in the inner city: graffiti were removed and cheerful murals were commissioned; rest areas were set aside; and the main streets were decorated with flower containers and ornate lamp-standards. Money being spent on the Lagan Walkway at lower Ormeau might have been better spent on tackling pollution, for those who swim in the vicinity of Shaw's Bridge on hot summer days undoubtedly put their health at risk. The 'Blackstaff nuisance' remained: the BBC programme 'Tonight' put that stream first in its 'Finger of Filth' competition to find the most polluted waters in the United Kingdom. It was just as well, then, that fine new swimming pools and leisure centres were dotted about the city by the end of the period.

Characterised as it was by violence, inner-city decay and an alarming growth of unemployment, this period in Belfast's history was unquestionably one of decline; yet, in some respects, these were years of achievement. Belfast acquired some of the best medical facilities in the United Kingdom: these included the Musgrave Park Hospital Orthopaedic Department (1970); geriatric units and other extensions to the Royal Victoria Hospital, and to the Ulster Hospital, in 1979–80; and new health centres at the Holywood Arches (1978) and Dunluce Avenue (1979). The Royal Victoria Hospital became renowned for its expert treatment of heart disease and of injuries dealt by bomb and bullet.

Against this bleak background a surprisingly vigorous cultural life continued. Under the direction of Michael Barnes, the Queen's University Festival, founded in the 1960s by Michael Emmerson, attracted top performers to Belfast for an annual fortnight of international music and theatre. For the rest of the year, citizens were entertained with considerable élan by the youthful Ulster Orchestra; in addition to its regular Ulster Hall concerts, the Orchestra played for the annual week of 'Grand' opera during which visiting principals sang in works from the traditional repertoire, backed by a local chorus.

In the visual arts, there was a proliferation of styles and effects, some slavishly copied from international sources. In Belfast, however, some of the more serious painters rejected this rigid adherence to London and New York fashions. Colin Middleton, although apparently eclectic, continued to excite the Ulster audience with his surrealistic images and vivid expressionistic colours. While the paintings of Gerard Dillon remained figurative, they experimented with the prospect of abstraction in his sad but exuberantly coloured pierrots. The tensions and social disturbance of the period produced some response among painters, most notably in the work of Joe McWilliams; although fundamentally a lyrical landscape painter, McWilliams produced some of the most significant images of the Troubles.

Local writing experienced a new stimulus with the establishment of two Belfast publishing houses, Blackstaff Press (founded by Jim and Diane Gracey) and Appletree Press (founded by John Murphy). The literary output of these houses, and indeed cultural life in the province generally, was strongly supported by financial assistance from the Arts Council of Northern Ireland.

The remarkable literary flowering of these years was most striking in poetry. The reputations of Heaney, Hewitt, Longley and Mahon continued to grow, while the work of poets like Frank Ormsby, Paul Muldoon, Medbh McGuckian, Tom Paulin and Ciarán Carson drew international critical attention. To a remarkable extent, poetry seemed to be concentrated around Queen's University, particularly the English Society under the clear-sighted direction of Edna Longley.

Of the fiction writers to emerge in this period, Bernard MacLaverty has the widest reputation with work published in Ireland, Britain, America, Switzerland and Sweden. Sam McAughtry, with his stories about life in Belfast's dockland between the wars, is regarded by many as the authentic voice of the northern working class.

The Lyric built a handsome new theatre in Ridgeway Street by the lower reaches of the Lagan; there the policies established in Derryvolgie Avenue were unflinchingly maintained with a steady growth of professionalism – most striking in the recent appointment as writer-in-residence of Martin Lynch, a young political activist from Turf Lodge, whose plays *Dockers* and *The Interrogation of Ambrose Fogarty* had electrified audiences of an unusually wide social range. Graham Reid had his first play, *The Death of Humpty Dumpty,* performed at the Abbey; like Lynch, he has a sharp ear for Belfast working-class speech and draws on memories of his Shankill childhood and employment as a hospital worker and teacher to write plays which engage the real substance of experience in these troubled times, plays which are full of intelligent ideas and satiric humour. The Lyric absorbed most of the Arts Council grants to theatre until the end of the 1970s when the Arts Theatre (a self-supporting popular theatre in the previous decade) re-opened with its help. The Group had closed during the early years of the Troubles; then it was completely refurbished by the City Council and re-opened in 1980 for the use of amateur groups at a very reasonable charge – an inspired decision which was immediately successful.

Real progress was made in education, which by 1970–1 was absorbing 42.8% of the city's rates allocated to services. Older schools, such as McQuiston, Wolfhill and Perth Street, were closed; new primary schools, such as Holy Cross, Vere Foster, Ligoniel and St Bernadette's were built; most areas were belatedly provided with nursery schools; the Queen's University Teachers' Centre was opened, and outcentre and other support services were greatly improved; and, with the fall in the size of classes, teaching methods became more imaginative and enlightened. In 1952–3 there were 669 classes with more than 40 pupils each in the Education Committee's primary schools (32 classes had more than 54); in 1962–3 there were 186 such classes; and by 1982 there were no classes larger than 40 in all the schools managed by the Belfast Education and Library Board. Expected change, in other respects, did not come. Attempts to introduce comprehensive secondary education were successfully resisted and the temporary adoption of a 'transfer procedure' in place of 11-plus qualifying tests merely made it easier for some grammar schools to maintain their enrolment at a time when the city's school population was falling. Also, as Norman McNeilly rightly observed: 'Lord Londonderry's original vision of 1923 had disappeared into the mists of time, and the dual system of Roman Catholic and Protestant schools was the grim reality.' It was right not to attempt to force integration at a time of strife but more could have been done to make facilities available to those parents of both traditions who did want their children educated together – the only determined effort in this direction, the setting up of Lagan College in 1980, was made by private enterprise.

The rapid expansion of further education in these years did much to promote the non-sectarian education of young people over the age of sixteen. The College of Art was completed in 'Blitz Square' (opposite the York Street Co-operative store) in 1968; the College of Technology so increased its work that even after the departure of art, business and commercial courses and the completion of its Millfield building, it was forced to use other annexes in the city centre; Rupert Stanley College not only extended the range of its courses but also established a network of evening centres across the city; and the College of Commerce, detached from the College of Technology in 1965, became the College of Business Studies in 1970, with a large new building housing its catering, business, secretarial, and academic courses. The decision made in 1968 to build the Ulster College at Jordanstown greatly improved opportunities in higher education but also contributed to over-capacity in teacher training; proposals to merge Belfast's colleges of education in 1981–2 were strenuously and successfully opposed by the Catholic Church and the *Irish News*.

The Belfast Education and Library Board replaced the Belfast Education Committee in 1973, a year which saw radical changes in the government of the city. Local government reorganisation and direct rule from Westminster deprived councillors of many of their previous powers when Belfast City Council took the place of Belfast Corporation. Irreconcilable political differences did not prevent a steady rise in the prestige of the city fathers, an increasing number of whom were drawn directly from the working classes. From 1973 councillors' discussions were less often characterised by bitter disputation; this, to a large extent, was because little real power remained with them after the imposition of direct rule from Westminster. Nevertheless, the conscientious way in which those who were elected Lord Mayor from 1973 carried out their duties improved the standing of that office in the whole community, and many detected a new sense of civic pride and responsibility in the City Hall.

'Changes. . . among the most fundamental to affect Belfast since its early days'

City churches are closing. The existence of schools with fewer pupils continues to be threatened. Houses in the wasteland of redevelopment are bricked up. Areas like Cromac, Crumlin and Central show dramatic population losses. These changes, which are among the most fundamental to affect Belfast since its early days, will have a crucial bearing on the way in which the city is administered by the Council and financed by the ratepayers.

This editorial comment was made by the *Belfast Telegraph* on 8 July 1982, the day that the results of the April 1981 Census were published. The population of Belfast had fallen by a quarter in a decade, that is, from 416,679 to 305,763 – 40,000 more of a drop than the experts had estimated. Having closed Ulsterville Primary School a few days before, officials in the Academy Street education offices were probably least surprised by the census figures: the number of five-to-nine-year-old children at school in the Belfast area had dropped by almost 14,000 between 1971 and 1978, and secondary school enrolment had fallen by over 10,000 between 1969 and 1982. Not only is the population diminishing as a result of emigration and redevelopment; it is also steadily ageing. Is Belfast dying?

William Black, in a trenchant survey of the province's economy published in the December 1981 issue of the *Irish Banking Review*, came to the bleak conclusion that, even if there is a rapid recovery elsewhere, here 'it is questionable whether there are a sufficient number of potential expansion points in the existing industrial structure to provide the basis for a substantial recovery in manufacturing employment'. In April 1982 the Belfast Junior Chamber of Commerce invited experts to its conference, 'Belfast 2000', to speculate about the city's future to the end of the century; though there was much talk of the transformation which could follow from technical progress, not a single speaker foresaw a significant fall in unemployment in Belfast for many years to come. Indeed, Belfast has shown so many symptoms of political, social, and economic malaise that the city, together with Naples, was picked out for special consideration by the EEC; so far, curiously little has come of this.

Belfast's predicament is by no means unique. If the city's economy is in difficulty so too is that of almost every major urban area in Britain north of Birmingham. In 1982 the whole of the western world is in recession and Belfast's unemployment rate is almost exactly that of Chicago. If there are substantial areas of Belfast where more than half the school leavers are unemployed, there are similar areas in other British and Irish cities, and 52% of black people between the ages of 15 and 23 are unemployed in July 1982 in the United States of America. Present unemployment figures are indeed as bad as those of 50 years ago, but living standards are far higher, and immeasurably higher than those prevailing in developing countries. While Belfast is afflicted by inner city decay this problem is universal in advanced industrial states. The

310

scale of the housing problem is far greater in London and, unlike the metropolis, Belfast enjoys unified housing management; the quality of recent publicly-controlled estates is exceptionally high, and the Housing Executive began 1,900 dwellings in 1981–2 – the highest number in Belfast for several years. Though Belfast is still disfigured by bloodshed and communal divisions, the total number of fatalities in the past fourteen years, each one tragic in itself, is nonetheless smaller than the death toll among civilians alone in Beirut in the summer of 1982.

Postscript

'So bitterly cold was it that Parson Woodforde recorded in his diary that the contents of his chamber pot under his bed had frozen solid.' It was essential to introduce lively detail into a history class, meeting on a dark evening in the city centre in 1972. I was describing the invasion of Holland in 1794–5 when the French revolutionary armies advanced across the frozen Waal and the cavalry galloped over the frozen Zuider Zee to capture the Dutch fleet. I continued: 'The British troops came under sudden and unexpected attack,' and with that there was a burst of automatic gunfire close by. The evening students merely groaned; by now they had become used to explosions and shots, being able in some cases to identify the weapons used by the sounds they emitted. The firing continued and became general, and the evening supervisor gently suggested that all classes should close early. The supervisor and Fred, a burly mature student, quickly took joint command and ensured that every student and employee found a place in a car. I was in Fred's car; the pointer on the speedometer touched 75 m.p.h. as he drove through Shaftesbury Square, his racing engine failing to drown the sound of gunfire. The shooting continued all night and I learned next day that almost all parts of the city had been affected. Not one student or employee had been injured, and not one provocative comment had been made throughout, though our political views must have been very varied as we came from all parts of the city.

The incident demonstrated for me that an important minority refused to be divided and that the greatest enemy of those who sought to change or to defend the province through violence was the determination of so many in Belfast and elsewhere to carry on a normal life as far as possible. Educational institutions remained open both in the city centre and in the most disturbed areas throughout the Troubles. Cinemas, theatres and discos continued to attract customers. Even in the worst periods of violence people came into the city centre for entertainment. I remember emerging from the 'Duke of York' late one evening in 1972 to find two drunk men supporting each other and wading through a sea of broken glass. 'Watch yourself, Charlie,' said one, 'it's desperate frosty tonight; don't slip on that ice.'

The re-opening of the Arts Theatre and the Group Theatre marked the turning of a corner, and the Ulster Hall won back its audiences for popular music. Van Morrison – the man who made Cyprus Avenue renowned across the civilised world – returned to enthral devoted fans in his native city. The queues for Disney's *Snow White* (which, to the indignation of the *Irish News,* had been banned for children in Belfast in 1938) outside the city centre cinemas in Christmas 1981 were longer than the queues I had seen in Dublin. For many, the refurbishing of the Grand Opera House and its reopening with Brian Friel's play *Translations* in the autumn of 1980, was the most striking outward and visible sign of the city's refusal to die.

The Grand Opera House could not have been restored by local funds alone. By 1982 Belfast had become a city ever more dependent on a kind of drip-feed from Westminster. Damaged as the city is by indigenous violence, world-wide recession and the austere economic policy of central government, it is still a living entity with the power of growth and renewal. Throughout its turbulent history it has shown a capacity for stoic endurance, adaptation and creativity. We have lived and are living through dark days in our community which may be regarded as a microcosm of an embattled planet facing the intractable problems of the arms race, the inequitable distribution of world resources and the abuse and thoughtless destruction of those resources; if we believe the problems are insoluble we make them so. A slough of despond provides a poor vantage point. To lose hope would be to betray the past and destroy the future.

Oh, my country! when wilt thou learn to feel, that only shame and ruin can spring from thy intestine broils: when will thy children love as brethren, and thy fair fields cease to be reddened by fratricide blood – blood shed to slake the insane thirst of party, pride, and power, and shed often at the bidding of men who trample thy rights and glory in the dust – thy disgrace, thy bitter, taunting foes? Sir, I look on every man as an enemy to our land, be he Protestant or Romanist, who cherishes the spirit of faction, who seeks the domination of a party, or who, to further what he may even conscientiously deem a good cause, will kindle and inflame the bad passions of an ignorant and imbruted mob. Such is the wretched practice which has been pursued for centuries in this unfortunate island, and which has made Ireland a hissing and a scorn to the whole civilized world. Is this to last for ever?

Rev W.M. O'Hanlon,
Walks among the poor of Belfast, 1853

Select Bibliography

Belfast before 1820, a bibliography compiled by Noragh Stevenson for the Linen Hall Library in 1967, contains a daunting 618 entries. Around 200 books on Northern Ireland since 1968 have been published, almost all of them directly relevant to the history of the city, and to total the number of works relating to Belfast for the intervening years 1820–1968 would be a formidable task. It follows that of necessity this bibliography must be highly selective.

General histories

J.C. Beckett and R.E. Glasscock (eds.), *Belfast: the origins and growth of an industrial city* (BBC, 1967) is the best concise general survey: there are sparkling chapters on the early history by E.E. Evans, J.C. Beckett, C.E.B. Brett and J.L. McCracken in particular; individual contributions on the later period are excellent but do not form a satisfactory chronological account; and, being written at an optimistic time, it does tend to pass over the darker side of Belfast's history. Ian Budge and Cornelius O'Leary, *Belfast: approach to crisis: a study of Belfast politics, 1603–1970* (Macmillan, 1973) is primarily a specialist work on political behaviour but the first 172 pages give a lively and informative account of the city's history, with invaluable detail on municipal affairs.

George Benn published *The history of the town of Belfast* (Mackay) in 1823 and then devoted the next fifty-five years of his life expanding this to become *A history of the town of Belfast from the earliest times to the close of the eighteenth century* (Marcus Ward, 1877). This monumental work must be one of the most impressive local histories written in the nineteenth century; the high quality of Benn's scholarship makes his book indispensable as a source book but, as his approach is that of an antiquarian rather than a historian, it is also somewhat exhausting for the general reader. Indefatigable to the last, Benn completed a second volume, *A history of the town of Belfast from 1799 till 1810* (Marcus Ward, 1880), useful mainly for sections on the leading families of the town. D.J. Owen, *History of Belfast* (Baird, 1921) is valued chiefly by those who cannot lay their hands on copies of Benn; on the earlier history it is rather tedious and adds little that is new but, in spite of infuriating omissions and uncritical admiration for the Corporation's achievements, it is a great store of information on nineteenth-century Belfast.

Problems of a growing city: Belfast 1780–1870 (Public Record Office of NI, 1973), 260 pages long, is probably the best value for £1.50 obtainable in Belfast at the time of writing. A collection of documents with a perspicacious introduction, it is in its own way as indispensable for the nineteenth century as is Benn for the earlier centuries; it is primarily the work of Peter Brooke though he is nowhere named in the volume. Cathal O'Byrne, *As I Roved Out* (Irish News, 1946; new edition, Blackstaff Press, 1982) is the best of many collections of newspaper articles on old Belfast, and is rightly popular. Other books of a similar character are generally less useful than their titles would seem to indicate; worthy of mention are S. Shannon Millin, *Sidelights on Belfast history* (Baird, 1932); A.S. Moore, *Old Belfast* (Carter, 1951); and Richard Hayward, *Belfast through the ages* (Tempest, 1952). Emrys Jones, *A social geography of Belfast* (OUP, 1960) is an important study based on years of impressive research and paints a vivid picture of the physical development of Belfast from its inception.

Earliest times to 1750

E.E. Evans is *the* authority on Belfast's physical setting; see especially: 'The site of Belfast', *Geography*, 22 (1937); 'Belfast: the site and the city', *Ulster Journal of Archaeology*, 3rd series, 7 (1944); and his contributions to *Belfast in its regional setting* (British Association, 1952), edited by E. Jones.

The *Ulster Journal of Archaeology* contains numerous articles on traces of early human settlement in the Belfast region; F.J. Byrne, *Irish Kings and High Kings* (Batsford, 1973) casts fascinating light on the obscure history of the Cruithin and Ulaid; T.E. McNeill, *Anglo-Norman Ulster: the history and archaeology of an Irish barony* (Donald, 1980) is a thorough account of the medieval background, giving much detail on the Clandeboye O'Neills; and Douglas Carson, *Ulster castles and defensive buildings* (BBC, 1977) provides valuable information on fortifications in and around Belfast. For the Elizabethan–Jacobean conquest and its consequences consult Grenfell Morton, *Elizabethan Ireland* (Longman, 1971); T.W. Moody, F.X. Martin and F.J. Byrne (eds.), *A new history of Ireland: volume III 1534–1691* (OUP, 1976); and D. Stevenson, *Scottish Covenanters and Irish Confederates: Scottish–Irish relations in the mid-seventeenth century* (Ulster Historical Foundation, 1981). Benn's 1877 volume is, nevertheless, still the only full survey – the books above help to interpret the events he described and the documents he quoted. The relevant chapters in J.C. Beckett and R.E. Glasscock (*op. cit*) for this period are outstanding.

The surviving records of the Corporation were reprinted in R.M. Young (ed.), *The town book of the Corporation of Belfast 1613–1816* (Marcus Ward, 1892) in a splendid edition illustrated with woodcuts executed by eighteenth- and nineteenth-century craftsmen of the town. The importance of Benn's work has overshadowed *Historical collections relative to the town of Belfast: from the earliest period to the Union with Great Britain* (George Berwick, 1817), almost certainly written and compiled by the Volunteer leader, Henry Joy junior: it contains Milton's long letter of denunciation and conveniently places documents in chronological order with terse linking commentary.

1750–1800

R.J. Dickson, *Ulster emigration to colonial America, 1718–1775* (Routledge and Kegan Paul, 1966) not only describes the 'Scotch-Irish' exodus from Belfast but also makes vivid comment on social conditions and rural discontent in and around the town. For an authorative examination of the causes of the 'Hearts of Steel', see W.A. Maguire, 'Lord Donegall and the Hearts of Steel', *Irish Historical Studies*, Vol. 21, 84 (1979). Benn is at his best describing the topography of Belfast in this period, but Joy's *Historical collections (op. cit.)* is to be preferred for political events. Joy collaborated with Dr W. Bruce to compile *Belfast politics; or a collection of the debates, resolutions and other proceedings of the town 1792–3* (Henry Joy, 1794; reprinted edited version Athol, 1974). For the origins of the Belfast Society of United Irishmen see A.T.Q. Stewart, '"A Stable Unseen Power": Dr William Drennan and the origins of the United Irishmen', in John Bossy and Peter Jupp (eds.), *Essays presented to Michael Roberts* (Blackstaff, 1976), and A.T.Q. Stewart's masterly *The narrow ground: aspects of Ulster, 1609–1969* (Faber, 1977). Mary McNeill, *The life and times of Mary Ann McCracken: a Belfast panorama* (Alan Figgis, 1960) is a delightful portrait of late eighteenth- and early nineteenth-century Belfast, excellent on Manson, Bunting, and Clifton House, though the radicals are viewed in rather romantic light. R.W.M. Strain, *Belfast and its Charitable Society* (OUP, 1961) provides further detail on Clifton House. The witty, gossipy and intelligent letters of Martha McTier can be read in D.A. Chart (ed.), *The Drennan letters* (HMSO, 1931). N.E. Gamble, 'The Business and Trade of Belfast 1767–1800' (unpublished Ph.D. thesis, University of Dublin, 1978) will be opened in January 1983 and was not therefore consulted by the author.

The nineteenth century

1. THE COTTON INDUSTRY No comprehensive survey is available but much can be gleaned from J.J. Monaghan, 'The Rise and Fall of the Belfast Cotton Industry', *Irish Historical Studies*, 3 (1942); E.E.R. Green, 'The cotton hand-loom weavers in the north-east of Ireland', *Ulster Journal of Archaeology*, series 3, VII (1944); E.E.R. Green, *The Lagan Valley, 1800–50* (Faber, 1949); the idiosyncratic and chaotic H. McCall, *Ireland and her staple manufactures* (Greer, 3rd ed., 1870); Rev J. Dubourdieu, *Statistical survey of the County of Antrim* (Dublin Society, 1812); and J.A. Beck, 'Francis Street Mill', *Fibres and Cordage*, Sept 1945. The views of many of the above have been effectively questioned by F. Geary in 'The Rise and Fall of the Belfast Cotton Industry: Some Problems', *Irish Economic and Social History*, VIII (1981).

2. THE LINEN INDUSTRY Astonishingly, there is no general survey of the industry in Belfast – information has largely to be dredged from trade and academic journals. The fascinating *Domestic industry in Ireland: the experience of the linen industry*, by W.H. Crawford (Gill and Macmillan, 1972) is concerned with the rural industry and C. Gill, *The rise of the Irish linen industry* (OUP, 1925) is less helpful on Belfast than the title suggests. D.L. Armstrong, 'Social and Economic Conditions in the Belfast Linen Industry 1850–1900', *Irish Historical Studies*, 7 (1951) is a *tour de force* which, incidentally, provides a succinct summary of the progress of the industry in the city; see also Emily Boyle, 'The linen workers' strike of 1872', *Journal of the Society for the Study of Irish Labour History*, 2; and J.M. Golstrom, 'The Industrialisation of the North-east', in *The formation of the Irish economy*, edited by L.M. Cullen (Mercier, 1969). For harrowing contemporary accounts of working conditions read John Moore, 'On the Influence of Flax Spinning on the Health Workers of Belfast', *Transactions of the National Association for the Promotion of Social Science* (1867) and C.D. Purdon, *The sanitary state of the Belfast Factory District (1864 to 1873 inclusive)* (Adair, 1877).

3. THE PORT, SHIPBUILDING AND ENGINEERING D.J. Owen, *Short history of the port of Belfast* (Mayne Boyd, 1977) is authorative; the author was secretary to the Harbour Board and criticisms made of his general history do not apply here. Extracts from contemporary government reports are printed in *Problems of a growing city (op. cit.)*. Shipbuilding in Belfast still awaits its historian. Contemporary newspaper reports and the *Shipbuilder* provide detail in plenty; L. Dunn, *Famous liners of the past: Belfast built* (Adlard Coles, 1964) is handsomely illustrated and is by far the most useful study; R. Anderson, *White Star* (Stephenson, 1964) tells the story of Harland & Wolff's best customer with infectious enthusiasm; J.G. Peirson, *Ship builders or the rise of Harland & Wolff* (Stockwell, 1935) is brief but excellent; and Edward Harland summarises his own achievement in 'Shipbuilding in Belfast' in Samuel Smiles, *Men of Invention* (Murray, 1884). See Dennis Rebbeck, 'The history of iron shipbuilding on the Queen's Island up to July, 1874' (unpublished Ph.D. thesis, QUB, 1950), but the papers of the shipbuilding firms otherwise await detailed analysis. For the growth of other engineering industries see W.E. Coe, *The engineering industry of the north of Ireland* (David and Charles, 1969), and H.D. Gribbon, *The history of water power in Ulster* (David and Charles, 1969): both are impressive studies. See also W.A. McCutcheon, *Wheel and spindle* (Blackstaff Press, 1977).

4. SOCIAL HISTORY *Mary Ann McCracken (op. cit.)* and *Problems of a growing city (op. cit.)* are essential for the first two-thirds of the century. P. Froggatt, 'Industrialisation and Health in Belfast in the Early Nineteenth Century', in D. Harkness and M. O'Dowd (eds.), *The town in Ireland* (Appletree, 1981) adds rigorous modern investigative techniques to contemporary accounts which include A.J. Malcolm, *The sanitary state of Belfast* (Greer, 1852) – a graphic report on the town's shortcomings – and Rev. W.M. O'Hanlon, *Walks among the poor of Belfast, and suggestions for their improvement* (Greer, McComb, 1853) – a compelling account of the congested working-class districts. Michael Farrell, *The Poor Law and the Workhouse in Belfast 1838–1948* (PRONI, 1978) is a thorough account, amply supported by extracts from contemporary documents, of the building of what is now the City Hospital and of the shortcomings of nineteenth-century poor relief. The liveliest description of social life in early nineteenth-century Belfast is T. Gaffikin, *Belfast fifty years ago* (Cleeland, 3rd ed., 1894), a lecture given in 1875; T. McTear, 'Personal Recollections of the Beginning of the Century', *Ulster Journal of Archaeology*, 2nd series, 5 (1899) is less vivid, but very informative on the northern suburbs especially; and see also 'Belfast Sixty Years Ago: recollections of a septuagenorian', *Ulster Journal of Archaeology*, 2nd series, 2 (1896) by Narcissus Batt who gave Purdysburn to the city.

5. POLITICAL HISTORY Owen's *History of Belfast (op. cit.)* and I. Budge and C. O'Leary (*op. cit.*) are the most convenient sources for municipal affairs and political developments in the city. C. O'Leary, 'Belfast Urban Government in the Age of Reform', in D. Harkness and M. O'Dowd (*op. cit.*), is witty and informative; P. Gibbon, *The origin of Ulster Unionism: the formation of Protestant politics and ideology in nineteenth century Ireland* (Manchester UP, 1975) is difficult reading but important because it challenges accepted explanations; and P. Buckland, *Irish Unionism 2: Ulster Unionism and the origins of Northern Ireland, 1886–1922* (Gill and Macmillan/Barnes & Noble, 1979) is the clearest guide to the late nineteenth-century resistance to Home Rule. Early sectarian outbreaks are categorised in parliamentary Blue Books under the quaint heading 'Outrage'; all the major Belfast riots were followed by commissions of inquiry and the report on 1886 is monumental; and of the many contemporary accounts by far the most

engaging is F. Frankfort Moore, *The truth about Ulster* (Eveleigh Nash, 1914) – because his stylish and wryly humorous memories were published at the outbreak of the Great War they have been largely forgotten. Andrew Boyd, *Holy War in Belfast* (Anvil, 1969), is a racy and detailed account of the riots. For some of the most thoughtful work on sectarianism see the section on the labour movement (below).

The twentieth century

1. THE EARLY LABOUR MOVEMENT H. Patterson, *Class conflict and sectarianism: the Protestant working class and the Belfast labour movement 1868–1920* (Blackstaff, 1980) is one of the most significant books to have been published on Belfast's history in recent years: it is the first comprehensive study of the early labour movement and finally dispels the widely-expressed view that Protestant workers were always the dupes of their employers. For alternative interpretations see Chapter 2 of Emmet Larkin, *James Larkin: Irish labour leader 1876–1947* (RKP, 1965; Nel Mentor, 1968); F. O'Hare, *The Divine Gospel of discontent: the story of the Belfast Dockers and Carters Strike 1907* (Connolly Bookshop, 1982); and Michael Farrell, 'The Great Belfast Strike of 1919', *Northern Star*, 3 (1972). Peter Brooke (ed.), *Robert McElborough: an autobiography of a Belfast working man* (Irish Congress of Trade Unions/PRONI, 1974) is a unique account of inter-union disputes by a gasworker and also paints a vivid picture of working-class Edwardian Belfast. See also J.W. Boyle, 'The Belfast Protestant Association and the Independent Orange Order', *Irish Historical Studies*, 13 (1962–3); and J.W. Boyle, *Leaders and workers* (Mercier, 1967).

2. POLITICAL AND SOCIAL HISTORY 1900–20 A.C. Hepburn and B. Collins, 'Industrial Society: the structure of Belfast, 1901' in Peter Roebuck (ed.), *Plantation to partition: essays in Ulster history in honour of J.L. McCracken* (Blackstaff, 1981), is a scholarly introduction to the new century. Sybil Gribbon, 'An Irish City: Belfast 1911', in Harkness and O'Dowd (*op. cit.*), is an essay of great charm – a lively yet learned portrait of the city at the height of its economic power. A.T.Q. Stewart, *The Ulster crisis* (Faber, 1967) is a gripping account of the resistance to Home Rule which reads like a thriller; it has a good claim to be the best-written book on twentieth-century Irish history. For the Great War, see Cyril Falls, *The 36th (Ulster) Division* (Linenhall Press, 1922); and J. Bardon, 'Ulster and the Somme', *Sunday News*, 3, 10, 17 and 24 April 1966. C.W. Breen, P. Buckland, and S. Kelly, *Irish Unionism 1885–1921* (PRONI, 1976) is a useful pack of documents, much of it directly relevant to Belfast.

3. POLITICAL HISTORY 1920–39 This period was largely ignored by historians until recently: books rushed to press to cash in on the interest generated by the violence since 1969 should be treated with caution. P. Buckland, *Factory of grievances: devolved government in Northern Ireland 1921–39* (Gill & Macmillan/Barnes & Noble, 1979) is an impressive study based on cabinet papers (some of which have since been denied to other researchers). While not uncritical, Buckland is broadly sympathetic to Unionism. On the other hand, Michael Farrell, *Northern Ireland: the Orange State* (Pluto, 1976) is frankly partisan and the book is by far the most informed and most lucid defence of the republican-marxist position; the author makes impressive use of ephemera and newspapers, provides ample detail on elections, and concludes with a full bibliography with terse, astringent comment. Budge and O'Leary (*op. cit.*) provides vital information on municipal affairs and helps to put the achievements described in the self-congratulatory *The Belfast Book* (Belfast Corporation, 1929) into perspective. St John Ervine, *Craigavon, Ulsterman* (Allen and Unwin, 1949) is a vehement and, at times, cantankerous defence of the Unionist record, valuable because it draws on the Craigavon papers. Paddy Devlin, *Yes we have no bananas: Outdoor Relief in Belfast 1920–39* (Blackstaff, 1981) is a passionate and limpid study – the most important book on the history of inter-war Belfast to have been published in recent years. For the 1920s Troubles see the last two chapters of P. Buckland, *Irish Unionism II* (*op. cit.*); G.B. Kenna, *Facts and figures of the Belfast Pogrom 1920–22* (O'Connell Publishing Co., 1922) – partisan nationalist; and J. Redmond, *Church and State in East Belfast* (privately published, 1965) – partisan loyalist. For the 1932 riots supplement Devlin (*op. cit.*) with J.J. Kelly, 'A journalist's diary', *Capuchin Annual* (1944); and J. Bardon, *The Belfast Outdoor Relief Riots 1932* (QUB Teachers' Centre, 1981). For the 1935 riots see Henry Kennedy, 'Riot at Lancaster Street', *Aquarius*, 5 (1972); and J. Bardon, *The Belfast Riots of 1935* (QUB Teachers' Centre, 1981). See also T.J. Campbell, *Fifty years of Ulster 1890–1940* (Irish News, 1941), the memoirs of a Nationalist leader; Patrick Shea, *Voices and the sound of drums: an Irish autobiography* (Blackstaff, 1981) – beautifully written memoirs of a Catholic in the civil service; Sir Arthur Hezlet, *The 'B' Specials: a history of the Ulster Special Constabulary* (Tom Stacey, 1972; Pan, 1973) – partisan but comprehensive, by a former USC commander; David Kennedy, 'Catholics in Northern Ireland 1926–1939', and J.L. McCracken, 'The Political Scene in Northern Ireland 1926–1937', in F. MacManus (ed.), *The years of the Great Test 1926–39* (Mercier, 1967), RTE radio talks; and J. Bardon, *The Stormont Election of 1938 in Belfast* (QUB Teachers' Centre, 1981) – documents with comment.

4. THE SECOND WORLD WAR J.W. Blake, *Northern Ireland in the Second World War* (HMSO, 1956) is the official history, finely written and exhaustive, with a great deal of material directly relevant to Belfast. P.C.J. Radcliffe (ed.), *Northern Ireland in the Second World War: a guide to official documents in the Public Record Office of Northern Ireland* (PRONI, 1976) has a good introduction; and Robson St C. Davison, 'The German Air Raids on Belfast of April and May 1941, and their consequences' (unpublished Ph.D. thesis, QUB, 1980) is a valuable supplement to Blake's researches. Douglas Carson's schools radio programme, *The Blitz* (in the BBC series 'Modern Irish History: People and Events') is a moving documentary on the air raids and is regularly repeated. J. Bowyer Bell, *The secret army: a history of the IRA 1916–70* (Blond, 1970) is the best history of the IRA before the present Troubles and contains much interview material and detail on armed republicanism in Belfast.

5. POLITICAL HISTORY 1939–68 Michael Farrell, *The Orange State* (*op. cit.*) is the only detailed narrative account of a period which has yet to receive the attention it deserves from historians. John F. Harbinson, 'A History of the Northern Ireland Labour Party 1891–1949' (unpublished M.Sc. thesis, QUB, 1966) and *The Ulster Unionist Party, 1882–1973: its development and organisation* (Blackstaff, 1973) are very useful works of reference, with much detail on Belfast. The second half of Budge and O'Leary (*op. cit.*) provides a minutely detailed analysis of political attitudes in Belfast in the 1960s. C.E.B. Brett, *Long shadows cast before: nine lives in Ulster, 1625–1977* (Bartholomew, 1978) is an interesting chronicle of a family connected with Belfast for more than three centuries and contains detailed reminiscences of the author's membership and chairmanship of the Northern Ireland Labour Party.

6. ECONOMIC AND SOCIAL HISTORY c.1920–68 K.S. Isles and N. Cuthbert, *An economic survey of Northern Ireland* (HMSO, 1957) is a daunting work, but as it is a searching analysis of the provincial economy from the inception of Northern Ireland, it repays careful study; a great part of the report is concerned with Belfast's strengths and weaknesses and Appendix G, 'Cyclical Variations in the Linen Industry', by William Black, is a rigorous examination of that industry on the eve of its collapse. Betty Messenger, *Picking up the linen threads: a study in industrial folklore* (Texas University Press 1978, Blackstaff, 1980) is a unique and delightful book which deserves to be more widely read: it not only contains extensive transcripts of interviews with those who worked in the mills from the beginning of the twentieth century but also gives a lucid explanation and description of techniques of production. For shipbuilding refer to the works quoted for the previous century but, in general, finding accessible detail for this period is a frustrating business. H. Jefferson, *Viscount Pirrie of Belfast* (Mullan, 1947) is a muddled biography, deficient in specific information; as articles in municipal publications are primarily concerned with past glories, newspaper reports (particularly those by the *Belfast Telegraph* shipbuilding correspondent at the close of every year) are invaluable for this period. The history of the Belfast aircraft industry, by contrast, is succinctly chronicled in John Corlett, *Aviation in Ulster* (Blackstaff, 1981). For other aspects of the city's economy see *Belfast Harbour Commissioners, centenary volume, 1847–1947* (Belfast Harbour Commissioners, 1947); E.D. Maguire, *The Sirocco story* (Davidson & Co, 1958); *Belfast industrial handbook 1951* (Belfast Corporation, 1951); and P. Buckland, *The factory of grievances* (*op. cit.*), chapters 4 and 5.

Some of the very best social history has been written and compiled by local historical societies and schools. Fred Heatley is indisputably the most accomplished and dedicated of local historians in Belfast, with a passionate belief that enthusiasm is the principal quality required: his parish histories, *St. Joseph's centenary 1872–1972: story of a dockside parish* (Irish News, 1972) and *The story of St. Patrick's, Belfast 1815–1977* (Bethlehem Abbey Press, 1977) are models of their kind; and *Ligoniel: the last of the mill villages: written by the people of Ligoniel* (Workers Educational Association, 1981), edited by him, was (deservedly) sold out in a city-centre bookshop in two hours. Heatley has been the main driving force behind *Outline Annual*, the journal of the West Belfast Historical Society; the first edition of 1975 is now a collector's item. Carmel Gallagher (ed.), *All Around the Loney-O* (St. Louise's Comprehensive College, 1978) is a delightful history of the Pound which makes skilful use of street directories, songs, interviews and documents from the PRONI; it is but one of many informative publications by schools and teachers' centres. See also the School Curriculum Project publications edited by Robert Crone, *Belfast – rise of a city* (1974), *The Blue Flower* (1974), and *Local Studies* (1976) which draw heavily on contemporary material; and *Ballymacarrett Past and Present* (Rupert Stanley College, 1972).

7. ARCHITECTURE, BUILDING DEVELOPMENT AND TRANSPORT W.A. Maguire is the acknowledged expert on the Chichester and Hill families whose misfortunes played such an important part in the nineteenth-century development of Belfast: see especially, 'The 1822 settlement of the Donegall estates', *Irish Economic and Social History*, 3, (1976); 'Ormeau House', *Ulster Journal of Archaeology*, 42, (1979); and *The Downshire Estates in Ireland, 1801–1845* (Oxford University Press, 1972).

C.E.B. Brett, *Buildings of Belfast 1700–1914* (Weidenfeld and Nicolson, 1967) is handsomely illustrated and written with such wit and verve that it becomes only slowly apparent that it is based on very extensive research. E. Jones, *A social geography of Belfast* (*op. cit.*) provides the best general survey of housing development from earliest times to 1960. P.G. Cleary, 'Spatial expansion and urban ecological change in Belfast with special reference to the role of local transportation 1861–1917' (unpublished Ph.D. thesis, QUB, 1980) is the product of nearly ten years research and contains material for several books; it provides what the general reader has sought for so long: detailed information on when and by whom the streets and houses of the city were laid out and built during Belfast's Victorian and Edwardian heyday. Cleary's survey of trams, railways and omnibuses in the period is exhaustive; see also R.A. Hunter, R.C. Ludgate and J. Richardson, *Gone but not forgotten: Belfast trams 1872–1954* (Irish Transport Trust, 1979) and J.M. Maybin, *Belfast Corporation Tramways 1905–1954* (Light Rail Transit Association, 1981), both fully illustrated, with texts pulsating with the most harmless and appealing of fanaticisms.

Education and public services to 1968

For a selection of books on schools and colleges see under Institutions (below). Mary McNeill, *Mary Ann McCracken* (*op. cit.*), [P. Brooke] *Problems of a growing city* (*op. cit.*), and W. Gray, *Science and art in Belfast* (Northern Whig, 1904) between them provide a general survey of educational developments in the eighteenth and nineteenth centuries. Norman McNeilly, *Exactly 50 years: the Belfast Education Authority and its work 1923–73* (Blackstaff, 1973) is most comprehensive. D.H. Akenson, *Education and enmity: the control of schooling in Northern Ireland 1920–50* (David and Charles, 1973) is a *tour de force* – an incisive description and analysis of sectarian squabbling in education; for a partisan view of the same issue see W. Corkey, *Episode in the history of Protestant Ulster 1923–47* (Dorman, 1965).

For a masterly examination of the development of social services in the city from a Unionist viewpoint see R.J. Lawrence, *The government of Northern Ireland: public finance and public services, 1921–1964* (OUP, 1965). See also P. Devlin, *Yes we have no bananas* (*op. cit.*), P. Buckland, *The factory of grievances* (*op. cit.*), *The Belfast Book 1929* (*op. cit.*), and R. Marshall, *The book of Belfast* (*op. cit.*). In the absence of detailed government investigation in the inter-war years, A. Beacham, *Report of a survey of living conditions made in a representative working-class area in Belfast November 1938–February 1939* (Social Service Committee, Presbyterian Church in Ireland, 1939) is very revealing.

A select list of works consulted for the period 1969–82

Arthur, P. *The People's Democracy, 1968–73* (Blackstaff, 1974).
Black, R., Pinter, F. and Overy, R. *Flight: A report on population movement in Belfast August 1971* (Northern Ireland Community Relations Commission, 1975).
Black, W. 'The Effects of the Recession on the Economy of Northern Ireland', *Irish Banking Review* (December 1981).
Boal, F.W. 'Territoriality on the Shankill/Falls Divide', *Irish Geography*, 6, 1 (1969).

Boal, F.W., Doherty, P. and Pringle, P.G. *The spatial distribution of some social problems in the Belfast urban area* (Northern Ireland Community Relations Commission, 1974).

Darby, J. and Williamson, A. (eds.) *Violence and the social services in Northern Ireland* (Heinemann, 1978).

Clark, W. 'What's driving the Irish linen trade up the walls?' *Irish Times*.(12 April 1982).

Deutsch, R. and Magowan, V. *Northern Ireland: A chronology of events 1968–74* 3 vols (Blackstaff, 1973–75).

Devlin, P. *The fall of the Northern Ireland Executive* (privately published, Belfast, 1975).

Evans, R.W. (chairman) *Belfast 2000* (papers of conference 12–23 April 1982, Belfast Junior Chamber of Commerce/Royal Town Planning Institute).

Evason, E. (ed.) *Poverty in Northern Ireland: facts and figures* (Community Information Service, N.I.C.S.S., 1979).

Fisk, R. *The point of no return: the strike which broke the British in Ulster* (André Deutsch, 1975).

Flackes, W.D. *Northern Ireland: a political directory 1968–79* (Gill and Macmillan, 1980).

Holland, J. *Too long a sacrifice: life and death in Northern Ireland since 1969* (Dodd, Mead & Co, 1981).

Kelly, H. *How Stormont fell* (Gill and Macmillan, 1972).

Longford, Lord and McHardy, A. *Ulster* (Weidenfeld and Nicolson, 1981).

Magee, J. *Northern Ireland: crisis and conflict* (RKP, 1974).

McCreary, A. *Survivors* (Century Books, 1976).

McCullagh, M. 'The political and sectarian significance of changes in the occupation structure of Northern Ireland', *Social Science Teacher* (to be published March 1983).

McGuffin, J. *Internment* (Anvil, 1973).

O'Connor, F. *Housing in Belfast* (Northern Ireland Housing Executive, 1982).

Rowthorn, B. 'Northern Ireland: an economy in crisis', *Cambridge Journal of Economics, 5* (1981).

Sunday Times 'Insight' Team *Ulster* (Penguin, 1972).

Townsend, P. *Poverty in the United Kingdom* (Penguin, 1979).

Wiener, R. *The rape and plunder of the Shankill* (privately published, Belfast, 1975).

**Planning publications relating to the Belfast urban area:
relevant to Chapters 10 and 11**

Belfast regional survey and plan 1962 [Matthew Report] (HMSO, 1964).

Economic development in Northern Ireland, including the report of Prof Thomas Wilson (HMSO, 1965).

Belfast urban area plan: Vol 1, Main report; Vol 2, Appendices, Building Design Partnership (HMSO, 1969).

Belfast transportation plan, R. Travers Morgan & Partners (HMSO, 1969).

Review of transportation strategy, Department of the Environment NI (HMSO, 1978).

Belfast areas of special social need, Project team (HMSO, 1978).

Poleglass area statement, Department of the Environment NI (HMSO, 1978).

Belfast household survey 1974 (NI Housing Executive, 1975).

Belfast household survey 1978 (NI Housing Executive, 1979).

Belfast urban area: planning statement and progress report, Department of the Environment NI (HMSO, 1981).

Economic and industrial strategy for Northern Ireland [Quigley Report], Review team (HMSO, 1976).

Tenth annual report, NI Housing Executive (1981).

Publications on institutions, churches, etc.

Allison, R.S. *The Seeds of Time: being a short history of the Belfast General and Royal Hospital 1850–1903* (Brough, Cox and Dunn, 1972).

Anderson, J. *History of the Belfast Library and Society for Promoting Knowledge* (McCaw, Stevenson and Orr, 1888).

Barkley, J.M. *A short history of the Presbyterian Church in Ireland,* 1959).

City Hall, Belfast: short guide (Strain, n.d.)

Blair, May *Once upon the Lagan: the story of the Lagan Canal* (Blackstaff, 1981).

Fisher, J.R. and Robb, J.H. *Royal Belfast Academical Institution: Centenary Volume, 1810–1910* (McCaw, Stevenson and Orr, 1913).

Henderson, J.W. *Methodist College, Belfast, 1868–1938* (Governors, MCB, 1939).

Jameson, J. *The history of the Royal Belfast Academical Institution, 1810–1960* (Mullan, 1959).

Knox, W.J. *Decades of the Ulster Bank 1836–1964* (Ulster Bank, 1964).

Loudan, Jack *In Search of water* (Mullan, 1940).

Loudan, Jack *The Crown Bar* (Nicholson and Bass for Bass Ireland, 1981).

Magee, J. *The Linen Hall Library and the cultural life of Georgian Belfast* (Library Association of Belfast, 1982).

Malcolm, A.G. *The History of the General Hospital, Belfast, and other medical institutions of the town* (Agnew, 1851).

Marshall, R. *Methodist College, Belfast: the first hundred years* (Baird, 1968).

McConnell, J. *Presbyterianism in Belfast* (Davidson and McCormack, 1912).

McCusker, Mary 'Richmond Lodge – The Story of a Belfast School', in *Outline Annual 1975* (*op. cit.*) pp.21–7.

Moody, T.W. and Beckett, J.C. *Queen's Belfast, 1845–1949: the history of a university,* 2 vols. (Faber, 1959).

Nesbitt, Noel *A Museum in Belfast* (Ulster Museum, 1979).

The Northern Banking Co Ltd: an historical sketch: Centenary volume 1824–1924 (Linenhall Press, 1925).

O'Laverty, J. *An historical account of the Diocese of Down and Connor,* 5 vols. (Duffy & Sons, 1895–8).

Rodgers, P. *St Peter's Pro-Cathedral* (Howard, 1967).

Shearman, H. *Belfast Royal Academy, 1785–1935* (Governors, BRA, 1935).

Simpson, N. *The Belfast Bank 1827–1970* (Blackstaff, 1975).

Strain, R.W.M. *Belfast and its Charitable Society* (OUP, 1961).

The Presbyterian Historical Society of Ireland *A history of congregations in the Presbyterian Church in Ireland 1610–1982* (Presbyterian Church in Ireland, 1982).

Tyrell, W.E. *History of the Belfast Savings Bank* (Belfast Savings Bank, 1946).

Vinycomb, J. *An enquiry into the history and authenticity of the Belfast arms* (Marcus Ward, 1896).

Books containing historical photographs

Bombs on Belfast 1941 (Baird, n.d.)

Brett, C.E.B. *Buildings of Belfast 1700–1914* (Weidenfeld and Nicolson, 1967).

Evans, E.E. and Turner, B. *Ireland's eye: the photographs of Robert John Welch* (Blackstaff, 1977).

Hamilton, P. *Up the Shankill* (Blackstaff, 1979).

Shearman, H. *Northern Ireland 1921–71* (HMSO, 1971).

Walker, B.M. *Faces of the past: a photographic record of Ulster life 1880–1915* (Appletree, 1974).

Walker, B.M. *Shadows on glass: a portfolio of early Ulster photography* (Appletree, 1976).

A selection of publications on theatre, art, creative writing, etc.

Bell, S.H. *The theatre in Ulster* (Gill and Macmillan, 1972).

Campbell, A.A. *Belfast newspapers, past and present* (Baird, 1921).

Catto, M. *Art in Ulster 2* (Blackstaff, 1977).

Dawe, G. (ed.) *The younger Irish poets* (Blackstaff, 1982).

Ervine, St J. *Ulster: the real centre of culture in Ireland* (Baird, 1944).

Foster, J.W. *Forces and themes in Ulster fiction* (Gill and Macmillan, 1974).

Hammond, D. (ed.) *Songs of Belfast* (Gilbert Dalton, 1978).

Hewitt, J. *Art in Ulster 1* (Blackstaff, 1977).

Milroy, J. *Regional Accents of English: Belfast* (Blackstaff, 1981).

O'Hare, C. *What do you feed your donkey on? Rhymes from a Belfast childhood* (Collins, 1978).

Ormsby, F. (ed.) *Poets from the North of Ireland* (Blackstaff, 1979).

Patterson, D. *The Provincialisms of Belfast and the surrounding districts: pointed out and corrected* (Mayne, 1860).

Quinn, H. 'Belfast street songs', *The Bell* 1, 5 (February, 1941).

Smith, A.G. *Belfast Literary Society 1810–1901* (Linenhall Press, 1902).

Wilson, Judith C. *Conor 1881–1968: the life and work of an Ulster artist* (Blackstaff, 1981).

Note to young researchers

The best starting points are the street directories and newspapers. The Belfast Central Library has newspaper scrapbooks dating from 1890 (classified under Newspaper Cuttings, Local) which are more durable and easier to consult than the bound volumes of newspapers, which have to be ordered several days in advance. Comprehensive local newspaper collections are held in the Linen Hall Library, the Belfast Central Library, and the Public Record Office for Northern Ireland; the very useful *Northern Ireland newspapers: a check list with locations,* edited by J.R.R. Adams (Library Association of NI/PRONI, 1979) may be consulted at all three establishments; the Linen Hall Library conveniently keeps all its Belfast books in one case in its Irish Section; the Belfast Central Library has the Biggar Collection (an almost complete collection of books on the early history of Belfast); the *Belfast News-Letter* up to 1924 can be consulted and photocopied on micro-film in the Belfast Central Library, the Linen Hall Library and the Public Record Office of NI.; and librarians in local branch libraries (delighted to find someone not seeking out yet another thriller) are unfailingly helpful and can often arrange inter-library loans.

Index to text

Note: While most items are indexed individually, some are included under general headings: for example, 'Lyric Theatre' appears under 'Theatres', *'Titanic'* under 'Ships', 'Anderson & McAuley' under 'Shops and stores', etc.

320

Acknowledgements

To Barbara Fagan and Dorothy Barham who typed the manuscript.

To Gerry Cleary for permission to consult his unpublished Ph.D. thesis, without which the sections on transport and building development in the late nineteenth and early twentieth centuries could not have been written.

To Jim McConville who wrote for us detailed recollections of his youth, and to Hugh Finnegan for permission to quote from his unpublished memoirs.

To A.T.Q. Stewart, for his incisive and encouraging criticism of the typescript.

To John Carlin, James Dennison, Andy and Maureen Fagan, Micky Maguire, Aileesh McGirr, Bella O'Hara and Bob Turkington who gave interviews, and to Pat Devlin and Mary McCluskey who converted tape-recordings into typescript.

To the following who lent printed and manuscript material or provided valuable advice and assistance: John Auld, Victor Blease, Andrew Boyd, Oliver Boylan, Deirdre Brown, Pat Brown, Douglas Carson, Andrew Crockart, Mary Douglas, Michael Foy, Charlotte Gault, Vera Gillespie, Nevin Harris, Richard Hawkins, Gerry Healy, Paul Kane, Campbell Kell, John Keys, John Killen, Hamilton Laird, Maureen Larmour, Fred Law, Mary McClean, Leslie (J.L.) McCracken, Michael McCullagh, Philip McDonagh, Ann Mitchell, Seamus Murphy, Helen O'Donnell, John Patterson, Helen Ross, Thompson Steele, Sam Watt, Anthony Weir and Barry White.

None of the above bear any responsibility for opinions expressed or errors which may have crept into the text.

To Michael Collins and Ivan Little for invaluable assistance in taking and preparing photographs for reproduction.

To the following who lent or helped to trace photographs and other illustrations: W.J. Anderson, Dorothy Barham, Brian Barton, Eileen Black, Douglas Carson, Gloria Dreen, Rowel Friers, John Gray, Ruth Greene, David Hammond, Tony McAuley, Walter Macauley, Noel Nesbitt, Cecil Nimmons, Trevor Parkhill, Vici Topping, Robert J. Trainor, Patrick Walsh and Cynthia Wilson. Every effort has been made to acknowledge all those whose illustrations and photographs have been used; if there have been any omissions in this respect, we apologise and will be pleased to make the appropriate acknowledgement in any future editions.

To the staff of the Linen Hall Library, the Belfast Central Library, the Belfast Harbour Commissioners, the Public Record Office of Northern Ireland, the Library of the College of Business Studies, the Ulster Folk Museum, the Ulster Museum, the Queen's University Library, the Queen's University Teachers' Centre, Harland & Wolff Ltd and the *Belfast Telegraph* for their patient assistance.

To Carol Bardon who prepared the index with meticulous care and offered constructive criticism and constant support at every stage in the writing of this book.

Jonathan Bardon
Henry V. Bell